MINERVA SERIES OF STUDENTS' HANDBOOKS

No. 19

General Editor

PROFESSOR
BRIAN CHAPMAN
MA, D.PHIL (*Oxon*)

THE SCIENCE OF SOCIETY

Minerva Series

THE SCIENCE OF SOCIETY

AN INTRODUCTION TO SOCIOLOGY

By

STEPHEN COTGROVE

Professor of Sociology
University of Bath

Third Edition

London

GEORGE ALLEN & UNWIN LTD

RUSKIN HOUSE   MUSEUM STREET

FIRST PUBLISHED 1967
SECOND IMPRESSION 1967
THIRD IMPRESSION 1968
FOURTH IMPRESSION 1968
FIFTH IMPRESSION 1968
SIXTH IMPRESSION 1969
SEVENTH IMPRESSION 1969
EIGHTH IMPRESSION 1970
REVISED EDITION 1972
THIRD EDITION 1975

© *George Allen & Unwin Ltd, 1967*

ISBN 0 04 3000541

PRINTED AND BOUND IN GREAT BRITAIN BY
REDWOOD BURN LIMITED
TROWBRIDGE & ESHER

PREFACE TO THE FIRST EDITION

If sociology is a relatively new star in the academic firmament, it is one which is rising rapidly. It lacks therefore the settled and established perspectives of the older disciplines. It is also a subject with a voluminous literature, and the task of selecting what is most appropriate in an introductory text is especially difficult.

Two main criteria, therefore, have guided the selection and presentation of the material. Firstly, there is the claim that sociology is a science; that it is, in fact, possible to apply the perspectives of science to the study of social systems. Throughout, the emphasis had been on getting across the sociological perspective rather than conveying a mass of factual information. Science is essentially analytical. It involves the isolation of variables, tracing their relations with other variables, and in this way mapping out systems and sub-systems of interrelated elements. The 'rag-bag' notion of sociology as being the study of the odds and ends left over by economists, historians, and political scientists has been decisively rejected. Nor is sociology simply 'political arithmetic', counting heads and providing demographic data for governments. But if it is developing a distinct perspective, it must of necessity develop a special language. It is no more possible to undertake sociological analysis without special language symbols than it is possible to study physics or chemistry.

There has been no hesitation then in using the vocabulary of sociology. But technical terms have been introduced in a context which indicates their meaning and have been italicized when first used. Where the word italicized is a familiar word, such as *culture*, this serves also to draw attention to the fact that it is being given a precise and special meaning.

There is one further guiding principle. Science, like other intellectual activities, can be exciting. The excitement of discovery, of pitting one's intellectual resources against a tough problem, is one of the most rewarding aspects of science for the scientist. It is not easy to preserve this excitement in an introductory text. But it is perhaps easier in sociology than in some subjects because its study inevitably involves new ways of looking at familiar things. Attention has been directed, therefore, wherever possible to recent researches and to the problems that are now attracting the interest of sociologists, in the hope that students may catch some of the excitement of scientific research by some exploration at the frontiers of knowledge.

Finally, the emphasis throughout is on the sociological study

7

of industrial society, with particular reference to modern England. It is hoped that this text may be one of an increasing number which attempts a more systematic and analytical approach, and tries to tread a middle way between highly theoretical and abstract studies and the all too voluminous largely descriptive literature whose relations to sociological perspectives are hard to find.

It will be necessary for the advanced student to undertake some further reading, selected from the recommendations for each chapter. The aim has been to provide a systematic framework to which wider reading can be related. There is little point in incorporating detailed summaries of readily available texts. Moreover, the exercise involved in relating the perspectives of this book to the sometimes differing approaches of the supplementary reading is an essential experience in developing a critical approach. No attempt has been made to keep footnotes to a minimum. On the contrary, these are important indications to the student of where to look for a more detailed development of the points briefly made in the text.

The indebtedness of the textbook writer to others is always extensive. The footnotes and references are some indication of this. But this book owes more than most to the help and encouragement of others. In particular, I must acknowledge my debt to a group of former students, who became the founder members of a graduate seminar at the Polytechnic in which many of the perspectives to be found in this text were hammered out. Distinctions are always invidious, but I must mention in particular Steven Box, Penri Griffiths, Stanley Parker, Noel Parry and Douglas Young, some of whom have still further increased my gratitude by reading and criticizing draft chapters. I am also grateful to Anthony Taylor for his valuable assistance with Chapter 5, and to Mary Couper, Theo Nichols and Dr Ram Srivastava for reading draft chapters. Any inadequacies and errors are, of course, my own. I would also like to express my appreciation to Mrs Avril Fordham who patiently typed a none too legible manuscript, and, by no means least, to my wife and family for their forbearance during the many months of intensive pre-occupation with its production.

Finally, I wish to thank *New Society* and Dr S. Parker for permission to reproduce in Chapters 2 and 4 parts of an article written jointly with Dr Parker, 'Work and Non-Work'.

Bath University of Technology
July 1966

PREFACE TO THE SECOND EDITION

Revising a text is more than up-dating the material to reflect the advances in the subject. It is a test of the adequacy of the organizing framework to accommodate the new material. And it is a fascinating exercise in stock-taking—in becoming conscious not only of developments in the subject, and in one's own perspectives, but also of changes in the social context in which the subject has evolved.

The world of the early 1970s does not seem the same as that of the mid-1960s. How much this is because the world has changed, and how much because we have come to see the world differently, is problematic—and indeed, one of the themes of this book. One can no longer write 'poverty has been largely abolished'—a phrase which no reviewer challenged then, but which would certainly not get by now. If the 1960s thought of themselves as an age of affluence, the 1970s have been labelled the age of 'the permissive society'. The re-emergence of political radicalism in the 1960s has taken new forms in the 1970s. The Bomb has been replaced by technology as the 'enemy' by the proponents of the 'alternative society'. Students not only wear their hair as long as Isaac Newton, but they now sit on senates.

It is no task of sociology to provide simple solutions to the problems of the world (though it is sad that we are not better at predicting them); but it cannot but help reflect the society in which it flourishes. Nor should an introductory text be over-preoccupied with current intellectual fashions (or it will quickly become as dated as yesterday's newspaper), though it may contribute to their analysis and understanding. One way in which topicality and relevance can be saved from obsolescence is to relate contemporary issues to larger themes. Problems of order and freedom, of the extent to which man is moulded by society or is able to shape his destiny—such are the perennial themes of philosophy which can be illuminated by sociological analysis. Debates about permissiveness and 'women's lib' are in this sense as old as society itself. Assumptions and speculations about the nature of man are similarly not the exclusive preserve of the theologian and philosopher, but part of the world-taken-for-granted reflected not only in letters written to *The Times* but also in the work of sociologists, economists, psychologists and historians.

It is such reflections which have flavoured the current revision. Throughout, an attempt has been made to draw attention to alternative views about the nature of man and society; to the functionalist emphasis on the consensual nature of society and its almost overpowering dominance over the life of the individual; to the mounting criticisms of those who stress the lack of consensus and the ubiquity of conflict; to the increasingly sensitive exploration of the subtle interaction between man and society which offers hope of escape from sociological determinism. Such themes can be illuminated by topics as diverse as work, stratification and delinquency.

The very substantial re-writing of Chapter 4 on the economic system reflects the publication explosion in this area. The equally drastic revision of Chapter 6 to include a discussion of radicalism, youth culture, and the culture of poverty reflects in part a change in the social context, in my own interests, and in my views as to how the material can best be organized. The inclusion of a more extended discussion of roles and interactions in Chapter 8 is an attempt both to integrate a burgeoning literature and to make up for a deficiency in the first edition.

Acknowledgements are ritual, but like other rituals they symbolize some reality. And in my case this is the real debt which any teacher owes to generations of students. It is in the lecture room and seminar room as well as in research that issues are explored, ideas thrashed out, and enthusiasm for the sociological enterprise sustained.

University of Bath
February 1972

PREFACE TO THE THIRD EDITION

Apart from up-dating the reading lists, two main changes have been made to the revised text. Firstly, a discussion of the social construction of scientific knowledge, (deleted from the second edition), has been reinserted. Secondly, an extended analysis of the impact of technology on society and its implications for social change has been added to Chapter 9. Both these changes reflect a growing critical relationship between science, technology and society and emerging doubts about the future of industrial societies.

University of Bath.
August, 1974.

CONTENTS

TABLES AND FIGURES

ABBREVIATIONS

A.J.S.—*American Journal of Sociology*
A.S.R.—*American Sociological Review*
B.J.S.—*British Journal of Sociology*
Soc. Rev.—*Sociological Review*
Soc.—*Sociology*

Chapter 1

THE SCIENCE OF SOCIETY[1]

It is logical to start with the question: What *is* sociology? But it is not easy to answer it. Indeed, the reader is warned that this may be the most difficult chapter in the book. It may certainly be helpful to return to re-read some sections after the issues have been more fully illustrated in subsequent chapters.

This chapter will try to answer three main questions. Firstly, what is the subject-matter of sociology? Secondly, how is this subject-matter approached? And thirdly, why do we study it—what is its justification?

The answer to the first question can be deceptively simple. It is really no answer to say that sociology studies human society, because so do history and anthropology. Nor is it enough to say that it studies human social behaviour, because so does social psychology. We really want to know what is its distinct perspective. What is the distinctive way in which sociology looks at man and society and their interactions? What is the distinctively sociological perspective on, for example, marriage and the family?

SOCIOLOGICAL PERSPECTIVES

A marriage seems at first sight to be an intensely personal affair. Boy meets girl, they fall in love, marry, set up house together. After a few years she stops working and has a baby, followed by a second and possibly a third at intervals of about two years, while the husband continues to work.

But although each feels that he is freely choosing, each is, in fact, fitting into a pattern which would be quite different in other societies. In India, for example, boy does not meet girl and fall in love. Parents arrange marriages, and will choose a husband or wife for their daughter or son after consulting horoscopes and entering into negotiations with the other family.

Every step in this complex process is, in fact, regulated by powerful social pressures. Courtship, marriage and subsequent relations between wives and husbands, all are the subjects of laws, convention and expectations, which if broken will bring a variety

---

[1] I am indebted to Penri Griffiths for valuable suggestions for the organization and content of this chapter.

of sanctions ranging from imprisonment to ridicule. It is this coercive nature of society which Durkheim saw as its chief characteristic. For Durkheim,[1] sociology is the study of such *social facts*, which he defined as ways of acting, thinking and feeling, general in a society, which exert coercion on the individual to conform. Birth-rates are a good example of such social facts. In the nineteenth century, for example, wives usually had three or four children, sometimes ten or more. Today, the majority have one, two or three. Such facts cannot be explained simply by reference to individuals. Wives today are just as capable of having large families. But society today is different in many ways from Britain in the nineteenth century. And it is to these differences in their social context that individuals are responding when they take steps to limit their family size.

'Boy meets girl' then is a social fact. The biological changes which are involved in this event are common to healthy men and women in all societies, but there will be considerable differences in the permitted ways of sexual behaviour. Some societies permit plural mating (polygamy) and allow husbands to have more than one wife (polygyny) or wives to have more than one husband (polyandry).

'Boy meets girl' within the context of a set of rules and usages or *institutions* which define what is considered 'normal' by any particular society. The social grouping which results from this regulation of sexual behaviour is the family. At each stage in its formation, and throughout its life, the behaviour of boy and girl, husband and wife, parent and child, will conform more or less closely to a pattern of norms and expectations which will define the way in which each will act out his *roles*. 'Boy' will have learnt what is expected of him as a 'lover' (and even ways of making love vary in different segments of society). He will expect to experience the emotions of romantic love with one particular girl, whom he will then ask to enter into a life-long (monogamous) relationship with him in which he will expect her to look after his home, cook his meals, possibly defer to his judgement on major issues and probably give up her career. She in turn will expect him to keep alive his romantic attachment by remembering wedding anniversaries, and any deviation from a strictly monogamous relationship may be interpreted as a fatal blow to the marriage, and until recently was recognized by the law as a 'matrimonial offence' giving grounds for divorce.

We learn to play adult roles during childhood. During play, for example, we engage in *anticipatory socialization* by acting as mothers and fathers, or teachers. Indeed, it is instructive to watch

[1] E. Durkheim, *Rules of Sociological Method* (1950).

children at play to see just how they define adult roles. To say that we play the role of husband or wife implies that this is simply an act. At first it is, and we may not feel the emotions which we have come to expect. But with time, the 'act' becomes a part of us, an element in our *identity*, just as the newly qualified doctor at first self-consciously plays a part very different from that of his student days, but comes in time to *be* a doctor, thinking and behaving like one. Social systems are, in fact, remarkably successful in moulding people who will fill a wide variety of social roles—assembly-line workers, research scientists, witch-doctors, warriors, hunters. Such differences can certainly not be explained as inborn.

It is perhaps a somewhat exaggerated analogy to liken individuals to puppets, pulled by social strings, and acting out parts written for them by society. But they have come to know their parts so well that they are no longer aware of the pulls and pushes, and, unlike puppets, an internal machinery has taken over and moves them from inside. They have *internalized* their roles. All of this is an oversimplification, but it serves to illustrate an important element in the sociological perspective—the coercive nature of social systems which structure the behaviour of individuals in their pursuit of biological and other satisfactions.

Social systems

Perhaps the key concept in the sociological perspective is the notion of a *social system*. A system is a whole whose parts are interrelated. A simple example is Boyle's law in physics, which states that under certain conditions there is a mathematical relationship between the temperature, pressure and volume of a gas. An increase in temperature is a *function* of an increase in pressure, as, for example, when you blow up a bicycle tyre and the valve gets hot.

This brings us back to the question: What precisely are the elements of social systems, and what are its boundaries? All science involves an abstraction of certain aspects of complex phenomena. In the example just quoted, the physicist has abstracted certain measurable aspects—temperature, pressure and volume— and has ignored odour and colour. To some extent the question of what constitutes a system is a question for empirical study. For example, researches have discovered an association between social class and early school leaving: the children of working-class parents are more likely than the sons and daughters of the middle class to leave school early. To investigate this more fully, we would have to translate the notion of social class into variables which could be observed and measured. The earliest inquiries simply related early leaving to fathers' occupation. But not all boys whose fathers are unskilled workers leave early. If we compare the early leavers

17

with those who stay on, we discover other variables. For example, boys whose mothers had a secondary grammar-school education are less likely to leave early. In this way, we will uncover the elements in the system, and when we have accounted for all the variance in early leaving we will have isolated the 'system'.

It would be more precise to say that we have isolated a sub-system, because many elements in the system will be functions of larger systems. Whether a school practises streaming or not, for example, will depend on a number of variables, including the current state of educational theory and whether the school is in a predominantly middle- or working-class area. In sociology, it is usually difficult to isolate a system to discover its boundaries, and to deal with it as though it were a closed system. For this reason, the concepts 'internal' and 'external' system are preferred by some sociologists.

There are, of course, other major systems in society. We can identify distinct systems of action organized around the major functions which must be performed in any society if it is to survive. The family maintains the flow of new recruits for society, not only through procreation, but also plays an important role in transmitting the values and norms of society, thus contributing to the *socialization* of children for their future adult roles. In addition to the kinship system, there are the economic and political systems, each of which will be the subject of more detailed study in later chapters of this book.

Not only are sub-systems such as schools and factories related to the major systems of which they are parts, but the major systems themselves are interrelated. We shall see later, for example, that the family greatly influences a child's scholastic attainments, the school socializes the child to perform work roles in the economic system, while the job a man does influences his family life and relations with his wife. This, in fact, is the major task of sociology —to bring to light the interrelations between the elements in systems and sub-systems. As a framework for such analysis, the vocabulary of sociology provides a number of other useful concepts which enable us to identify the major components of social systems.

Structure

If we focus attention on a major sub-system of society, such as the economic system, we can identify a number of separate *organizations*, such as firms and trade unions. Each of these will have a definable *structure*. That is to say, there will be a hierarchy of *positions* or *statuses* such as managing director, secretary or bench worker. Moreover, there will be recognized norms defining what is expected of each position. When an individual acts according to such expectations, he is carrying out his role as managing director or secretary. *Role* is the acting out of *status*.[1]

The notion of structure, then, serves to emphasize the relatively stable and enduring framework within which social action takes place. When we speak of the *social structure*, therefore, we are referring to the total pattern of interrelated systems—the kinship, political, educational and economic systems which constitute the broad framework within which individuals occupy positions and act out roles.

Culture

The behaviour of actors in a social system will be influenced by their perceptions of what others expect of them. Actions will also be oriented towards the pursuit of valued ends or goals. Members of a trade union, for example, join to achieve better wages and conditions. The shared norms and values of members of a social system are a most important aspect of a society. Shared norms, values and beliefs are referred to as the *culture* of society—and here the word is being used in a technical sense.

In the small group such as the family, as well as in the wider society, activities will be directed towards the achievement of valued goals. In a society in which material possessions such as cars, TV sets and refrigerators are highly valued, individuals will be motivated to want them. Such shared goals help to integrate the activities of individuals in a social system. Members of a family who all want the same kind of holiday will all bend their energies in the same direction. But there must also be agreement on means as well as ends. Norms of conduct prescribe some means and prohibit others. Only some means of achieving valued goals are legitimate. Morals, fashions, conventions, laws—all regulate conduct according to prevailing norms. Consensus on means (shared norms) together with consensus on ends, channel social actions and help to promote integrated systems of action. Where such shared norms exist, regulating the behaviour of actors in a specific context, we refer to the existence of a *social institution*.

Types of persons

Both *culture* and *structure* are highly abstract concepts. In the last analysis, a school, or a factory, is a collection of individuals. They may indeed share a range of beliefs about the importance of certain objectives, and agree on a set of rules for the conduct of affairs, and in this sense we may speak of the *culture* of the school.

[1] See L. A. Coser and B. Rosenburg (eds), *Sociological Theory: a Book of Readings* (1964), Chapter 8.

But a culture only exists to the extent that beliefs and values are shared among members of a group. We must therefore look at the social system from the perspectives of the individual actors. For the sociologists, this means looking at *typical*, not isolated, individuals. It is the family life of car-workers, or the educational achievements of working-class students, that interests us. And when sociologists analyse the family life or political behaviour of car-workers, they normally do so in the language of statistics, which makes it possible to estimate probabilities within clearly stated limits.

When we look at the social system from the perspective of typical individuals, we can start by locating their *position* or *status* in the social system (manual workers in the economic sub-system, for example). We may then explore the personal qualities, skills, capacities, beliefs (about trade unions, for example) which are characteristic of the individuals occupying such positions (*role incumbents*). Finally, we may describe the way in which the role is acted out. To do this, we must take account not only of how the individual is expected to behave by others but also how the individual perceives the expectations of others. Indeed, the way in which an individual acts in a social situation will depend on the way *he* defines it. If a child believes that his mother does not love him, this is the *real* situation for him.

Many theories of society have, in fact, stemmed from certain assumptions about the characteristics of the individuals who compose it. Theories of economic behaviour, for example, influenced by the utilitarians and classical economists, have assumed that man is motivated primarily by the desire to maximize his material satisfactions. 'Economic man' rationally pursues economic goals. For Thomas Hobbes,[1] man was primarily a 'security seeker'; for some sociologists, he has been defined primarily as a 'status seeker', while for Freud, sex instincts were seen as the primary explanation of a variety of social phenomena, including religion and civilization.

Such explanations are clearly an over-simplification of human motivation. Moreover, they fail to take account of other characteristics of the individual actor in a social system, such as his definition of the situation. Manual workers, for example, may restrict output and thus fail to earn production bonuses and to maximize income. But this does not mean that they are uninterested in economic rewards. It may be that they prefer to sacrifice income for security. They define the situation as one which calls for restrictions on output.[2]

[1] T. Hobbes, *Leviathan*.
[2] See Chapter 4 for a discussion of 'occupational strategies'.

But in any case, we cannot adequately explain the behaviour of a social system simply in terms of the characteristics of the individuals who compose it.[1] The actor is himself the product of a social system. His motives and perspectives, and the ways in which he legitimizes and justifies his actions can only be understood as a result (in part) of the lengthy processes of *socialization* which has moulded his characteristics. We must take account, too, of the actor's position in the social structure, the roles that he occupies and the complex expectations which these generate. And finally, the prevailing culture will influence the ways in which he defines situations, the goals he values and the means which he accepts as legitimate. The total *social system*, that is to say, embraces structures, culture and persons (Figure 1.1).

Of course, this discussion should not be taken to imply that consensus is the only basis for social order and integration. Men can work together for what appear to be common goals from quite different motives. And conflict is not necessarily disruptive. It may lead to the search for new solutions, and in this way it may promote greater integration. Such problems of order, conflict and change will be explored more fully in the final chapter.

FIGURE 1.1
A MODEL OF A SOCIAL SYSTEM

Social structure	*Culture*
Political system	Values (ends)
(Machinery of government, parties, pressure groups)	Norms (means)
Economic system	Knowledge, beliefs,
(Firms, the market, trade unions)	ideologies
Kinship system	
(Families, kinship networks)	
Cultural system	
(Schools, colleges, churches, broadcasting corporations)	

Types of persons
(e.g. manual workers, middle-class students)

Roles	Characteristics
(Activities, interactions)	(Values, motives, definitions of self and situations)
	Identity

[1] This approach is known as psychological reductionism.

21

Social processes

This model of a social system is not, however, entirely satisfactory. It suggests a somewhat static picture. We need, in addition, to look at societies from another more dynamic perspective and to examine the *processes* of interaction, organization, differentiation and change. Interaction, for example, takes place in schools, workshops, parliaments and prisons. There are a number of agencies in addition to the family which contribute to the socialization process. So, in the second section of this book, the focus will switch to a study of such social processes.

Social and non-social

When we discuss courtship patterns in sociology, we take as given the biological basis of courtship—puberty and sexual maturation. What interests us is the fact that different societies impose different patterns of courtship, and channel and control the biological sexual drive in different ways. We can never overlook the biological basis of human behaviour. But biology cannot explain the social expectations which result in distinctive courtship patterns, differing between societies. Biology cannot explain *social* facts. Sex is a biological drive; monogamy or celibacy are social facts.

Quite elaborate theories have been developed which attempted to explain social movements in biological terms. Racial theories of history, for example, have tried to explain the rise and fall of civilizations as due to changes in the racial (inborn biological) composition of peoples. One weakness of such theories apart from the lack of evidence is the fact that social changes frequently take place far too quickly for them to be due to biological changes which take scores of generations. We cannot, for example, explain the fall in the size of the family from 1870 in biological terms. This has been far too large to be explicable as the result of any decline in reproductive capacity.[1]

Geographical factors, too, have entered into sociological explanations. And in some ways, the sociologist must take them into account. We may observe, for example, that suicide rates are higher in hot than in temperate climates. If we could demonstrate that climate was indeed the significant variable, then we would need to turn to biology and possibly psychology to determine how the human organism responds to temperature in ways which affect the tendency to suicide. The explanation would not then be sociological. In fact, we find a number of other variables which are not themselves causally related to climate but which are associated

[1] For a review of such theories, see M. Ginsberg, *Sociology* (1934); P. Sorokin, *Contemporary Sociological Theories* (1928).

22

with suicide—such as social norms on the morality of suicide, and the degree of integration between the individual and society. These are all sociological variables. This does not mean that sociologists can ignore geographical or biological factors. They constitute factors which individuals in societies have to take into account. But it is the differential response of societies to, for example, arid conditions, or skin colour, which interests the sociologist. A lack of rainfall is a geographical fact; an irrigation system is a social product. A hand is a biological non-social phenomenon; and handshake is a social fact, a symbol, communicating meaning and intention from one individual to another.

Sociology and the social sciences

The relation between psychology and sociology is obviously close. The basic unit of society is the individual. And it is the behaviour of the individual that preoccupies the psychologist. He studies, for example, the ways in which inputs of sensory experience are translated by the brain into meaningful perceptions. The sociologist, too, is interested in these phenomena, but only in so far as he needs to take account of them in studying the interaction between individuals in social situations. There are, however, some areas where the distinction is harder to draw. For example, both are interested in exploring the meaning and satisfaction of work. Such areas of overlap need not worry us unduly. There need be no academic demarcation disputes. Rather, there is much to be gained from interdisciplinary collaboration and exchange of ideas and data.

In general, sociologists and psychologists are concerned with different levels of analysis. The sociologist is interested in the individual as an element in a social system. He needs to take account of the way in which an individual perceives a situation, since this will influence his reaction to it. But he leaves the study of the mechanisms of perception to the psychologist. Sociologists, in other words, are trying to build a body of theory to explain the behaviour of social systems—while psychologists want to explain the behaviour of individuals. Individuals, in fact, are always parts of social systems. Both psychology and sociology involve different ways of looking at individuals. This is what science is—a way of looking at and talking about phenomena. It involves abstracting certain elements from complex reality (e.g. whether a man dominates his wife) and trying to relate these to other elements. For example, wives who are economically dependent are more likely to be subordinate. This is a sociological explanation—relating typical unemployed wives with a typically subordinate role. We are not, in this case, concerned with whether any particular wife has psychological characteristics which can be described as a submissive personality.

It is less easy to differentiate between sociology and anthropology. The simplest basis of distinction is to say that anthropology has concentrated on the study of pre-literate societies. Because of the small size of such societies, the absence of a shared culture with the investigator, and the absence of written records specific techniques of inquiry have had to be developed, in which observation and interviewing have played a dominant role.

Economics, unlike sociology, studies only one segment of society. But it also differs in its perspectives.[1] Classical economics was largely deductive, starting with basic assumptions about economic rationality, and deducing from these an elaborate theory of economic behaviour. The theory of price, for example, assumes that individual buyers will buy less if the price rises and that producers will produce more. Price under perfect competition is determined by the interaction of the curves derived from plotting changes in supply and demand in relation to price movements. The theory of the firm shows how profits can be maximized given various relations between fixed costs, average costs and marginal costs. Whether managers actually behave in this way, is another matter.

Economics, then, provides us with models of behaviour in limited circumstances and under stated assumptions. It has developed more sophisticated theory than sociology, and has also gone further in the use of mathematics. But sociology and economics are coming closer together. In trying to bring its models more closely into line with what actually happens in the real world, economists have increasingly tried to measure economic behaviour (econometrics) and to modify their theories in the light of empirical data. On the other hand, there has been a growing interest among sociologists in the study of the economic system.

The convergence between sociology and economics can be seen in a number of ways. Problems of economic growth in under-developed countries have forced economists to widen their perspectives and to pay attention to the non-economic context of production—the way in which the extended family, for example, may hinder mobility of labour. On the other hand, the possibility that models of economic behaviour may be capable of computer analysis, and the more sophisticated theories of economics are tempting sociologists to work more closely with economists and to try to apply some economic perspectives, such as input–

[1] For a fuller discussion, see N. J. Smelser, *The Sociology of Economic Life* (1963), Chapter 2.

24

output analysis, to the study of social systems. A particularly interesting example of convergence is the use of the economist's notion of exchange to explain various social phenomena, such as power. All social interactions involve an exchange of benefits. Where the interaction is one-sided, one party can regularly use the threat of withdrawal of favours to achieve compliance: that is, a power relationship exists.[1]

History and sociology have a long and close association. The difference is mainly in the kind of question asked. The historian asks 'what happened?' and strives to achieve a chronological reconstruction of events. One extreme view of history would be that its task is simply to describe the minutiae of events. Sociology places more emphasis on 'how' questions, and on building general theories of social systems. Many historians would adopt a more analytical, rather than purely descriptive, approach, and seek to establish relations between events and to investigate the causes of events. Many works by historians and by sociologists, in fact, are indistinguishable in their approach. Indeed, it may be that historians will increasingly adopt a sociological perspective in their study of the past.[2] Similarities, however, are largely confined to the works of those sociologists who have studied historical societies. But to the extent that sociologists are mainly concerned with the study of contemporary societies, their perspective is becoming increasingly distinctive as they concentrate more and more on distinguishing the elements in social systems and formulating and testing theories about the relations between them.

THEORIES AND METHODS

How then does the sociologist study social systems? What kinds of explanation does he attempt? It has been generally claimed that sociology is a science. But there is by no means consensus on the implications of this for sociology. Moreover, problems about the nature of scientific explanation are questions of current philosophical debate. Such problems cannot be discussed in detail here, but it is important to stress right at the outset that an introductory text must of necessity over-simplify in the interests of clarity. A rather more pressing and practical question is: How far can the ways of studying phenomena which have proved so

[1] For a brief account and discussion, see P. S. Cohen, *Modern Social Theory* (1968), pp. 121–5.

[2] See, for example, the recent studies at Cambridge: P. Laslett, 'The History of Population and Social Structure', *Int. Soc. Sci. J.*, Vol. 17, 1965, No. 4, and *The World We Have Lost* (1965). See also A. Marwick, *The Nature of History* (1970).

successful in the natural sciences be applied to the study of man and society?

Science claims superiority over other kinds of knowledge on the grounds that it is derived from the observation and recording of phenomena. The ultimate test of a scientific proposition is its verifiability. This means that scientific propositions are limited to statements that are capable of verification. The proposition 'Five million angels can dance on the head of a pin' is not verifiable. Nor is the statement 'You ought not to gamble'.

Theory versus empiricism

Much social research has been mainly of a fact-gathering kind into the 'condition of Britain' question, to discover, for example, exactly how many people were living in poverty, and the factors such as low wages and irregular employment which led them to this condition. Such inquiries into the health of towns, labour conditions in factories and the conditions of the poor have been undertaken largely outside the universities, by government departments, by amateur investigators like Booth and Rowntree or by statisticians like Bowley. They have provided a mass of factual data which has had a substantial influence on social legislation.[1]

Current researches closely related to this tradition includes studies of family life in industrial cities, and the researches into the problems of old people, widows and poverty. But it would be misleading to describe such recent studies simply as political arithmetic—counting heads—although they are certainly concerned with providing data for legislators. Such studies have also been influenced by the perspectives of anthropology and have placed great stress on the use of interviews as the method of making extensive inquiries into various aspects of the life of the community. Their approach has, however, been mainly descriptive.

Now it can be argued that science is more than observation and recording. And however important political arithmetic may be, it does not as such contribute greatly to the development of a science of society. It undoubtedly provides us with much raw material. The difficulty in sociology is that in the past there has often been an inverse relation between the significance of an inquiry and its methodological and theoretical rigour. Inquiries into important questions of family life have been theoretically naïve, while many theoretically rigorous researches have investigated trivial questions.

Recent studies of family life can be taken to illustrate the relations between theory and empirical research. Young and Willmott,

[1] M. Abrams, *Social Surveys and Social Action* (1951).

for example, have shown that kinship is still a powerful force in East London. Married daughters still visit their mothers a good deal; in fact, much of the leisure-time of the women is spent with mothers and close relatives. When the young families are moved to new housing estates in outer London, these ties with 'Mum' are weakened. But this is not the only change. The role of the husband and his relations with his wife also change. Husbands participate more actively in the household tasks, and are to be seen pushing the pram at weekends.

These studies raise some interesting questions. Why do husband–wife relations and roles change when families move to new housing estates? We could formulate a number of hypotheses. It may be that new estates have fewer pubs, and so husbands are forced back into the home. Or the new houses encourage them to spend more on furniture and decorations or to work in the garden, so they become home-centred. At about the same time as the Young and Willmott study, Elizabeth Bott was asking questions of this kind. She came to the conclusion that it was the existence of strong kinship ties beyond the conjugal family which explains the relations between husbands and wives (conjugal roles). Such strong ties persist after marriage and prevent the development of joint activities. Hence, spouses continue to lead separate lives—a pattern of *segregated conjugal roles* persists. In the new housing estates, the pull of kinship is weakened and husbands and wives develop changed patterns of integrated activities.

If we are to discover the relations between elements in a social system, we need to approach our inquiries with this aim in mind. If we set out simply to collect and record data, we find all too often that much of the data is useless and cannot make possible any advances in theory. Theoretically oriented studies are generally greatly superior to descriptive studies in their economy of effort. If we have a definite hypothesis in mind, we can collect data specifically to test it. The social survey approach frequently collects a large amount of descriptive information which cannot be related to any theoretical perspective.

The sociological imagination
What has been said is not meant to imply that only theoretically rigorous analyses are of use to the sociologist. The break-throughs in scientific theory are the result of hunches and guesses that may be triggered off by the most unlikely events. If we are to be intellectually creative, we have to cultivate our ability to see relations which are often far from common sense. To stimulate our 'sociological imagination',[1] we may talk to experts in other

[1] C. W. Mills, *The Sociological Imagination* (1959).

disciplines. We may get clues on the working of social systems by discussions with experts in cybernetics. Or we may read novels. Sillitoe's *Saturday Night and Sunday Morning*, for example, suggests that the way in which Arthur Seaton spends his weekends is very directly the result of the boredom and tedium of his work at the lathe from Monday to Friday. A rigorous inquiry to test this hypothesis is likely to yield more useful results than a large-scale survey which can do little more than relate the statistics of leisure activity to previous education, occupational categories and income. But what differentiates the imaginative insights of the novelist and the activities of the sociologist, is that the latter must eventually put his theories to the test of the most rigorous empirical inquiries that he can devise. This, in turn, does not decry the value of the more speculative and interpretative studies such as Hoggart's *The Uses of Literacy* or Whyte's *Organization Man* or Riesmann's *Lonely Crowd*. It does mean that we have to be aware of the fact that studies have varying degrees of reliability.

Types of explanation

Sociology seeks to analyse the relations between variables in social systems. We can, for example, demonstrate that there is a relation between a boy's social class and his educational achievement. We could say that class is a *cause* of under-achievement, meaning that working-class boys fail to achieve the same degree of success attained by middle-class boys of comparable ability. To take another example, if we observe that there is a relation between whether a wife works and the extent to which she is dominated by her husband, we could say that the employment of wives is a *cause* of their emancipation from male dominance. But we could equally well say, that it is their emancipation from being tied to the kitchen ('a woman's place is in the home') which has *caused* more of them to go out to work. One way round this difficulty is to refer to a functional relation between female employment and male dominance. This leaves open the question of the direction of causation, and indeed, whether there is, in fact, a direct causal relation between the two variables at all. This is to use the word *function* in a mathematical sense—a way which has not, in fact, been favoured by social scientists. If a mathematician says that A is a function of X, he simply means that there is a regular relationship between A and X.

In the social sciences, the concept of function has more generally been used in a way borrowed from biology. We may speak of the function of the digestive system, meaning the contribution which it makes to the maintenance of the body as a functioning system.

In the same way, sociologists talk about the function of, for example, religion in society. This particular usage has given rise to a number of difficulties, which will be examined later in the discussion on *functionalism*.

Two other kinds of explanation are widely used in sociology. Suppose, for example, that we are interested in exploring the factors which lead wives to go out to work, or which lead some young people to become delinquent. As we have seen, the explanation of a social action requires an analysis of two main variables. We need to discover the characteristics of the actors, and we also need to know something about the situation to which they are responding. We may, therefore, compare numbers of delinquents with numbers of non-delinquents to see whether the delinquents possess any specific characteristics, either innate (genetic) or acquired. We would also need to compare all those who have similar characteristics, who become delinquent with those who don't, to discover whether there are situational (environmental) factors which can account for the adoption of delinquent behaviour. This approach attempts to account for the *aetiology*[1] of delinquent acts, that is to say, the antecedent factors which lead to the emergence of delinquent behaviour. This is the approach used in medicine when an explanation is sought for the causal factors leading to a specific disease.

We may, on the other hand, be interested rather in the distribution of some particular kind of behaviour. We may observe that delinquency is concentrated in the lower working-class areas of cities. Or we may wish to explain why fertility rates were high in the nineteenth century, and very low in the 1930s, or why middle-class boys have high rates of educational achievement. This corresponds to the interest of medicine in epidemics, and leads to an *epidemiological* explanation.[2] Here, we try to discover what characteristics of the social system in the nineteenth century were associated with high fertility rates and the corresponding conditions of the social system in the 1930s associated with low fertility rates. A sociological explanation, that is to say, explains rates as functions of a social system.[3] A pioneer and classical study of this kind is Durkheim's analysis of suicide, discussed more fully in Chapter 9. If we use the concept of function in the mathematical sense, such explanations are of course, functional explanations.

[1] In American texts, this is spelt 'etiology'.
[2] See Chapter 9.
[3] For an example of this approach, see the analysis of reproduction in Chapter 2.

Concepts, models, theories

Science involves the abstraction of some characteristics (variables) from complex reality and the attempt to establish laws about the probability of there being regular relationships between such variables. Boyle's law, for example, provides a mathematical formula for the relations between the temperature, pressure and volume of a gas. 'Temperature', 'pressure' and 'volume' are each *concepts*. They are verbal symbols which stand for characteristics. If such characteristics are to be observed, and if possible measured, we have to translate them into criteria which can be perceived by the senses—whether it be the movement of a dial on a pressure gauge, or the thread of mercury in a thermometer. Similarly, if we are to investigate social systems, we must formulate concepts which symbolize the variables we wish to examine, and state the criteria by means of which such characteristics can be observed.

Suppose we are interested in the relations between husbands and wives (conjugal roles) and the influence of the husbands' occupation. We would need to decide what aspects of husband–wife relations might possibly be related. We can identify a number of possible variables, such as the power relations between spouses (equality/dominance), the evaluation of wives by husbands (intrinsic/instrumental) and the kinds of functions wives perform for their husbands (companions, hostesses, servants). The next step would be to decide on criteria which would provide us with indices of such variables for research purposes (to 'operationalize' the concepts). Out of such concepts, it might be possible to construct a *model* which described in a systematic way all the variables we would need to investigate in exploring our problem. We could go further than this and hypothesize some possible relations between the variables. For example, 'where the husband is dominant, the wife is more likely to be a "servant" than a "companion".' Or 'where the husband's occupation involves influencing others, his wife is likely to function as a "hostess"'. The formulation of concepts and models, and the further step in hypothesizing relations between variables, are all steps in the process of theory building—the hallmark of the scientific perspective.

Models are a half-way house in theory building. They are very tentative descriptions of what a system looks like, and suggest possible relations between variables for empirical research. Figure 1.1, for example, is a tentative model of a social system which will be used for the subsequent analysis in this text. Concepts and models are *heuristic* devices—essential aids in the process of analysis. The fact that subsequent researches prove them to be

30

faulty does not matter. What is important is that they provide us with first approximations which we can test and out of which we can build theories which have more powerful explanatory value. The fact that the Niels Bòhr model of the atom (neutron with electrons in orbits) is no longer acceptable to modern physics in no way detracts from the fact that it was a major step with enormous power to generate further theory and research.

Verification and refutation

This brings us back to some of the current controversies in the philosophy of science. This chapter has inevitably taken a position on some of these questions. It implies, for example, that the perspectives of the natural sciences can be applied to the study of society. At this point it may be useful to direct attention to some recent ideas on the nature of science which are particularly relevant to the social sciences.

It was argued earlier that science goes beyond the simple description, collection and presentation of facts. This itself was an over-simple distinction between facts and theories. Every concept that we use involves going beyond simple sensory data. There is no such thing as an 'innocent, unprejudiced observation'.[1] If we explore, for example, conjugal roles, we are selecting from the sum-total of interactions between spouses certain actions and investing them with a special meaning—as evidence of shared or segregated patterns of activity. And if concepts involve imposing a meaning on sense inputs, theories go even further than facts. A hypothesis is a conjecture, and as such goes beyond the facts—it is indeed an imaginative leap. Now, in order to test such conjectures, we may construct an experiment or collect data, to *prove* our theory. The danger is immediately obvious. In order to guard against this, Karl Popper has argued that our task should be to seek to disprove our theory, to look for data which, if found, would show that we were wrong. Indeed, no amount of piling fact on fact can ever conclusively prove a theory to be right. Science is the graveyard of discarded theories, not usually because the facts were wrong, but because better ways of explaining more of them have been found. Indeed, scientists interpret the data within the framework of the prevailing *paradigms*, that is, accepted theoretical frameworks such as the atomic theory of matter in chemistry.[2] It is the existence of such paradigms which indicates the existence of a science.

This brings us to a crucially important characteristic of science:

[1] P. B. Medawar, *The Art of the Soluble* (1967). His essay on 'Hypothesis and Imagination' is a challenging statement by a distinguished scientist.
[2] T. S. Kuhn, *The Structure of Scientific Revolutions* (1962).

it is essentially a social and not an individual activity (however important individuals may be in the process of discovery). Scientists publish their findings in learned journals. Their reports are read critically by other members of the *scientific community* working in the same or related fields. If the paper is found to be convincing, it will be cited, or used as the basis for further work, and another brick will have been built into the growing edifice of scientific knowledge. In short, science is above all 'public' knowledge, as distinct from the 'private' experience of a work of art; 'its goal is a *consensus* of rational opinion over the widest possible field'.[1]

It is clearly more difficult to achieve a 'consensus of rational opinion' in sociology. Not only is the data complex, but the subject is still at the stage where it is difficult to be sure what are the 'prevailing paradigms', if any. But although the task is difficult, only time will tell whether the goal can be achieved. The outlook is certainly hopeful, judged by the progress of recent years.

Prediction and probability

The claim by sociology to be a science does not go unchallenged. It implies that it is possible to construct models and establish theories that will enable us to predict the behaviour of social systems—and this means ultimately, of individuals. This conflicts with our deep conviction that we are each free and self-determining.[2] In its more extreme form, such a view is clearly untenable but some measure of predictability is essential in normal human relations. We come home from school or work knowing that the bus or train can be relied upon (within limits) and that a meal will be served at the usual time. We know that the chances of a boy achieving good 'A' levels whose father is a professional are about thirty times better than those of an unskilled worker's son with the same IQ.[3]

The argument may shift. In each of these cases, we are dealing with probabilities. We cannot say for certain that John Smith will leave school without good 'A' levels, only that the chances are say 30:1 that he will. But the natural sciences, too, deal in

[1] J. Ziman, *Public Knowledge* (1968), p. 9. (Italics mine.) See also W. O. Hagstrom, *The Scientific Community* (1965) and N. W. Storer, *The Social System of Science* (1966).
[2] For a thought-provoking discussion of the implications of sociology for the problem of free-will, see P. Berger, *An Invitation to Sociology—a Humanist Perspective* (1963).
[3] Statistics provide us with methods of establishing whether such differences are greater than could be expected by chance. Chi-squared tests, for example, may be used under some circumstances to enable us to say that 'the probability is only 1 in 100 (or 1,000, etc.) that the difference could occur by chance'.

probabilities. When, however, you are dealing with millions of molecules which are relatively simple, statements can be made with a very much higher order of probability than when you are analysing a system made up of a few hundred very complex men and women.

Interpretation and understanding

A more fundamental attack on the position that sociology is a natural science comes from those who argue that human beings differ in a crucially significant way from molecules—they are conscious beings whose actions have meaning for them. When the natural scientist studies molecules, he can only do so from the outside. When the social scientist studies individuals in social systems, he wants to know, among other things, why the individual behaves as he does—what meaning his action has for him. Some social scientists[1] have argued that a sociological explanation must therefore go beyond the kind of explanation sought by the positivists, who considered that the task of sociology was to establish statistical regularities. We also need to *understand* the meaning which the action has. Now this does not necessarily amount to an attack on sociology as a natural science. In the form in which the view was originally stated, it does put sociology in a different category. It was argued that meaning could only be grasped by intuition and empathy. Because the sociologist is like the individuals he is studying, he can put himself in their shoes and intuit the meaning of their actions—can understand them in terms of the motives and feelings which he shares with those he is studying. This is something the natural scientist cannot do, but the social scientist must do.

There are some obvious objections to this procedure. In the first place, the 'intuition' of meanings or motives is frankly guesswork. There is no harm in guessing, and indeed we may turn to the insights of novelists, politicians, magistrates or anyone else for ideas about possible motives. But science is concerned with verification, and it would be essential to discover some way of verifying our 'intuition' empirically. There is, however, a more fundamental objection. When we say we 'understand', we are referring to a subjective state in which we feel that things make sense. This, it can be argued, is a long way from scientific proof, which depends on the demonstration of interrelations. Indeed, in some fields such as cosmology, the explanations of science are very far

---

[1] Notably Weber, influenced by Dilthey and Ricket. For a more recent re-statement of this position, see P. Winch, *The Idea of Social Science* (1958). For a discussion of the positivist position, see the work of A. Comte, the inventor of the word 'sociology', and J. S. Mill, *Logic* (Book 6).

from 'understandable'. (Those who take this position then would reject the Weberian view that sociology is concerned with understanding human action.) But it does not follow that we are not interested in the meaning and significance which a social action has for the individual. Thus, if we observe that boys in 'C' streams in schools leave at age 15, we want to go beyond the statistical correlation between streaming and early leaving. We will want to know how such boys define themselves, see the school, and their image of the world outside, that is to say, the meaning which their action has for them. But intuition is not enough. We must establish their 'definition of the situation' (to borrow W. I. Thomas's term) by empirical investigation, by interviews, questionnaires and the various other tools of social research. In this way, we can fill in the intervening variables between 'C' stream and 'early leaving', and this in turn will enable us to see in more detail whether this is likely to be an invariant relationship.

Ethnomethodologists go further than this. The social world, they argue, can only be known subjectively as it is experienced by the actor. Sociology is limited simply to discovering the ways in which actors come to know and understand their world and to forging methodological tools for this purpose. There is in fact no objective knowledge of society, but only the subjective commonsense knowledge of individuals. In short, there are only 'definitions', and no 'situations'. And sociologists, they argue, hold no privileged position to claim any special validity for their definitions: there can be no interpersonal knowledge of society, and no possibility of distinguishing between 'true' and 'false' meanings.[1]

None of this is meant to imply that sociology does not face special difficulties in its attempt to apply the methods of science to the study of social phenomena. A more detailed study of some of these difficulties is to be found in textbooks on methods of research. A few may be mentioned briefly. The fact that the objects of sociological study are aware that they are being investigated may well change their conduct. A person being interviewed may well give replies which he thinks will please the interviewer. But such problems, though more frequent in social science, have their parallels in the natural sciences. Electrons, for example, are affected by the light which is used to observe them (Heisenberg's principle of indeterminancy). Sometimes a result may be brought about simply because it is expected. Children put into 'C' streams in schools sometimes do less well because little is expected of them. Their poor achievement then confirms the original impression

[1] For a critique, see Z. Bauman, 'On the Philosophical Status of Ethnomethodology'. *soc. Rev.* (Feb 1973) For a more detailed account, see R. Turner (ed.), *Ethnomethodology* (1974).

34

that they are less able. This is what Merton calls a *self-fulfilling prophecy*.

Varieties of sociological theory

'Sociology comes into being with the extension of the scientific method . . . to the social world of man himself.'[1] It was during the early part of the nineteenth century that systematic attempts to evolve a science of society led to the emergence of sociology as a distinct perspective, different from philosophy, history, political economy and other social sciences. From this date on, sociology's search for a distinct identity has been accompanied by the formulation of a variety of theories about the nature of social systems and the methodology appropriate for their study.

There is no space in an introductory text to do more than to mention some of the earlier theories, and to sketch a little more fully models and theories of more contemporary interest. Many of the perspectives of contemporary theory have their roots in the work of the 'founding fathers' of the nineteenth century. The germ of the idea of society as a system whose parts are interrelated is to be found in the work of Comte (*Cours de philosophie positive*, 1830–42). Herbert Spencer elaborated the concept of society as an organism with structures which become differentiated as society evolves and performs increasingly specialized functions.[2] Durkheim's emphasis on the way in which society exercises constraints on the individual is, as we have seen, one of the most forceful statements of the existence of social factors as distinct from biological, geographical or psychological facts.

This 'holistic' approach which emphasizes the influence of the whole over the parts (individuals) who make up society is, in fact, one of two major theoretical approaches which have dominated sociological thinking.[3] It has come to be known as *functionalism*. By contrast, the *action* approach stresses the role of the individual in explanation. These two approaches are more than differences of emphasis. They reflect one of the basic problems which has long beset attempts to explain society: the problem of the nature of the relation between the individual and society—the part and the whole. One objection to the functionalist approach[4] is that it makes it difficult to take account of the properties of the individual actors in a social system which cannot be explained simply in

[1] Don Martindale, *The Nature and Types of Sociological Theory* (1960).
[2] L. A. Coser and B. Rosenburg, op. cit., Chapter 15.
[3] Alan Dawe, 'The Two Sociologies', *B.J.S.*, 1970, in K. Thompson and J. Tunstall, *Sociological Perspectives* (1971), pp. 542–54.
[4] There are, in fact, a number of objections, particularly its alleged weaknesses in dealing with conflict and change. We return to these issues in Chapter 9.

terms of their roles and statuses. On the other hand, the action approach presents similar difficulties; it cannot easily explain the characteristics of social systems which can exert such a powerful influence on the individual. Social wholes indeed differ from systems in the natural sciences precisely because neither the parts nor the wholes can be satisfactorily explained in isolation. It is the interaction between them which accounts for the *emergent properties* of the systems which cannot be explained simply in terms of the characteristics of the parts. There is no such thing as a 'part' which does not at the same time have properties which reflect its relations with the whole. A cog in a machine is a cog, whether it is part of the machine or not. A man in society is a 'man', a father, worker, voter, precisely because he is a part of a society. It is society which prescribes his role as father, worker, voter.

Of course, one solution to any one-sided emphasis is to develop an *interactionist* approach, which explores actors in interaction with systems. And this is precisely what is happening in sociology. Indeed, it is perhaps surprising that partial approaches should have generated so much heat and have been defended with such fervour. This serves to remind us that the relation between sociology and ideology is still close. The functionalist position, for example, has been attacked particularly strongly by those whose political views are to the left, and mostly for what its antagonists see as an over-emphasis on consensus as the basis of order and integration. It is, of course, true that some 'functionalists' have stressed the integrative role of norms and values, and have neglected to explore conflict and coercion. On the other hand, conflict theorists could equally be accused of neglecting co-operation and consensus. The question is, in any case, best resolved by formulating testable hypotheses.

Such differences in broad theoretical perspectives are rooted in more fundamental philosophical issues and reflect different assumptions about the nature of man. Marx and Durkheim exemplify this basic difference in perspective between the action approach and functionalism, and illustrate the quite different assumptions about the relations between man and society which inform their analyses. For Durkheim, the main problem was the problem of order. He feared that industrialization would threaten the integration of society by bringing about a decline in moral consensus, or agreement on the norms which constrain and regulate social relations—a condition which he described as *anomic*. For Marx, by contrast, the basic problem was to liberate the individual from the conditions of capitalist society which prevented him from self-realization by separating him from the

36

products of his labour (*alienation*). 'Marx wanted to humanize society, to organize the actual world so that man could experience himself as man (free and autonomous in his human or productive activity). Durkheim proposed to humanize Hobbesian man through the extension of social control.'[1] He dreamt of a society in which conflict had been eliminated through consensus on the objectives and rules of social life. Marx's vision was of a 'society of artists', in which each was free to do his own thing— to act spontaneously and creatively.[2] Hence it could be argued that both sociologies are *doctrines*, in the sense that one sees the problem as *order*, while for the other what is problematic is *control*. And any definition of a problem implies a value.

Enough has been said here to give some indication of the range of theoretical explanations in sociology and to underline the point that precisely because conflicting theories still exist, sociology is still at the *pre-paradigmatic* stage of development, although it could be argued that there are now only two competing paradigms. There are excellent texts which can guide the student clearly through this complex maze.[3] The approach adopted in this text will be eclectic—to present data within whichever theoretical frameworks appear most useful, and in this way to illustrate the explanatory use of theory. In general, functionalism and systems analysis is helpful at the macro-level, while the action approach and interactionism comes into its own at the micro-level. In the hands of writers such as Erving Goffman, for example, this perspective has proved to be a powerful tool for understanding hospitals, asylums and prisons,[4] as well as a variety of ways in which the self interacts with society in day to day situations.[5]

Science and values

Science is concerned with questions of fact. Propositions about values—prescriptive propositions—are logically distinct from descriptive propositions. Of course, in making a judgement about what is good, or what ought to be done, we need to take account of all the relevant facts. But the distinction remains. Most philosophers would agree that we cannot derive an 'ought' proposition from an 'is' proposition. This is to commit what Moore called the

[1] John Horton, 'The Dehumanization of Anomie and Alienation: A Problem in the Ideology of Sociology', *B.J.S.*, December 1964. Hobbes argued that life for man before civil society regulated his conduct was 'solitary, poor, nasty, brutish and short'.

[2] See Chapter 9 and Alan Dawe, op. cit.

[3] P. Cohen, op. cit., will be found to be an excellent, clear, authoritative guide.

[4] E. Goffman, *Asylums* (1961).

[5] E. Goffman, *Where the Action Is* (1969).

naturalistic fallacy. Crime is a fact which exists in all societies and is in this sense 'natural'. Pain is 'natural'. In neither case can we logically jump to propositions about the goodness or badness of such phenomena.

Sociology then is concerned with studying the nature of social systems, not with passing moral judgements about what it finds. Of course, sociologists are themselves members of a society, and will have moral attitudes towards the questions they study. What is clearly important is that they carefully distinguish between facts and values. When engaged in scientific research into social questions, they will need to take every precaution to avoid bias both in collecting and interpreting data. Indeed, scientific method devises techniques to minimize distortions. In writing up a report, for example, on the effects of divorce on children, it would be essential to avoid mixing up statements about the observed consequences which can be verified, with moral judgements which cannot.

Of course, this is not meant to imply that the only worthwhile propositions are those which are capable of verification. It may be prudent to base our behaviour so far as possible on knowledge of this kind. All we are saying is that science involves a distinct kind of discourse. And since sociology claims to be the application of the scientific perspective to the study of society, this involves efforts to maximize detachment and objectivity.

Some sociologists will argue that impartiality is impossible. O. R. McGregor, for example, in his book *Divorce in England*, states that it 'does not claim to be impartial (whatever that may mean); it does claim to be candid because throughout it attempts to distinguish between cant and opinion. . . . But there can be no excuse for unscientific explanations of such data as exist or for the substitution of dogma for empirical knowledge in this crucial area of human behaviour.'

One way in which values do enter into the work of the sociologist is in his selection of topics which he thinks are worth study. McGregor thinks that divorce is a 'crucial' area of behaviour. He has studied it because he thinks it is important. Moreover, he clearly has definite views on the subject. But this has not prevented him from taking a cool analytical look at the facts.

Some sociologists would go further than this and argue that sociology ought to concern itself with problems which are significant for the human condition, and not simply of academic interest. But however much values may influence the choice of areas for study, it is clearly important that the researches themselves must be carried out and reported in ways which accord with the conventions of science. There is a danger that 'committed' sociology may become caught up in ideological controversy, to the exclusion of any possibility of achieving a 'consensus of rational opinion'.

One way in which values are likely to intrude unnoticed is in the use of value-loaded terms. Many words used in sociology are taken over from public language. A word like 'civilization', for example, is very difficult to define in a purely descriptive way. It includes not only reference to certain characteristics of society, but to those which are highly valued. What is a civilized society? The answers would be a list of those characteristics which the individual values, and although this may tell us something about the individual's values, such a term is of little use for classifying types of society. 'Democracy', 'psychopath', are further examples of such words.

There is a more subtle way in which assumptions certainly, and possibly values, may underly much of the work of the sociologist. We have already discussed major differences between the perspectives of Marx and Durkheim. These could be described perhaps as differences of judgement about the nature of the human problem. But judgements shade imperceptibly into values. Underlying the view that the problem is how to liberate the individual from the social constraints which prevent him from realizing his human potentials, is the belief that the individual is more important than society. And implicit in the idea that society ought to provide conditions for self-realization are assumptions about the *ontological* nature of man or what man is capable of becoming. Indeed, as we shall see, much sociology rests on value assumptions of this kind; that it is *better*, for example, for a man to work at jobs which provide opportunities for self-actualization.

There is no shortage of critical literature drawing attention to the values and assumptions implicit in sociological analysis. Such criticism is clearly important in enabling us to become aware of our assumptions and implicit values and to make them explicit. We certainly cannot avoid such assumptions, and in this sense, the critics of the value-free sociology have a case. Indeed, it is important to be reminded of the more fundamental issues which may be brushed aside by those preoccupied by middle-range survey research.[1]

What is more dangerous is the current fashion to believe that the 'myth of a value-free sociology' has been exploded. But no one who has read carefully Alvin Gouldner's challenging exploration of the issues can take so simple a view. Indeed, Gouldner draws attention to the important part which the value-free principle has

[1] See, for example, John Horton, op. cit., pp. 294–8, and A. W. Gouldner, *The Coming Crisis of Western Sociology* (1970).

39

played in enhancing the autonomy of sociology and its freedom (but not in all countries) from political pressures. It 'provided the foundation for the development of more reliable knowledge about men. Moralistic reflexes suspended, it was now more possible to sift conscience with the rod of reason and to cultivate moral judgements that expressed man's total character as an adult person: he need not now live quite so much by his past parental programming, but in terms of his more mature present.'[1] True, Gouldner goes on to castigate those who shelter behind the need for objectivity in the sociological enterprise as an excuse for not acting on their knowledge, and failing to speak out on social issues. But this brings us to the final issue, the 'uses of sociology'.

THE USES OF SOCIOLOGY

Finally, we come to the question: Why study sociology? There are three main answers to this question—conservative, revolutionary and pragmatic. Sociology came into existence as an essentially conservative answer to the problems of revolution and change at the beginning of the nineteenth century.[2] For both Comte and Spencer, society was a natural system with its own laws of evolution and change. In the hands of Spencer, sociology lent strong ideological support to nineteenth-century *laissez-faire* economics. Any attempt at social amelioration, for example, would be an interference with the laws of natural selection and the survival of the fittest, and would threaten the health of the social organism. Much contemporary American sociology is basically conservative and anti-revolutionary, or at least stems from implicit value commitments to the American conception of democracy.[3]

Not surprisingly, this has stimulated a concern with a more radical sociology, seeking inspiration from Marx, and 'committed' to radical comment. Such commitment has little patience with the scientific claim to a 'value-free' sociology, and is impatient with empiricism and its preoccupation with the smaller issues. Its preference is for involvement with the fundamental problems of war and peace, and concern with the broad drift of capitalist society.[4]

The prevailing tradition in Britain has been pragmatic—to find an answer to social problems. This is best exemplified by the

[1] Alvin Gouldner, 'Anti-Minotaur: The Myth of a Value-Free Sociology', in I. L. Horowitz (ed.), *The New Sociology* (1965), Chapter 13.

[2] D. Martindale, op. cit., p. 122.

[3] See, for example, D. Bell, *The End of Ideology* (1960).

[4] One of the most powerful and challenging exponents of this position is C. Wright Mills. See his *Power Elite* (1946) and *The Causes of World War III* (1958). See also I. L. Horowitz, op. cit.

Fabians, and the investigations of philanthropists such as Booth and Rowntree into the 'condition of Britain' question. Studies of poverty, factory conditions and urban living have, to a large extent, been pioneered outside academic sociology, which has until recently shown little interest in such questions, having its roots rather in the nineteenth-century philosophy of history and a concern with the broad pattern of social change and development. Largely under the influence of Professor Titmuss, the investigation of social problems has now become academically respectable and is exemplified by the work of the Institute of Community Studies.

There is one further source of disenchantment with sociology. Some students find the constraints of a 'scientific' approach to the study of society irksome and cramping. They wish to range more freely in their thinking and discussion, and find the pressures to relate and justify their ideas by rigorous empirical testing unduly restrictive.

To some extent, this difficulty springs from a misunderstanding of the nature of science. Science is *not* just collecting facts: it involves creative and imaginative thinking. It differs from the arts in that it is not concerned simply with communicating private experience, but goes further and seeks to establish a body of accepted 'public' knowledge. Some are better at generating ideas, and some at testing them. There is room for both in the sociological enterprise.

For those whose interests lie in the bigger issues—in the search for understanding about the ontological nature of man, the problem of freedom, the challenge of existentialism and similar moral and humanistic issues explored by the traditional 'humanities'—there is much food for thought, not only in the writings of the founding fathers such as Durkheim and Weber but in the more recent work of Merton, Goffman and Berger.[1] Goffman, for example, paints a picture of human interactions as a 'con' game, in which individuals 'manage' the presentation of the self.[2] None reading Goffman can be quite as confident that they know their real selves or the real identities of those they interact with most frequently. And as Peter Berger[3] argues so convincingly, *homo sociologicus* would appear to be depressingly unfree. Not only is he a puppet acting out the script that society has written for him, but he has internalized the part so well through socialization that he is not even aware of his captivity. Berger uses Sartre's notion of

[1] For a most readable and challenging discussion of the contribution of sociology to humanistic issues, see R. P. Cuzzort, *Humanity and Modern Sociological Thought* (1969).
[2] E. Goffman, *The Presentation of Self in Everyday Life* (1969).
[3] P. Berger, op. cit.

41

'bad faith' to get us off the hook. An awareness of our condition, he argues, is the first step towards freedom. Not to exercise such choice as we have is 'bad faith'. But such heady excitements are only part of the diet of sociology. Those who wish solely to explore ideas, and to eschew the more painstaking and sometimes tedious enterprise of testing them, had best look elsewhere.

This brings us to the final difficulty—the distinction between knowledge and action. The knowledge that we are 'prisoners of society' does not absolve us from the responsibility of exercising choices and acting 'morally' so far as we are able. But however much knowledge may influence action and be a basis for action, the task of the university is the advancement and dissemination of knowledge, not involvement in action. Sociology *is* an academic subject, pursued by academics in universities and colleges. What unites all scholars of sociology is the attempt at a rigorous, objective pursuit of knowledge. The enterprise is dispassionate in the sense that every effort is made to avoid distortion, not of course with complete success. (This does not mean that there is no passion as a driving force behind the dedicated preoccupation of an academic with poverty, or the problem of order, or the attempt to build a theoretical model of a social system.)

What people *do* with sociology is, of course, another matter —and their own concern. Some come to university to learn sociology to equip them to teach, or to be more competetent social workers, or to be more effective in striving for fundamental structural changes in society or to find a personal philosophy of life. What unites them, whether they are temporary student members of the community of scholars, or whether they have devoted their lives to it, whether they are reactionaries or revolutionaries, is the pursuit of knowledge. They may agree to choose to concentrate on studies which have relevance and application to the contemporary world. But they would not agree on action. Any attempt by universities to become committed to courses of action would split them into fragments and destroy them as communities of scholars. This does not absolve the scholar from social responsibility or from active involvement in the community. But it does require him to keep his personal uses of sociology out of the lecture room.[1]

But even if we maintain the distinction between knowledge and action, there remains the problem of how far the universities should focus their studies on knowledge which is relevant for action.

[1] There are exceptions which prove the rule. Professional schools such as medical schools do educate and train students for action. But they also ensure through rigorous selection that all agree on the action for which they are being trained—all intend to practice medicine.

'Paradoxically there is much in common between technocrats who have no use for free intellectuals and clamour for the production of ever more mental technicians, and supposedly radical students who cannot understand the needs of disinterested inquiry and clamour for the regimentation and politicizing of the intellect. . . . If the mind is chained to the immediate demands of the practicalities of the hour, it loses that autonomy without which it becomes a simple machine for "doing things".[1]

DISCUSSION

Any academic discipline involves looking at the world from a particular point of view. The sciences have several distinctive features. Firstly, they are concerned only with the kinds of propositions and explanations which can be verified by reference to observable and measurable data. Secondly, they are an attempt to reach 'a consensus of rational opinion' among the members of a discipline by communicating and checking the findings of research. Thirdly, they attempt to construct general theories which can explain a wide variety of phenomena.

Clearly sociology has a long way to go. Indeed, it is a measure of its immaturity as a science that dissension seems to dominate rather than consensus. Perhaps this is because in debate sociologists tend to emphasize their differences. It could equally well be argued that there has been remarkable progress. At the theoretical level, there are signs of marked convergence. And the split between empiricism, 'collecting facts for governments', and theory has narrowed as, on the one hand, there is more usable theory available, and, on the other, new generations of sociologists show increasing sophistication in designing research projects within theoretical frameworks.

Whether the social sciences will ever be able to develop the theoretical rigour and consensus of the natural sciences, only time can tell. After all, it is only in the last decade or so that biology has begun to emerge as a 'hard' science. Prior to the Jacob-Monod theory in genetics, the biological sciences were largely descriptive and classificatory. We cannot predict what new knowledge the future will bring. But the enormous explanatory power of theory applied to the study of natural phenomena suggests that the attempt to develop a science of society may be equally worth-while.

Finally, no attempt has been made to give any account of research methods, though not because they are unimportant. It is not the methods of collecting data which distinguish the sciences.

[1] Lewis A. Coser, *Men of Ideas* (1965), p. xvii.

And the methods used in sociology are, in general, common to other social sciences. So the interested student is referred to the excellent texts recommended in the Reading.

READING

P. Berger, *An Invitation to Sociology: A Humanist Perspective* (Doubleday, 1963).

E. Chinoy, *Sociological Perspectives* (Random House, 1964).

L. A. Coser and B. Rosenburg (eds), *Sociological Theory* (Collier-Macmillan, 1964).

P. S. Cohen, *Modern Social Theory* (Heinemann, 1968).

M. Coulson and D. S. Riddell, *Approaching Sociology* (Routledge, 1970).

R. P. Cuzzort, *Humanity and Modern Sociological Thought* (Holt, Rinehart and Winston, 1969).

M. Duverger, *Introduction to the Social Sciences* (Allen and Unwin, 1964).

D. G. MacRae, *Ideology and Society* (Heinemann, 1961).

D. Martindale, *The Nature and Types of Sociological Theory* (Routledge, 1964).

C. W. Mills, *The Sociological Imagination* (Oxford University Press, 1959).

C. A. Moser, *Survey Methods in Social Investigation* (Heinemann, 1959).

Robert A. Nisbet, *The Sociological Tradition* (Heinemann, 1972).

K. Thompson and J. Tunstall, *Sociological Perspectives* (Penguin, 1971), Part 5.

P. Worsley (ed.), *Modern Sociology: Introductury Readings* (Penguin, 1970), Parts 1 and 2.

THE SOCIAL SYSTEM

Chapter 2

THE FAMILY

There are few areas of social life in which we are more conscious of change than in the family and sexual behaviour. Moreover, rising divorce rates, an increase in illegitimate births and in extra-marital sexual behaviour, are seen by some as signs of the impending breakdown in family life and even as threats to the social order. Some will stress the need for change—to discard outworn conventions and codes which stifle the realization of rich and spontaneous human relations, while others will emphasize the need for some framework of norms and rules as a condition for stability and the development of deep and enduring relations.

Family life, from one perspective, is intensely personal and private. Yet there are few areas where the relations between the individual and society are brought into sharper focus. Whatever may be the preferences of individuals for children, society cannot remain indifferent. Threats of population decline or of over-population will press governments to seek to influence such personal and intimate decisions. How free are individuals to choose how many children they will have, and even whom they will marry, and what kind of relationship they will build with their spouse?

The fact that many aspects of family life are seen as problems, and the emotive and value-laden nature of many issues, present special difficulties for the sociology of the family. The definition of divorce as a 'problem' is itself a value judgement. The question could be phrased: What are the consequences of lifelong mono-gamous marriages compared with other forms of marital relation-ship? In short, this is an area where it is particularly important to distinguish between social and sociological problems.[1] The socio-logical study of the family has understandably reflected its

[1] See Chapter 9 for a further discussion of this issue. See also M. Anderson (ed.), *Sociology of the Family* (1971), Introduction.

problematic features as well as the dominant position of structural functionalist theory, with its stress on consensus and on the normative control of interaction. It is only recently that studies have begun to explore the processes of exchange and bargaining[1] as a means of understanding the differing patterns of marriage within the framework of prevailing norms. And it is only recently, too, that we have begun to explore the interaction between the family and other areas of social life, notably work roles and education.

THE FAMILY AND THE SOCIAL SYSTEM

One thing we can be sure of: the family takes a wide variety of forms in different societies. In Western societies, for example, it would be strongly condemned if a husband took a second wife without divorcing the first. Yet in some Middle Eastern societies up to four wives are allowed. Or again, Western civilization is almost unique in the stress which it places on romantic love as the basis of marriage.[2] There are some societies in which the traditional roles are reversed, women are the dominant sex and regulate the economic life of the community.[3] And there have even been some attempts to remove the child-rearing and socializing functions from the family.[4]

In spite of such wide variations, it would seem that the family in some form or another exists in most societies. And the changes in contemporary society may herald changes in the form and functions of the family rather than its breakdown or disappearance. Our task is then to explore the relations between the family and society in order to explain the characteristics of the family and if possible to predict changes in its form and the part which it plays in society.

The family and culture
Part of the explanation, as we have already seen, is to be found in the *culture* of society. In every society, culture defines the rules which pattern the relations between husbands and wives, parents and children. Thus, there are norms about the selection of partners (including courtship and incest taboos), about husband/wife and parent/child roles (including numbers of partners to the marriage, division of labour between husbands and wives, and the distri-

---

[1] Such processes are explored more fully in Chapter 8.
[2] K. Little, 'The Basis of Marriage', in E. Butterworth and D. Weir (eds), *The Sociology of Modern Britain* (1970), pp. 28–30.
[3] M. Mead, *Sex and Temperament in Three Primitive Societies* (1964).
[4] See N. W. Bell and E. F. Vogel (eds), *A Modern Introduction to the Family* (1960), Chapter 5.

bution of authority within the family). Norms also lay down what are socially acceptable forms of sexual behaviour, including the tolerance or condemnation of extra-marital sexual relations.

Culture then defines both what we can expect and what is considered legitimate. The relations between husband and wife are structured by their mutual expectations as to what constitutes 'wifely' or 'husbandly' conduct. Each acts out his role within the prescribed limits, or suffers the sanctions applied to deviants. Moreover, each thinks that his or her behaviour is perfectly 'natural', yet the wide differences in family roles between societies, or even between different segments of the same society, underline the *social* structuring of family life.

Culture, then, goes some way to explain the persistence of family patterns. But it cannot explain how the specific patterns of behaviour emerged in the first place. In the West, we accept monogamous marriage as the only conceivable form of marriage. The existence of entrenched cultural norms, underpinned in this case by law and religion, may explain the persistence of monogamy. But how can we account for the decline in the patriarchal family, and a world trend towards conjugal family patterns? To do this, we must look for those factors which reinforce or challenge existing practices. We shall find, for example, that a number of changes in the nineteenth century led to a challenging of the prevailing norms condemning the practice of contraception and eventually to a change in the norm. We also find a shift to a more equalitarian relationship between husbands and wives. For a clue to such changes, we shall later examine the interaction between the family and other parts of the social system, particularly its interactions with the economic system.

The foregoing paragraph may be taken to imply that culture is a passive, dependent variable, adjusting to pressures to change. Although this may be true in the long run, in the short run we have to treat culture as an independent variable, exerting an extremely powerful influence. Moreover, cultural beliefs and norms do not exist in isolation. Beliefs about the family, for example, are frequently associated with religious beliefs. In fact, in some societies, the latter may determine the former, resisting pressures for change.

A major determinant of monogamy in the West derives from the influence of religion. Long before the Christian era, both Greek and Roman religion exerted a powerful pressure towards life-long monogamy. It was believed that the spirits of the dead depended for their well-being on the care of the living. The veneration and care of ancestors constituted the religion of the family, but such tasks could only be carried out by the sons of a 'religious' marriage. Consequently, irregular sexual relations by wives were severely punished.[1]

The traditional Christian doctrine has stressed the inherent sinfulness of sexual behaviour and has sought to confine it within the marriage relation and to direct it towards the procreation of children.[2] Such doctrines have had a substantial influence on marriage laws, and on marriage relationships. The contemporary family then is in part a function of such normative and legal elements in society.

Of course, we could go farther back and ask why Christianity came to teach particular views on marriage and the family. But we have to draw a line somewhere, and this particular question is not of major relevance for the study of contemporary social systems. A more significant question would arise from the observation that contemporary religious views on the family are undergoing change. In 1908, for example, the report of the Lambeth Conference of the Church of England condemned the practice of birth control.[3] In 1956, the same conference concluded that family limitation was compatible with Christian doctrine. The sociological issue here is how far religion can be treated as a dependent variable, and how far social changes will bring about further modifications of religious teaching on the family. It will clearly be difficult for society to accommodate a substantial discrepancy between precept and practice. Meanwhile, we can observe that pressure from religious organizations and viewpoints has considerably shaped legislation, especially on the question of divorce, and that religious views on such issues vary among the churches and are undergoing change.

This stress on the institutional pressures which structure the family has led some to argue that the stability of the family derives very largely from such a legal framework and system of moral rules. The 'institutionalists' argue that any weakening of such rules, by liberalizing divorce laws for example, would lead to a fatal weakening of family ties and would contribute substantially to the disintegration of family life. In short, it is law and morality which hold the family together. This is precisely the kind of question which requires empirical sociological investigation, and to which we will return later.

Within this framework of legal and social rules, there are con-

[1] F. de Coulanges, *The Ancient City* (1956).

[2] O. R. McGregor, *Divorce in England* (1957). Chapter 1 reviews the history of divorce and marriage in England.

[3] 'The Conference regards with alarm the growing practice of the artificial restriction of the family, and earnestly calls upon all Christian people to discountenance the use of artificial means of restriction as demoralizing to character and hostile to national welfare.'

siderable variations in the patterns of marriage and family life. In some localities, for example, husbands and wives share a variety of activities, and arrive at important decisions such as budgeting the family income after joint discussion. In other areas, husbands share few activities with wives, treating the home mainly as a place for bed and board, and a base from which they go to work or for leisure activities which they share with their work-mates. Their wives do not know what their husbands earn and receive a fixed 'wage' for housekeeping.[1]

One explanation of such differences would be that the traditions of family life vary. Men and women will have learnt particular ways of playing roles as husbands and wives through their up-bringing and will perpetuate these in their own marriages. Moreover, they will respond to the 'sub-culture' of their locality where there will be generally accepted *norms* or rules of family behaviour (the husband should be the boss), *values* attached to various aspects of married life (companionship is one of the most rewarding aspects of family life) and various *beliefs* about marriage (that men are by nature polygamous). Different segments of society certainly vary, and such sub-cultures will exert pressures on those who live within them. They will reinforce some patterns of conduct and inhibit others. Where the men spend their eve-nings in the pubs, leaving their wives at home, it will be difficult for one to be odd-man out. But this does not explain why the patterns differ, only the fact that, once established, they will be resistant to change.

The influence of culture must not be exaggerated. Uniformity of conduct is not by itself evidence of normative consensus. For example, there is a mass of evidence to show that the selection of a mate is generally *homogamous*—that is to say, like marry like. Such similarities of education, class, religion between spouses were attributed to normative pressures. More recent research, however, has thrown doubt on this and has stressed the importance of opportunity. Quite simply, interaction, and therefore choice, is most likely to be with those of similar background.

Family and kinship

Some have tried to explain different patterns of marriage by relating them to social class.[2] A number of studies of working-class areas, such as Bethnal Green[3] have described the three-

[1] M. Anderson (ed.), op. cit., Part 3.
[2] The concept of class will be examined in Chapter 7. The terms 'working class' and 'middle class' will be used to refer to manual and non-manual occupations.
[3] M. Young and P. Willmott, *Family and Kinship in East London* (1957).

generation 'mum-centred' family, in which married daughters remain closely related to their mothers, while husbands spend much of their leisure-time outside the home. Such facts have been used as evidence that kinship is still a powerful force in the older industrial areas. Young and Willmott noticed, however, that when Bethnal Green families moved to new housing estates on the outskirts of London, the close ties with 'mum' weakened. Mogey[1] observed a similar change in his study of Oxford families. But more significant, the relations between husbands and wives changed. Husbands began to spend more time in the home, and to share in the household tasks, including care of the children. In more technical terms, *segregated conjugal roles* became *joint* or *integrated*, and marriages became *home-centred* instead of *mum-centred*.

Why was this? In posing such questions, we can begin to move from description to analysis. We can begin to identify a number of variables and to ask questions about the relations between them. Elizabeth Bott,[2] for example, considers that the extent to which the nuclear family of husband and wife is caught up in a wider network of relationships is the main factor shaping the relations between husbands and wives. In Bethnal Green, for example, both spouses are caught up in a network of close ties with kin and community. Marriage is super-imposed, as it were, on a previous pattern of social ties, interactions and interrelations, and these are so strong that they persist after marriage. Each spouse continues to be pulled outside the home so that the development of joint activities is inhibited. Conjugal roles follow the segregated pattern. Removal to a new housing estate then will weaken the links binding husband and wife to the social network, and the emotional support, which this provides, making it more likely that each will turn to the other for help and support. In this context joint or integrated conjugal roles are more likely to develop.

More recent studies have questioned Bott's interpretation of the nature of the relationship between the social networks and conjugal roles. According to Bott, it is the connectedness of the social network which prevents the development of joint conjugal roles. We can certainly agree that where spouses, especially the wife, interact frequently with her kin, that this would be incompatible with joint conjugal roles.[3] A rather different interpretation

---

[1] J. M. Mogey, *Family and Community* (Oxford, 1956).

[2] E. Bott, *Family and Social Network* (London, 1957).

[3] C. Rosser and C. Harris, *The Family and Social Change* (1965), p. 207. It could also be argued that in traditional working-class areas, role segregation within the elementary family is accompanied by role segregation in the social network, and that it is the latter which maintains the high degree of connectedness in the social network. See H. Fallding, 'The Family and the Idea of a Cardinal Role', *Human Relations*, Vol. 14, 1961, No. 4.

is given by Rosser and Harris. They argue that a major factor is the domestic involvement of the wife. Segregated roles have been particularly characteristic of working-class families in the past, with 'the wife tied down at home with frequent pregnancies and a prolonged involvement in child-rearing while the husband went off to long, arduous hours at work and thence with his work-mates to club or pub. The more women are involved in domestic affairs, the more likely they are to lead separate lives from their husbands, and the more probable that they will interact with their mothers in an exchange of domestic tasks made possible by proximity of residence. The extended family is for such wives a 'mothers' union', in which husbands are only marginally involved.

The debate on the extent of kinship ties has not been confined to the working class. But in the middle class, it is the link between father or father-in-law and son or son-in-law which is particularly important as a source of financial aid and support, especially during the early years of family building.[1] The extensive kinship connections at the upper levels of society undoubtedly exist but have been less fully documented and explored.[2]

The family and the economic system

The discussion so far suggests that social class is one important variable associated with the existence of extended kinship ties beyond the elementary family. This leads to the more specific question: In what ways does the husband's (and possibly wife's) role in the economic system affect family structure? The husband's occupation is a major determinant of the family's market situation. And in the past, especially in those areas where opportunities for female employment have been limited, the family has been economically extremely vulnerable, and even among the better paid workers, separated from poverty by little more than one wage packet. The extended kinship network has, in these circumstances, performed an important function as a mutual aid society, providing some small measure of insurance against unemployment or illness of the wage-earner.

The relationship between the *work-situation* and the family can be seen most dramatically in studies of what can be called 'extreme' occupations: those that make extreme demands on the individual. Data exists on two of these—coal-mining[3] and distant-water fishing.[4] In both cases we have a picture of work, at the coal face,

[1] C. Bell, *Middle-Class Families* (1968).

[2] T. Lupton and C. S. Wilson, 'The Kinship Connections of "Top Decision Makers"', in P. Worsley (ed.), *Modern Sociology: Introductory Readings* (1970), pp. 151–64.

[3] N. Dennis *et al.*, *Coal is Our Life* (1956).

[4] J. Tunstall, *The Fishermen* (1962).

and on trawlers, which is dangerous and damaging, and demands close co-operation on the job, where one man's mistake can cause the death of others. The men are strongly attracted to a job which pays well and which they define as virile, manly work. But they also hate many aspects of it and seek the forgetfulness of alcohol in the long round of pub visits on Saturday and Sunday, wives left at home. To repair the damages exacted by his work, the miner expects a wife who will feed and comfort him, making few demands in return. Indeed, the relationship can be conceptualized as that of 'servant'. About the trawlermen, Tunstall says, 'Some men quickly come to regard their wives mainly as providers of sexual and cooking services in return for a weekly wage.'

There is only scanty evidence on the influence of other occupations on the family. But what there is suggests that the extent to which a man finds his work absorbing will be related to the significance of family life for him. The less a man is work-centred, the more likely he is to be home-centred and to treat his wife as a 'companion'.[1]

The extent of the husband's involvement in work is similarly used by Edgell to explain conjugal role relations in middle-class families. Those who are strongly committed to occupational advancement, *spiralists*, are likely to develop segregated conjugal roles and to exercise a dominant influence in the family, while those who are not strongly oriented to success are more likely to develop joint conjugal roles and equalitarian relations.[2]

A man's occupation will also determine his *market situation* (income, security, chances of promotion), and this in turn has been shown to be a significant variable influencing the relations between husbands and wives.[3] Husbands higher up the occupational ladder have more resources available to bring to the family situation. Goode refers to this process as *role-bargaining*.[4] The control which a family can exercise over its members depends in part on their relative bargaining power—the reciprocal rewards which each can offer others. The working-class family has few resources by which it can control its members. Unlike an agricultural community, in which sons are economically dependent on fathers, industrial society offers economic independence to sons and the chance of bettering their father's position. More-

[1] S. Cotgrove, 'The Relations Between Work and Non-Work Among Technicians', *Sociological Review*, Vol. 13, July 1965, No. 2.

[2] S. Edgell, 'Spiralists: Their Careers and Family Lives', *B.J.S.*, September 1970.

[3] R. O. Blood and D. M. Wolfe, *Husbands and Wives* (1960).

[4] W. J. Goode, 'The Process of Role Bargaining in the Impact of Urbanization and Industrialization on Family Systems', *Current Sociology*, Vol. 12, 1963–4, No. 1.

over, the creation of thousands of new jobs makes it less likely that the kin group can obtain appropriate jobs for its members.

By contrast, upper-class fathers can offer both economic advantages and social position to their sons, who cannot strike a better bargain outside the family, which retains therefore a greater hold over them. 'Thus we have the apparent paradox resolved, that the families that are most successful in the industrialized and urbanized system are precisely those families which are farthest removed in pattern from the conjugal family which is thought to be so harmoniously adjusted to industrialization.'[1]

The economic position of both wives and adolescents has been greatly improved in recent years by economic expansion and full-employment. More wives are now working than at any time this century and young people are receiving relatively higher wages than ever before. Both now have more bargaining power in the family and this may well have contributed to the decline in the power of the husbands over wives and parents over children. Working wives are likely to try to change the division of labour within the family and to gain more co-operation from their husbands in household tasks. We can expect then in such families, a further shift towards joint conjugal roles, and away from the 'servant' towards 'companionship' relations. American researches suggest that the wife going to work is the most important single factor determining the decline in the power of the husband and a change in the division of labour between husbands and wives.[2]

Working wives

The entry of women into the labour market has important consequences for the family. Two main trends can be noted. Firstly, there is an increase in the proportion of married women employed from 10 per cent in the 1930s to over 33 per cent in the 1960s. Secondly, and closely related, married women now constitute a much larger proportion of the labour force than hitherto, and a much larger proportion of all working women are married.

Demographic changes are part of the explanation. The percentage of women never married is steadily falling, from 15 per cent in 1900 to (an estimated) 5 per cent in the 1970s. Moreover, younger marriages mean that the number of single women is also declining. In 1951, one-sixth were married by the age of 20. By

[1] Ibid. There is a considerable literature which explores the similarity or contrast of forms ('isomorphism' and 'heteromorphism') between work and family life. See R. and R. Rapoport, 'Work and Family in Contemporary Society', in M. Anderson (ed.), op. cit., pp. 272–96.

[2] R. O. Blood and D. M. Wolfe, op. cit.

1973, this proportion will have increased to around one-quarter. These changes mean that the numbers of single women available for recruitment to traditional female occupations such as teaching and nursing are declining, and such jobs will increasingly have to rely on married women.[1]

The growth of family planning, smaller families and the concentration of child-bearing during the early years of marriage mean that more women are free to enter gainful employment after the age of 40. Indeed, women are now faced with many years of active life after the completion of their traditional child-bearing function, which is no longer a full-time job.

Changes in the economic system have also contributed to the increased employment of women, both single and married. Full-employment in the post-war period has led many employers (often reluctantly) to employ married women, sometimes on a part-time basis. Changes in the economy have also increased the numbers employed as clerks, shop assistants, social workers, medical auxiliaries and similar occupations which lend themselves particularly to female employment. Women now outnumber men in employment in shops and offices, while nearly 50 per cent of all employed women are in non-manual jobs, compared with less than 30 per cent of males.

But such changes do not necessarily imply a shift of interest on the part of women away from their traditional role as wives and mothers to a growing interest in and preoccupation with work. Although this may be a trend for women who have a professional training and career,[2] the great majority of working wives use work instrumentally as a source of income to be spent on the home— on refurnishings and decorations, durable consumer goods, holidays and clothing for the family, and only secondarily because they are lonely or bored. They work to raise the standards of their families, and some regard those who stay at home as muddlers and lazy-bones.[3] The increase in working wives is, in fact, perfectly consistent with the growth in home-centredness. Such women put their families first, and are not interested in promotion. This purely instrumental involvement is confirmed by the fact that the peak year for working wives is around age 42, with a steady decline after 45. By age 55–9, only 16 per cent remain employed.[4]

[1] C. M. Stewart, 'Trends in the Employment of Married Women', *B.J.S.*, March 1961.
[2] For a discussion of this predominantly middle-class group, see A. Myrdal and V. Klein, *Women's Two Roles* (1956), and M. Fogarty, et. al., *Sex, Career and Family* (1971).
[3] V. Klein, *Britain's Married Women Workers* (1965).
[4] *Census of Population*, 1951. One per cent sample tables.

The consequences of the increase in working wives for conjugal roles have already been noted. As one husband expressed it, 'it makes [marriage] more of a partnership somehow'.[1] There is no evidence to suggest that for most women, the performance of two roles as wives and workers damages their family functions, though, of course, many find the situation one of strain. Social workers have failed to discover any adverse effects on the families of the majority of working wives, though there are exceptions, especially where mothers of pre-school children are forced to work from economic necessity. Nor is there evidence that delinquency rates are higher for the children of working mothers.[2] On the contrary, some research indicates that children may be harmed by excessive maternal care or over-protection.[3]

FUNCTIONS OF THE FAMILY

So far we have been looking at the ways in which the social system influences the family and kinship systems. But the relationship is not one-way: the family and kinship systems also perform important functions in the social system.

Reproduction
Every society must ensure that an adequate number of children are born. Furthermore, such children must acquire the personal characteristics which are necessary for them to carry out their roles in adult society. These functions—reproduction and socialization—are the major functions which the family performs. In a few societies, such as the Israeli Kibbutzim,[4] the nuclear family may play only a small part in the subsequent upbringing and socialization of the child. But most societies ensure that children are born to parents who are in a stable relationship, reinforced by the norms of society—that is, are married.

The reproductive function of the family is in many ways the most fully documented aspect of its behaviour in industrial societies. Governments need statistics and forecasts of population growth to enable them to plan school buildings, houses, to make provision for the elderly and for a variety of other decisions on economic and social issues. Census data is available in Britain from 1801, and demographers have amassed volumes of statistical data.

[1] V. Klein, op. cit. (1965), p. 79.
[2] For a detailed discussion of this group, see B. Thompson and A. Finlayson, 'Married Women Who Work in Early Motherhood', *B.J.S.*, June 1963.
[3] B. Wootton, *Social Science and Social Pathology* (1959).
[4] See N. W. Bell and E. F. Vogel, *The Family* (1960).

The main trends are clear enough. Since the 1870s the birth-rate (numbers of children born per thousand population) has been declining. Behind this decline, the salient fact is a reduction in the average number of live births per married woman. Compared with an average of six children for those married in the 1870s, the typical family size for those married in the 1920s was a little over two, and has more recently gone up to rather less than three. At the earlier date, 24 per cent of mothers had 0–3 children, compared with 81 per cent for those married in 1925.[1] And while 33 per cent of Victorian mothers had eight or more children, only 2·3 per cent of those married after the First World War had similarly large families. In other words, today the typical family is two or three children (50 per cent come in this category). In Victorian times, families varied all the way from no children at all (9 per cent) to ten or more children (10 per cent) with about an equal percentage in all the intervening categories. However, because of the extension of education, the total number of years of dependency has declined less dramatically.

Now one conclusion emerges fairly clearly. Such a decline in *fertility* cannot be due to a decline in reproductive capacity. The contemporary mother, who has one, two or three children (usually in the first ten years of marriage), could obviously, in the majority of cases, go on to have the six, eight or ten as her great-grandmother. The fact that child-bearing is concentrated in the early years of marriage, and then ceases fairly abruptly, leaves little doubt that the smaller contemporary family is the result of delib-erate decisions on the part of parents to limit conception. This conclusion is confirmed by an inquiry into family limitation which shows that the use of various methods of contraception has gone up. Only 15 per cent of wives married before 1910 practised some form of birth control, compared with 55 per cent of those married during 1940–7.[2]

Such facts do not explain why parents decide to limit their families. They suggest simply that the increasing availability and use of effective contraceptive means has enabled the typical family to be dramatically reduced in size. To discover why parents now limit their families, we have to ask in what ways the interaction between the family and society before the 1870s differs from the situation in the 1900s.

There was one main reason why the motive to use contraception was greatly strengthened in the nineteenth century. Advances in

[1] Royal Commission on Population (1946). For demographic data, see also A. M. Carr-Saunders, D. Caradog Jones and C. A. Moser, *Survey of Social Conditions in England and Wales* (1958).
[2] *Papers of the Royal Commission on Population*, Vol. 1, Table 37.

hygiene and medicine had resulted in a marked decline in mortality, particularly among infants. A much higher proportion of children survived birth and were reared to maturity. In other words, in the past, mortality had effectively limited family size. The lesson of the nineteenth century is that centuries of established patterns of family behaviour could not be changed in a hurry— a lesson which is reinforced by the great difficulties in establishing population control in the developing countries, where the decline in infant mortality, unaccompanied by any compensating changes in the behaviour of married couples, is causing an explosive growth in population.

To understand what seems to us to be the not very sensible practice of having ten children, we must examine the interaction between the family and the social system. Part of the explanation is to be found in the interaction between the family and culture. Pre-industrial societies are characterized by high levels of mortality. Moreover, the population is threatened and periodically reduced by famines, epidemics and wars. It is not surprising that such societies should urge child-bearing as a duty and condemn practices which aim at the limitation of fertility. And England was no exception. Even today, although families of the magnitude of Victorian times would be condemned, the idea of marriage includes the idea of children, and few voluntarily abstain.

Moreover, such cultural values have been incorporated into religious beliefs and in this way have come to be part of religious dogma and underpinned by religious sanctions. The marriage service of the Church of England puts the procreation of children as the first of its aims. The Church, too, has in the past strongly condemned contraceptive practices. Those who advocated the use of birth control were prosecuted, and until 1967 local authority clinics were permitted to give advice only to women for whom a further pregnancy would be detrimental to health.[1]

Despite such prohibitions and condemnations, the practice of birth control has spread. And concomitantly, the culture has been modified and now adopts a more permissive attitude, as exemplified by the encouragement to family planning in the report of the Lambeth Conference of 1958. We still have to explain, therefore, why the practice has increased. One important fact provides a

[1] Quoted by O. R. McGregor and G. Rowntree in A. T. Welford *et al.*, *Society* (1962), p. 404. See also D. V. Glass, *Population Policies and Movements in Europe* (1940), Chapter 1, for an account of the birth-control movement. Since the 1967 Act, family planning may be provided on social as well as medical grounds.

starting-point. Family limitation in the latter part of the nineteenth century was predominantly a middle-class practice. It was not until the 1920s that the wives of skilled manual workers report contraceptive practices as frequently as non-manual workers.[1] For those married in the early 1930s, there are no class differences (although these re-emerge subsequently). What then, led the middle classes to limit their families in the 1870s? And why did the manual workers not follow suit until a lapse of nearly fifty years?

The interaction between the family and the economic system provides the main clue. In an industrial society, the family ceases to be the main unit of organized production. Its economic function shifts from production to consumption. It is the family unit which consumes food, clothing and shelter, and such goods are bought mainly with the income of the male wage-earner. The larger the household, the more thinly a single income has to be spread,[2] unlike the agricultural family, where each child soon grows into a hand to work on the farm. In industrial England, child labour was gradually prohibited, first by the factory acts and then by the extension of compulsory education. As an increasingly high proportion of children survived birth, the total burden of pregnancies increased.

But it was not those who could least afford children who took the first steps to have fewer. Nevertheless, J. A. Banks[3] has argued that it was economic pressures which contributed to the decline in middle-class fertility after 1870. The middle class had experienced rapidly growing prosperity in the 1850s and 1860s. But the 1870s saw the beginnings of a relative decline in the rate of growth of profits and increasing foreign competition. Moreover, many items in middle-class budgets, such as domestic servants and housing, were becoming increasingly expensive. Faced with the desire to maintain and continue to improve their standards of living in a context of economic stringency and of families far larger than many parents desired, one practical solution was to limit family size. Moreover, the Bradlaugh–Besant trial and public controversy over birth control drew attention to this as a possible solution. Once begun, such practices gradually spread. Lower paid white-collar workers were under particular pressure to limit

[1] *Papers of the Royal Commission on Population*, Vol. 1, Table 37.
[2] Even in middle-class homes, 'a large family still involves relative, if not absolute deprivation'. In larger working-class families, disadvantages are reflected in the lesser average height of children and a greater incidence of respiratory infection. O. R. McGregor and G. Rowntree, in Welford, op. cit., pp. 411–12.
[3] J. A. Banks, *Prosperity and Parenthood* (1954).

family size. As education became increasingly important for entry to middle-class occupations, middle-class parents became more anxious to bequeath the only inheritance within their means to ensure that their children would be able to continue in middle-class occupations—a good secondary education. And this meant a very small family.

It is less easy to explain the tardiness of the manual workers in adopting family limitation on a similar scale. Skilled workers were enjoying rising wages in the last decade of the century. But about one-third of the manual workers in industrial cities were living under conditions of poverty. Over-crowding, and poverty are not conducive to the foresight and planning which contraception involves. Short-term hedonism and passive acceptance of fate were the typical reactions to poverty.[1] These are not the conditions which favour a break from tradition and the introduction of innovating practices. And the subordinate 'servant' role of the manual-workers' wife tended to make her feel helpless at the prospect of successive unwanted pregnancies, and unable to take steps in the face of opposition and possible hostility from her husband. The segregated conjugal role structure of manual-workers' families defined the children as the wife's responsibility. Husbands paid over a fixed wage to their wives and it was for them to do the best they could.

The more recent increase in the birth-rate must also be explained. In part, it is due to the fact that a higher proportion of women are married,[2] to the younger age at marriage (from 23 in 1931 to 20 in 1962, for women), and the fact that women are having children at a younger age. Children who would have been born later are arriving earlier and the gap between generations is decreasing. These changes are themselves the result of rising incomes and the improvements in the supply of housing.[3] But the increase in fertility is not simply 'borrowing' children from the future. There is also evidence of an increase in family size. Younger marriages, of course, increase the risk of pregnancy, and married women are now faced with a longer potential childbearing period. There is some evidence that parents now want larger families. Incomes have risen, and welfare services have reduced, though

[1] See Chapter 6 for a more detailed discussion of working-class sub-culture.

[2] Higher male infant mortality, plus the effects of the First World War, skewed the sex ratio so that in 1921 there were 894 males per 1,000 females. In 1951 the ratio was 1,089 per 1,000 females.

[3] Overcrowding has been greatly reduced since 1930, except in a few large cities. The current shortage of housing reflects the increase in effective demand due to rising incomes. Improved contraception and earlier physical maturation may also have contributed.

not eliminated, the relative disadvantage of parenthood. Now that more can enjoy the material pleasure of affluence, some may begin to invest more in family life—becoming home-centred as a refuge from the anonymity of urban living and the meaninglessness of work. Such explanations must remain largely speculative until they have been tested by research.

The interaction between the family and the economic system is therefore very complex. There is no simple relation between poverty and fertility. There tends to be an inverse relation between wealth and family size. The high level of unemployment in the 1930s was accompanied by the rapid spread of contraception among manual workers. But the practice declined among those married from 1935 to 1947, and manual workers continue to have larger families than non-manual, although they can less well afford the cost. But other variables also operate, notably culture. And the relative value of children must be weighed against the sacrificed alternatives. The final equation will depend on both values and costs.

Illegitimacy
One corollary of the reproductive function of the family is the social condemnation of conceiving children out of wedlock. And a substantial increase in illegitimacy would indicate a change in the family's child-rearing function. Moreover, it would indicate a rejection of the norm which condemns extra-marital sexual intercourse. Crude illegitimacy rates indicate a substantial increase in illegitimacy during the Second World War, and larger numbers in the 1950s and 1960s compared with pre-1939. But all statistics require care in interpretation. Some maternities are conceived out of wedlock, but subsequently legitimized by the marriage of the pregnant bride. There has been a decline in the percentage of extra-marital conceptions thus legitimized. If the

TABLE 2.1

ILLEGITIMATE MATERNITIES AND PRE-MARITALLY CONCEIVED LEGITIMATE MATERNITIES, 1938–1956 ENGLAND AND WALES*

	Illegitimate maternities	Pre-maritally conceived legitimate maternities	Total conceived extra-maritally %	Extra-maritally conceived legitimized %
1938	27,440	64,530	14·4	70·2
1946	55,138	98,626	11·8	44·1
1956	34,113	54,895	12·6	61·7

* Based on Table XI, Registrar-General's *Statistical Review of England and Wales*, 1956, Part 3.

60

increase in the numbers of legitimate conceptions is also taken into account, we find that the percentage of all extra-marital conceptions was less in 1946 than in 1938 and remained lower in 1956 (Table 2.1). However, total illegitimate births have since increased to 69,806 by 1968, and of these, there has been a very marked increase in recent years of the proportion born to mothers under 20, so that these now constitute nearly one-third of the total. Of course, such facts may reflect charges in patterns of extra-marital sexual behaviour or in contraceptive practice. By the age of 18, one-third of boys and one-sixth of girls will have experienced sexual relations at least once.[1] But whether this is more or less frequent than their parents we cannot say. We do know that among boys experiencing sexual intercourse, less than half always use contraceptives and a quarter never use them. Moreover, 40 per cent of experienced boys are unconcerned whether their partners become pregnant. Although girls are more concerned, few do anything about it.[2]

However, illegitimacy is not primarily a teenage problem. Most illegitimate births are to mothers aged between 25 and 29. The 'problem' could be tackled either by achieving a reduction in extra-marital sexual behaviour, by the more widespread use of effective contraception, or by a change in social attitudes and arrangements for the children of unmarried mothers. The solution favoured will depend on the values and norms of society.[3]

Socialization

The family is not simply concerned with child-bearing. Child-rearing involves socializing the child to adopt the modes of behaviour appropriate for its age and sex in any particular society. We now know from anthropological studies that human personality is immensely pliable. Out of the biological raw material, a variety of different types of persons can be produced. We learn to play a variety of roles. Boys, for example, learn through identification with their fathers, how the behaviour of men differs from that of women in their society. Of course, societies have quite different norms of male and female behaviour. In one, the sex roles are the exact opposite of those in Victorian middle-class England. It is the men who sit idly gossiping and intriguing, putting flowers in their hair, and wondering what woman will glance in their direction, while the women work and hold the purse-strings.[4] Whatever the

[1] M. Schofield, *The Sexual Behaviour of Young People* (1965), p. 51.
[2] Ibid., pp. 227–9.
[3] For a comprehensive analysis of illegitimacy, see V. Wimperis, *The Unmarried Mother and Her Child* (1960).
[4] M. Mead, *Male and Female* (1964).

norm may be, men and women will grow up believing that the sexual roles they have learnt are 'human nature'. This process whereby society builds itself into our personalities and teaches us specific ways of acting, thinking and feeling, is the *socialization* process.

The socialization process is, in fact, very complex, and can only be briefly sketched here in order to indicate the role which the family plays in socializing the child.[1] From the day the child is born, he will begin to be socialized. For example, until recently mothers were urged to feed their babies only at strictly regulated intervals. The majority of middle-class mothers followed such rigid feeding schedules, while working-class mothers did not. Anthropological studies indicated, however, that demand-feeding may produce more secure personalities and fashions have swung in the opposite direction. Although rigid feeding schedules may not by themselves have a decisive effect on personality, they are a part of a pattern of '*deferred gratification*', which middle-class children are likely to experience. At a later age, for example, they will be urged to sacrifice immediate pleasures to get on with their homework in order to pass exams which will ensure them a better job in the future.

The American philosopher, G. H. Mead, and the founder of psychoanalysis, Sigmund Freud, have both contributed a good deal to our understanding of the socialization process. Mead stressed the great importance of language. If a mother wishes to stop a baby from some dangerous action, she will have to use physical restraint. An older child will respond to the verbal symbols 'Come back Johnny, you'll hurt yourself.' In fact, most social interaction is reaction to symbols, either verbal or expressive. It is, that is to say, *symbolic interaction*.

The role of the family in the socialization process is clearly crucial, particularly in what can be called *primary socialization*, that is, the development of those relatively stable elements in personality such as a sense of basic security. It has been observed, for example, that the middle class are not only more likely to practise *deferred gratification*, but are more strongly motivated towards achievement. Researches show that this results when parents set high goals for their children, expect high standards of excellence, stress independence and instil confidence.[2] By contrast, achievement motivation is not developed in authoritarian 'father-centred' families, in which children receive little training in independence and achievement. Authoritarian fathers thwart their

[1] See also Chapter 8.
[2] B. C. Rosen and R. D'Andrade, 'The Psychosocial Origins of Achievement Motivation', *Sociometry*, September 1959, pp. 185–218.

sons' efforts to be autonomous and self-reliant.[1] In other words, the family plays an important part in producing types of persons who have the characteristics appropriate for certain social roles.

Differences in the child-rearing practices between social classes have long been observed.[2] Recent studies[3] have brought to light some of the mechanisms involved in such differential socialization, and help to explain the more aggressive and severe socialization of working-class fathers. Fathers whose work gives them little autonomy, and who are controlled by others, exercising no control themselves, are found to be more aggressive and severe. Their sons less frequently admire such fathers or gain emotional support from them. These factors are in turn related to occupational aspirations. Mobility is maximum where socialization is moderate, parents share authority, sons identify with fathers, and fathers are involved in their boy's emotional life.[4]

In all societies, other agencies besides the family contribute to socialization. In advanced industrial societies, formal educational institutions become very important indeed. The child is also exposed to other socializing media, such as TV. But the family remains extremely important, particularly at the level of primary socialization. Children whose home-life has been seriously disturbed are much more likely to become delinquent and to fail to achieve a satisfactory adjustment to society.[5]

Economic and sustaining functions
In pre-industrial society, production is usually organized on a family basis. The domestic system in Britain is a good example. Industrialization takes production out of the household into factories and offices. As a result, as we have seen, wives and adolescents are no longer completely dependent on the head of the family, with the resulting loss in his power. But the family remains the unit for consumption, consuming housing, food and to some extent leisure on a household basis.

However, as we have seen, the supportive function of the family has been more important for manual workers in recent history. The mutual aid provided by the extended family in times of misfortune underlies some of the significance attached to kinship ties in traditional working-class areas.

Not only does the family provide physical sustenance and

[1] Bernard C. Rosen, 'Socialization and Achievement Motivation in Brazil', *A.S.R.*, Vol. 27, October 1962, No. 5. Also in W. J. Goode (ed.), *Readings on the Family and Society* (1964), Chapter 22.
[2] See J. Klein, op. cit., Vol. 2 for a summary.
[3] D. G. McKinley, *Social Class and Family Life* (1964).
[4] See also Chapter 7 for a fuller discussion of the mobility process.
[5] B. Wootton, op. cit. (1959).

shelter, it also cares for its members when they are ill and old. It is true that the resources of the family have been reinforced by the growth of specialized medical services, hospitals and clinics, but it is still the husband, wife or parent who calls in the doctor, and receives the convalescent from hospital. Nor is there any evidence that children have ceased to care for their ageing parents.[1]

Affective functions

According to the marriage service of the Church of England, among the causes for which marriage was ordained, third place is given to 'the mutual society, help, and comfort, that the one ought to have of the other. . . .' Most married couples would probably place this somewhat higher on the list.

In some societies, especially primitive agricultural societies, the procreation of children to ensure the continuance of the male line is of overriding importance, and a wife may well be selected for her husband by his parents with this aim paramount. Without a male heir, there will be no one to inherit the family estate and to care for the ancestors' shrine.

Today, the emphasis is increasingly on companionship and compatibility therefore becomes more important. We have already noted the shift towards a more equal relationship and the sharing of tasks in the home-centred family. In this context, husbands and wives become more and more dependent on each other for support and primary relationships. With increasing leisure, and the weakening of social networks, a wife becomes not only her husband's best friend, but also the one with whom he will spend an increasing amount of time. In one American research, 48 per cent of wives rated companionship as the most valuable aspect of marriage.[2]

Of course, as we have seen, some wives are *servants* rather than *companions*, where their role is to make good the damage done by his occupation. But a husband's occupation can make demands on his wife which are compatible with companionship. She may, for example, help her husband get ahead by entertaining business associates, acting as *hostess* companion, or may actively collaborate with her husband in his work. Hostess-wives appear to be most satisfied with their husband's companionship and working-wives least.[3]

Recent researches suggest that the family may provide an important outlet for the pent-up frustrations generated by the work situation. Semi- and unskilled workers enjoy few positive rewards from work, and little or no autonomy. One possible outlet for

[1] M. Young and P. Willmott, op. cit.
[2] R. O. Blood and D. M. Wolfe, op. cit.   Ibid.

such frustrations is the family, and this may account for the more aggressive relations with wives and the more severe socializing techniques adopted by working-class fathers.[1] Thus in an industrial society, the family may become increasingly important for its tension-management function.

THE FAMILY AND SOCIAL CHANGE

It has already been indicated that industrialization has had a considerable impact on the family. But its precise consequences are still a matter of some controversy. Many argue that the family has been stripped of its functions. Some (usually moralists rather than sociologists) have gone so far as to say that the contemporary family is disintegrating. There is much more agreement on the fact that the process of industrialization is accompanied by the break-up of the traditional extended or joint family systems. But much depends on the definition of the extended family. If by this is meant joint households, then recent studies show that the nuclear family is traditional in pre-industrial Europe, and that the 'multi-generational family of kin living under the same roof or in close geographical proximity may even be somewhat commoner in the contemporary industrial city than it was among the peasantry.'[2]

As we have seen, kinship plays a more important part than some have supposed, not only in the more traditional working-class areas, but also in middle- and upper-class families. Family connections still count in getting jobs and accommodation in Bethnal Green. And in some trades, notably printing, family connections are almost essential for entry to apprenticeship. But there is already a wide range of jobs, including, for example, the civil service, where entry is no longer by patronage and family connections but by passing competitive examinations. Moreover, house agents would be out of business if the kinship network could get us accommodation.

How many of these changes can be attributed to the industrialization process, it is difficult to say. But it can be argued that the nuclear or conjugal family is a relatively good 'fit' with the needs of an industrial society. Industrialization certainly requires a mobile labour force, and the resulting geographical and social mobility will strain extended kinship ties.

In discussing the effect of industrialization on the extended kinship ties, it is important to distinguish the control which the kin may exercise over its members from the affective bonds which

[1] D. G. McKinley, op. cit.; R. Titmuss, *Essays on the Welfare State* (1961).
[2] P. Laslett, 'The History of Population and Social Structure', *Int. Soc. Sci. J.*, Vol. 17, 1965, No. 4, and *The World We Have Lost* (1966).

may unite them. It may be perfectly true, as Litwak argues,[1] that occupational and geographical mobility does not necessarily weaken the affective ties which unite members of a family. But the changes discussed by Goode would appear to weaken the power which the kin can exercise over individuals in many segments of industrial societies. Rosser and Harris[2] have shown that in South Wales, the extended family is still strong, in the sense that children still feel strong ties of affection to their parents and close kin. The three-generation family in which the elementary family still has strong affective links with the families of origin of the spouses persists. True, the structure is less close-knit, but it still performs an important function as a source of identity. And although the importance of the supportive function has declined, middle-class parents still provide important economic aid for their married children,[3] while upper-class fathers, as Goode has argued, have continued to provide economic advantages and social position for their sons.

The thesis that industrialization has brought about the decline of the extended family depends to some extent on definitions and criteria. Geographical mobility certainly reduces the frequency of interaction—the criterion employed by Young and Willmott. Moreover, there is increasing social and cultural heterogeneity among its members, as sons less often follow in their father's footsteps. But this has not destroyed the very real sense of identity, which results in frequent visits, telephone calls or letters.[4] It is not, perhaps, surprising that the strong emotional ties with parents and siblings generated by long years of childhood dependency, are not suddenly severed on marriage. Moreover, the importance of kinship ties as a source of identity is not confined to manual workers, but as Rosser and Harris show, characterizes middle-class families too.

One result is that the individual is forced to make his way with less family support—kinship places no hindrance on industry employing the individual where he is needed. Moreover, the more close-knit conjugal family knits in with the needs of industry by its emphasis on affective support, which helps to restore the emotional balance of individuals facing the strains and frustrations of industrial work. Furthermore, the conjugal family specifies the status obligations of its members in less detail than the extended family which assigns specific tasks according to family position.

[1] E. Litwak, 'Occupational Mobility and Extended Family Cohesion', *A.S.R.*, February 1960; 'Geographic Mobility and Extended Family Cohesion', *A.S.R.*, June 1960.

[2] C. Rosser and C. Harris, op. cit., pp. 226–33.

[3] C. Bell, op. cit.   [4]Ibid.

Thus, the conjugal family makes possible the wider variations in role performance which are demanded by an industrial society with its emphasis on achievement.[1]

Industrialization may also go some way to explain the decline in arranged marriages, and the increase in divorce and re-marriage. Families are not only less able to control their young, but as land becomes less important, the advantages of family alliances have declined. In the past, family lineages have had strong reasons for fearing divorce and re-marriage because of its possible consequences for alienating property or confusing inheritance.[2]

But this does not mean that the family will remain in its present form. Divorce statistics indicate that for some the pattern may be shifting from lifelong to serial monogamy; from one partner for life to a series of partners.

Divorce and family stability

It is important, however, to get divorce statistics in perspective. In the first place, they are not the only index of family stability. A marriage may be terminated by death. There was, in fact, a smaller percentage of divorced and widowed women in 1951 than in 1931, despite the enormous increase in divorce. Moreover, a wife who is no longer living with her husband may seek a maintenance order from the courts. Table 2.2 shows that whereas divorce petitions increased by more than thirty times, if these are aggregated with maintenance orders, the increase in legally recognized marital breakdowns becomes about six times. It must also be remembered that the number of married persons has nearly doubled. The corrected ratio should therefore show a three-fold increase in breakdowns per head of population. Since 1951, there has been a further increase to over 45,000 and the rate per thousand married has gone up from 2·6 to 3·6.

TABLE 2.2

PETITIONS FOR DIVORCE AND MAINTENANCE ORDERS, E. AND W.*

	Petitions for divorce	Maintenance orders	Total
1911–15	1,000	7,600	8,600
1951–4	33,100	14,500	47,600

* From O. R. McGregor, op. cit., p. 51.

[1] W. J. Goode, *World Revolution and Family Patterns* (1963), Chapter 1.3, 'The "Fit" between the Conjugal Family and the Modern Industrial System'. For a more extended discussion, see B. F. Hoselitz and W. E. Moore, *Industrialization and Society* (1960).
[2] W. J. Goode, op. cit., p. 376.

Divorce statistics and court orders do not enable us to say anything about either the happiness of marriage or its *de facto* stability. They represent only those who for one reason or another have decided to seek legal recognition of the termination of their marriage. Changes in the law have, in fact, removed many barriers to the resort to divorce. The most important of these changes are the extension of grounds resulting from the Herbert Act in 1937, and the Legal Aid Act of 1949, which reduced the financial barriers. Under the 1969 Act, irretrievable breakdown of the marriage is the sole ground for divorce. This marks a sharp break with the legal tradition that divorce could only be granted on evidence of a matrimonial offence. There has also been a change in public attitude and divorce no longer carries the stigma that it once did nor can it any longer threaten a career in public life. As a result of these changes, divorce is no longer the prerogative of the well-to-do, but is distributed proportionately through all sections of society. In fact, the increase in divorce and maintenance orders since 1911 can be explained almost entirely as being due to the growth of population and the removal of economic and social barriers.

The question remains which was raised earlier. Are the institutionalists right when they argue that any further liberalization of marriage laws would fatally weaken family ties? Historical evidence suggests that there could well be a further increase in divorce. But whether this would contribute to an increase in broken marriages is problematic. It might simply mean that more existing broken marriages become legally terminated.

The evidence also suggests that marriage may be becoming increasingly important and rewarding for the individual with the growth of the home-centred family in which companionship is increasingly valued. Satisfaction with the love, understanding and standard of living provided by husbands is high even in America with its high divorce rates.[1]

On the other hand, it is arguable that the changing structure and functions of the family make stable marriage more difficult. As we have seen, in industrial societies, with the weakening of extended kinship networks, the conjugal family becomes increasingly important as a source of affective support for its members. With the shift from segregated to integrated conjugal roles, and the growing importance of companionship, husbands and wives interact more frequently and become more dependent on each other's company. These changes make greater demands on compatability, compared with the more restricted interaction of husbands and wives characterized by a 'servant' or 'colleague'

[1] R. O. Blood and D. M. Wolfe, op. cit.

relation. Moreover, the tension management function can only be adequately discharged within the context of strong emotional bonds. However, in a highly segregated role relationship, the partners expect less, but also get less from the marriage, making separation easier.[1] Mobile couples will be faced with particular problems. As we have seen, when families move from stable traditional working-class areas, there is a change from segregated to joint conjugal roles. Such new relationships have to be worked out by the couples. There is no close-knit network to define conjugal roles, and the subsequent uncertainties are likely to generate strains.[2]

There is some evidence that the shift to joint conjugal roles and loose-knit social networks is accompanied by an increase in marriage breakdowns. The divorce rate is higher in large urban communities and decreases with size, being lowest in rural communities. It is also particularly high in boroughs with transient populations.[3]

As could be expected, farmers have a very low divorce rate, and there is support for the view that traditional working-class occupations are also less prone to divorce. But when we turn to occupational differences within broad socio-economic categories, these are very marked. Rates for actors, lorry drivers, cooks, company directors, authors, painters, hotel-keepers are all very high. The occupations at high risk certainly include many which demand a high degree of personal involvement; husbands will be strongly 'work-centred'. But just how far the demands of the occupation generates strains, or how far the occupation attracts those with personality characteristics which make them divorce-prone, is problematic.[4] Whatever the explanation, it would appear that inter-occupational differences are powerful factors predisposing to stability or divorce.

Finally, we must note that an increasing proportion of divorces takes place between those who have been married for over twenty years,[5] and that an increasing proportion of divorcees re-marry. Marriage is more popular than ever, but the more exacting demands made upon it can only be discharged by spouses more adequately matched than the chances of cupid's bow necessarily

[1] E. Bott, op. cit., p. 220.
[2] T. Noble, 'Family Breakdown and Social Networks', *B.J.S.*, June 1970.
[3] Ibid.
[4] Ibid.
[5] This is in part due to an increase in the expectation of life. As McGregor says, 'the divorce court is now taking over functions which, in the past, were the undertaker's prerogative', op. cit., p. 50.

ensure.[1] Moreover, there are always likely to be some who simply cannot match up to the heavy demands that marriage makes upon them.

DISCUSSION

Sexual roles are structured to a very high degree by the culture of the society, that is to say, by its norms, values and beliefs. The recognized patterns which result constitute the institutional complex of marriage and the family, and reflect the normative expectations of members of society, some of which are reinforced by legal sanctions. But such expectations are themselves undergoing change. The *Women's Liberation* movement has sought to increase the consciousness of women to the limitations and disabilities which the female role still imposes and to encourage women to challenge and break out of such constraints.[2]

Within this broad framework, there are variations on the major themes. Husbands may be dominant, as in the patriarchal family, or the relationship may be more equalitarian. There may be a rigid sex division of labour or a sharing of household tasks. Such differences can be explained partly by the relations between the conjugal family and the extended kinship-networks. The interaction between the family and the economic system also influences conjugal roles. The increasing employment of married women outside the home has increased their bargaining power and contributed to their liberation within the family. The nature of the husband's occupation and the demands which this makes on his married life may influence husband/wife relations: wives performing roles as 'servants' or 'companions'.

The family performs important functions both for its members and for society. Among the most important of these are not only procreation but also the socialization of the child to fit him for adult roles. Furthermore, changes in the reproductive behaviour of the family and differences in the socialization process are influenced by the interactions between the family and the economic and cultural systems. The evidence suggests that the socialization process in each stratum of society produces the personal qualities necessary to function in that stratum. It suggests that the upwardly mobile working-class boy is hampered by much more than the relatively low income of his parents—as subsequent chapters will demonstrate.

[1] Researches into the factors associated with marital failure enable predictions to be made on the basis of data supplied by engaged couples. F. W. Burgess and L. S. Cottrell, Jr, *Predicting Success or Failure in Marriage* (1939).
[2] This issue is also discussed in Chapter 7.

The main trends in family life may be tentatively summarized as a decline in the close-knit extended kinship network, and in the supportive function of the kin, resulting in the privatization of family life, but the persistence of loose-knit affective kinship ties as a source of identity. The changing sex division of labour, the increasing integration of conjugal roles, and the emergence of more equal relations between spouses reflect the decreasing demands of child-bearing and domesticity, expanded opportunities for wives to work and the break-up of stable communities. The growing importance of the affective functions of the elementary family, and the emergence of companionship as a major functional relationship between husbands and wives reflect a growing investment in family life with the declining saliency of work. The increasing frequency of the legal termination of unsatisfactory marriages results from the removal of barriers to divorce, and is consistent with the increasing saliency of satisfying marital relations in an urban industrial society.

READING

M. Anderson (ed.), *Sociology of the Family* (Penguin, 1971).

N. W. Bell and E. F. Vogel, *The Family* (Free Press, 1960).

R. O. Blood and D. M. Wolfe, *Husbands and Wives* (Free Press, 1960).

E. Bott, *Family and Social Networks* (Tavistock, 1957).

E. Butterworth and D. Weir, *The Sociology of Modern Britain* (Collins, 1970).

N. Dennis, F. Henriques and C. Slaughter, *Coal is Our Life* (Tavistock, 1956).

R. Fletcher, *The Family and Marriage* (Penguin, 1962).

M. P. Fogarty, R. Rapoport and R. Rapoport, *Sex, Career and Family* (Allen and Unwin, 1971).

H. Gavron, *The Captive Wife* (Routledge, 1966).

W. J. Goode, *The Family* (Prentice-Hall, 1964).

W. J. Goode, *World Revolution and Family Patterns* (Collier-Macmillan, 1963).

C. C. Harris, *The Family* (Allen and Unwin, 1969).

G. Hawthorne, *The Sociology of Fertility* (Collier-Macmillan, 1970).

J. Klein, *Samples from English Culture*, Vols 1 and 2 (Routledge, 1965).

V. Klein, *Britain's Married Women Workers* (Routledge, 1965).

O. R. McGregor, *Divorce in England* (Heinemann, 1957).

D. G. McKinley, *Social Class and Family Life* (Collier-Macmillan, 1964).

C. Rosser and C. Harris, *The Family and Social Change* (Routledge, 1965).

M. B. Sussman, *Source Book on Marriage and the Family* (Houghton Mifflin, 1968).

P. Willmott and M. Young, *Family and Class in a London Suburb* (Routledge, 1960).

P. Worsley (ed.), *Modern Sociology: Introduction Readings* (Penguin 1970), Part 3.

M. Young and P. Willmott, *Family and Kinship in East London* (Routledge, 1957).

S. Yudkin and A. Holme, *Working Mothers and their Children* (Michael Joseph, 1963).

Chapter 3

THE EDUCATIONAL SYSTEM

Social issues and problems have inevitably influenced the intellectual preoccupations of sociologists. Indeed, much social investigation into poverty and urban living has been an exercise in collecting facts to influence policy rather than an attempt at a more fundamental analysis of the nature of society. In this sense, such 'political arithmetic' has a somewhat doubtful claim to be considered as sociology. It is this tradition which has had a predominant influence on the sociology of education. Hogben's researches in the 1930s revived a debate about the relative importance of nature compared with nurture in human achievement. It challenged the view that intelligence was a major factor determining human achievement and stimulated a series of inquiries into the social determinants of educability. The findings of post-war reports on education such as Plowden have further reinforced the view that the pursuit of equality of opportunity presents problems of great complexity. Indeed, the influence of sociology on policy has been very considerable.

It is only as recently as the 1960s that the sociology of education has broken out of its preoccupation with stratification and focused on the more theoretical perspectives of role analysis and organization theory in an attempt to understand the dynamics of interaction in the classroom and school. And it is more recently still that attention has turned to look at the way in which society shapes the very content of the curriculum, and at the interactions and negotiations between the child and the teacher out of which the pupil arrives at his own construction of reality.[1]

Societies and governments have a strong interest in the influence of schools as major socializing agencies. Without necessarily subscribing to the functionalist view that societies are held together by consensus about ends and means,[2] such consensus ensures at least some measure of articulation between the actors in a social system. Socialization, in this sense, is a mechanism of social control. This faces every society with the need to ensure adequate

---

[1] See Chapters 6 and 8 for a further discussion of the sociology of knowledge and of symbolic interactionism.

[2] On this, see D. Wrong, 'The Over-Socialized View of Man', in N. J. Smelser and W. J. Smelser, *Personality and Social Systems* (1963). This issue is discussed more fully in Chapter 9.

machinery for the socialization of the young into the prevailing culture; not simply rules of conduct and expectations about future behaviour, but also the accumulated know-how for planting crops, making dwellings, dealing with sorcery or calculating logarithms. And those who wish to challenge the existing social order will seek to promote an alternative view[1] of social reality.

In pre-literate societies, the cultural heritage is limited by what can be remembered and passed on from father to son, although even in such societies there may be some division of labour, and some individuals (priests, magicians) who specialize in the preservation and transmission of often esoteric knowledge. The invention of writing marks a major development since it permits cultural accumulation and preservation on a scale never before possible. And it necessitates the emergence of a class of learned men, either sacred or secular, who are the guardians and transmitters of knowledge.

Advanced industrial societies differ in other important respects even from early literate societies. Firstly, the rate of cultural innovation is greatly accelerated, due largely to the institutionalization of innovation with the growth of organized science research institutions, and a growing emphasis on the research function in the universities.[2] Secondly, they are characterized by universal literacy, which greatly extends the possibilities of cultural communication beyond a narrow class of literati. And thirdly, technological advances have made possible new and powerful cultural agencies in the form of radio, television and the cinema.

EDUCATION, CULTURE AND SOCIAL STRUCTURE

Schools and colleges are obviously major agencies of cultural preservation and transmission. But however important they may be in modifying the knowledge and beliefs, the norms, and the values of individuals, it would be somewhat arbitrary to limit discussion to such cultural agencies, and to ignore broadcasting, the press and the cinema. This chapter, therefore, will look at all those agencies which are primarily concerned with cultural preservation, transmission and innovation.[3] It will examine the way in which the main cultural agencies articulate with other major structural elements in society, notably the political and economic

[1] See Chapter 6.

[2] D. S. L. Cardwell, *The Organization of Science in England* (1957).

[3] Other agencies such as the family and churches are also involved in cultural transmission. But this chapter will concentrate on the systems of schools and colleges and those agencies such as the press and broadcasting whose activities are closely articulated.

systems. Secondly, it will examine in particular schools and colleges as social systems, and the cultural transformations brought about by the mass media. In this analysis, we shall not be concerned with actual knowledge and belief systems, that is, with a study of the actual content of culture and its determinants. This is a subject for separate study in Chapter 6. But we must begin by noting that what is taught in schools involves selection from the sum total of culture. Indeed, the very word 'culture' is ambiguous.[1] We must turn first, therefore, to an examination of the interaction between the educational system and culture.

Education and culture

Universities do not teach carpentry, though a few teach architecture. Courses on Marxist–Leninist philosophy are not generally included in the USA but they are in the USSR. Workers' movements have challenged classical economics,[2] and students have criticized the mystifications of 'bourgeois' sociology, and have set up 'free universities'.

What is defined as knowledge, in short, is not beyond debate. The natural sciences have been described as 'a consensus of rational opinion over the widest possible field'.[3] It is clearly much more difficult to achieve such a consensus in the social sciences. And arts subjects are more concerned with communicating private experiences and personal judgements.

Several questions emerge. How are bodies of knowledge constructed? Why is some knowledge, such as music, included in the notion of 'culture' but not carpentry? How does this come about? —who decides? And who decides what shall be taught in schools and colleges?—that is to say, how is the curriculum determined, for it is the curriculum which shapes the social distribution of knowledge. It is such questions which direct attention to an exploration of the relations between knowledge and power.[4]

A full discussion of the social construction of knowledge and beliefs will have to be postponed until Chapter 6. But the crucial question of the factors shaping the notion of culture is central to an understanding of the functions of educational institutions. It is fairly obvious that if we say that history is a part of 'culture',

[1] Throughout this chapter, wherever the meaning is ambiguous, the word *culture* in italics indicates that it is being used in a technical sociological sense; in quotation marks it indicates the use of the term to refer to valued intellectual products.

[2] M. T. Hodgen, *Workers' Education in England and the US* (1925).

[3] J. Ziman, *Public Knowledge* (1968), p. 9. See also A. F. Blum, 'The Corpus of Knowledge as a Normative Order', in M. F. D. Young, *Knowledge and Control* (1971), Chapter 4.

[4] M. F. D. Young, op. cit., Introduction.

but carpentry is not, that the word is being used prescriptively to indicate what kinds of knowledge we ought to value and acquire. It is not so long ago that some would have excluded science from the body of knowledge that 'ought' to be acquired by a cultured man. Certainly, some branches of knowledge are more prestigious than others: technology, for example, in this country has not enjoyed the same status as pure science.

To understand this, we must explore more fully the role which the men of knowledge and their organizations play in the social structure. Much early knowledge has grown out of the attempts to solve practical problems. Early knowledge of astronomy, for example, grew from navigation and from the problems of devising a calendar which was essential for the more detailed regulation of agriculture. Similarly, geometry grew from the problems of architecture and building. Pythagoras' theorem provides us with a simple method for constructing a right angle, and π gives a formula for measuring the length of iron necessary to make a 'tyre' for a wheel.

Advances in technology made possible a more elaborate division of labour. But under the conditions in which early civilizations emerged, they also made possible a differentiation within society whereby a relatively leisured aristocracy was supported by the labours of a large subordinate stratum with varying degrees of slavery and freedom. It was this division of society which came to be reflected in the values attached to different kinds of knowledge. The leisured aristocracy in Greece, for example, speculated on politics and ethics, while mathematics became an intellectual activity divorced from its practical applications. Manufacture, agriculture and mining were carried on by slaves, and the knowledge related to such affairs came to be considered inferior. The value placed on various kinds of knowledge will be related to the needs and interests of different strata in society. Thus, the intellectual interests of the upper stratum have been related to their functions: to government, warfare and leisure. Politics, philosophy, literature and music have been valued by them and defined as 'culture', while technology has been excluded. The dominant stratum in society will be in a strong position to define what is 'cultural'. What is taught, therefore, will reflect in part the prevailing definition of culture. For example, German universities refused to include technology in the nineteenth century, while English universities have in the past only acted as reluctant hosts.

The second main question asks to whom is knowledge distributed, and what kinds of knowledge? The social distribution of knowledge is determined in part by the system of schools and colleges—that is, the structure of the educational system. But it is shaped also by the curriculum—the particular package of knowledge that is formally transmitted by teachers and lecturers. These two questions are, in fact, closely related. 'What' is taught depends also on 'to whom'. To understand this, it is important to remember the way in which culture functions not only as a source of 'know-how', but also provides meanings and legitimations. In other words, what is taught in schools plays an important part in constructing the way in which pupils come to see and understand the world: it shapes their construction of reality and provides them with meanings and legitimations. It is this aspect of socialization which is stressed by the control theorists, and it is for this reason that schools have been used as important agents of social control. Indeed, throughout most of human history formal education has been received by only a small section of society. Knowledge has been seen as a source of power and influence, and on these grounds jealously preserved and guarded by a small elite. Priest and scholar have usually been closely related roles. The extension of education raises new problems of content. What is appropriate for the administrator or landowner is not fitting for the artisan or labourer. The spread of education, therefore, has been accompanied by a growing differentiation of structure and content.

Some indication of the way in which social factors shape the curriculum can be seen from the extension of education to the labouring classes in the nineteenth century. At a time of social unrest and fear of revolution, it is not surprising to find that a major aim was to 'gentle the masses'. The early Bible classes of the Nonconformists aimed at teaching reading simply as a means of Bible study. The denominational societies later extended their provision by setting up day-schools, and the influence of the churches was strengthened by the fact that the colleges to train teachers for the labouring classes were also denominational. In the words of one of the speakers in a parliamentary debate in 1820, every poor man 'ought to be made sensible that there is an attainable good in this life superior to animal gratification . . . and that a life of faith and obedience affords hope of a happy immortality. Of this every poor man in the nation should be made sensible, and for this purpose the humble schools prepared for him are sufficient; for I believe they never neglect reading the Scriptures, catechetical instruction, and daily supplication.'[1]

This stress on the control function has not, of course, been the only factor shaping the curriculum. Education functions not only to develop personal qualities but also to impart special knowledge and skills,[2] for example, in the education of doctors and engineers.

[1] Quoted in J. W. Adamson, *English Education, 1789–1902* (1930), p. 54.
[2] This distinction between personal qualities and expert knowledge was

This aspect is explored more fully later. Moreover, philosophies of education have stressed its role in developing human potentialities and see it as a liberating process. Such views have been particularly influential in the infant school, and more recently in the demands for the abolition of formal curricula and examinations in universities as a protest against the constraints on intellectual development which, it is argued, they impose. Codified bodies of knowledge taught and examined as traditional disciplines are indeed a form of control over teaching and learning.[1] The demand for participation in the formulation of curricula is in this sense an understandable response of students seeking to extend the areas of human freedom.

Until recently studies of the curriculum attracted little attention from sociologists, although Banks has argued that the literary emphasis of the grammar schools in the inter-war years has reflected social pressures to provide an education relevant for the more prestigious white-collar occupations.[2] Another important aspect of the relations between culture and education which has not so far been explored is the role of ideologies of education, which might be expected to play much the same role as managerial ideologies discussed in the next chapter as guides and legitimations. Courses in the principles and philosophy of education might well be studied by sociologists as sources on this important aspect of the educational system.

One final point. In this section we have focused on two main questions: What factors influence the value placed in different kinds of knowledge? and what structures the social distribution of knowledge—the curriculum? This leaves largely unexplored the equally basic question: What determines what passes for knowledge, that is, how is knowledge constructed? This is an issue to which we return in Chapter 6. Furthermore, knowledge in the sense of what is formally taught is only a part, and one would argue, a somewhat insignificant part of what we know. Each individual possesses a mass of information, his own construction of reality, without which he could not possibly find his way in social interactions. This world-taken-for-granted owes more to informal

developed by Max Weber. The Chinese literati, for example, did not acquire a knowledge of administration, but the literary and stylistic education which they received was believed to confer on the mandarins special qualities and authority which were essential in an administrator. See H. H. Gerth and C. W. Mills, *From Max Weber: Essays in Sociology* (1947).

[1] On this, see B. Bernstein, 'On the Classification and Framing of Educational Knowledge', in M. F. D. Young, op. cit., Chapter 2.

[2] O. Banks, *Parity and Prestige in English Secondary Education* (1955). See also S. F. Cotgrove, *Technical Education and Social Change* (1958), Chapter 3.

learning through interaction than it does to schools.[1] But it may well have a very important influence in the process of interaction between teacher and pupil—as we shall see later in this chapter.

Education and the economic system

The growth of knowledge (not only science and technology, but also of accounting, architecture and the social and behavioural sciences) has been accompanied by its increasing application to production, administration and the provision of specialized services such as medicine. There has been increasing division of labour and the growth of a variety of intellectual occupations for the application of such specialized knowledge to practical affairs. These occupations include the 'professions', such as medicine, the law, engineering, accountancy, and a wide range of intellectual occupations, such as radiographer, teacher, nurse and technician. There are in fact nearly 200 occupations for which qualifications can be gained by passing the written examinations of qualifying associations.[2] In addition, there are a large number of occupations for which qualifications may be important for promotion, such as national certificates in engineering for draughtsmen and technicians or City and Guilds certificates for operatives and craftsmen, but which are not awarded by qualifying associations. The implications for education are obvious. Educational qualifications have become increasingly important for occupational advancement.

We have a situation then where a considerable proportion of those in the elite educational institutions are reading subjects which have little relevance to practical affairs, while the bulk of the educational preparation for industry is by part-time study in technical colleges and by correspondence courses. The clue to this situation is to be found partly in the way in which society has defined culture and therefore influenced the activities of educational institutions. As we have seen, the prevailing notion of culture in the nineteenth century certainly excluded knowledge of manufacture. A second factor was the existence of traditional institutions for the transmission of knowledge of practical affairs. From the lawyer to the craftsman, apprenticeship had become the traditional vehicle for educating the novice. This had one advantage, among others, in that it allowed a profession to safeguard the 'secrets' of its practice and so strengthen its market situation against the entry of unauthorized parvenus. The rapid expansion of intellectual occupations in the nineteenth century occurred in this context, in which the idea of the university excluded vocational

[1] P. L. Berger and T. Luckmann, *The Social Construction of Reality* (1967). This issue is examined more fully in Chapter 6.
[2] G. Millerson, *The Qualifying Associations* (1964).

79

studies for business, and manufacture (but not the Church and politics), and in which apprenticeship[1] was the traditional vehicle for vocational education and training.

As more and more professions introduced written examinations as a test of competence, the problem of providing the necessary education was solved in a variety of ways. The chartered accountants, for example, turned to correspondence courses, and have until recently strongly resisted attempts to provide full-time courses in colleges.[2] Solicitors followed a similar practice, supplemented by short intensive cram-courses. Engineering drew some of its members from the universities, but between the wars, an increasing number had studied part-time at technical colleges. The technical colleges expanded rapidly after the 1880s to meet a growing demand for paper qualifications in a wide range of manufacturing and business studies. They were essentially a product of the nineteenth century with its deeply rooted belief that practical experience was the best teacher for practical affairs and that educational institutions could contribute little. The demand came from ambitious students anxious to acquire a paper qualification which they could use as a lever for promotion. It is from this that we have inherited the 'night-school' tradition of part-time study to supplement practical experience. As knowledge has grown, this situation has been increasingly challenged. Rapid advances in electronics, for example, have made it more and more difficult for the engineer to acquire the necessary knowledge by part-time study. Moreover, as the demand for qualified manpower has exceeded the supply in many fields, traditional part-time methods have been under pressure to change.[3]

One important function of examinations[4] is to confer a licence to practise. In medicine, for example, examinations test the fact that the doctor has the knowledge necessary for competent practice. But in many such occupations, it is believed that various personal qualities are also necessary. Where the examination confers a licence to practise, it will be important to try to select first for personal qualities those who are to be accepted for education and training. Social work students are a further example. Where qualification is not a licence to practise, selection can take place afterwards and not all who qualify are admitted to the occupation.

---

[1] G. Williams, *Recruitment to Skilled Trades* (1957). See also Chapter 4 for a discussion of apprenticeship as an occupational strategy.

[2] S. F. Cotgrove, op. cit., Chapter 11.

[3] S. F. Cotgrove, op. cit.

[4] For a detailed analysis of the various functions of examinations, see S. Wiseman (ed.), *Examinations and English Education* (1961).

The impact of the economic system on education has led not only to the emergence of new institutions for vocational education. The occupational significance of education has also influenced the structure and content of secondary education. The growing demand for grammar-school places over the last fifty years reflects the recognition not only by middle-class, but increasingly by working-class parents that the grammar school provides the key to entry to the coveted, secure, black-coated and professional occupations. The occupational significance of the grammar school is confirmed by the large-scale research into social mobility carried out by the London School of Economics after the Second World War.[1] This concludes that a grammar-school education is strongly associated with the achievement of higher status occupations. Banks has also shown that the occupational significance of secondary education has influenced the school curriculum where attempts in the inter-war years to establish a technical curriculum oriented towards careers in industry failed because of the relatively lower status and poorer chances of upward mobility associated with technical jobs. It also accounts for the failure of the secondary-modern school to achieve parity of esteem. The grammar school borrows prestige from the occupations for which it prepares,[2] and buildings and equipment alone cannot earn parity of esteem in the eyes of society for schools which lead to the lower rungs of the occupational ladder.

Pressures from the economic system can distort educational processes in other ways. If the emphasis shifts from studying for examinations as a means of improving one's performance in a job to seeking qualification as a means of achieving promotion, there may come to be little relation between the content of the curriculum and the occupation for which it is ostensibly intended. Studies of the craft examinations of the City and Guilds illustrate this process. An analysis of the content of craft courses in the mid-1950s[3] brought to light a rather surprising finding, that a high proportion of these so-called 'craft' courses were pitched at technician level. A possible hypothesis is that this situation has resulted from the fact that such courses have functioned in the past as a basis for selecting technicians rather than training craftsmen. In order to test this hypothesis, a follow-up study was made of men who had sat a City and Guilds examination some years earlier. It was found, as predicted, that the majority of those who had passed had left the bench and become technicians, while most

[1] D. V. Glass (ed.), *Social Mobility in Britain* (1954).
[2] O. Banks, op. cit.
[3] S. F. Cotgrove, 'Technicians and the City and Guilds', *Technology*, December 1958.

of those who failed remained craftsmen.[1] Further research may show that other occupational qualifications function as a basis for selection rather than as a vehicle for the transmission of occupationally relevant knowledge.[2]

Education and the political system

In Britain, the relations between education and the political system have attracted little attention from sociologists,[3] who have been mainly preoccupied with exploring educational opportunity. The state has itself been primarily responsible for determining educational opportunity, since it is the political system which allocates resources to education, and determines who shall be educated. 'The series of education acts are all examples of state intervention, mainly to extend the provision of various forms of education to wider classes of individuals. In doing so, the political system has responded to a variety of pressures, including the demand from more and more individuals for an extended education, partly because this is defined as good in itself and should therefore be available to all, but more important because of the growing recognition of the value of education for social advancement.[4]

Apart from its role in the provision of educational opportunity, the state in Britain has allowed a considerable degree of autonomy to the educational system. This situation is itself largely the result of historical forces which shaped the relations between the educational and political systems during the formative years of the state system in the nineteenth century, and the struggle for control between the religious denominations and the state. The growth of new knowledge after the Renaissance was in any case a challenge

[1] Incidentally, this research brought to light an unexpected finding. Those who had passed no longer thought of themselves as being simply craftsmen; passing the examination had modified their identities. They felt that they were worth a better job than those who had failed or never even studied, and this had motivated them to seek promotion from the bench.

[2] City and Guild courses have now been revised, and the multifunctional courses which functioned to promote those who passed, and to provide some relevant knowledge for those who failed have been replaced by separate courses more closely geared to the occupational needs of craftsmen and technicians. But in the light of the above evidence, it can be predicted that unless the majority of craftsmen are expected to have passed exams, those who have qualified will continue to seek promotion and may well be lost to the ranks of craftsmen.

[3] The trend report by J. Floud and A. H. Halsey, 'The Sociology of Education' (*Current Sociology*, 1958, No. 3), does not include any systematic discussion of the relations between education and politics.

[4] See M. Ginsberg (ed.), *Law and Opinion in the Twentieth Century* (1959), pp. 319–46, especially the chapter by D. V. Glass, for an account of the extension of educational opportunity.

to the religious monopoly of culture in the Middle Ages. But the struggle between the Anglicans and the Nonconformists delayed the establishment of a state system of education for half a century. The free churches feared that a state system might lead to the imposition of Anglicanism.[1] Consequently, Anglicans, Nonconformists and Roman Catholics all provided their own schools and their own teacher-training colleges, lest their rivals should extend their influence over the minds of the young.[2] When state education was finally introduced, the system of control first by school boards, and then by local education authorities of local government gave a maximum of local autonomy, reflecting not only the fears of the Nonconformists of state dominance, but also the prevailing *laissez-faire* ideology. Indeed, the first board schools were seen as an extension of the poor law, intended only for the children of manual workers, and not for the middle classes who could afford to provide for the education of their own children.[3]

The trend, however, is to strengthen the powers of the government. The 1902 Act was largely permissive. It empowered local authorities to provide education. The 1944 Act established a Minister for Education, with the duty to promote education and to ensure the execution of a national policy under his control and direction. This reflects the increasing role of the government in an industrial society to mobilize human and material resources and to allocate them to socially desired goals. It reflects, too, the increasing demand for educational opportunity from below.[4] But the local authorities still retain some autonomy in deciding on the extent and nature of provision and the form which the organization of local education may take. However, even here there has been growing pressure for reorganization along comprehensive lines, and the possibility of some action to integrate the public schools.

The measure of autonomy of the education authorities from central government control does not, of course, mean that teachers enjoy autonomy in the classroom. On the contrary, pressures from the universities at the upper levels of secondary education largely determine the curriculum, while the influence of central government inspectors has probably been considerable. A major source

[1] The Anglicans for long refused a licence to teach to non-Anglicans: while at Oxford and Cambridge, those who were not members of the Church of England were excluded until 1871. See W. O. Lester Smith, *Education* (1957), for a brief account.
[2] For a more detailed analysis of the relations between religion and education, see N. Hans, *Comparative Education* (1949).
[3] For an account of the extension of elementary instruction, see G. A. N. Lowndes, *The Silent Social Revolution* (1937).
[4] W. O. Lester Smith, op. cit.

of control over the teacher, however, especially at the lower levels, comes from his selection, education and training in, until recently, mainly single sex institutions, segregated from other forms of post-secondary education for other professions. The teacher's role in socialization and the inculcation of values make his work the object of anxious scrutiny. The close association between the churches and teacher-training exemplifies the concern of society with the role of the teacher who is expected to transmit culture without challenging prevailing moral standards and religious beliefs.[1]

MASS MEDIA AND THE SOCIAL STRUCTURE

The relations between the mass media and the social structure are generally very different from those of schools and colleges. The press, for example, is mainly privately owned and controlled. And it is this which is at the root of much of the anxiety which has given rise to two royal commissions on the press.[2] A major fear underlying these inquiries is that there may be a growing concentration of ownership, which would reduce the range of opinion. The 1949 report concluded that there was nothing approaching a monopoly in the press, and that the largest single aggregation of newspapers under one ownership (Kemsley Newspapers Ltd) accounted for 17 per cent of the total of daily and Sunday papers. But by 1962, the commission reported a marked increase in concentration. Seventeen daily or Sunday papers had ceased production since 1949 and only four new ones had started.[3] The 1962 commission concluded that there is still a considerable range of choice, but it would be better if there were more.

Advertising constitutes a substantial proportion of the revenue of the press. This is the key for understanding relations between the press and the economic system. The ability of a publication to compete for advertising depends not only on the size of its readership, but also on its character. 'Quality' papers, for example, have a smaller circulation, but they are read by the higher income groups and by those in positions which enable them to control substantial expenditure. Such papers, therefore, are able to charge

[1] Community control over teachers especially in rural areas in the United States penetrated far into their private lives in the recent past. See L. A. Cook, *Community Backgrounds of Education* (1935).
[2] *Royal Commission on the Press*, 1947–9 (1949); *Royal Commission on the Press*, 1961–2 (1962). For a historical account of the press and its place in society, see F. Williams, *The Dangerous Estate* (1959), and R. Williams, *The Long Revolution* (1965).
[3] 1962 report, op. cit., p. 112.

much higher rates. Such dependence on advertising revenue has inevitably raised the question of the possibility that advertisers may seek to influence the expression of opinion. The 1949 commission had some evidence of such attempts, though it considered them to be infrequent and largely unsuccessful. The main aim of a paper is to increase its circulation. It is more likely, therefore, to be influenced in what it prints by the interests of its readers than of its advertisers. Nevertheless, the 1949 commission considered that a paper will 'probably avoid taking a line detrimental to advertisers' interests unless by so doing it can increase its interest to the public'.[1]

There are two main keys to the content of the press. Firstly, there is the influence of the proprietors. Most papers are consistent adherents of a particular political party. Partisanship occurs in all papers to some degree. 'The press is part of our political machinery, which is essentially partisan.'[2] Although proprietors will seldom exercise day to day control over their editors, they will choose men whose views coincide with the policy which the proprietors wish to pursue.[3] But the distortions of truth and excessive bias were not confined to any one form of ownership. The 1949 report concluded that all the popular papers and some of the quality papers fell short of the standard achieved by the best through excessive partisanship or distortion in the interest of news value.[4] The second main influence is the pursuit of large circulation, the main root of the second major criticism of the press—its triviality and sensationalism. Neither of these shortcomings was peculiar to newspapers with any particular form of ownership, and occurred in papers owned by co-operative societies, as well as those where political control is formally divorced from commercial policy.

THE EDUCATIONAL SYSTEM

So far we have examined the articulation between the educational system and other elements of the social structure. We turn now to an examination of the interaction between the sub-systems within the educational system itself. A full treatment would require an analysis not only of the various educational and cultural structures, such as schools, colleges, universities, newspapers, broadcasting companies, but also the interaction between them;

[1] 1949 report, op. cit., p. 143.
[2] Ibid., p. 151.
[3] For a more detailed discussion of the press and politics, see F. Williams, op. cit.
[4] 1949 report, op. cit., p. 151.

between, for example, universities and grammar schools, television companies and schools.

In examining schools and colleges as social systems, a major focus of interest is to obtain some kind of measure of their functioning. It is in the classroom and lecture hall, at the grassroots of the system, that the function of the cultural transformation of students and pupils takes place. Fortunately, we have such measures, crude though they may be, in the shape of statistics on examinations and other indices of educational performance. These provide us with some measure of the result of the interaction process between child and teacher, student and lecturer. And it is important to stress that in order to understand this interaction process, we need to explore the characteristics not only of pupils, in terms of their potential for learning, their attitudes and motives, but also the characteristics of the teachers with whom they interact in the classroom, and the total school environment. Moreover, as the child also interacts with his family and neighbourhood as well as with the school, the educational process cannot be understood without taking account of the family and the neighbourhood influence.[1]

The school as a social system
As we have seen, education functions to instil the values and norms of society and to develop personal qualities. Secondly, it transmits knowledge—or rather, those aspects of knowledge which society defines as part of culture. These are two primary goals which constitute the *charter* of the educational system. To these must be added a third. Attendance at school is compulsory up to the statutory school-leaving age. The schools have, therefore, to ensure attendance and to perform a custodial function.

Schools may attach varying degrees of importance to these goals. In other words, we can conceptualize the culture of the school as being predominantly 'academic', 'missionary' or 'custodial', according to the emphasis it places on academic achievement, developing the personal qualities of the child (child-centred) or simply maintaining order and discipline. The culture of the school will reflect not only the expectations of society but will also be influenced by its interaction with its environment. Academic goals are the main objective of many schools, particularly grammar schools in middle-class areas. Such schools will be characterized

[1] The educability of the child 'depends as much on the assumptions, values and aims embodied in the school organization into which he is supposed to assimilate himself, as on those he brings with him from his home'. Jean Floud and A. H. Halsey, 'The Sociology of Education', in *Current Sociology*, Vol. 7, 1958, No. 3, p. 184.

by a predominantly academic sub-culture, shared by staff and pupils. By contrast, a secondary-modern school in a working-class area will find it extremely difficult to pursue academic goals. Its pupils have been defined by the selection process as unacademic, and the values of working-class culture do not place the same premium on academic achievement. Two main strategies seem to be adopted by such schools. Firstly, they may adopt a custodial role, aimed primarily at keeping the children in order. Alternatively, they may stress the socializing function of the school and pursue a primarily missionary role.[1]

A grammar school in a working-class area is less likely to abdicate academic goals. One way in which it may solve its problems is by adopting rigorous streaming and by sponsoring selected pupils to ensure that some, at least, achieve the academic goals which are the criteria for success of the grammar school. But such strategies will also have consequences for those who are demoted and labelled as failures; they are likely to promote the development of anti-school and delinquent sub-cultures.[2]

A third sub-culture has been described by students of American high schools which may also be applicable in Britain. Researches indicate the existence of a 'fun' sub-culture in addition to the 'academic' and 'delinquent' sub-cultures already discussed. The fun sub-culture attaches value to good personality, being friendly, good reputation, being an athlete, good grades and being smart —although the latter accounts for only 12 per cent of the response. Indeed, the competition for recognition and status in such a sub-culture does not include academic success. The prevailing norms are against working too hard.[3] Thus, although the fun sub-culture may be supported by the school with its emphasis on athletics as a means of achieving identification and integration, it also functions to inhibit the pursuit of academic goals.

Studies of American college life have similarly brought to light the existence of four comparable student sub-cultures, differing in the importance attached to collegiate life and to involvement with ideas.[4] The 'collegiate' sub-culture involves strong attachment to

[1] M. Carter, *Home, School and Work* (1962), Chapter 3, describes a number of schools which could be fitted into these categories.

[2] C. Lacey, *Hightown Grammar* (1970), and 'Some Sociological Consequences of Streaming in a Grammar School', *B.J.S.*, September 1966. See also D. A. Young and W. Brandis, 'Two Types of Streaming and Their Probable Application in Comprehensive Schools', in B. R. Cosin *et al.*, *School and Society: A Sociological Reader* (1971), pp. 148–51.

[3] James S. Coleman, 'Academic Achievement and the Structure of Competition', *Harvard Educational Review*, Vol. 29, 1959 (summarized in Burton R. Clark, *Educating the Expert Society* (1962)).

[4] Burton R. Clark, op. cit.

college life, to sports, college societies and other extra-curricular activities. It is, however, resistant to excessive involvement in studies or ideas beyond what is necessary to pass examinations. Its most active supporters come from the upper and upper-middle classes, and it flourishes only in residential colleges. The 'vocational' sub-culture sees the college courses as leading to diplomas and degrees and the better jobs which these can command. It is resistant to intellectual demands beyond those necessary for passing examinations and to active involvement in college life. Its supporters are usually students from lower middle- or working-class homes. The 'academic' sub-culture identifies with the value of the academic staff. Knowledge and ideas are intrinsically valuable and the excitement of intellectual study is the main motivation. The 'nonconformist' sub-culture is critical of the 'establishment' and detached from the college. Such students may be deeply involved with the ideas of the classroom, and even more with current issues in literature, politics or art. They are often seeking identity and are likely to adopt distinctive styles of dress.

With the increasing proportion of boys from lower middle-class homes, the collegiate sub-culture is declining and the vocational becoming dominant. The problem facing the colleges now is not whether students will study or play, but whether they will concern themselves with narrow studies for a job. Student peer-group cultures have been shown to exert a powerful influence on the activities and interests of students and to enable them to resist the influence of faculty members.[1] This raises an interesting question. One result of encouraging the development of a strong student community by residential accommodation may be to reduce the impact of the intellectual challenge of college life. Some supporting evidence for this comes from a study of a college of education.[2] Here a strong student culture existed which lead them to identify strongly with teachers in the schools, stressed the importance of techniques and the irrelevance of educational theory.

A second major element in the school system will be the allocation and definition of roles. The teacher's role is in part defined by society and the educational system. But the goals of the school will also generate role expectations to which the teacher will be under pressure to conform. In the 'custodial' school, his role will be what Webb[3] has conceptualized as the 'drill-sergeant', with

[1] J. H. Bushnell, 'Student Culture at Vassar', in N. Sanford (ed.), *The American College* (1962), Chapter 14.

[2] Marten Shipman, 'Education and College Culture', *B.J.S.*, December 1967.

[3] J. Webb, 'The Sociology of a School', *B.J.S.*, September 1962.

its emphasis on discipline, punishment and routine. In this way, the goals of the school will influence the strategies which are developed both inside and outside the classroom, and the responses of the pupils. Drill-sergeant techniques, for example, are likely to generate high levels of aggression which spill over into delinquency after school. Such a school is likely to exhibit the characteristics of a 'blackboard jungle', requiring even more stern repressive measures and the further dominance of custodial functions. It will exhibit a strongly developed delinquent sub-culture.[1]

Two factors will modify this over-simplified picture. Firstly, the personal qualities of teachers will influence the 'style' with which they play their roles. A teacher with considerable flair may be able to play a custodial role in a way which is compatible with the pursuit of academic or missionary goals. Secondly, a process of selection and self-selection may occur. 'Academic' teachers who find themselves in 'missionary' schools will be under pressure to change, but it is unlikely that all teachers even in a long-established school will adopt the same goals.

EDUCATION AS A SOCIAL PROCESS

Recent developments in theories of organization and interaction have resulted in new ways of looking at the classroom. The relations between pupils and teachers may be seen as a process of negotiation and bargaining. Although the roles of each are broadly defined, negotiation takes place over, for example, the amount of neatness or quietness. Once an order has been negotiated, the teacher, like his pupils, will be expected to comply.[2] The relation between teacher and pupil also involves an exchange of knowledge. And again, recent advances in the sociology of knowledge[3] can usefully be applied to an understanding of the process of transforming knowledge. Such studies emphasize the importance of the world-taken-for-granted which constitutes the individual child's construction of reality. Moreover, this reality is socially constructed in the sense that it is formed from the informal interactions of everyday life, and especially in the family and peer group. It is the differences in these constructions of reality which play such an important part in the learning situation, in which teachers and

[1] See Burton R. Clark, op. cit., for a more detailed account. This discussion of the existence of high-school and college sub-culture raises the more general question of the extent to which these articulate with a more pervasive youth culture. The evidence for this will be examined in Chapter 6. The school as an organization and the role of the teacher will be discussed in Chapter 8.

[2] These notions are explored more fully in Chapter 8.

[3] See Chapter 6.

pupils from different backgrounds face each other with the different views of the world. At the centre of the socialization process, the individual is faced with the problem of developing a satisfactory identity or self-concept out of interaction with others. It is this which presents the child stigmatized by allocation to the 'D' stream with such problems. It is to the outcome of this process of interaction that we now turn.[1]

Scholastic attainments

There is now a wealth of data which demonstrates the fact that social background plays a large part in determining educational attainment. A much higher proportion of the children of non-manual workers have attended grammar schools, and gone on to university (Table 3.1). Moreover, the children of unskilled workers are not only under-represented on entry to grammar school, but gradually fall farther behind in their educational achievements.[2]

Such differences may, of course, reflect differing levels of ability or financial and other barriers. However, the abolition of fees since 1944 has not resulted in any levelling-up. The chances for the sons of a manual worker still remain small compared with those for the sons of a professional or manager (Table 3.1). Educational opportunities have greatly increased, but the class differences in achievement remain. Indeed, although there was some narrowing of differentials in the inter-war and early post-war period, they may have widened slightly rather than narrowed in more recent years, with the declining importance of standardized ability tests in selection at eleven-plus.[3]

In the nineteenth century, it was widely assumed that the lack of achievements of some strata in society were due mainly to their inferior genetic endowment. Galton, for example, attributed the high levels of achievement of some outstanding families to their inherited genius. The development of intelligence tests offered a promising line of inquiry, but it became increasingly apparent that these were not, in fact, measuring a genetic factor uninfluenced by environment. Attempts to unravel the relative importance of 'nature and nurture' and the influence of other non-genetic factors such as motivation in the determination of measured intelligence have proved only partially successful.

In recent years, the attack has shifted to a study of those environmental factors which influence educational achievement. There is

[1] For the approach to the study of the school outlined in this paragraph see especially B. R. Cosin *et al.*, op. cit., Sections 1 and 2.
[2] Central Advisory Council, *Early Leaving* (1954), Tables J and 7 and 8.
[3] A. Little and J. Westergaard, 'The Trend in Class Differentials in Educational Opportunity in England and Wales', *B.J.S.*, December 1964.

little doubt that the relatively inferior educational achievements of children from working-class homes are due to factors other than ability. Researches by Douglas indicate that fewer working-class boys are admitted to the grammar school than middle-class boys in the same groups of measured ability. The difference is particularly marked for those with test scores of 54 or less, where the percentage declines from 40 per cent of the upper middle-class to 7·9 per cent from lower working-class homes.[1] At the grammar school, the

TABLE 3.1

PROPORTION IN DIFFERENT CLASSES OBTAINING GRAMMAR-SCHOOL AND UNIVERSITY EDUCATION (BOYS)*

		Born		
		1910–19	1920–9	Late 1930s
		%	%	%
Prof./managerial:†	Gram.	44	54	62
	Univ.	8½		19
Skilled manual and other non-manual:	Gram.	13	15	20
	Univ.	3½		3½
Semi/unskilled:	Gram.	4	9	10
	Univ.	1		1

* For grammar schools, these occupational categories refer to Hall-Jones 1–3, 4–5 and 6–7 pre-1929, and to Crowther Report groups post-1930. For universities, the pre-1929 are Hall-Jones 1–4, 5, 6–7 and post-1930 Registrar-General's Classes I and II, III, and IV and V.

† Compiled from A. Little and J. Westergaard, op. cit. This study drew on data from A. H. Halsey, *Ability and Educational Opportunity* (1961), the Crowther Report, and R. K. Kelsall, *Report on an Inquiry into Applications for Admissions to British Universities* (1957).

achievements of working-class children fall steadily behind middle-class children who were in the same ability groups when they were admitted to the school. Morover, nearly eight times the proportion of sons of professional fathers go on to further education compared with the sons of the unskilled.

These findings are reinforced by the Crowther Report. A survey of national-service recruits found that 42 per cent in the top ability group (out of six) did not attempt the sixth-form course to advanced level. The percentage was significantly higher for the sons of manual workers at 63 per cent.[2] Similar results are quoted in the Robbins Report. Of those in the top ability group (IQ 130-plus) who are the sons of non-manual workers, 37 per cent went

[1] J. W. B. Douglas, *The Home and the School* (1964).
[2] *15 to 18* (1960), Table 4.

on to degree-level courses, compared with 18 per cent of the sons of manual workers.[1]

This association between educational achievement and social background does not tell us which are the causal factors. Although fees have been abolished, this does not rule out the operation of financial considerations. Family allowances, for example, cease at age sixteen. The Early Leaving Report considers that shortage of money affects 11 per cent of the boys and 18 per cent of the girls who leave early. There is little doubt 'that poverty affects the decision to leave in an appreciable number of cases'. The Crowther Report found that 34 per cent of the boys and 43 per cent of the girls who wanted to stay on at school left because they needed or wanted to earn money.[2] There was also a strong association between parent's income and early leaving. Seventy-three per cent of the boys whose fathers earned less than £10 per week left grammar and technical schools by age 16, compared with 53 per cent of those whose fathers earned more than £16.

Two main variables affect both measured intelligence and educational achievement; the home and the school. The influence of the home includes both material conditions and more complex characteristics such as parental attitudes and encouragement. A study in Merseyside concluded that in summer, 27 per cent and in winter 44 per cent of children had to do homework under definitely bad conditions.[3] Parental interest not only has a marked effect on the child's attitude towards school and willingness to work hard, but even brings about an improvement in intelligence-test scores between age 8 and 11. The professional's son is more likely to plan a career for which an extended education is essential. The combined effect of future careers and parental attitudes is seen in a particularly marked way in the very different academic achievements of boys compared with girls coming from skilled and semi-skilled workers' homes. Such differences certainly cannot be explained in terms of differential ability.

Recent studies have begun to probe in more detail the intervening variables between family background and educational achievement. It has long been known that children from lower working-class homes score significantly lower on verbal test of intelligence, compared with their performance on non-verbal tests. Researches by Bernstein[4] have brought to light class differences in mothers' conceptions of the use of toys which have implications

[1] *Higher Education* (1963), Appendix 1, Table 5, p. 43.
[2] *15 to 18* (1960), Vol. 11, Table 10.
[3] *Early Leaving*, p. 36.
[4] B. Bernstein and D. Young, 'Differences in Conceptions on the Use of Toys', *Sociology*, May 1967.

for the development of measured intelligence. Middle-class mothers see toys as important for helping children to find out about things and as helping the child when he goes to school. Differences in measured intelligence were found to be related to such conceptions.

Bernstein's major contribution has been to focus on class-related differences in the way in which language is used to convey meanings.[1] Put very simply, Bernstein distinguishes between two ways in which language can be used. In the first form, meanings are spelt out and made explicit. The second form can best be understood in contrast with the first. Here the meanings are derived only in part from speech itself, and in part from clues provided by the context. So, for example, husbands and wives who have been married for a length of time may develop a more restricted 'public' language in which meanings are implicit rather than explicit, against a backcloth of shared experiences. There is no need to verbalize fully: an expressive movement of hand or head may suffice to convey meaning. The first ('formal' language) conveys universalistic meanings, while the second ('public' language) communicates particularistic meanings which are specific to particular contexts. Now the school transmits uncommon knowledge—universalistic knowledge. So the teacher using a universalistic mode of speech will not convey meanings adequately to the child who is geared mainly to a particularistic mode of speech. To communicate, the teacher will need to use the child's dialect. And it is this particularistic speech with which the working-class child is more likely to be familiar.

Bernstein's argument is complex. To make it clearer, it is important to stress what he is not saying: '... it does not mean that the resultant speech and meaning system is linguistically or culturally deprived, that the children have nothing to offer the school, that their imaginings are not significant. Nor does it mean that we have to teach the children formal grammar. Nor does it mean that we have to interfere with their dialect. .... The introduction of the child to the universalistic meanings of public forms of thought is not "compensatory" education; *it is education*.'[2] It is the failure of teachers to provide a linkage between the school and the world outside, which contributes to the under-achievement of the working-class child.

The second main group of variables in educational achievement

[1] B. Bernstein, 'Social Structure, Language and Learning', *Educational Research*, June 1961, and 'A Socio-Linguistic Approach to Social Learning', in P. Worsley (ed.), *Modern Sociology: Introductory Readings* (1970).

[2] B. Bernstein, 'Education Cannot Compensate for Society', in B. R. Cosin *et al.*, op. cit., pp. 61–6.

is the school and the interaction between the child and the school. In the Douglas inquiry, schools were classified according to their past record in academic achievement. Those with a good record improved the test scores of all but the top ability group, while in the poor schools, the top and most of the intermediate ability groups decline, although the lowest ability group shows a gain. Even controlling for parental interest and related variables, by age 11, the school is second only to parents' interest in its effects on ability scores, and good teaching can make up for parental indifference.[1]

If the task of the school is to transmit culture, this will be hindered by any marked discontinuities between its attitudes and values and those of the home. A study of eighty working-class grammar-school boys[2] suggests that the conflict between the culture of home and school can, in fact, exert a very powerful influence on educational achievement. The working-class boy will find that many of the values and attitudes of the grammar school differ sharply from those of the home. Faced with the need to choose, he frequently rejects the values of the school, withdraws from involvement in its activities, and seeks support by identification with a peer group of boys with similar backgrounds. So strong is this conflict that Jackson and Marsden found that the only working-class boys who successfully completed the grammar-school course were those with middle-class connections—a mother, for example, who came from a middle-class home. There is also evidence to suggest that parental indifference and hostility hinders the entry of working-class boys into universities.[3]

The existence of a distinctive youth culture whose values are opposed to those of the school has been argued persuasively, notably by Parsons[4] and Coleman.[5] Youth culture, it is claimed, emphasizes 'having a good time', and athletic prowess. Sugarman measured commitment to teenage culture by such indices as regular listening to pop music, wearing teenage fashions, smoking and going out with girls. He found that those scoring high had unfavourable attitudes towards school, emphasized having a good time now and not worrying about the future, and were more likely to be under-achievers academically.[6] What is problematic, of course, is whether relative academic failure is the cause or the

---

[1] J. W. B. Douglas, op. cit., Chapter 14.

[2] B. Jackson and D. Marsden, *Education and the Working Class* (1962).

[3] C. T. Sandford, M. Couper and S. Griffin, 'Class Influences in Higher Education', *Brit. J. Educ. Psych.*, June 1965.

[4] T. Parsons, *Essays in Sociological Theory* (1954), Chapter 5.

[5] J. S. Coleman, *The Adolescent Society* (1961).

[6] Barry Sugarman, 'Youth Culture, Academic Achievement and Conformity', *B.J.S.*, June 1967.

consequence of commitment to the teenage scene. The existence, extent and causes of youth culture will be discussed more fully in Chapter 6.

Educational achievement is influenced, too, by the way in which the school is organized and the techniques of teaching adopted. These are sociological variables, since they reflect the culture of society—the knowledge and, more important, the assumptions which a society has about the educational process, and the value which it attaches to various goals. In a 'sponsored' system, for example, ability streaming is a device which enables resources to be concentrated in an attempt to maximize the achievement of the most able children.

Evidence on the effects of ability streaming on achievement is somewhat scanty, but in general it supports the conclusion that streaming functions as a self-fulfilling prophecy.[1] Those who are *labelled* as less able, in fact achieve less, even though the label may fail to reflect ability as measured by IQ tests. High IQ boys from working-class homes, for example, are less likely than middle-class boys to be placed in 'A' streams.[2] In streamed schools, the lower streams score progressively lower in a variety of tests, and the gap between the lowest and highest streams widens.[3] Douglas found an increase in the measured ability of those in upper streams from age 8 to 11, which was particularly marked for the lower-ability groups. A corresponding decline in the scores of those in lower streams was most marked for the upper-ability groups.[4] Division into grammar and modern streams has comparable results. In all ability groups, there are increases in the measured ability between the ages of 11 and 15 of those attending grammar schools and a decline in those at modern schools. This is particularly marked for the children of manual workers in the top ability group (scores 58–60) attending modern schools whose score drops four points.[5]

There is less evidence to explain the relatively poor performance of the lower streams. It is likely that the 'best' pupils are given the 'best' teachers. They certainly do more homework. Being labelled as failures is related to emotional disturbances, and the development of an anti-school sub-culture in which prestige is obtained from cheeking a teacher, playing truant, smoking and drinking. Thus, membership of such a group contributes to further failure.[6]

[1] See R. K. Merton, op. cit., for a discussion of this concept and examples.
[2] J. Ford, *Social Class and the Comprehensive School* (1969).
[3] B. Jackson, *Streaming: An Education System in Miniature* (1964).
[4] J. W. B. Douglas, op. cit., p. 115.
[5] *Higher Education*, Appendix 1, p. 50.
[6] C. Lacey, op. cit. (1966).

Moreover, academic failures do not even gain any compensatory status by success in games.[1]

Evidence on the educational consequences of comprehensive secondary education is equally scanty. On theoretical grounds, great differences would not be expected. Most comprehensive schools practise ability streaming. Transfer between grammar and non-grammar streams is, of course, theoretically easier than between schools, but less frequent in fact than teachers believe to be the case. Since an increasing proportion of modern schools have grammar-school streams, and are likely to concentrate their resources on these, the advantages of comprehensive schools for purely educational achievement may not be great. Indeed, Julienne Ford's[2] study confirms that the chances of a working-class boy with a high IQ reaching the 'A' stream are somewhat better in a comprehensive school than in a grammar school (35 per cent), though still well below those of a boy from a middle-class home and with the same IQ (68 per cent). Moreover, a much smaller proportion (13 per cent) of working-class boys in the 'A' stream of the comprehensive school in her study intended to stay on in the sixth form, compared with those in the grammar school (72 per cent).

The organization and administration of examinations is a further factor contributing to success or failure. Studies of university pass rates show that these vary widely between faculties in the same university, and between the same faculties in different universities. Venables[3] has shown that many technical college examinations have built-in failure rates. A high level of failure results when students are not allowed to proceed to the next year of a course until they have passed sessional examinations. Moreover, there is evidence to suggest that a relatively stable failure rate is applied from year to year in spite of the varying merit of examination scripts.

Attitudes and values

The effect of the school on other aspects of behaviour is less well demonstrated. There is, however, data which suggests that such consequences differ considerably according to the type of school and the ability stream experienced. Allocation to grammar or modern school has a considerable effect on vocational aspirations.[4]

[1] K. B. Start, 'Substitution of Games Performance for Academic Achievement', *B.J.S.*, September 1966.
[2] J. Ford, op. cit., Chapters 2 and 3. See also D. A. Young and W. Brandis, op. cit.
[3] E. Venables, *The Young Worker at College* (1966).
[4] H. T. Himmelweit, A. H. Halsey and A. N. Oppenheim, 'The Views of

And although aspirations are higher among working-class comprehensive school boys compared with those attending modern schools, they are still well below the grammar-school attenders, even among those in the 'A' streams of the comprehensive school.[1] Modern schoolboys are more likely to want good wages and are less likely to stress intrinsic rewards such as interest and autonomy.[2] Grammar-school boys see their future status as being mainly achieved through work and dependent on their own exertions. Few secondary-modern school boys see efforts at work as the determinant of future status, while a substantial proportion have fantasies in which future status is achieved in the field of sport or entertainment. The success through effort pattern is more marked in the 'A' than in the 'B' streams of both grammar and modern schools.[3] There is some evidence, too, that assignment to a low status in school affects the pupil's self-esteem and generates a sense of inferiority, contributing to the under-utilization of mental abilities (which has been discussed earlier).[4] Moreover, working-class boys with a grammar-school background are more likely than those attending modern school to vote Conservative. Ex-modern schoolboys were also more likely to be politically apathetic, and less likely to believe that 'Big Business', the 'House of Commons' and similar institutions were working well.[5] Elder concludes: 'A large number of modern school attenders, regardless of their occupational status, seem to be somewhat alienated from the economic and political life of the country. Frustration of the achievement needs of these youths may result in the search for meaning and satisfaction in delinquent, sexual, and religious activities.'[6]

The mass media
Although the effects of education on behaviour have attracted little attention, this is far from true for the mass media. Indeed, it is the very massness of the cinema, newspapers, radio and television that has generated fears about their impact on society.

Adolescents on Some Aspects of the Class Structure', *B.J.S.*, June 1952. Factors affecting achievement motivation will be analysed in more detail in Chapter 7.

[1] J. Ford, op. cit., Chapter 4.

[2] Gallup Survey quoted in Glen H. Elder, Jr, 'Life, Opportunity and Personality: Some Consequences of Stratified Secondary Education in Great Britain', *Soc. of Educ.*, Spring 1965.

[3] Ibid.

[4] Gallup Survey, quoted in G. H. Elder, op. cit. See also J. W. Staines, 'The Self-Concept in Learning and Teaching', in D. F. Swift (ed.), *Basic Readings in the Sociology of Education* (1970).

[5] T. Veness, *School Leavers* (1962).   [6] G. H. Elder, op. cit., p. 199.

Unlike more individual and personal forms, mass communications are directed towards large public, heterogeneous audiences, and the relationship between communicator and audience is impersonal and one-way. Consequently, the media have been charged (particularly by those on the left who emphasize a conflict view of society) with contributing to the emergence of a mass society[1] in which primary relationships with family and local community have decayed and an atomized mass is at the mercy of the 'image makers'.[2]

The immediacy and potential power of television, in particular, has generated further fears. There is the fear that economic interest groups may use the media to minimize social criticism and to ensure conformity to the economic *status quo*. There is also anxiety lest a desire to attract mass audiences causes a deterioration in cultural standards. Finally, there is the fear that the media are producing passivity, dependency and escapism.

The evidence is somewhat complex.[3] Many individuals with anxiety tendencies do seek fantasy and escape, and for these, television meets a need, and probably reinforces their escapist tendencies. Himmelweit, Oppenheim and Vince have not found evidence that TV makes children passive. But Belson discovered that television reduced the activities and initiative of viewers. Lazarsfield and Merton in America, however, argue that television does have a narcotic effect, and that 'the commercially-sponsored mass media indirectly but effectively restrain the cogent development of a genuinely critical outlook.'[4] There is little doubt that violence on TV does not have the cathartic effect frequently claimed for it by reducing aggression vicariously. On the contrary, such material would appear to be especially dangerous for delinquents for whom such characters have been found to provide heroes, and models for action, while heavy exposure to violence on the screen heightens the possibility that someone will behave aggressively.[5]

The long-term effect on tastes and interests is more difficult to discover. Himmelweit found that when there was only one channel, television did extend tastes, but with the opportunity for selective viewing offered by a second channel, there was a marked narrowing of tastes and preferences. American studies have similarly found evidence for a hardening of taste at a level which reflects its own

[1] This concept is examined more fully in Chapter 5. See also Leon Bramson, *The Political Context of Sociology* (1961).
[2] Denis McQuail, *Towards a Sociology of Mass Communications* (1969), p. 15.
[3] For a detailed discussion, see Denis McQuail, op. cit., Chapter 3.
[4] *Mass Communication, Popular Taste and Organized Social Action, 1948*, quoted in J. D. Halloran, *The Effects of Mass Communication With Special Reference to Television* (1964), p. 23.
[5] J. D. Halloran, op. cit.

search for a common denominator of taste. Himmelweit found that it widened tastes only for the bright ten- and eleven-year-olds, and for the average thirteen- and fourteen-year-olds.[1]

The effects of television, though significant and important, do not appear to be dramatic. But it is difficult to come to any firm conclusions from the available evidence of its cumulative and long-term effects. The fact that the impact of television in a three-week election campaign is slight[2] does not rule out the possibility that it may have more marked effects on political attitudes over a greater length of time. More research will be needed before this can be judged with any degree of certainty.

The influence of the press is difficult to assess on the available evidence. The reports of 1949 and 1962 concluded that the popular press and, on occasion, the quality press, fell short of the highest standards, and were guilty of excessive partisanship, distortion, triviality and sensationalism. But the complex nature of the communication process does not enable conclusions to be drawn based simply on the content of communication. However, the 1949 report concluded that with few exceptions, newspapers 'fail to supply the electorate with adequate materials for sound political judgement'.[3] The fact that collectively the press represents the whole spectrum of political opinion does little to help the average reader who is not in a position to perform the very complex task of comparing a number of partial and distorted accounts in order to extract an unbiased conclusion. The most probable result is that in those areas where the reader has direct experience, the press is unlikely to have a major influence. But where he relies almost entirely on the press, its distortions could have more significant effect.

The view that an audience is an atomistic mass passively accepting the message of the communicator has been sharply challenged by researches into *uses and gratifications*.[4] This approach stems from the perspectives of social action theory, and postulates that individuals have specific needs (for information, escape, reassurance) which will influence behaviour towards the media. From a substantial volume of research on the impact of television, it is clear that both the consumption of television and its impact is heavily patterned, and that 'the level and direction of consumption varies sharply with age, sex, intelligence, education, social class, parental habits and social relations. The effect of television depends on these variables. We must get away from the habit of thinking in terms of what television does to people and substitute for it the

---

[1] H. Himmelweit *et al.*, *Television and the Child* (1958).
[2] J. Trenaman and D. McQuail, *Television and the Political Image* (1961).
[3] 1949 report, op. cit., p. 154.   [4] D. McQuail, op. cit., p. 91.

idea of what people do with television.'[1] The impact of television on leisure, for example, depends to a considerable extent on what people did with their time before they had TV. Himmelweit[2] has noted what she calls a 'displacement effect'; television viewing replaces comparable activities such as reading comics, cinema visits and radio listening. On the other hand, it has little effect on reading books, and sports activities.

The atomistic 'mass society' view has also been challenged by researches into the actual flow and channels of communication, which show that recipients are typically members of groups which provide them with norms and frames of reference for the evaluation and interpretation of messages. Studies of propaganda in the Second World War, for example, showed that the affective ties between soldiers and other members of their combat units protected them from the effects of propaganda.[3] It was this *camaraderie* which maintained the cohesion of army units rather than any commitment to official ideology. Hence, propaganda aimed at discrediting political and ideological beliefs was ineffective. Similarly, studies of election campaigns suggest that the perception and interpretation of communications are structured by the recipient's membership of groups, which lead him to interpret the communication in a way which makes it congruent with the norms and beliefs of his reference groups.[4] The *two-step flow* hypothesis of Lazarsfield and his associates[5] has similarly focused attention on the role of opinion leaders who act as intermediaries in a communication network of interconnected individuals.[6] In other words, communications must always be seen as a part of a total pattern of interaction between individuals and groups.

Studies of audiences focus on only one component in the communication process. News flows through channels, and the 'gatekeepers'—journalists, producers—influence what will be channelled to the recipients.[7] Moreover, the whole question of the

[1] J. D. Halloran, op. cit., p. 20.

[2] H. Himmelweit, *et al.*, op. cit. In the USA television does appear to have reduced the time spent in reading books and magazines.

[3] E. Shils, 'Primordial, Personal, Sacred and Civil Ties', *B.J.S.*, June 1957; E. Shils and M. Janowitz, 'Cohesion and Disintegration in the Wehrmacht in World War II', *Pub. Op. Quart.*, Vol. 12, 1948.

[4] J. W. Riley and M. Riley, 'Mass Communication and the Social System', in R. K. Merton, L. Broom and L. S. Cottrell, *Sociology Today: Problems and Prospects* (1965).

[5] P. F. Lazarsfield *et al.*, *The People's Choice* (1948). For a summary of related researches, see J. W. Riley and M. Riley, op. cit.

[6] See Cauter and Downham, *The Communication of Ideas* (1954), for comparable English material on communication structures.

[7] D. McQuail, op. cit., pp. 64–5, and M. Warner, 'Decision-Making in Television Network News', in J. Tunstall, *Media Sociology: A Reader* (1970).

systems of controls and values within which the communicators operate has recently attracted the attention of researchers. A study of BBC staff[1] brought to light three main views about the functions of broadcasting. For the pragmatists, the BBC exists to inform, educate and entertain the public; for the 'platonists', the BBC performs an important normative function in its observance of moral standards and in the authority attached to its comment and criticism; while thirdly, for the 'mirror on society' view, the task of the BBC is to reflect swiftly and forcibly, contemporary events, society and culture.

In practice, producers (especially television) have a good deal of autonomy and are largely responsible for the content of transmissions. In his inquiry, Burns found a strong professionalism among producers. The role requires intense commitment and generates considerable strains. 'The producer must immerse himself in the particular unreality in which his show exists. . . . The professional role of television or radio producer requires him, therefore, to insulate himself. . . .'[2] This insulation even extends to insulation from the audience. Apart from intense anxiety about audience ratings, there is singularly little curiosity or research into the impact of the programme. The criteria by which programmes are judged are those of the professional producer and his peers. This 'private world', Burns argues, is a necessary device to protect those who are intensely committed to their occupational roles from the intolerable strains of external pressures. Studies of journalists and editors similarly show their relative indifference to the needs of the audience compared with the constraints of the in-group of newsmen.[3]

Studies of the content of programmes suggest that what is reflected by the media is a somewhat distorted image of society with an emphasis on conventional conservative values. The analysis of trends over time confirms the general conclusion that by and large the content mirrors changing reality and that the media tend towards conservation and reinforcement rather than functioning as active agents of change. And the most plausible explanation of this tendency is the attempt by the communicators to respond to what they *believe* the audience to want.[4]

[1] Tom Burns, 'Public Service and Private Worlds', in J. Tunstall (ed.), op. cit., p. 136.
[2] Ibid., p. 154.
[3] D. McQuail, op. cit., p. 66. See also, M. Warner, 'Decision Making in Network Television News', in J. Tunstall, op. cit., pp. 158–67.
[4] J. Tunstall, op. cit., pp. 68–70.

The functionalist perspective on education stresses its importance in socializing individuals for a variety of social roles. That is to say, education is an important part of the control mechanisms of society. The more society can ensure that individuals internalize the norms and values appropriate to their social roles, the less the need for external controls in the shape of rewards and punishments. But the greater the division of labour and the specialization of roles, the more need there is for structural differentiation within the educational system. And as the expertise required for the performance of roles increases, so educational qualifications become more important criteria for recruitment. It is to these functions of education in socialization, control, social selection and recruitment that we now turn.

Socialization and social control
It has already been argued that at one level a primary objective for the education of the labouring poor was to 'gentle the masses' —to socialize them to their subordinate roles in society. At another social level, a major emphasis of the rapidly expanding public schools was on devising educational regimes which would develop qualities of character and leadership in the children of the emerging middle class. Even in the relatively undeveloped field of vocational education, there was a major emphasis on the colleges and schools producing 'intelligent workmen' who would 'understand the principle underlying their trade'. Specialized knowledge, it was argued, would be learnt on the job, not in the educational institutions.[1] Similarly, the reform of recruitment to the civil service reflected the same approach. The administrative grade took men with good honours, not because the knowledge acquired could be applied to administration but because, like the mandarins of China, their diplomas were indications of qualities of mind.

If the educational system was to perform the function of socializing for a variety of social roles, differentiation of structure was essential. The structural differences reflected, of course, social rather than educational criteria such as ability. Indeed, the Schools Inquiry Commission of 1868 proposed that there should be three distinct types of secondary education, and that the differences would be grounded in social distinctions. The third grade, for example, was to be for the sons of middle-class parents of straitened means, destined for careers in business, leaving at 14, and receiving a more practical education than that intended for the sons of the well-to-do who would leave at 18 for university.

[1] S. F. Cotgrove, op. cit. (1958).

There was no question of secondary education for the children of the labouring classes. It was during the nineteenth century, too, that the public schools became the preserves of the middle and upper classes. They had originally been established and endowed with funds to provide poor scholars with an education which would enable them to enter the Church. As the rising industrial middle class became increasingly dissatisfied with the education provided by the local endowed schools, a number of such schools gradually emerged as pre-eminent, attracting boarding scholars from further afield, while the local foundationers became a diminishing element in such schools.[1]

The educational system of the nineteenth century then was closely related to the class-structure, both by the source from which the various types of schools drew their pupils and by the curriculum. The efforts of the two-year trained elementary school teachers to raise their status and the level of education in the working-class schools were effectively hindered by administrative action, notably by Low's system of payment by results in 1861 which ensured that only reading, writing and reckoning should be taught.[2] Even the achievement of literacy was hindered by the sterility of the curriculum forced on the elementary schools. It was feared that too much education would make working-class children unfit for their station in life. But even this limited intellectual diet was thought to be too literary, producing clerks and not artisans, and was consequently extended to include manual instruction for training the co-ordination of hand and eye following the recommendations of the Cross Commission of 1888. Even subjects such as political economy were used as vehicles for moral education. The syllabus for Social Economy of the London School Board for 1871 included such topics as 'thrift, temperance, and economy and their bearing on general wages. Honesty, trustworthiness and fore-thought and their influence on the wealth of the community . . .'[3] What the elementary schools did then was to cultivate personal qualities essential for workers in an industrial society with an emphasis on punctuality, regularity, obedience and habits of industry.

Although the schools are no longer so explicitly oriented towards 'gentling the masses', they continue to perform important socializing and control functions. In Britain, religious instruction is the only item in the curriculum which is mandatory. In the USSR, instruction in Marxist–Leninist philosophy is an integral

[1] *The Public Schools and the General Educational System* (Flemming Report), (1944).
[2] A. Tropp, *The School Teachers* (1957), Chapters 5 and 6.
[3] From the *Report of the School Board for London*, 1904.

part of education. School history books in all countries tend to be written from an ethnocentric viewpoint, and to inculcate nationalistic attitudes. UNESCO is currently engaged in trying to get such texts re-written from a world view point. The recent increase in delinquency and illegitimacy among young people has prompted the Newsom Report to propose extending the operations of the school into leisure-times, thus taking over from the family and extending the school's socializing influence.

The socializing function of the primary school is particularly important. It is here, for example, that the child is exposed to social norms and values beyond those which are available for learning in the family. In the family, individuals are judged by what Parsons calls particularistic standards in which feelings predominate, while in the school the child is expected to conform to universalistic standards which are applied impartially to all. Furthermore, while in the family, ascriptive roles based on age and sex predominate; that is to say, the child is expected to behave according to the norms for his age and sex. School, however, reflects the orientation of the wider society, in which roles are allocated on the basis of achievement. The emphasis placed on achievement legitimizes selection and reduces the strains imposed by differentiation.[1]

The school, argues Parsons, plays an important role in developing the achievement orientation necessary to generate the high levels of motivation required by an industrial society.[2] But a latent function of such pressure to achieve may be to produce a youth-culture which includes anti-intellectual elements. In particular, high ability low status children are likely to rebel against a situation in which the stakes are high, and to express their protest against the adult world by rejecting the intellectual values which they are being pressured to achieve.[3]

The socializing function, however, does raise problems. It assumes a measure of agreement on what personal qualities society wishes to cultivate. Rapid social change makes these less certain. But it also suggests a major objective for education for the future—to fit the future generation to adjust to social change. There is certainly pressure to introduce a more occupationally and socially relevant curriculum in the schools. Newsom proposes that 'the final year ought to be deliberately outgoing—an initiation into the adult world of work and leisure', and the fourth and fifth years should include 'a range of courses broadly related to occupa-

[1] T. Parsons, 'The School Class as a Social System and some of its Functions', A. H. Halsey, J. Floud and C. A. Anderson, *Education, Economy and Society: A Reader in the Sociology of Education* (1962), Chapter 31.

[2] Achievement motivation is examined more fully in Chapter 7.

[3] T. Parsons, op. cit.

tional interests . . .' F. Musgrove,[1] however, has warned against a curriculum for the grammar school which is too closely geared to the needs of the locality. The grammar-school boy is occupationally and geographically mobile, and needs an education which will extend his horizons and experiences.

Selection and mobility promotion

If education functioned in the nineteenth century mainly to socialize the children of the various social strata for their station in life, this is no longer an adequate explanation of the structure and function of education. In the nineteenth century, status was predominantly ascribed. The sons of artisans were expected to become artisans, and were educated accordingly. By a series of steps, society has moved to a position where achievement plays a very much larger part. The growth of knowledge and its application to the performance of increasingly specialized roles means that talent is largely replacing kinship as the basis for recruitment. As certificates and diplomas are more and more the means of entry to the better paid, more secure, higher status jobs, education becomes increasingly important as a basis for occupational achievement and upward social mobility. The emphasis has shifted from socialization to selection.

However, despite its changing functions the English educational system has retained many of its nineteenth-century features. Until recently we have kept distinct types of school educating for distinct levels in the social system. The grammar school leads to white-collar, professional and managerial posts, while the secondary modern leads mainly to manual work. Within the comprehensive schools, streaming perpetuates the same divisions. But we have modified the method of selection and recruitment to such schools. The Act of 1944 abolished fees for secondary education and rounded off the process of change whereby selection by ability to profit has gradually replaced selection by ability to pay.

It must not be concluded that the selective functions of the schools have determined the particular structure of education which we have in this country. Rather, an essentially aristocratic structure has been modified so that schools which once educated a social elite now educate an intellectual elite. Much the same can be said of other elements in the educational system, such as the universities which have similarly come to be places for the education of an intellectual elite. But the structures have been largely inherited from the past. It is the sources and methods of recruitment to elites which have been modified.

By comparison, other societies, such as America, have evolved

[1] F. Musgrove, *The Migratory Elite* (1963).

somewhat different systems of mobility, and the contrast enables us to see the ways in which other elements in the educational system are related. Turner[1] suggests that there are two polar types of mobility systems, which he calls *sponsored* and *contest* mobility, each of which is related to characteristic types of education. In a sponsored system, potential recruits to elite positions are selected and allocated as early as possible to elite educational institutions so that they may be exposed to the lengthy socialization necessary to develop elite qualities. The system may be likened to a series of escalators. The most able are placed on the bottom step of a long and fast moving escalator which carries them up and drops them off at the top. The selection process also goes on within the school with the allocation of the most able to higher 'streams' (ability groups) where once again they are carried along at a faster pace.

The contest system is exemplified by the American system. This, by contrast with the sponsored system, can be likened to a race in which everything is done to give the outsider a fair chance. The race is not won until the winner passes the post, so everyone must be allowed to stay in the race. There is no question of selection. To change the metaphor, the educational system is comparable to a broad ladder up which anyone can climb and carry on climbing until he decides to give up. In America, for example, there is no early selection of the likely winners. All go to common schools. And whereas in a sponsored system, much research effort is devoted to devising the most efficient selection procedure, in a contest system the problem is to motivate the student to keep trying, since his achievement will depend heavily on his own efforts. He is not carried along by the educational escalator which in the sponsored system is constantly buttressing and reinforcing his efforts by defining him as successful and expecting high levels of achievement (unless he is in a 'C' or 'D' stream).

The system has consequences, too, for the curriculum. In the sponsored system of Britain, the elite has opened its doors to the recruitment of the carefully selected and socialized parvenu. In order to preserve its status it fosters an elite culture, which stresses correct syntax, distinctive speech styles and the acquisition of non-utilitarian knowledge, all of which require a lengthy socialization process. By this technique, the elite stratum can preserve its distinctive characteristics. In the contest system of America, there is no such distinctive elite culture. The door must be left open to the outsider, and early selection and special socialization are not

---

[1] R. Turner, 'Modes of Ascent through Education', in A. H. Halsey *et al.*, op. cit. (1961) and also in P. Worsley (ed.), *Readings* (1970). For a critique of Turner, see A. H. Halsey, *A.S.R.*, June 1961, pp. 454–6.

possible. Consequently, there is less stress on the status value of non-utilitarian knowledge, and the way is open for educational institutions to foster the growth of studies related to practical affairs. The much larger number of vocational courses in American universities, and particularly the large numbers of engineering students contrast with the small proportion in English universities. Once again, we see that the character of the elite influences the concept of 'culture', and therefore the activities of educational institutions.

If education is to function to promote upward social mobility, it will be necessary for those born into the lower status groups to have access to mobility-promoting educational institutions, and the chance to win the certificates and diplomas which are the mark of educational achievement. This as we have seen is far from being the case. It is, however, important to emphasize that education is only one of a number of factors which determine the achievement of higher status occupations. There are other means of upward mobility apart from the educational ladder, and high educational achievement will not by itself determine recruitment to elite positions. This will be examined more fully in Chapter 7.

EDUCATION AND SOCIAL CHANGE

It is clear that in an industrial society, the links between education and occupation become increasingly important. The functions of the educational system shift from conferring charisma on priests or mandarins, to an emphasis on socializing and controlling the masses during the early unsettled phase of industrialization, and then to preparing an increasing range of specialists for their occupational roles and so selecting for upward mobility. Concomitant with these changes in function there are changes in the structure of the educational system with the growth of secondary schools, technical and teacher-training colleges and universities, and the changes in the curriculum as the notion of culture is slowly modified with the increasing importance of science, technology and practical knowledge and the accompanying increase in the influence and status of scientists and technologists.

The relations between the educational system and the social structure are very complex and not yet fully understood. We can certainly see some ways in which changes in the social structure exert pressures for change on the educational system. The growth of political democracy, for example, leads to the demand for greater equality of opportunity. This demand in turn, springs in part from the increasing importance of education for occupation, and reflects changes in the economic system of production which increasingly applies specialized knowledge, making the possession of diplomas more rewarding in economic terms.

The present pressure towards a comprehensive 'contest' system of education is a further example of change in the educational system in response to forces largely external to the system, and to some extent resisted by parts of the educational system. It has already been explained that the tripartite system of grammar, modern and technical schools which emerged as a result of the 1944 Act[1] was a continuation of the essentially aristocratic system of the nineteenth century. The main change was in the more democratic method of recruitment which substituted ability to profit for ability to pay. This change, however, gave rise to mounting criticisms of tripartism focused on the methods of selection used to allocate children to the coveted grammar-school places. This system excluded many middle-class children who would previously have attended as fee-payers having passed the less-rigorous selection test imposed on those not dependent on a free-place. Moreover, there was the growing evidence that many admitted were failing to complete the grammar-school course, while the chances of admission to a grammar school varied considerably according to locality, with ratios varying from under 10 per cent to over 50 per cent.

The occupational significance of a grammar-school education was alone enough to generate great anxiety in the middle-class parents at the possibility of failure at the 'eleven-plus'. Reinforced by the evidence of the weakness in selection procedure, social pressure has led to a widespread acceptance of the desirability of 'ending the eleven-plus'. But since some form of selection is essential if separate types of secondary school remain, such a policy can only lead to the introduction of some form of 'comprehensive' education, in which the common school catering for all ranges of ability continues in some form at the secondary stage. Furthermore, the rigid distinctions of tripartism have been eroded in recent years by the marked increase in GCE courses in secondary-modern schools and the development of a variety of school-leaving examinations. Again, social pressures deriving from the occupational significance of educational qualifications eventually overcame the persistent refusal of successive Ministers to introduce leaving examinations in the modern schools.[2]

Changes in the economic system which increasingly applies

[1] The act did not specify the form which secondary education should take, but tripartism was strongly supported by the Ministry of Education and by many LEAS. The Minister, in fact, has intervened on occasion to prevent the abolition of some grammar schools.

[2] W. Taylor, *The Secondary Modern School* (1963).

specialized knowledge to production have led to a growth in the demand for qualified manpower. As a result, the possession of diplomas has become more economically rewarding and therefore more highly sought, thus still further increasing the demand for educational places. It is this mechanism which underlies the educational explosion in the advanced industrial societies.

But this 'feed-back' from the economic system to the educational system does not necessarily produce an equilibrium between the demand for qualified manpower and the supply. Other elements in the social system exert an influence. For example, the inferior status of technology and its limited acceptance as a part of culture have hindered the growth of technological studies in Britain.[1] The newly industrializing societies of Africa and India are faced with especially difficult problems. High status occupations such as politics attract large numbers of students to the study of law, while there are serious shortages of engineers and technicians. In India, the high status of education plus the keen competition for jobs resulting from the shortage of appropriate occupations meant that a university degree came to be a qualification for clerical work, thus producing an even greater demand for graduate qualifications. The over-production of graduates in many European countries similarly produced a discontented intellectual proletariat who tended to support extremist political movements.[2]

The precise relationship between economic development and the expansion of education is only partially understood. There are two main possibilities. The expansion of educational opportunity may reflect mainly the growing consumer-demand for education by individuals for a variety of reasons, particularly the value of education for social mobility. It may, on the other hand, be due to the growing demand for qualified manpower from the labour-market reflecting the rising level of expertees required by modern industry.[3] Available data suggest that both factors have been at work, although there is some evidence that the supply of education has in some occupations outstripped the demand. Analysing data for the United States, Folger and Nam conclude that 'the evidence favours the hypothesis that within-occupation rises in education exceed in magnitude the shifts in educational requirements resulting from shifts in occupational structure'.[4] Although the expanding occupations are those requiring higher educational

[1] D. W. Hutchings, *Technology and the Sixth Form Boy* (1963), and S. F. Cotgrove, op. cit. (1958).

[2] W. M. Kotschnig, *Unemployment in the Learned Professions* (1937).

[3] J. K. Folger and C. B. Nam, 'Trends in Education in Relation to the Occupational Structure', *Soc. of Educ.*, Vol. 38, No. 1.

[4] Comment, *Soc. of Educ.*, Vol. 38, 1965, No. 2.

levels, the evidence suggests that the educational up-grading of occupations is greater than shifts in the occupational structure in a direction requiring higher educational levels. This conclusion would not necessarily apply, of course, to Britain where the median length of education is less than that in the USA. But even here, the evidence suggests that the expansion, at least until recently, has been due to consumer-demand rather than to industrial pressures affecting the labour market.[1] There is also some evidence to suggest that it is such an increase in the supply of educated personnel which has acted as a stimulus to economic growth, rather than the reverse relationship. The growth of an educational system supplying qualified scientists would appear to have played a major role in the expansion of scientific industries in Germany in the nineteenth century. By contrast, England lacked a class of professional scientists, and failed to respond to the challenges in the dyestuffs and electrical engineering industries in the nineteenth century.[2] Technological advances in industry depend on prior developments in the educational system. The presence of scientifically qualified men in key posts in industry is essential if industry is to be in a position to apply science to production. And a class of scientists is the product of the educational system. A somewhat analogous situation exists today in the social sciences. The Heyworth Committee,[3] for example, has had some trenchant things to say about the utilization of social science research findings. The Treasury, which is responsible for the efficient running of the machinery of government, employed (at the date of the inquiry) no social scientists other than economists to advise on the techniques of management. Industry similarly fails to employ social sciences in a professional capacity where they could identify problems and feed in research knowledge where appropriate. The growth of the social sciences owes little to the demands of industry and government for their services in these fields.

It would appear then that the educational system does not perform a purely passive role, responding more or less slowly to societal pressures. New knowledge is itself a function of the educational system. And it is this which has contributed so much to the transformation of society. As the rate of growth of new knowledge increases, universities and research institutes become increasingly influential as generators of new ideas. Technological needs have certainly played an important part in the growth of science in the past,[4] but with the institutionalization of science and

[1] S. F. Cotgrove, op. cit. (1958).
[2] D. S. L. Cardwell, op. cit.
[3] *Report of the Committee on Social Studies* (1965).
[4] R. K. Merton, *Essays in Social Theory and Social Structure* (1957).

the growth of science as a profession,[1] new knowledge is generated by relatively autonomous educational institutions, with all the repercussions of nuclear fission and electronics on the social structure and international relations. In fact, so important are developments in knowledge as agents of social change that Popper argues it is impossible to predict long-term social change, because we can never know what new knowledge we will discover.[2] What we can say with reasonable certainty is that the rate of social change brought about by new knowledge will increase, because the rate of growth of knowledge corresponds to a geometric rather than to an arithmetic progression.

This shift in the role of the universities[3] from cultural preservation to innovation faces them with new problems. Once institutions are established, they are resistant to change. Their practices will generally be legitimized by beliefs that they are morally right. A suggestion that the universities should concern themselves more with practical affairs and with the after-careers of their students brought the reply from one group of dons 'To have such a solemn, humourless, Benthamite pawing with the basic moral assumptions of university life fills one with horror.'[4]

DISCUSSION

The relevance of sociological research in education to both policymakers and professional teachers is obvious. But the gap between knowledge and action is often considerable. Teachers and governments have to get on with the job before all the data is in. And in any case, educational policy and classroom teaching involve much more than a knowledge of sociology.

The debate around equality has both influenced and been influenced by social and sociological inquiry. And as with a number of other issues on the one hand there are those who stress the need to change the individual, and, on the other hand, those who argue that it is the 'system' or the context in which the individual acts which is the crux of the problem. The first point of view is exemplified by those who have seized on the data which documents the under-achievement of the working-class child to promote a policy of compensatory education. The child from a

[1] D. S. L. Cardwell, op. cit. Promotion depends increasingly on publication. The academic market-place motivates academics to higher levels of research effort. Caplow and McGee, *The Academic Market Place* (1961).

[2] K. Popper, *The Poverty of Historicism* (1957).

[3] A. H. Halsey, 'The Changing Functions of Universities', in A. H. Halsey *et al.*, op. cit. (1961).

[4] *Observer*, 5 March 1961. See S. F. Cotgrove, 'Education and Occupation', *B.J.S.*, March 1962.

culturally-deprived home, who lacks parental support must receive special help to compensate for his own and his parents' inadequacies. By contrast, the opponents of this view argue that it ignores the substantial evidence on the paucity of resources devoted to education in the school which such an allegedly 'deprived' child attends. In short, it is not compensation but a square deal which is needed. One cannot help suspecting that there are ideological commitments underlying these alternative interpretations of the evidence. Can the issue be resolved in the light of present knowledge? This is a question best left for the student to settle for himself.

Attempts to apply organization theory and role analysis to the school have not yet gone very far. The application of interactionist perspectives and the ideas of exchange and bargaining between teachers and pupils, and the closely related studies of the uses of television, hold out promising and exciting prospects. They are in line with the growing emphasis on the need to organize 'learning situations' and the shift away from didactic authoritative teaching at all levels. The view of pupils passively assimilating knowledge is no more tenable than the picture of an atomistic mass TV audience manipulated by the hidden persuaders. But this is not to say that neither teachers nor programme producers are without influence, only that the degree of influence is problematic.

At the macro-level, the socialization and control functions of education have been highlighted by recent challenges to the curriculum—'free universities' and notions of 'alternative societies'. In spite of the penetrating work of Durkheim on the ways in which societies structure knowledge, it is only very recently that sociologists have paid much attention to these issues. The recent revival of interest in the sociology of knowledge promises to have a considerable impact on this aspect of the study of education. Here again, those who stress the conflict view of society argue that those in a dominant position in society will seek to control the definition of culture—what counts as 'knowledge'. There is nothing new in such ideas of course. They have simply not been taken up and explored in any systematic way by main stream sociology of education.

O. Banks, *The Sociology of Education* (Batsford, 1968).

M. Carter, *Home, School and Work* (Pergamon Press, 1962).

B. R. Clark, *Educating the Expert Society* (Chandler Publishing Company, 1962).

B. R. Cosin, (ed.), *Education: Structure and Society* (Penguin, 1972).

S. F. Cotgrove, *Technical Education and Social Change* (Allen and Unwin, 1958).

J. W. B. Douglas, *The Home and the School* (MacGibbon and Kee, 1964).

J. Ford, *Social Class and the Comprehensive School* (Routledge, 1969).

J. D. Halloran, *The Effects of Mass Communication with Special Reference to Television* (Leicester University Press, 1964).

J. D. Halloran, *et al.*, *Television and Delinquency* (Leicester University Press, 1970).

A. H. Halsey, J. Floud and C. A. Anderson, *Education, Economy and Society: A Reader in the Sociology of Education* (Free Press, 1962).

D. H. Hargreaves, *Social Relations in a Secondary School* (Routledge, 1967).

J. Holt, *The Underachieving School* (Pelican, 1971).

B. Jackson, *Streaming: An Education System in Miniature* (Routledge, 1964).

B. Jackson and D. Marsden, *Education and the Working Class* (Penguin, 1962).

C. Lacey, *Hightown Grammar: The School as a Social System* (Manchester University Press, 1970).

K. Liepmann, *Apprenticeship* (Routledge, 1960).

D. McQuail, *Towards a Sociology of Mass Communications* (Collier-Macmillan, 1969).

W. Taylor, *The Secondary-Modern School* (London, 1963).

J. Tunstall, *Media Sociology: A Reader* (Constable, 1970).

R. Williams, *The Long Revolution* (Penguin, 1965).

M. F. D. Young, *Knowledge and Control* (Collier-Macmillan, 1971).

Chapter 4

THE ECONOMIC SYSTEM
AND OCCUPATIONS

There are few areas in which the conflicts between the needs of the individual and those of society are more dramatically apparent than in the world of work. In some societies, manual labour has been forced upon a slave class who have been defined in various ways as sub-human. In the Christian mythology, man is expelled from the Garden of Eden for the sin of Adam and forced to earn his bread by the sweat of his brow. Marx dreamt of a 'society of artists' in which man is liberated from the tyranny of mindless labour and from the limitations of a particular occupation: '. . . communist society . . . makes it possible for me to do one thing today and another tomorrow, to hunt in the morning, fish in the afternoon, rear cattle in the evening, criticize after dinner, just as I have a mind, without ever becoming hunter, fisherman, shepherd, or critic.'[1]

At the level of sociological inquiry, we find the same basic issues reflected in major emphases in the sociology of economic life. Managerial sociology has often tended to assume a basic consensus between the needs of the individual and those of the firm, and has explored a variety of ways in which conflicts which disrupt such consensus may be removed. The social action approach has focused more explicitly on the needs which the worker brings to his job, the meaning which it has for him, and has examined ways in which work may become a source of self-realization. The debate not only raises basic issues about the nature of man and what man is capable of becoming, but also questions about the centrality of work in industrial society. Even sociologists sometimes accept the assumption that 'man the worker'—fulfilling himself in his daily labour—is the highest form of man.

Nevertheless, there is little doubt that work is a major influence on the individual in an industrial society. For some, occupation *is* a major source of *identity*. If we know that a man is a doctor, lawyer, engineer, priest, artist, we feel that we already know quite a lot about the kind of person he is. Why is this? Do occupations attract particular types of persons? Or does the occupation

[1] K. Marx and F. Engels, *The German Ideology*, quoted in L. S. Feuer (ed.), *Marx and Engels* (1959).

imprint its influence on the individual? Researches suggest that both factors must be taken into account. Furthermore, they support the view that the kind of work that a man does has a profound influence on non-work areas of life, on family life (as we saw in Chapter 2), on leisure, and on class and political attitudes.

WORK AND NON-WORK

This relation between work and non-work is scarcely surprising. Industrialization has been so conspicuously successful in increasing wealth precisely because it has mobilized armies of workers by hand and brain to regular and systematic work, so that work has become a dominant influence in the life of the individual, taking up the major part of his energies five or more days a week, for most of the year, and for most of his life. It is probable that at no previous time in history have so many worked so hard and for so long as in nineteenth-century Britain. And the more recent reduction in the demands of work from the seventy or more hours fifty-two weeks in the year of the nineteenth-century factory worker, to a forty-four hour week in most industrial societies still compares unfavourably with the working hours of the urban artisan in pre-industrial society. According to Wilensky[1] the skilled artisan in the thirteenth century worked as little as 194 days a year. Moreover, professionals and administrators today certainly work considerably longer than in pre-industrial society.

But it is not simply a question of the changing distribution of time between work and non-work. The nature of work itself has undergone profound changes. The mechanization of work has resulted in its concentration in factories. The majority of occupations now involve working in large-scale organizations, and this has produced complex problems of the relations between individuals and organizations. Moreover, growing division of labour and the application of science to production have changed work tasks so that we have a decline in old skills and the disappearance of the traditional craftsman, raising questions about the impact of mass production on the life of the worker. On the other hand, we have a growing demand for highly trained mathematicians and scientists and this in turn generates new problems. For example, researches suggest that the outlook and values of scientists may differ from those of the administrators and the organizations for which they work. Such conflicts, it is believed, may hinder the intellectual

[1] H. L. Wilensky, 'The Uneven Distribution of Leisure: The Impact of Economic Growth on Free Time', in E. O. Smigel (ed.), *Work and Leisure* (1963).

creativity of scientists and in this way threaten the efficient growth of scientific knowledge.[1]

In this chapter we shall examine work from a particular perspective. We will be looking at types of work-roles in the social system; that is to say, at the typical roles which individuals occupy in the processes of production, distribution and exchange. We will, moreover, be concentrating here on the individual, on his experiences, the meaning which these have for him, and the consequences of these work experiences for non-work behaviour. But this does not mean that we have shifted from a sociological to a psychological perspective. Our interest is not in individuals as such, but in types of work-roles which exist in particular societies. That is to say, we are interested in specifically social facts.

But what is work? At the outset there is the problem of definition. If we talk to some writers, artists, scientists and other professionals, we may find that they have difficulty in saying where their working day begins and ends. They may say, 'Well, I don't consider what I do is really work. I thoroughly enjoy it; it's what I want to do.' This suggests one important dimension of work-roles—the element of compulsion which characterizes them. But to exclude the scientist from our study because he has freely chosen to do his job would clearly be unsatisfactory. A second dimension of work-roles is the fact that we are paid for what we do. Does this mean that when the scientist papers the living-room at the weekend this is not work? He is much more likely to define this as work than his activities in the laboratory. Moreover, it is an economic activity just as much as his laboratory work, for he is earning money in the sense that he would otherwise have to pay someone else to do the job.[2] Similarly, the housewife 'works' even though she is not paid by an employer.

This discussion reminds us of the difficulty already encountered, that sociology uses an existing vocabulary which frequently emerges as unsatisfactory for scientific analysis. We have to arrive at an 'operational' definition, which clearly identifies the phenomena for study. For this purpose we can define work as any activity which is directed towards the production of goods and services which typically have a value in exchange and which are carried out for a valuable consideration. Moreover, although the degree of

[1] Although occupations cannot be understood except in an organizational setting, this chapter will concentrate on their study from the perspective of the individual, while Chapter 8 will take up the theme of the operation of organizations.

[2] N. Anderson, *Work and Leisure* (1961), suggests the term 'non-work obligations' for such activities. For a more extensive discussion of the distinction between work and leisure, see S. Parker, *The Future of Work and Leisure* (1971), Chapter 2.

compulsion which enters into such activities varies widely, we cannot define work simply as compulsory activities. In practice, we can largely avoid these problems of definition by studying 'occupations', that is to say those roles which determine a man's *market situation*: his ability to command goods and services for a consideration (monetary or otherwise).

The following table indicates the possible combinations between the variables and locates leisure activities in relation to (a) market situation (b) the nature of involvement in the activity, whether it is undertaken for purely 'instrumental' reasons or whether it is an 'expressive' activity which is intrinsically satisfying.

FIGURE 4.1
WORK AND NON-WORK

	Market	*Non-market*
Expressive	After-hours reading of scientist	Hobby—e.g. painting (Leisure)
Instrumental	Form-filling	Helping to wash up (Non-work obligations)

THE ECONOMY AND THE SOCIAL SYSTEM

Every society has to solve the problem of getting work done. This involves socializing individuals in order to produce the skills, capacities and motivation necessary. It also requires machinery for the selection and allocation of individuals to work-roles, and for organizing the relations of production, distribution and exchange. In simple terms, the basic problem which societies have to solve is 'How do we ensure that people work?'

Work, the economy and the political system
One extreme solution to the production problem is the use of coercion in slave systems. Here the monopoly of coercive means in the hands of the politically and economically dominant stratum is used to enforce the maximum exploitation of servile labour, as in the chattel slavery of the Southern States of America until the mid-nineteenth century. But even in the early phases of industrialization, the power of the employer to extract a maximum effort was strongly reinforced by the political system which conferred on the employer a variety of legally (coercively) enforceable rights, while at the same time limiting the protective measures which could be taken by workers, by limiting their rights of assembly, and organization.

A major variable in the relations between the political system and the economy is the extent to which governments allow autonomy

117

to economic units. A maximum of autonomy existed under *laissez-faire* capitalism[1] in nineteenth-century Britain. Here, the means of production were privately owned, and the property laws conferred extensive powers on property owners. Property rights can most simply be conceived as a bundle of legally enforceable claims to use and control things. In the last analysis, property rights depend on the extent to which the state is prepared to use its monopoly of coercive means to enforce such claims. Property laws, therefore, provide the main mechanism for the control of both ownership, production and distribution. In the nineteenth century, the rights of property gave almost unlimited powers of use and control. And since most were dependent on the property of others (such as factory and land-owners), for access to the means of earning a livelihood, the powers of property include the control over persons through things. Factory owners had almost unlimited powers to hire and fire whom they chose. In the face of such powers, workers were individually weak, but were prevented from taking collective action by the Combination Acts. Thus, even in a *laissez-faire* economy, the state intervened in a decisive way to determine the relations between employers and employees.

The growth of industrialization has been accompanied by the gradual extension of political protection to the worker. The right to form trade unions, the right to strike, industrial legislation and arbitration courts, factory legislation, redundancy agreements, unemployment benefits, severance pay, have all increased his relative bargaining power and restricted the economic and physical demands that can be made on the worker.[2] Although there is still a coercive element in work for most, this now derives from the fact that the individual needs to sell his labours to earn an income. But political action is still significant in shaping the relative bargaining power of the two sides. The state determines the framework within which the power-struggle over the amount and conditions of work and its rewards takes place. The 'distribution of economic, or purchasing power is one aspect of the distribution of social power'.[3] Much of the literature on industrial relations is, in fact, a description of the collective bargaining machinery which has been set up and of the roles of government, employers' associations and trade unions.[4]

[1] The word is used here in a strictly descriptive sense to refer to an economic system in which the private ownership of the means of production predominates.

[2] For a detailed analysis of changes in property laws, see W. Friedmann, *Law in a Changing Society* (1964).

[3] D. Lockwood, 'Arbitration and Industrial Conflict', *B.J.S.*, December 1955.

[4] For a brief account, see I. C. McGivering *et al.*, *Management in Britain*

The key significance of property laws in determining the exercise of control in the economy can be seen by a more detailed study of one particular form of property—the joint-stock company which is now the dominant form of productive property. This was an invention of the nineteenth century to make possible the mobilization of capital in more permanent forms for large-scale enterprises. The joint-stock company is a legal person in whom is vested the property of the company. The powers of the company are exercised on its behalf by its legally appointed officers. The shareholders own shares in the company, not the walls and machinery of the factory. A share carries with it a right to distributed profits, and (with the exception of non-voting shares) the right to determine the risk-taking policy of the company through a vote at shareholders' meetings, including the election of the board of directors. The control of the affairs of the company therefore is, in theory, in the hands of the shareholders' meeting and the board of directors.

It can be seen that the various rights of control which ownership confers are distributed in a complex way. Only the board of directors and the officials of the company whom they appoint can exercise the powers of control. As a result, it has been argued, the major consequence of the dominance of the joint-stock company has been to divorce ownership from control.[1] Moreover, by devices such as holding-companies and interlocking directorates, it is argued, a relatively small number of individuals owning only a fraction of the total share capital can control vast industrial empires. In other words, a few individuals can control that which they do not own.[2]

A modification of this theory put forward by J. Burnham[3] argues that the running of giant corporations is an increasingly complex business requiring specialized knowledge. Moreover, with the increasing public ownership of the means of production, control is passing into the hands of the expert managers on whose know-how production is more and more dependent.

The complex issues can, to some extent, be clarified by empirical data on shareholding. A study of ninety-two very large companies in Britain[4] shows that in thirteen companies the largest twenty

(1960), Chapter 3. Industrial relations at plant level will be examined in more detail later in this chapter in the discussion of occupational strategies, and in Chapter 8 as an illustration of the processes of organizations.

[1] This is a further example of the division of labour and specialization of roles which characterizes industrial societies.

[2] A. A. Berle and G. C. Means, *The Modern Corporation and Private Property* (1932).

[3] J. Burnham, *The Managerial Revolution* (1941).

[4] P. S. Florence, *Ownership, Control and Success of Large Companies* (1961).

shareholders own more than 30 per cent of the shares and that more than 10 per cent of the shares are owned by the board. That is to say, in these companies only, there is substantial concentration of ownership on the board. These companies include those controlling press and cinema such as Rank and Kemsley and brewery firms, together with a chemical firm, and an aircraft firm. In another twenty-one firms, there is a substantial share concentration (the largest twenty shareholders owning more than 30 per cent, but the board own less than 10 per cent). In over one-third of the large companies, share distribution makes possible ownership control.

No firm conclusion can be drawn from such data. Some have argued that the evidence indicates the separation of management and control from ownership, and the emergence of an influential class of professional managers whose interests do not coincide with those of either the shareholders or labour. In one-half of the large companies, for example, the directors own less than 2 per cent of all shares. On the other hand, it can be argued that the fact remains that most directors are substantial shareholders, that one-quarter of the directors are among the twenty largest shareholders, and this together with the various emoluments which directors enjoy results in substantial congruence between their interests and those of the shareholders.[1] There is, in fact, no divorce between the ownership of property and the management of industry. On the contrary, relatively small amounts of property give control over great concentrations of economic power. Nor is there any evidence that the direction of industry is increasingly in the hands of technocrats and professionals. Except in the very largest companies, the majority of directors have no formal qualifications; indeed, only 1·4 per cent have PhDs. Moreover, the majority do not regard themselves as professional managers.[2]

It is possible to argue that what has happened in recent years is the separation of control over access to the means of production (which is increasingly in the hands of career managers), from control over preferential distribution of the proceeds from production (which is exercised by large shareholders, directors and financiers).[3] Whether this will mean that the control over distribution will eventually shift to the managers, as Burnham has argued, remains a matter of controversy. But it must be stressed that in the last analysis, it is the political system, by its property legislation, which determines the exercise of economic power.[4]

[1] T. Nichols, *Ownership, Control and Ideology* (1969).
[2] T. Nichols, op. cit., Chapters 7 and 8.
[3] I. C. McGivering, op. cit.
[4] The problem of whether the political elite is dominated by men of property

120

The extension of the political control of the economy is not only reflected in the decline in the rights of private property, the regulation over investment, the location of industry and labour relations, but also by the growth of the public sector of the economy through nationalization.[1] One-third of all assets of companies are now in the hands of public corporations. In socialist societies, the public ownership and control of the means of production has been carried much further, so that in the USSR the party machinery effectively controls the entire production process. But most industrial societies have substantially reduced the autonomy of the economic system, and the traditional labels of 'capitalist' and 'socialist' are no longer particularly useful for characterizing such economies.[2] Moreover, political control is not limited simply to regulating production and ownership. Distribution also takes place within the framework of a legal system regulating relations between buyers and sellers, controlling currency and weights and measures, and more recently, seeking to protect the consumer by indicating standards of quality. Furthermore, much government action takes the form of co-ordinating or stimulating economic action, rather than regulating or controlling it in a restricted sense.

So far, some of the ways in which the political system structures the economic system have been examined. There are also a number of ways in which the economic system influences the political system. Both employers and employees form pressure groups to exert influence on the government, and more recently consumers have formed similar pressure groups. But this aspect of the interaction between the economy and the polity will be examined within the context of analysing the political system in Chapter 5.

Work, the economy and the cultural system

Even the most coercive system of production will have difficulty in relying on coercion alone. Apart from the practical difficulties of getting hard work out of slaves, a slave society is faced with the problem of justifying its actions and salving its conscience. It will

---

will be examined in Chapter 5. See also R. Dahrendorf, *Class and Class Conflict in Industrial Societies* (1959), for a statement of the view that property derives from power.

[1] It is important to avoid confusion between capitalism and industrialization. Much of the early literature on the determinants and consequences of industrialization failed to make such a distinction. See J. W. Sombart, 'Capitalism', *Encyclopedia of the Social Sciences*.

[2] The control of the nationalized sector may still remain substantially in the hands of those who also control the private sector. See C. Jenkins, *Power at the Top* (1959).

be necessary for there to be a set of shared beliefs and values which legitimize the practices of slavery. Where the slaves constituted a distinct ethnic group, such as the Negroes in the Southern States of America, it was possible to develop a rigid out-group morality and to believe that they did not possess the same qualities as whites. The 'Sambo' personality of servility and dependence was believed to be essentially inborn. Moreover, it was possible to find scriptural justification for slavery, and for the churches to lend their support to its practice.[1]

In the early stages of industrialization, there was still a substantial coercive element in work. But in a relatively more free society, it was necessary to attempt to reinforce the drive to work with moral (normative) pressures. According to Max Weber,[2] the cultural imperatives necessary for the emergence of industrial capitalism were generated by the puritan sects of the sixteenth century. These stressed the connection between hard work, thrift, and abstinence and religious salvation, and hence made an essential contribution to the growth of the 'capitalist spirit'. We do not necessarily need to agree with Weber that it was the protestant sects which generated this new ethos of capitalism. But there is no doubt that religion served to legitimize the values of a capitalist society and helped to socialize workers to play their roles in the new machine economy. Unlike the traditional Christian condemnation of wealth, the new ethic saw riches as the reward of a life of diligence, thrift and sobriety. Poverty, on the other hand, was viewed as indicating a weakness of moral fibre rather than as a concomitant of holiness. Furthermore, the ideas of Social Darwinism with its doctrine of the survival of the fittest in the competitive social struggle legitimized the authority of the captains of industry. The mere fact of their success was sufficient evidence of their fitness to govern industrial empires and to demand the obedience of their workers.[3]

The crucial significance of private property for maintaining the control of production and distribution in private hands was also legitimized and supported by an elaborate ideology. Private property was justified by the philosophers as the basis for freedom and for the development of personality, and defended as a natural and inalienable right.[4]

In the more developed economies of the later nineteenth and

[1] S. M. Elkins, *Slavery* (1959).

[2] M. Weber, *The Protestant Ethic and the Spirit of Capitalism* (1930).

[3] See R. Bendix, *Work and Authority in Industry* (1956), for a detailed analysis of economic ideologies and their metamorphoses in Britain, America and Russia.

[4] See, for example, the works of John Locke and Bishop Gore, and the Papal encyclical, *Rerum Novarum* (1891).

twentieth centuries, the organization of production undergoes structural changes. Large-scale corporations dominate the economic system, and account for the bulk of production. The growth in scale gives rise to new problems, particularly those of co-ordinating the activities of large numbers of workers and maximizing their output. Industry employs an increasing number of specialists, and as a consequence, there has been a marked increase in the numbers, prestige and power of managers,[1] who now occupy the key roles in the economy and have displaced the entrepreneur of early capitalism. But the qualities which ensure success for the organization man are very different from those necessary for survival in the early stages of capitalism. The manager needs to be a good committee man, skilled in inter-personal relations, and a good company man, loyal to the corporation and willing to pursue its goals with single-minded enthusiasm. It is this social ethic of conformity to the corporation which Whyte[2] argues is becoming dominant, replacing the rugged individualism of the protestant ethic. These 'other directed' men of the giant corporations are in sharp contrast with the 'inner directed' industrialists of early capitalism.[3]

Bendix has documented in considerable detail the subtle changes by which the 'entrepreneurial ideology' of the nineteenth century has gradually become transformed into a 'managerial ideology', which has functioned to legitimize the managerial exercise of control in large-scale organization. Components in this managerial ideology have included the scientific management movement inspired by Frederick Taylor in the 1920s and the more recent 'human relations' school.[4] In Britain the new ideology was associated mainly with the capital-intensive industries, notably chemicals and iron and steel. Here, labour disputes might lead to expensive shut-downs of large amounts of valuable plant. Sir Alfred Mond, chairman of ICI, was an insistent proponent in the 1920s of a new approach to labour questions. He argued that industry was no longer dominated by a few, but was now run by managers whose task it was to act as arbitrators between the claims of capitalist, labour and the public. All in industry are employees, even the directors, and their interests coincide. The task of management is to educate the workers into identifying their interests with those of management, and to win their willing co-

[1] I. C. McGivering et al., op. cit. Comparisons between the composition of the American business elite born in 1801–30 and 1891–1920 show an increase in the percentage of managers from 16 to 48 per cent and a decline in entrepreneurs from 68 to 18 per cent. R. Bendix, op. cit., p. 229.

[2] W. H. Whyte, Organization Man (1957).

[3] D. Riesman, The Lonely Crowd (1950).

[4] These approaches are discussed more fully in Chapter 8.

operation and loyalty by such schemes as profit-sharing and co-partnership.[1]

This ethic of social responsibility, however, does not appear to be dominant among businessmen. The most prevalent ideology stresses the responsibility of managers to promote the long-run economic growth of the company, in the belief that such a policy is in the best interests of all and that in this way industry can best discharge its responsibilities to its workers, shareholders and society.[2]

The views so far discussed have all agreed in viewing work as a painful necessity and even a moral duty—as *instrumental* in promoting the health of body and soul, or as a form of divine service. But a quite different justification for work found expression in the writings of Marx, William Morris and Ruskin in the nineteenth century, and has since received renewed and influential support in the work of the self-actualization school in psychology (notably Maslow and Herzberg)[3]. This view sees work as intrinsically valuable—as a means towards the realization and expression of the self and of personal growth through the exercise of choice and responsibility. 'A musician must make music, an artist must paint, a poet must write if he is to be ultimately happy. What a man can be, he must be. This need we call self-actualization.'[4]

Such a view raises obvious difficulties for its advocates. Indeed, it was against the dehumanizing consequences of capitalist forms of production that the early Marx wrote so powerfully. It is because the worker sells his labour, and is thus subject to an alien will that he is no longer able to satisfy his needs, and experiences alienation. Subsequent debate, however, has focused rather on the dehumanizing effects of the division of labour and fragmentation of work. The remedy sought is a policy of job-enlargement and job-enrichment, together with worker participation, and it is the psychology of self-actualization with its stress on intrinsic rather than on instrumental involvement which is currently influential in managerial ideologies.[5]

Not all, however, would accept this view. There are still many who reassert the instrumental view of work, and argue not simply that work is not (empirically) a central life interest, but that there is no particular reason why it should be: meaning and self-actualization may be found in other spheres—in family life or

[1] I. C. McGivering *et al*. op. cit., pp. 91–101.
[2] T. Nichols, op. cit., Chapters 14–16.
[3] F. Herzberg, *Work and the Nature of Man* (1968).
[4] A. H. Maslow, *Motivation and Personality* (1954).
[5] Managers, unlike academics, must act. It is in this sense, not in any perjorative way, that we can speak of management ideologies—as systems of belief which provide a basis and legitimation for action.

creative living. Or again, an increasing emphasis on man's role as a consumer rather than as a producer is similarly consistent with an instrumental attitude towards work.[1] These are issues to which we return later.

In addition to their role in legitimizing ownership and managerial control, ideologies also play an important part in regulating the process of distribution. Social philosophers[2] have long sought to arrive at a satisfactory set of principles for distributive justice. And such ideas enter into all discussions on the problem of fair wages. But although in contemporary society most agree on the desirability of pursuing the goal of distributive justice, there is little consensus on the relative importance to be attached to human need, skill, effort, achievement, comparability and what industry can afford. It is the lack of such consensus which underlies much industrial conflict and inhibits the achievement of incomes policies.[3]

Our analysis so far has examined the relations between the economic system and other major sub-systems. But in the last analysis, production, distribution and exchange are activities carried out by individuals. And it is to the interaction between the individual and the economic system that we now turn. Or rather, it is to the study of types of economic roles, since it is social types and not individuals as such who are the subjects of sociological study. That is to say, we are especially interested in occupational roles, such as those of skilled workers, managers, scientists and teachers.

OCCUPATIONS AND THE ECONOMY

The more speculative 'philosophies of work' which we have been examining are important as legitimations, justifications and guides to action. Indeed, their influence on conduct may be out of all proportion to their empirical validity. For example, if men are socialized into an instrumental attitude to work, their expectations and therefore satisfactions may largely reflect such culturally derived meanings. We turn now to such empirical questions as: Why, in fact, do men work? What are their motivations and satisfactions? And how are these influenced by orientations to work? Equally important, what does work do to people?—for it can be argued that work is one of the most powerful influences

[1] For a more detailed discussion of philosophies of work, see Alan Fox, *A Sociology of Work in Industry* (1971), Chapter 1.

[2] See, for example, S. I. Benn and R. Peters, *Social Principles in the Democratic State* (1959).

[3] D. Lockwood, op. cit.

over the life of the individual in industrial societies. It is the main determinant of income and status and therefore of the life-chances of the worker's family.[1] But we are interested, too, to discover how far work provides opportunities for self-development or is damaging and alienating in its consequences. And finally, how far does a man's job influence his social and political attitudes and the way in which he seeks recreation or recuperation in leisure?

Technology and work

The technology of the assembly-line epitomizes in its most extreme forms the division of labour and fragmentation of tasks which characterizes a dominant mode of industrial production.[2] It is the machine which sets the pace, tasks are repetitive, take about one minute to perform and require little or no skill. The fragmentation extends to the relations between workers who do not work in teams, while the noise makes talking difficult. In short, the worker becomes a thing—an appendage to the machine.

It is this kind of work which the early Marx described as *alienated*—'the work is *external* to the worker . . . consequently he does not fulfil himself in his work . . . has a feeling of misery, not of well-being, does not develop freely a physical and mental energy but is physically exhausted and mentally debased. The worker therefore feels himself at home only during his leisure. . . . His work is not voluntary but imposed, *forced labour*. It is not the satisfaction of a need, but only a *means* for satisfying other needs.'[3] For Marx, the main source of alienation was the wage-contract.[4] When a man sells his labour, he completely subordinates himself to another: in Marx's view, wage-labour was virtually synonymous with slavery. Such forced labour, he argued, cannot be a source of intrinsic satisfaction and self-realization but only a means to an end. However, most subsequent studies have focused on the technology as the source of alienation, and it is to this evidence which we now turn.

Studies of assembly-line and repetitive work have documented the intense dislike which such work generates. Harvey Swados, an American writer who has worked in factories, emphasizes the differences between manual and middle-class non-manual work, despite their superficial similarities: 'there is one thing that the

[1] The relation between occupation and stratification is discussed in Chapter 7.
[2] E. Chinoy, 'Manning the Machines: The Assembly-Line Worker', in Peter L. Berger, *The Human Shape of Work* (1964).
[3] T. B. Bottomore and M. Rubel (eds), *Karl Marx: Selected Writings in Sociology and Social Philosophy* (1963), p. 177.
[4] For a detailed discussion of 'alienation', see Richard Schacht, *Alienation* (1971), especially Chapter 4, and S. Cotgrove, 'Alienation and Automation', *B.J.S.* (Dec. 1972).

worker doesn't do like the middle class; he works like a worker. . . . The worker's attitude towards his work is generally compounded of hatred, shame, and resignation. . . . It is not simply status-hunger that makes a man hate work that is mindless, endless, stupefying, sweaty, filthy, noisy, exhausting, insecure in its prospects, and practically without hope of advancement. . . .'[1] A study of assembly-line workers concluded that they viewed their jobs with a mixture of anger and resignation, and complained bitterly of overwork, monotony and physical strain.[2]

C. Wright Mills[3] argues that the alienating conditions of modern work now extend to the salaried employee. The breaking-down of jobs into small, repetitive and uninteresting parts decreases skill, and destroys the autonomy and craftsmanship of work in office as well as factory. The office-worker is as chained to the commuting timetable as the factory worker is to clocking-on. For such men, too, work is significant only as a source of income or prestige.

Not all production, however, has the same characteristics as the assembly-line. Blauner[4] has attempted to identify four major dimensions of alienation[5] and to investigate the extent of alienation among workers in different technologies. (1) 'Powerlessness' he defines as the inability to control work, such as the inability to influence management decisions, lack of control over conditions of employment, and lack of control over immediate work processes. (2) 'Meaninglessness' is the inability of the worker to develop a sense of purpose by seeing the relationship between his job and the overall production process, and is determined by the scope and span of the work tasks. (3) 'Isolation' is lack of membership of industrial communities and is reflected in impersonal adminis-tration and the absence of informal groups. (4) 'Self-estrangement' is the failure to become involved in work as a means of self-expression. It is reflected in the isolation and separation of work from the totality of social life, and in work being simply instru-mental (a source of income) rather than a source of intrinsic satisfaction.[6]

[1] See M. R. Stein et al., Identity and Anxiety (1960).
[2] L. Lipsitz, 'Work, Life and Political Attitudes: A Study of Manual Workers', Am. Pol. Sc. Rev., December 1964, p. 953.
[3] C. Wright Mills, White Collar (1951).
[4] R. Blauner, Alienation and Freedom: The Manual Worker in Industry (1963).
[5] For a more detailed discussion of the concept of alienation, its history and influence, see I. L. Horowitz, The New Sociology (1965), Chapters 15 and 16, and R. Schacht, op. cit.
[6] It does not follow that alienation in the work situation is accompanied by 'global' alienation from the individual's total social milieu.

Conditions in modern industry vary widely in the extent to which they contribute to the alienation of the worker in these ways. The printing industry, for example, is still predominantly based on craft technology. The craft printer has substantial control over his work situation, and can control the pace, quality and quantity of the product. His work is not subdivided and he can enjoy an intrinsic satisfaction in contributing to a product with which he can identify. Moreover, in the small shops which are characteristic of the printing industry, there is an absence of the sense of anonymity and isolation which typifies large-scale mass-production industries.

Other studies confirm that the technology affects the meaning which work has for the individual and the satisfaction he derives from it. Baldamus[1] shows that differences in skill and the length of the work-cycle are responsible for enormous discrepancies in turnover rates. Enamellers, for example, who receive a two-week training and whose job-cycle is completed in five minutes, have a turnover rate of 96 per cent (that is, avoidable leavers in a year are 96 per cent of the total number employed). By contrast, pattern-makers with a training period of five years, and a job-cycle of one to twelve weeks, have a turnover rate of only 4 per cent.

Among the more specific factors producing attachment to the job is 'line-traction', where the object passes through a series of operations carried out by different workers, with or without the help of a conveyor belt. 'Process-traction' is experienced where the tasks are determined by the chemical or physical nature of the production process, for example pottery-throwing, welding, forging. 'Object-traction' derives from the mental picture of the work-object, and 'machine-traction' occurs where the worker feels drawn along by operations on machines which are constantly running. Each of the components of the task is determined by technology and by organizational factors, and all produce varying degrees of physical and psychological strain reflected in turnover rates and other expressions of dissatisfaction.

Socio-technical systems

The view we have so far discussed attaches considerable importance to the technology. Indeed, it amounts almost to a form of technological determinism.[2] But the relations between men and machines

[1] W. Baldamus, 'Types of Work and Motivation', *B.J.S.*, March 1951.
[2] Blauner does recognize the role not only of technological organization, but also the social organization of the factory, but he argues that the social organization is largely a product of the technology. See D. Silverman, *The Theory of Organizations* (1970), Chapter 5.

are not rigidly determined by the technology. The nature of the work-tasks and the use of machines is also in part a result of managerial decisions about the organization of production.

The socio-technical systems approach explores the relations between the technology, the organization and its environment. Each influences the other. For example, Woodward found marked differences in the organization and management structure of firms involved in different types of technology. In mass production, control is more highly centralized and bureaucratic[1] in form than in process production (automation), where there is much more need to innovate and where a highly centralized administration would be slow. Again, in mass production, where the product is highly standardized, staff (experts such as research and development scientists) tend to be separated from line management (administrators), while in process production such as automated chemical plants, it is more difficult to distinguish between specialists and administrators.

Clearly the technology sets limits to the forms of organization that are possible. But there is considerable room for manoeuvre. In a nylon-spinning factory, management, influenced by the ideas of Herzberg, deliberately introduced a number of changes in the organization of work. Throughout the process of change there was an emphasis on involving supervisors and operatives in planning the changes. The main change was to abolish the rigid rules which laid down every step. 'You had a book more or less like a Bible and it told you everything. . . .'[2] The responsibility for deciding when various tasks were to be performed, and for checking the quality of the yarn was transferred from the supervisors to the operatives. More flexibility was introduced so that operatives could move about more freely and help out teams on other machines. They also now carry out minor repairs.

The extent of *job enlargement* (extending the range of activities) and *job enrichment* (increasing the skill content and responsibility) was not great. But even these modest changes resulted in quite substantial increases in job satisfaction. 'It was pretty monotonous —the same thing over and over again. You were watching the clock all the time before, working to time, and the time dragged. It's not that much more interesting now, and yet the time seems to go a lot quicker.'[3] But as this comment shows, there were limits set by the technology. Heat and noise remained major sources of

[1] This concept is discussed more fully in Chapter 8.
[2] S. Cotgrove, J. Dunham and C. Vamplew, *The Nylon Spinners* (1971), p. 43.
[3] S. Cotgrove *et al.*, op. cit., p. 83.

complaint, and the job was still relatively monotonous, compared with, for example, work in chemical process plants.[1]

Orientations and meanings

So far a very over-simplified picture has been presented. It is a picture of men more or less passively moulded by and reacting to the pressures which flow from the social structures in which they occupy roles. As we shall see in more detail in Chapter 8, more recent thinking about behaviour in organizations has been very much coloured by the influence of social action theory. This is an illustration of the theoretical dilemmas mentioned in Chapter 1. The functionalists, we saw, have tended to emphasize the view that society shapes man. More recently, there has been a growing interest in exploring the ways in which individuals respond to and influence situations. This *social action* approach[2] has focused on the characteristics which actors bring to social roles. Behaviour in social situations, it is argued, can only be explained if we take account of the interaction between social actors and the structures in which they are located.

This action frame of reference can be illustrated by studies of the world of work. In the nylon-spinning plant, for example, most of the operatives had never had the opportunity for self-actualizing work. The modest improvements were for them a source of considerable satisfaction. But for the small minority who had previously been employed in more skilled jobs, the impact of the changes was slight. Most had deliberately traded intrinsic interest for pay.[3] Similarly, Goldthorpe and his associates have argued that the relatively high level of satisfaction with jobs which are intrinsically boring can be understood in the light of the predominantly instrumental orientation which the workers bring to their jobs; '. . . the effects of technologically determined conditions of work are always *mediated* through the meanings that men give to their work.'[4]

At this point, we need to make a further distinction. The notions of orientations to work and satisfactions from work contain some ambiguities. We need to distinguish between what attracts a man to a job, the satisfactions he derives from doing the job and the reasons for staying in the job.[5] The Luton studies have

[1] For a more detailed discussion of the socio-technical systems approach, see D. Silverman, op. cit., pp. 109–25.

[2] Ibid., Chapters 6–10.

[3] S. Cotgrove *et al.*, Chapter 5 and p. 135.

[4] J. Goldthorpe *et al.*, *The Affluent Worker in the Class Structure* (1969), p. 181.

[5] W. W. Daniel, 'Industrial Behaviour and Orientation to Work: A Critique', *Jour. of Management Studies*, October 1969.

established that some workers' attachment to their jobs is predominantly instrumental. This is why this particular sample of highly-paid workers have chosen their jobs and this is why they stay. It is in this sense that they are 'satisfied' with their jobs, even though those working on assembly-lines showed the usual dislike of many aspects of the job itself.

A second distinction may help to clarify what we mean when we talk about satisfaction. Herzberg has demonstrated that the aspects of work which are reported as sources of satisfaction are not the same as those which give rise to dissatisfaction. Though inadequate wages, job security and working conditions may be sources of dissatisfaction, they cannot be major sources of satisfaction. Like clean water, and good living conditions, such aspects are necessary conditions for good health: hence he refers to them as *hygiene* factors. But it is aspects of the job itself (job content) such as achievement, recognition and responsibility which are the sources of positive satisfaction, and which provide the opportunities for *self-actualization* or personal growth. It is these which are the *motivators* and provide the positive motivation to do the job itself and to work well. In short, the absence of positive satisfaction is not 'dissatisfaction' but 'non-satisfaction'.[1]

Now subsequent researches have not entirely supported Herzberg's two-factor theory. There is evidence that the two factors are not as clear-cut as he has claimed, particularly in his later writing: wages can be a source of positive satisfaction. But his work does lend broad empirical support for the distinction between work as a source of positive satisfaction and the absence of dissatisfaction, and of the existence of instrumental and intrinsic orientations to work. The 'affluent' workers, then, can be seen as hygiene seekers, attached to their jobs by the high pay. But this is not the same as positive satisfaction. And there is no evidence that their instrumental orientation blinds them to the intrinsically unsatisfactory nature of their work. It does not provide positive opportunities for self-actualization, or, in Blauner's terms, they remain self-estranged.

This brings us to a further problem. It is by no means clear from Blauner's work whether alienation is to be thought of as a characteristic of the objective conditions of work or of the subjective response. He defines it as a syndrome of 'objective conditions and subjective feeling states'. If, as Goldthorpe has argued, the predominant orientation to work is instrumental—that is, if the

<hr/>

[1] F. Herzberg, op. cit. Herzberg has built on Maslow's theory of a hierarchy of needs. At the base are physiological needs, then needs for safety, love, esteem and finally self-actualization. See A. H. Maslow, *Motivation and Personality* (1954).

workers do not expect work to be intrinsically interesting—then they may not experience alienation as a subjective response. 'Thus these workers are disposed to define their relationship with their firm more as one of reciprocity and mutual accommodation rather than as one of coercion and exploitation. And in this sense at least, they are far from being "alienated".'[1] Indeed, there is mounting evidence that for most, work is not a 'central life interest'. For the great mass of industrial workers, and for many white-collar workers, too, work is not a significant area of life.[2] Dubin found in his study of several hundred American industrial workers that work was a central life interest for only a small minority. Lafitte interviewed 300 factory workers in Melbourne, and came to the same conclusion; that the activities most valued are found chiefly outside work. The factory worker is seldom work-centred. Work for him is not something on which he centres his interests, his hopes and aspirations, nor even his worries. It is simply *instrumental* in providing him with an income. That is, the typical worker is neither alienated nor involved: rather he is dissociated and apathetic. Work is non-salient. For the 'privatized' worker, the salient areas of life are to be found outside the factory, above all in family life.

We have focused particularly on the working lives of manual workers. In part, this reflects the direction of sociological interest, resulting in a substantial volume of published research. The lives of managers and professionals have attracted less attention, or proved less amenable to study. More exotic and extreme occupations such as those of jazz musicians and deep-sea fishermen are more attractive, too, as sources of theoretical insights. The large 'grey' area of routine clerical work, sales and transport generates little theoretical or intrinsic excitement.[3] Scientists, by contrast, have received much attention, particularly in the USA and will be cited to exemplify other aspects of occupational studies.

How then, can we account for the prevalence of instrumental orientations to work? Or, by contrast, the intense commitment to his occupational role of the priest, scientist, artist, and to a lesser extent the social worker, policeman and teacher? In the affluent worker study, the sample was limited to those aged between 21 and 46, most with dependent children, and had taken

[1] J. Goldthorpe et al., *The Affluent Worker* (1968), p. 144.

[2] R. Dubin, 'Industrial Workers' Worlds: A Study of the "Central Life Interests" of Industrial Workers', in E. D. Smigel, op. cit., Chapter 3, and in A. M. Rose, *Human Behaviour and Social Processes* (1962).

[3] There are notable exceptions, for example D. Lockwood, *The Blackcoated Worker* (1958), remains one of the most penetrating and theoretically insightful studies of clerks. See also R. M. Blackburn, *Union Character and Social Class* (1967).

their present jobs 'as a result of feelings of family responsibility or wifely pressure'. And it is family life which is the major source of expressive and affective satisfactions. This home-centred style of life was reinforced by the fact that not only were the workers themselves predominantly geographically mobile but Luton contained a high proportion of mobile workers and lacked the characteristics of the traditional solidary local community. The family takes precedence over membership in other groups, such as those based on the place of work. Furthermore, many were downwardly mobile in the sense that many had siblings of white-collar status and hence may experience *relative deprivation*, while their relatively high pay would lead to *status incongruency*—or a discrepancy between status deriving from their jobs compared with the relatively high pay comparable to that of higher status occupations. Such considerations would further reinforce the dichotomy between working and non-working lives and encourage an emphasis on family rather than work.

The market system and occupations
The occupation of an individual enables us to locate him in the market—a sub-system of the economic system. The market is the mechanism which regulates the supply and demand of economic goods, including labour and skills. The manual labourer who offers his skills for sale in the labour market receives a wage which is determined by a complex of forces which include the extent to which his occupation is organized and its effectiveness in bargaining, the economic strength of the industry and the scarcity of his skill. But it will also be influenced by more specifically sociological factors such as the customary notions as to what constitutes a fair wage; what he is morally entitled to. Thus, in general, non-manual workers think that they ought to be paid more than manual workers, even though the job they are doing may require less skill.

Although economists have specialized in the study of market behaviour, we may observe here that it is not in fact possible to isolate the market from the social system in which it functions, except perhaps in the very short run, when all the non-economic factors are constant. The rights to organize and to strike which are confirmed and safeguarded by legislation clearly affect the bargaining position of workers in the market. The economic system is related to the political system in a number of ways which affect the market situation of the worker, that is to say his ability to command goods and services.

A major distinction can be made between those who derive an income from the ownership and control of productive resources and those who sell their labours for a wage or salary. This was, of

133

course, the basic dichotomy drawn by Marx between the bourgeoisie and the proletariat. But it cannot explain all the variables in which we are interested. Craft printers and assembly-line workers are equally members of the proletariat in the Marxian sense, but as we have seen, the differences between them are very considerable.

The market situation involves not only the size of income, but also its security. Moreover, income includes non-monetary rewards such as sickness benefits and welfare facilities. Work, in fact, carries with it the right to rewards which can differ in both size and security of enjoyment. The complexity of the differences can be simplified somewhat if we use the language of the property market. Property consists of the enjoyment of recognized rights. The tenant, for example, has strictly limited rights of enjoyment. He cannot alter the fabric of his tenement, while his tenancy is terminable at relatively short notice. By contrast, the freeholder enjoys a much more extensive range of rights and almost complete security. He can be dispossessed, but only after lengthy legal process and with safeguards for adequate compensation.

Jobs are property in much the same sense.[1] The factory owner, or the independent professional, is a freeholder, while the factory worker is a tenant. But the tendency in the more advanced societies is for more and more jobs to shift to the intermediate position of leaseholder.[2] Salaried jobs such as those of teachers and employed accountants enjoy considerable security of tenure, while firms are extending the range of rewards to which office-holders are entitled with a variety of welfare benefits, and even paying fees for the sons of executives to attend public schools. Similarly, the extension of the machinery of protection to manual workers, with increasing rights of severance pay as compensation means that more and more workers are moving from vulnerable tenancies to more secure lease-hold occupancy of jobs. Careers, as distinct from jobs, are characterized by leasehold rights. A career offers a reasonably secure expectation of continued employment, with regular promotions according to formal criteria and with predictable salaries at each stage.

Occupations and the status system
Society attaches different values to different occupations. Manual work, for example, carries low prestige, while non-manual work is highly esteemed. Social status is the social evaluation of roles. And

[1] I am indebted to Douglas Young for this notion.
[2] This reflects the strategy increasingly adopted by employers to win the loyalty and co-operation of workers (see R. Bendix, op. cit.) as well as the efforts of trade unions to gain security for their members.

occupational roles are the main determinants of the social status of the individual.

Empirical studies show that there is considerable social consensus on the relative standing of occupations. Ranked in order of prestige, we have medical officer of health, company director, school teacher, insurance agent, policeman, carpenter, bricklayer, railway porter, agricultural labourer, road sweeper.[1] Moreover, there is considerable agreement on the prestige ranking of occupations in all industrial societies. Power, influence, wealth and moral worth are all criteria which contribute to the formation of the complex judgements of social standing. Income alone is not enough. It does not lead to the acceptance on an equal footing of well-paid manual workers by blackcoated workers who may earn less. Moreover, service occupations such as those of teachers and clergymen enjoy a relatively high standing in society, compared with their relatively low incomes. One very important factor in the social evaluation of an occupation is the position which it occupies in the authority structure of industry. The inferior status of the manual worker to the clerk, despite his often superior income, probably derives from his inferior position and lack of autonomy in the work situation. His subordinate role on the job spills over and influences his off-the-job standing.[2]

There are, however, important sub-cultural differences in prestige rankings. Young and Willmott found in their inquiries in Bethnal Green that a substantial minority of lower status workers rejected the more general prestige rankings and adopted the criterion of usefulness to society which resulted in a dustman, for example, ranking his occupation on equal terms with a medical officer of health. Company directors were demoted to an inferior position on the same grounds.[3]

Occupational socialization and choice
Some explanation of the existence of instrumental orientations to work is clearly to be found in the previous experiences which led to the choice of that particular occupation. For a fuller understanding of the meaning of work, we need then to look at the whole process of occupational socialization and choice.

There is one difficulty at the outset. 'Choice' is too strong a word to describe the process of drift and frequent job change which

[1] C. A. Moser and J. R. Hall, 'The Social Grading of Occupations', in D. V. Glass (ed.), *Social Mobility* (1954), Chapter 2.

[2] J. H. Goldthorpe and D. Lockwood, 'Affluence and British Class Structure', *Soc. Rev.*, Vol. 11, July 1963. The question of status and status consistency will be explored in more detail in Chapter 7.

[3] M. Young and P. Willmott, 'Social Grading by Manual Workers', *B.J.S.*, December 1956.

characterizes the early work experience of many young people. It is the minority who become doctors, teachers, accountants, solicitors, engineers. The large grey area of routine work offers little positive attraction. Most workers, attracted to their jobs for instrumental reasons, find little or no opportunity in their work for self-fulfilment or expression. Thus, while the few *embrace* their occupational roles, many are *dissociated* from work, and some *alienated*.

However, it is still useful to think of the individual choosing a job, having tried to match up what the job can offer against his needs and interests, even though, in fact, he chooses it for the money and his major interests are elsewhere. 'The child has to build up a role map of his society so that he can locate occupational names on it and can know the role prescriptions associated with these names. . . . This knowledge eases his task at the point of entry to the labour force of choosing an occupation that more or less matches his wishes from amongst the limited range available.'[1] To understand choice, therefore, we need to go back to the socializing influences which have helped to shape his *identity*. Among these influences, education is particularly important, especially selection at eleven-plus for entry to the grammar or modern school, each of which carries its stream of children on to broad groups of occupations.

Carter's[2] study of school-leavers provides a striking demonstration of this socializing process. For the less able child in the lower forms of the modern school, the dominant picture that emerges is one of school as a source of boredom and frustration. In many schools the imposition of dull, mechanical tasks, which lack any apparent significance or relevance to the life of the child, effectively train him to accept the routine demands of industry. The transition from school to work involves little more than a change of routine. Many expect little from work and are satisfied with what they find, even though the work is repetitive and makes few demands. The secondary-modern boy leaving school at 15 has received early training in dissociating himself from the demands which 'they' make upon him. He simply does not care. It is not surprising that psychologists have discovered that many are content to carry out routine tasks. Dissatisfaction is a measure of the

[1] P. W. Musgrave, 'Towards a Sociological Theory of Occupational Choice', *Soc. Rev.*, Vol. 15, 1967, pp. 32–46. See also J. Ford and S. Box, 'Sociological Theory and Occupation Choice', *Soc. Rev.*, Vol. 15, 1967, pp. 287–99. S. Box and S. Cotgrove, 'Scientific Identity, Occupational Selection, and Role Strain', *B.J.S.*, March 1966, and S. Cotgrove and M. Fuller, 'Occupational Socialization and Choice: The Effects of Sandwich Courses', *Sociology*, January 1971.

[2] M. Carter, *Home, School and Work* (1962).

gap between aspiration and achievement. For many, no such gap exists—their expectations and aspirations are centred on the world outside the factory.

The same socializing and selection mechanism can be seen very clearly in the recruitment of Hull fishermen. Most of the boys who become fishermen originate from the lower stream of the modern school near the docks. Here the boys have learnt to see themselves as future unskilled workers, and the teacher as the prototype of the white-collar world which oppresses the manual worker. Whether they go straight from school, or after a variety of unskilled jobs, fishing is seen as an escape into a world of virile men with money in their pockets. 'One reason why these boys want to go on trawlers . . . is that they are trying to say "No" to their inferior position in the class system. On a trawler . . . there are none of the wider distinctions of accent, vocabulary, social distance.'[1] During his first years, the young fisherman learns to be tough, to drink, to spend freely. He lacks education and position. But his job gives him manhood and money. By twenty-three, 'he has indelibly printed on him certain habits, reflexes, patterns of spending, attitudes to life . . . he cannot go back.'

Socialization can also influence the expectations which the individual brings to the job and the satisfaction which he gains from it. Technicians who have qualified by taking examinations, or have simply attended courses, are much more likely than those who have not studied to expect and to enjoy intrinsic satisfactions, such as an interesting job, and a chance to use abilities to the full.[2] Other studies show that professionals, who have undergone an extended education, are more identified with and satisfied with their work.[3]

Where an occupation requires particular personal qualities, we can expect a considerable amount of attention to be paid to socialization and selection. Military academies, for example, not only pay great attention to the social background of a recruit, but they also subject him to a rigorous education and training designed to develop military qualities of honour and loyalty, which includes detailed regulation of the recruit's daily routine, and indoctrination in military traditions and in professional etiquette.[4]

[1] J. Tunstall, *The Fishermen* (1962).
[2] S. Cotgrove, 'The Relations between Work and Non-work among Technicians', *Soc. Rev.*, July 1965.
[3] Morris Rosenburg, *Occupation and Values* (1957).
[4] For a detailed account of American military academies, and the discontinuities between professional education and the realities of military life, see M. Janowitz, *The Professional Soldier* (1960), pp. 127–45. On the socialization of doctors, see R. K. Merton *et al.*, *The Student Physician* (1957).

Some degree of socialization may also occur during employment. If the characteristics of the individual do not match up entirely with the demands of the job, he may adjust to the situation by changing his own values or norms. Merton[1] discusses the tendency in bureaucracies for officials to become over-conformist, to adhere rigidly to the rules and regulations for their own sake. A major structural pressure to behave in this way stems from the fact that the official's life is planned for him in terms of a graded career. The rewards for conformity are promotion, security and eventually a pension. These pressures to conform induce timidity and conservatism. Moreover, strict conformity to the rules protects the individual against criticism, and may be a device sought by the timid. The result is that importance comes to be displaced from ends to means; from organizational goals to rules. How far this process is the result of the re-socialization of the official and how far it is due to a tendency for bureaucracies to attract less adventurous types of personality cannot be determined in the light of present knowledge.

We have so far assumed that socialization and choice are fairly distinct processes: that the individual becomes a particular kind of person (develops an identity) and then looks for a job which matches his needs or enables him to realize and express himself. In practice, this distinction cannot be maintained. As the individual moves from preliminary fantasy choices through a series of stages of increasing certainty to the point where choice finally crystallizes,[2] so future occupation may feed back and influence the development of an appropriate identity. This process of *anticipatory socialization* can be seen, for example, in medical schools (and military academies) where the student increasingly identifies with his future role and in this sense *becomes* a doctor.[3] This process is most marked, of course, where the role is embraced and provides a major component in the individual's identity.[4]

But it is important to remember that for many, perhaps most, jobs are instrumental. They are hardly likely to provide 'a means of implementing a self-concept' in the way which is claimed by

[1] R. K. Merton, 'Bureaucratic Structure and Personality', in *Social Theory and Social Structure* (1957).

[2] On the stage of choice, see E. Ginzberg *et al.*, *Occupational Choice: An Approach to a General Theory* (1951).

[3] H. S. Becker and J. Carper, 'Elements of Identification with an Occupation', *A.S.R.*, 1956, pp. 341–89.

[4] Some roles such as a member of a closed religious community may be described as *total* roles, since the identity is totally embraced within the role: there is nothing of the self left outside. Socialization and identity are discussed in Chapter 8.

some influential psychological theories.[1] For such individuals, the search for a satisfactory identity must be directed elsewhere. For others, however, occupation may be a means of solving an identity crisis.[2] This important question of the search for identity will be explored more fully in the final chapter.

Occupational roles, role strain and role conflict

The process of socialization and selection ensures some measure of fit between the individual and his job. But the fit is seldom perfect. The job may fail to provide scope for the individual's particular needs and capacities, or the job may make conflicting or stressful demands resulting in marked strain and conflict.

The concept of *role* is particularly useful in this context. We have used it before to talk about the role of the husband or wife when we wanted to stress the fact that being a husband is in many ways like acting a part in a play which someone else has written.[3] Being a nurse in a hospital or a teacher in a school, a scientist in a research laboratory or a prison-officer—all involve playing a part, which in this case, has been written by the organization. The rules of the organization provide us with the script, define our tasks and the goals we are expected to pursue. *Role strain* is the felt difficulty in fulfilling role obligations.[4] *Role conflict* refers to conflicting demands made on the individual or to the conflict between the needs of the individual and the demands of the role, or to ambiguity and vagueness in the role prescription. The extent to which conflicts generate strains will obviously depend in part on the saliency of the job for the individual. An absence of conflict is particularly important for the individual where the role is embraced and is a major source of identity.

The script gives us our part. But the actor determines how he will play it. Each actor has his own *role style*. The way he plays the part will be shaped by his own characteristics. It will depend on how he perceives the role, as well as the skills and capacities he has for carrying out the tasks which the role requires.[5]

Although all members of occupations (such as teachers, scientists and social workers) experience a similar socialization in the latter stages of their education, there are subtle differences in their

[1] D. E. Super, 'Vocational Adjustment: Implementing a Self-Concept', *Occupations*, Vol. 30, 1951, p. 88.
[2] S. Box and J. Ford, 'Commitment to Science: a Solution to Student Marginality', *Sociology*, September 1967.
[3] See also Chapter 8.
[4] W. J. Goode, 'A Theory of Role Strain', *A.S.R.*, 1960, pp. 483–96.
[5] D. J. Levinson, 'Role, Personality and Social Structure in the Organizational Setting', in N. J. Smelser and W. T. Smelser, *Personality and Social Systems* (1963).

occupational identities which may have important implications for the ways in which they adjust to and perform their roles. It has already been pointed out in Chapter 3 that there are differences among teachers in the importance which they attach to the various functions of education. Academic teachers stress the pursuit of knowledge, while on the other hand, there are those who place more emphasis on the development of the child and can be conceptualized as child-centred. We could expect such differences to reflect differential socialization and selection.[1] University graduates, for example, will have become attached to an academic subject before deciding to become a teacher and being exposed to professional training. Moreover, graduate teachers more often come from middle-class homes, and a considerable proportion enter teaching only as a second choice. They are anxious to maintain their middle-class status and will cling to their connection with the university. Such teachers are more frequently subject-centred. By contrast, teachers from training colleges more often come from a working-class home, have chosen teaching as a means of achieving higher status, and have been educated in a professionally oriented course. Such teachers are more frequently child-centred. But in spite of such differences in the way in which teachers define their role, there do not appear to be any distinctive personality characteristics which differentiate teachers from other occupational types.[2]

Scientists, too, differ in the extent to which they become *academics*, dedicated to the advancement of scientific knowledge. Some indeed, have this single-minded dedication, and such will prefer to work in a university where they are free to research and publish and receive the recognition which confirms their contribution.[3] By contrast, such 'dedicated' scientists who identify the values of science and who work in industry are likely to experience strains, stemming from the conflict between their need to publish and receive recognition, and industry's needs to protect its products by restricting publication until it is covered by patents.

One important source of strain is likely to occur wherever professionals and 'semi-professionals' (such as teachers, social workers and nurses) are employed in organizations. Professionals have generally acquired a high level of expertise from their extended education and expect a correspondingly high level of autonomy and scope for the exercise of expertise. Organizations,

[1] J. Kob, 'Definition of the Teacher's Role', in A. H. Halsey, J. Floud and C. A. Anderson, op. cit., 1958.

[2] P. W. Musgrave, *The Sociology of Education* (1965), Chapter 16, 'The Role of the Teacher'.

[3] S. Cotgrove and S. Box, *Science, Industry and Society* (1970), Chapter 2.

on the other hand, seek to exercise control. The resulting tensions between professionals and organizations may generate severe strains and have an adverse effect on the morale and performance of the professionals.[1] This issue is discussed more fully in Chapter 8.

Strains, then, can be felt as a result of a lack of congruence between the needs which the individual brings to the organization and those which the organization can satisfy. But they can arise, too, when organizations make ambiguous or conflicting demands on individuals. The case of the foreman in industry provides examples of role strain from such sources.[2] His position in the management structure subjects him to conflicting demands. The first line supervisor is at the base of the authority pyramid and hence is likely to experience the full force of any conflicts between management and men. His role has become ambiguous and his status threatened by the development of staff functions which have eroded many of the foreman's traditional functions. Hiring and firing has become a specialized task performed by the personnel department. The increasing application of science to production and the growth of specialized research and development departments have challenged the foreman's traditional role as the custodian of accumulated know-how. Scientists and technicians are now taking the decisions he used to take.

The development of joint-consultation has been a further factor introducing an element of ambiguity into the foreman's role. Works committees in which higher management and workers meet face-to-face have weakened his position in the chain of communication. The growth of full-employment and the shop-stewards' movement have challenged and reduced his authority.

As a result of such changes, the foreman's position in the authority structure has become ambiguous, his powers weakened and his functions eroded. It is no longer always as clear as it once was that he is part of management. Moreover, piece-work and overtime under conditions of full-employment have greatly reduced the income differentials which were once a mark of his superior status.[3] He is a 'marginal man', sharing something of the perspectives of both management and men.

Teachers, too, are subjected to a number of (sometimes

[1] A. Etzioni, *The Semi-Professions and Their Organization: Teachers, Nurses, Social Workers* (1969).

[2] M. Dalton, 'Conflicts Between Staff and Line Management', in T. Burns (ed.) *Industrial Man* (1969).

[3] These are only a few examples of the many strains and conflicts which result from the employment of individuals in occupational roles. For a perceptive study of the conflicts between the values of art and the pressures of the market, see Griff, 'The Commercial Artist', in M. R. Stein *et al.* op. cit.

141

conflicting) pressures. The teacher's *role-set*,[1] that is to say, the complex of other roles with which his own role interacts, includes school governors, the local authority, inspectors and parents. Parents, for example, may seek to increase their influence over the teachers by the formation of parent-teacher associations. Some parents may have strong views on the adoption of progressive teaching methods and many would seek to reverse a decision to demote a child to a lower stream.

Wilson[2] has drawn attention to a number of other role-conflicts and sources of strain. There are those, for example, which derive from the diffuse nature of the teacher's role, the absence of any clear boundary whereby he can know when he had done his job. The task of socialization cannot be measured in the way that a doctor's or solicitor's role performance can be measured. The teacher must continually ask himself whether he has fully discharged his obligations and there is a tendency to over-extend himself. The socializing role also requires an affective relationship with his pupils. But his custodial role as a disciplinary agent may be jeopardized if he becomes too friendly.

Other strains arise out of conflicting commitments to role and career. If he is to 'get on', the teacher needs to be on the move, seeking promotion or moving to a more congenial school. Yet his commitment to the values of teaching may pull him towards staying in a tough school and certainly staying long enough to really know his pupils.

OCCUPATIONAL STRATEGIES[3]

Members of occupations adopt a variety of devices to protect themselves against the strains and conflicts to which their work exposes them. Some of these adaptations involve compensatory activities outside work, such as creative leisure pursuits. These will be examined later in this chapter. But they also adopt various strategies to exercise control over their work, market and status situations. These include restrictive practices on the shop floor at one end of the spectrum, through collective bargaining, to an

[1] R. K. Merton, 'The Role-Set: Problems in Sociological Theory', *B.J.S.*, June 1955.

[2] B. R. Wilson, 'The Teacher's Role', *B.J.S.*, March 1962, pp. 15–32. See also, L. Gross *et al.*, *Explorations in Role Analysis: Studies of the School Superintendent Role* (1958), and L. E. Watson, 'Office and Expertise in the Secondary School', in D. F. Swift (ed.), *Basic Readings in the Sociology of Education* (1970).

[3] I am indebted to Noel Parry for many of the ideas expressed in this section. For a summary of strategies, see A. Tourraine *et al.*, *Workers' Attitudes to Technical Change* (1965), pp. 109–13.

organized labour movement seeking to transform society at the other.

Strategies of independence[1]

A well-documented example is to be found in the famous Hawthorne investigations. Workers in the bank-wiring room (wiring banks of telephone terminals) had developed a strong informal organization which exercised control over the output of workers in the group, reinforced by a variety of sanctions including horseplay and mild physical violence. In this way, the group exercised some small measure of control over a largely management-determined working day, and offset to some extent the insecurity of their position which would be heightened if they worked themselves out of a job.[2] Absenteeism and some strikes are other examples of strategies to control the pressures of the work situation.[3]

Time study is widely adopted in industry as a technique for controlling the wage-effort bargain. Jobs are timed, and a rate fixed by management for what it considers to be a reasonable output. Roy has documented the ingenious devices which are adopted on the shop floor to achieve quotas which are felt to be unobtainable by 'fair' means. 'They time jobs to give you just base rates. It's up to you to figure out how to fool them so you can make out. You can't make any money if you run the job the way it's timed.'[4] Strategies for *making out* included running machines at lower speeds and embellishing performance with dustings, adjustments and the like, while being timed; time allocated for setting up and similar 'gravy' jobs could be used to gain a head start on timed jobs by delaying clocking.

Members of occupations share common interests which almost invariably leads to the formation of associations for their pursuit and promotion. Trade unions are familiar examples. They function to protect and improve both the work situation and the market situation of the manual worker. Since workers are freely inter-

[1] This term is used by R. Bendix, op. cit. See also C. Argyris, *Integrating the Individual and the Organization* (1964), Chapter 4.

[2] F. J. Roethlisberger and W. J. Dickson, *Management and the Worker* (1939).

[3] P. W. Musgrave, op. cit., suggests that teachers seek to protect themselves against parental pressures by not encouraging the formation of parent-teacher associations. See also H. S. Becker, 'The Teacher in the Authority System of the Public School', in A. Etzioni, *Complex Organizations—A Reader* (1961).

[4] D. Roy, 'Efficiency and "the Fix": Informal Intergroup Relations in a Piece-Work Machine Shop', *A.J.S.*, 1955, pp. 255–66, in T. Burns (ed.), op. cit. See also, 'Quota Restriction and Goldbricking in a Machine Shop', *A.J.S.*, Vol. 57, 1952, in W. A. Faunce, *Readings in Industrial Sociology* (1967). These issues are further explored in Chapter 8.

changeable, they are individually virtually powerless. Only by collective action have they been able to achieve a stronger bargaining position with their employers. Lockwood's[1] study of clerks illustrates the ways in which differences in work, market and status situations influence the strategies of occupations.

Clerks and trade unions

It is in the work-situation and not in market-determined incomes that Lockwood finds the main clue to understanding the strategies adopted by clerks. The typical clerk in industry is employed in a small office, and usually one in which his relationship to his employer is paternalistic. His functions, remuneration, promotion and pension will be determined by a personal relation with his employer. Such conditions do not promote a sense of common identity of interest among clerks essential for collective action. Moreover, clerical work is typically a stepping-stone to executive and managerial posts. The clerk will therefore tend to see his future dependent on his own efforts and the impression he can make on his employer. Collective bargaining is hardly likely to earn promotion.[2] He will be conscious, too, of the fact that membership of a trade union is inconsistent with middle-class status and values. Such clerks, therefore, have not been highly unionized. Moreover, where they have formed occupational organizations, such as in banking, they have in the past refused to affiliate to the TUC or to adopt strike action. By contrast, bureaucratic organizations establish uniform working conditions regulated by impersonal rules, which exclude all forms of personal consideration between employer and clerk. It is, in fact, in the bureaucratically organized civil service and local government service that clerical unions have flourished, whereas the unions catering for industrial clerks have hitherto made relatively little progress. It is where the work situation of the clerk corresponds most closely with that of the factory worker that he is most likely to adopt the union strategies of collective bargaining and the threat of strike action to improve his market situation. In short then, whether clerks are prepared to adopt collective bargaining or whether they prefer to rely on individual efforts will depend on the organization of the work situations and on the strategies which are most likely to achieve an improvement in their market situation.

Some white-collar occupations have a high level of membership,

[1] D. Lockwood, op. cit.
[2] A. J. M. Sykes, 'Some Differences in the Attitudes of Clerical and Manual Workers', *Soc. Rev.*, November 1965, found that 92 per cent of a sample of clerks preferred to bargain individually, and 92 per cent disapproved of trade unions for clerks.

but it would be misleading to think of these as highly unionized. Blackburn[1] draws a useful distinction between what he calls *completeness*, which refers to the proportion of the occupation who belong to the association, and secondly, *unionateness* which refers to the character of the association. The elements of unionateness include collective bargaining, militancy (including willingness to adopt strike action, declaration and registration as a trade union, affiliation to the TUC and Labour party affiliation). Occupational associations differ considerably not only in completeness but also in unionateness. Prestige associations, which may be largely learned societies, are clearly low on this index.

The recent increase in white-collar unionization can be explained in these terms. The growth in completeness among clerical workers may be the result of their increasing employment in large open-plan offices. Increasing unionateness reflects the weakening of their bargaining position in the market with the spread of education and the increasing employment of women which have threatened their claims to superior status and differential rewards. Moreover, management and executive posts are being increasingly recruited from university graduates and the chances of internal promotion reduced. More clerks, therefore, are coming to see union organization as instrumental in improving their market and work situation.

Professions
Differing again from both clerks and manual workers are a group of occupations which are referred to rather ambiguously as professions. There is no agreement as to precisely what are the characteristics of a profession.[2] There are no criteria which can be applied to all the occupations loosely included in this group. Their most general characteristic is the application of a body of knowledge to some practical occupation. Thus engineering, medicine, architecture, the law—all require the mastery of a body of knowledge, and most such occupations now insist on passing formal examinations as a condition of entry.

Professional occupations have generally formed associations of members, and one of the main functions of such associations has been to examine aspirants to practise and to confer qualifications necessary for entry. Furthermore, some have devised ethical codes to regulate the conduct of their members, as for example, medicine. The formation of associations conferring qualifications and regulating conduct then are features of this group of intellectual occupations.

[1] R. M. Blackburn, op. cit.
[2] G. Millerson, *The Qualifying Associations* (1964).

Now although they have common features, there are also considerable differences in both the work and market situations of, for example, doctors and engineers. Teachers and engineers are mainly employees, while doctors and solicitors are usually in private practice, either as individuals or as partners. Architects and accountants may be either principals of private practices, or employees. It is not surprising, therefore, to find that occupations which experience a variety of situations in the economic system differ in the strategies they adopt and defy all efforts to define them by a set of common characteristics.

The highest degree of control is achieved where the professional sells his skills direct to a client for a fee, determined by his own professional association, and where the profession obtains a monopoly of the market by 'closure'. This involves an Act of Parliament which restricts certain key professional activities, such as signing death certificates in medicine, to practitioners whose names are included on the register kept by members of the profession. Under such circumstances, the profession individually and collectively regulates every aspect of its market and work situation.

Where the professional is paid a salary rather than charging a fee, his market situation is weakened. With the introduction of the National Health Service, doctors' remuneration was fixed in relation to the number of patients on their books, the total amount available for distribution being fixed by the government. This has resulted in the BMA assuming trade union functions in bargaining for higher rates and threatening strike action. Doctors, then, have retained a high degree of autonomy in the work situation, but with the decline in private practice, their market situation has come to depend increasingly on collective bargaining.

Professional codes of conduct, and the activities of professional bodies to improve their status and the 'public image' are similarly related to the market situation. Status is the prestige attached to an occupation and reflects the value placed upon it by society. High status serves to legitimize both the authority which the professional exercises and also his economic rewards. 'Unethical conduct' threatens the standing of the occupation and weakens its claim to be worth more in economic terms.

These relations can be illustrated by researches carried out among scientists and engineers.[1] It is hypothesized that professional status serves to legitimize the high pay and dominant position occupied by professionals in the authority structure of the work situation. Those who occupy subordinate positions therefore can be expected to support trade union associations in which collective

[1] K. Prandy, *Professional Employees—A Study of Scientists and Engineers* (1965).

146

bargaining is the appropriate strategy rather than professional associations, which will place more emphasis on maintaining the high standing of the occupation. A study of qualified scientists and engineers confirmed these hypotheses. It concluded that a major function of the engineering institutions was to reinforce the status claims of those employed in positions of responsibility.

The success of occupations such as medicine and the law in achieving high rewards in terms of income and prestige has provided a model which others have sought to imitate. Wherever an occupation requires the acquisition of a specific body of knowledge for its practice, it offers possibilities for adopting strategies modelled on those of the older professions. With the growth of knowledge, specialization and division of labour, an increasing number of occupations have found themselves in a position to set up associations, whose prime function is to examine and qualify members. Qualifications provide a means of limiting entry to the occupations, and a basis for negotiating salary structures related to qualification. Such associations, however, differ from the independent professions mainly in that they lack a code of conduct. Such a code would be largely functionless in an occupation where conduct is governed mainly by the conditions of employment in organizations, and if devised could function only as a status symbol.

The term profession then has little descriptive value. It refers to a group of occupations whose practice involves the applications of specialized intellectual knowledge sufficiently extensive to warrant formal educational and examination procedures. Such occupations are more likely to enjoy autonomy in the work situation. Moreover, their desire for public recognition and esteem and the frequently fiduciary element in their relations with clients will lead them to stress the element of service rather than income. However, since income and status are closely linked, they will seek to promote the pursuit of both by strategies which include the use of qualifications to control entry and to provide a basis for differential incomes. The strategies open to them will depend on their market and work situations. It is doubtful, in fact, whether the professions represent a different type of occupation,[1] oriented to service rather than to profit, as has been argued by Carr-Saunders and Wilson, and by T. H. Marshall. This view has been challenged by Parsons[2] who sees the typical professional attitude with its

[1] See, for example, A. Carr-Saunders and Wilson, *The Professions* (1933), and T. H. Marshall, *Citizenship and Social Class* (1950).
[2] T. Parsons, 'The Professions and Social Structure', in *Essays in Sociological Theory* (1958).

147

emphasis on understanding and disinterested service and ethical conduct towards the client as functionally necessary requirements to maintain the delicate relationship between the professional and his client. Economists and political scientists have stressed the dysfunctional consequences of professional organizations, criticizing them for their monopolistic practices.[1] Kessel has shown that the practices of the American Medical Association including the opposition to advertising 'are essentially similar to measures adopted by monopolies (and cartels) and serve the same purpose'[2] —functioning as a means of raising the price of professional services.

Skilled workers and apprenticeship

Just as intellectual occupations use qualifications as a lever for improving their position, so skilled trades will seek to protect their skills and the bargaining strength which this confers. And the institution of apprenticeship plays a key role in this process. Investigations in the 1950s into the working of apprenticeship[3] brought to light the fact that it was largely failing as an institution for education and training. On the industrial side, only a minority of apprentices received systematic training, most being left to pick it up by the time-honoured method of 'sitting by Nellie'. On the college side, only about one in ten of those who began courses were successfully qualifying. Moreover, recognition as a skilled craftsman is not in any way dependent on passing examinations or on providing proof of competent and systematic training. If the 'charter' of apprenticeship is to train young people in industrial skills, and if, in fact, it is not functioning successfully, how can we account for the support which it receives from industry? The clue is to be found in an intensive study of apprenticeship by Dr K. Liepmann.[3] It appears from this that apprenticeship is important for its regulatory functions rather than for its training functions. With the rise of the trade unions, the institution has come to be used by them primarily as a strategy for protecting their market situation. It provides a basis for regulating entry into the occupation, for protecting jobs by demarcation lines between skills, as a cushion against unemployment by agreements to dismiss dilutees (non-apprenticed labour) before craftsmen, and as a basis for claims to differential wages. A latent (unintended and unrecognized) function of the Ministry's policy of linking education

---

[1] See D. Lees, *The Economic Consequences of the Professions* (1968).
[2] J. Ben-David, 'Professions in the Class System of Present-Day Societies', *Current Sociology*, Vol. 12, 1963–4, No. 3. This article includes a summary of the literature on the professions.
[3] K. Liepmann, *Apprenticeship* (1960).

to a predominantly regulatory institution has been the virtual failure of its plans to increase the supply of effectively trained skilled workers.[1]

Industrial relations

The occurrence of overt industrial conflict depends on a number of factors. Managerialist ideology stresses the fundamental community of interests within industry. Overt conflicts according to this view are more often than not the result of misunderstanding and failure of communication. But this does not prevent management from standing firm and taking a tough line. By contrast, the conflict view sees industry as two sides with irreconcilable interests. But such a view is perfectly consistent with the absence of strikes, and relative harmony on the shop floor.[2] In short, an interactionist approach will take account of both the orientations of the actors and the situation as it is perceived.

Relations between union and management take place within the framework of substantial normative agreement.[3] Indeed, the 'teamwork view' predominates over the conflict view that there are two sides in long-term opposition. One of the reasons for the extensive and prolonged strikes in the past has been that such normative agreement did not exist: the unions were struggling precisely for recognition of bargaining machinery. Once this is established the balance shifts to bargaining over substantive issues, especially disagreements over pay—the fair distribution of the 'cake'. Such bargaining takes place within the framework of agreed rules and procedures. And in so far as the outcome of the bargaining is acceptable, it restores consensus. In short, collective bargaining institutionalizes conflict through procedures for conflict regulation and resolution.[4]

Strikes are the resort to coercive means where discussion and persuasion have failed. It must be remembered that they are only the tip of the iceberg; the majority of disputes are settled by negotiation. Moreover, there are other ways of expressing discontent, such as absenteeism and labour turnover.[5]

The pattern of frequency varies considerably both over time and between different countries. In the international league, Britain has, until recently, lost fewer man-days through strikes than many other highly industrial societies such as the USA. The

[1] Industrial Training Boards have now been set up.

[2] S. Cotgrove and C. Vamplew, 'Technology Class and Politics: The Case of the Process Workers', *Sociology*, May 1972.

[3] Alan Fox, op. cit., p. 135.

[4] See Chapter 9 for a more extended discussion of the process of conflict.

[5] See A. Kornhauser et al., *Industrial Conflict* (1954), for an extensive discussion of this subject, especially Chapter 40.

149

broad trend has been a marked decline in the number of working days lost through strikes this century. Peak years were 1912 with 41 million days lost, 1920 with 27 million and 1921 with 86 million.[1] By contrast, the post Second World War years have had from 2 million to 3 million days lost.

The high figures for the early decades of the century were due to a relatively small number of strikes involving large numbers of workers for a long period. These were the days when industrial conflict came close to a class struggle. Indeed, the General Strike was an attempt to achieve political ends by industrial action. These were the years when miners were struggling for adequate basic wages, hours and conditions of work. The bitterness of the struggle reflected the relative poverty and insecurity of workers in basic industries such as mining and textiles, and the unwillingness of the employers to reach negotiated agreements. Strikes were a show of force in a conflict for power to control market and work conditions.

In more recent decades, there have been many more strikes, but most have been of much shorter duration and involving fewer workers. Part of the explanation is the growth of complex negotiating and consultative machinery,[2] so that more disputes are now settled through conciliation and few become overt strikes. There has also been a substantial measure of accommodation by the employers to the demands of the workers. Fewer strikes are over basic issues, and more are frictional disputes over working arrangements. In the strike-prone industries such as mining and textiles, which contributed a disproportionate share to the disputes of the early decades, workers faced special difficulties. These industries were located in areas where there were few alternative chances for employment. There was, therefore, no escape from frustrating circumstances and unemployment.[3] The post-war policy of industrial diversification has provided an escape for those who would otherwise be pent-up with little alternative. But the past has left a legacy in the form of much more widespread support for the dichotomous conflict view of industry as two sides rather than a team, and stronger and more active support for the unions.[4]

[1] K. G. J. C. Knowles, *Strikes: A Study of Industrial Conflict* (1952). The figure for 1926 (the year of the General Strike) is, of course, much higher but not typical.
[2] Strikes are more frequent in large pits where the immediate settlement of a dispute is more difficult. S. Wellisz, 'Strikes in Coal Mining', *B.J.S.*, December 1953.
[3] See also C. Kerr and A. Siegel, 'The Inter-Industry Propensity to Strike', A. Kornhauser *et al.*, op. cit., Chapter 14.
[4] S. Cotgrove and C. Vamplew, op. cit.

In the late 1960s and early 1970s there has been an increase in the number of extended strikes over pay involving large numbers of workers. A plausible explanation is the rising aspirations of workers after decades of economic growth, the existence of anomalies and inequalities, and impatience with cumbersome negotiating machinery.[1]

NON-WORK CORRELATES

Occupation is clearly a most important influence in the life of the individual. Yet the study of occupations and their influence is an area which has hitherto been largely ignored by sociologists. In Britain, in particular, researches have concentrated rather on social class as a variable. We have a number of studies of working-class life, particularly investigations of family life. Such studies provide us with a good deal of useful descriptive material. But they fail to discover the variables in the working-class situation which are interrelated. Hoggart,[2] for example, refers to some of the distinctive elements in working-class sub-culture, such as belief in fate, and the distinction between 'them' who decide and 'us' who passively carry out instructions. Such embracing descriptions of working-class life fail to take account of the very considerable differences in market, status and work-situations which exist, and consequently provide little insight into the significance of such differences in the lives of workers. In short, the term 'working class' includes a very wide range of variables, and does not refer to a homogeneous group of individuals. What we now need are more rigorous studies which relate variables in the market, status and work-situations to non-work variables. What, for example, are the consequences for family life, leisure activities and political attitudes of alienative work experience.[3]

Studies of particular occupations as distinct from studies of class groups make it possible to see much more clearly the way in which the kind of work that a man does influences his pattern of life. Both Dennis, Henriques and Slaughter's[4] study of a mining community and Clancy Sigal's *Week-End in Dinlock* present a vivid picture of a type of work which makes a powerful impact on the life of the community. The face-worker is deeply involved in his work and enjoys relative autonomy at the coal face. But it is dangerous and damaging work, demanding the closest co-operation, where one man's mistake can cause the death of others. It is

[1] A. Fox, op. cit., p. 149.
[2] R. Hoggart, *The Uses of Literacy* (1957).
[3] C. Argyris, op. cit., pp. 73–92, summarizes American data.
[4] N. Dennis, F. Henriques and C. Slaughter, *Coal is Our Life* (1956).

151

this dangerous man's world which makes its indelible imprint on life after work—the forgetfulness of alcohol in the long round of pub visits on Saturday and Sunday, wives left at home, the deep significance of the trade union. And to repair the damages exacted by his work, the miner expects a wife who will feed and comfort him, making few demands in return.

Jeremy Tunstall[1] shows that the work of the distant-water fisherman spills over in a similar way to influence leisure and home life. As with the miners, men who are thrown closely together at work and whose homes are work-based, spend their leisure together. It is a world which generates conservatisim and belief in fate. It is a world of virile men with money in their pockets, defying their inferior position in the class structure. While on shore, the fisherman can be 'king for a day, wearing new suits, riding in taxis, drinking whisky'. Within the family, the prolonged absences of men at sea for three weeks at a time further encourage husbands and wives to lead separate lives, and husbands to treat their wives as servants (see Chapter 2).

But the less exotic occupations of clerk and executive also leave their imprint. W. H. Whyte's impressionistic study, *Organization Man*, shows the man with a career looking forward to a succession of jobs, each carrying higher rewards in terms of income, prestige and the perquisites of office. His working life is broadly predictable. Success for the organization man depends on conformity, being 'other-directed', being a good company man. Career prospects encourage training, and the adoption of the long view.[2] Such men will be strongly committed to their careers, and will not draw any clear distinction between work and leisure, combining vacation trips with business, and social life with business contacts.

The relations between family roles and occupation have already been explored in Chapter 2. Later chapters will examine in more detail the influence of occupation on political and social attitudes, and on voting behaviour. The relations between work and leisure, however, are particularly close. Leisure, therefore, will now be explored more fully as an example of the influence of work on non-work.

Leisure
It is to be expected that occupation has a marked influence on leisure. A man's job determines in the first place the amount of free time he has left over for non-work activities. His market

[1] J. Tunstall, op. cit.
[2] Sykes, op. cit., found that 87 per cent of clerks compared with 9 per cent of workers expected promotion, while 94 per cent of clerks compared with 2 per cent of workers has attended night school.

situation is a factor in the amount of money he has in his pocket for different leisure activities. His status situation may similarly influence freetime, by providing opportunities for achieving status in non-work activities which he cannot achieve through his occupation. Office in voluntary associations,[1] such as trade unions or political parties, success in the fields of sport or entertainment, provide possible alternative bases for status denied by occupation. Moreover, leisure activities function as status symbols and are ways in which income can be spent in status-conferring ways.

The influence of the work-situation on leisure, however, is particularly marked. Parker[2] has suggested that there are three main types of association. The first, 'opposition', includes the leisure patterns of coal-miners, distant-water fishermen and alienated workers in assembly-belt production. Here there is a sharp distinction between work and leisure. Work is not a central life interest, and yields only extrinsic satisfactions or may even generate hostility. In the words of C. Wright Mills, 'Each day, men sell little pieces of themselves in order to try to buy them back each night and weekend with the coin of fun.' Or again, in the words of Arthur Seaton, 'If your machine was working well . . . You went off into pipe-dreams for the rest of the day. And in the evening, when admittedly you would be feeling as though your arms and legs had been stretched to breaking point on a torture-rack, you stepped out into a cosy world of pubs and noisy tarts that would one day provide you with the raw material for more pipe-dreams as you stood at your lathe.'[3]

Withdrawal to home-centredness offers compensations of a different kind. Here, a man is boss of his own small world and can engage in meaningful tasks of his own choosing. Somewhat differently, the hard drinking of miners and distant-water fishermen is less a reaction against tedium than an attempt to escape from the world of work which is dangerous, damaging and viewed with mixed feelings of attractions and dislike.

A second type of association between work and leisure identified by Parker is 'extension'. This relationship characterizes occupations in which work is intrinsically satisfying. Parker found, for example, that youth-employment officers and child-care workers did not draw any sharp distinction between work and leisure, and work related activities frequently penetrate into leisure-time.

[1] In practice, such associations function only to a limited extent as alternative avenues for status. Officers tend to be recruited mainly from the higher status groups. (D. V. Glass (ed.), op. cit., Chapter 13.)

[2] S. Parker, op. cit.

[3] A. Sillitoe, *Saturday Night and Sunday Morning* (1958), p. 31.

Gerstl[1] found that dentists tend to use their hands in jobs about the house, advertising men paint and write, while professors read[2] and listen to music. Between these two types of association, there is a third—'neutrality'. Bank clerks, for example, are neither so engrossed in their work that they want to carry it over into their spare-time, nor does their work generate needs for which leisure-time offers compensation. Their attitude towards work is rather one of indifference. Some indication that an element of apathy spills over into leisure can be seen in the relatively greater preference they express for relaxing and sleeping as a way of spending extra leisure-time. Wilensky[3] suggests an alternative form of opposition where the influence of work may 'spill over' into leisure. Here, the exhaustion and tedium of work penetrate into non-work time. The worker collapses in his armchair, and twiddles the knobs on his TV set. The mental stultification produced by work permeates leisure: alienation from work becomes alienation from life.

SOCIAL CHANGE AND THE ECONOMY

To explore all the sociological aspects of economic growth would be a task of great complexity. We would need to know, for example, the social conditions such as the kinship and political systems which make possible and stimulate economic growth. We would also need to explore in detail the effects of economic change on the social system. Some aspects of these questions have been touched on, for example the relations between changes in the economic system and culture, and the kinship system. We have also seen that economic change can be viewed in terms of changes within the economic system, such as changes in the composition of the labour force. The whole subject of economic growth, its conditions and consequences, will be re-examined in the final chapter on social change. Meanwhile, there are a few more limited issues that are relevant to an understanding of the probable trends in the next few decades.

It can be seen from the preceding analysis that the changes which are likely to be most sociologically significant are those which influence occupational roles, by changing the degree of autonomy and skill required and influencing the involvement and satisfaction of the worker by hand or brain. The broad pattern has been

[1] E. O. Smigel, op. cit., Chapter 8.

[2] If the professor's reading is connected with his lecturing or research, one would prefer to categorize this as work (see Table 4.1).

[3] H. L. Wilensky, 'Work, Careers and Social Integration', *International Soc. Sc. J.*, 1960, No. 4.

a shift from a predominance of primary extractive industry (hunting, fishing, mining) to a secondary manufacturing industry, and now in the economically advanced societies to tertiary service industries (transport, education, retail trade). With this trend, has come a shift towards a higher proportion of non-manual workers in the labour force, the increasing employment of women, the growth of intellectual occupations, and a general rise in the levels of skill.[1] The growth of large-scale factory production and giant corporations means that the independent craftsman and small *entrepreneur* have declined while an increasing proportion of the labour force is employed in organizations of varying size. Such changes offset the degree of economic autonomy of the individual. There are now fewer employers, and a smaller proportion of employees are in managerial positions. Any extrapolation of existing trends inevitably involves considerable uncertainty. Bearing this in mind, it seems probable that technological change will bring about further changes in the occupational structure, a shift to non-manual occupations with increased skill and intellectual content.

The effects of such changes are still a matter for controversy and await further research. Automation certainly results in the reintegration of work. And in some cases this leads to increased worker satisfaction. It is important to remember that automation takes a variety of forms and these have different consequences. Although it reverses the trend towards the fragmentation of tasks, it may increase the isolation of the individual worker. However, not all forms of automation have this consequence. A study of automated electricity generating stations showed that work teams became more united.[2] Automation has also given rise to a good deal of optimism about the humanizing and up-grading of work.[3] Again the evidence is conflicting. Some studies have found identification and pride in automated machinery, while others have reported increasing estrangement from the productive processes.[4] A further possibility is that the increasing skills and knowledge will lead to the professionalization of work—a shift from jobs to careers.[5] Finally, the impact of automation may well be related to

[1] For relevant statistics, see A. Carr-Saunders, C. Jones and C. Moser, op. cit.

[2] F. C. Mann and L. R. Hoffman, *Automation and the Workers: A Study of Social Change in Power Plants* (1960).

[3] D. Bell, *The End of Ideology* (1960), Chapter 11.

[4] W. A. Faunce, 'Automation and the Automobile Worker', in W. Galenson and S. K. Lipset, *Labour and Trade Unionism, an Interdisciplinary Reader* (1960), pp. 37–9.

[5] For a summary of the effects of automation, see A. Tourraine *et al.*, op. cit., pp. 43–9.

the characteristics which the worker brings to the job—especially his family life, previous education and work experience.

Such changes in socio-technical systems are accompanied by developments in occupational strategies. In highly automated systems, the worker can do little to affect production, and the link between production and wages is loosened. The level of wages comes to be determined more by comparison with other categories, and the emphasis shifts from a struggle on the shop floor to broader issues of wages and incomes policy. The various levels of labour strategy become more clearly differentiated, and collective bargaining shifts from preoccupation with resistance to change at plant level as the unions become increasingly involved in major social and economic decisions.[1]

On balance, it would appear that automation increases work satisfaction. This may well be accompanied by a decline in the demand for purely recuperative leisure activities in the increased leisure-time available, although this will be unevenly spread, with scientists and other intellectuals continuing to work long hours. Such conditions are likely to be accompanied by associated changes in social and political attitudes.

One conclusion seems reasonably certain. Occupation is a key variable, functionally related to family life, leisure, social and political attitudes. Significant aspects of occupations are, in turn, related to changes in the economic system. The rate of change in the economic system is faster than at any previous time in history, and we can expect, therefore, that the rate of social change which it stimulates will also increase.

DISCUSSION

An instrumental orientation to work is the dominant theme in studies of the meaning of work in industrial societies. Men go to work and remain attached to jobs mainly for the money. This should not perhaps surprise us. In a market economy where the sale of labour is the condition for command over goods and resources, the pressures, for most, are inexorable. But this is not the same as an instrumental involvement in the job itself. And for some, work offers varying degrees of satisfaction through opportunities for the exercise of human skills and capacities. Indeed, work in highly automated plants goes some way towards the rehumanization of work, though the assembly-line, whether for the production of cars or cosmetics, remains the archetypal form of dehumanized work.

[1] A. Tourraine, op. cit., pp. 110–11. Tourraine also emphasizes that different types of industrial society will evolve different labour strategies which can only be understood in the context of economic and political systems.

Job-enlargement and job-enrichment offer possibilities, but technology sets the limits. Here, the extension of automation could be a major factor, but it is doubtful whether this is likely on any scale in the foreseeable future. How far non-work activities —home and family life or creative leisure pursuits—may provide alternative avenues for self-realization remains problematic. However, whether it is justifiable to use so powerful and emotive a word as alienation to describe workers who find home life more satisfying and fulfilling than work, is again a matter for debate. What we can agree is that the whole issue about the meaning and centrality of work raises questions about the ontological nature of man—what man is capable of becoming—which go far beyond sociology.

Marx's dream of a 'society of artists' is certainly far from realization. But the data reviewed in this chapter suggests that the pessimistic view of man as the 'prisoner of society' is overdrawn. Choice of occupation may be circumscribed by lack of knowledge and opportunity. But there *are* options. From this perspective, the decision to invest in family life and to treat work as instrumental *is* a human choice. So too is the development of shop-floor strategies to extend some measure of independent influence over working life. And if this involves sacrifice of economic rewards, it may be a decision consciously taken in the pursuit of alternative values. The alternative of pursuing maximum economic growth at the cost of other satisfactions may be a choice which all industrial societies will be increasingly forced to face. Economic rationality assumes the primacy of economic goals—and these, in the last analysis, are matters of preference.

At the macro-level, there is little evidence to support the once influential views of the managerialists that the divorce between ownership and control would result in the emergence of a new class of managers and technocrats, committed to an ideology of social responsibility. The leaders of British industry are still recruited predominantly from the higher strata and in general lack formal qualifications, certainly in science and technology, though it could be argued that Britain is a case of 'arrested development' and that such trends have gone further in the USA and in some European countries. The larger question of the social and political influence of the business elite will be explored in the next chapter.

157

J. A. Banks, *Trade Unionism* (Collier-Macmillan, 1974).

P. L. Berger, *The Human Shape of Work: Studies in the Sociology of Occupations* (Macmillan, 1964).

R. M. Blackburn, *Union Character and Social Class: A Study of White-Collar Unionism* (Batsford, 1967).

R. Blauner, *Alienation and Freedom: the Manual Worker in Industry* (University of Chicago Press, 1963).

T. Burns (ed.), *Industrial Man* (Penguin, 1969).

J. Child, *British Management Thought* (Allen and Unwin, 1969).

S. Cotgrove and S. Box, *Science, Industry and Society* (Allen and Unwin, 1970).

S. Cotgrove, J. Dunham and C. Vamplew, *The Nylon Spinners* (Allen and Unwin, 1971).

J. E. T. Eldridge, *Industrial Disputes* (Routledge, 1968).

A. Etzioni, *The Semi-Professions and Their Organization: Teachers, Nurses, Social Workers* (Collier-Macmillan, 1969).

Alan Fox, *A Sociology of Work in Industry* (Collier-Macmillan, 1971).

J. Goldthorpe *et al.*, *The Affluent Wokrer: Industrial Attitudes and Behaviour* (Cambridge University Press, 1968).

J. Goldthorpe *et al.*, *The Affluent Worker in the Class Structure* (Cambridge University Press, 1969).

F. Herzberg, *Work and the Nature of Man* (Staples Press, 1968).

G. K. Ingham, *Strikes and Industrial Conflict*, (Macmillan 1974).

T. Johnson, *Professions and Power* (Macmillan, 1972).

D. Lockwood, *The Blackcoated Worker* (Allen and Unwin, 1958).

S. Marcson (ed.), *Automation, Alienation and Anomie* (Harper and Row, 1970).

G. Millerson, *The Qualifying Associations* (Routledge, 1964).

T. Nichols, *Ownership, Control and Ideology* (Allen and Unwin, 1969).

S. Nosow and W. H. Form (eds), *Man, Work and Society: A Reader in the Sociology of Occupations* (Basic Books, 1962).

S. Parker, *The Future of Work and Leisure* (MacGibbon and Kee, 1971).

S. Parker *et al.*, *The Sociology of Industry* (Allen and Unwin, 1972).

K. Prandy, *Professional Employees: A Study of Scientists and Engineers* (Faber, 1965).

A. Tourraine *et al.*, *Workers' Attitudes To Technical Change* (OECD, 1965).

J. M. Vollmer and D. Mills, *Professionalization* (Prentice-Hall 1966).

W. W. Williams (ed.), *Occupational Choice* (Allen & Unwin, 1974).

Chapter 5

THE POLITICAL SYSTEM[1]

It is at the level of the political system that the differing perspectives of consensus and conflict are most apparent. The functionalists are certainly aware of conflict, but they stress the integrating functions of political processes. Pressure groups and parties function to inject the interests of various groups into the political process, where differences are ironed out and a maximum of consensus is achieved through the formation of policies which command wide-based support. In this model of a pluralist system, government is weak and acts as an honest broker between conflicting interests in the pursuit of consensus politics. Those who focus on the deep-rooted conflicts of interest in society draw attention to the evidence for the existence of ruling classes and elites, recruited predominantly from the propertied and landed classes, using the machinery of government for the pursuit of their own economic interests, and manipulating consensus through the mass media. It is around such issues that the sociological analysis of political structures and processes may be organized.

THE POLITICAL SYSTEM AND THE SOCIAL SYSTEM

A major difficulty confronts us at the outset. What precisely are the boundaries of the political system? It's by no means easy to arrive at any agreement on what exactly politics is about. We found no great difficulties in delineating the economic system or the kinship system sufficiently clearly to examine a rough working model. But the sphere of politics is more ambiguous. If we argue, for example, that politics refers to the exercise of power, then political behaviour penetrates all segments of society. Power and influence are exercised within the family, in schools, offices, factories and universities.[2] Such an approach blurs the boundaries between the political and social system and is not very helpful in delineating the political system as a cluster of distinct structures performing political functions. A somewhat similar approach is adopted by

[1] I am much indebted to Anthony Taylor and Penri Griffiths for valuable suggestions for this chapter.
[2] P. Worsley suggests that we differentiate between governmental and non-governmental power as politics I and politics II. *Sociological Review Monograph No. 8.*

159

David Easton[1] who defines the political system as the authoritative allocation of values. The fact that policies or commands are authoritative, that is, defined as legitimate and promulgated by a legally constituted authority characterizes the policies of churches, universities and other agencies and does not by itself clearly demarcate the political system. Moreover, there are some political systems which enjoy little legitimacy, and rely substantially on naked coercion. The degree and type of legitimacy is, in fact, one of the variables which differentiates between political systems.[2]

The threat of physical compulsion is clearly an essential element in politics. But it is not enough to identify the political system with the state; that is, with the apparatus which maintains order by the use or threat of use of more or less legitimate force. This would exclude the role of parties, and pressure groups, and would exclude the study of political systems in underdeveloped societies which have not yet evolved a distinct apparatus of state government. Almond[3] attempts to integrate these two elements of legitimacy and coercion in his definition: '. . . the political system is that system of interactions to be found in all independent societies which performs the functions of integration and adaptation (both internally and vis-à-vis other societies) by means of the employment, or threat of employment, of more or less legitimate physical compulsion.'[4]

The distinguishing feature of the political system which emerges from both Easton's and Almond's approaches is that politics is the most generalized system for the maintenance of order in the social system. We can then identify two main elements in the political system. Firstly, there is the apparatus for decision-making and the execution and enforcement of policies. In Britain, this includes Parliament as the rule-making machinery; the civil service and local government, backed by the police and the army, apply the decisions and execute the policies of the government; while the judiciary and the courts adjudicate and contribute to rule enforcement as part of the machinery for applying the coercive sanctions of fines and imprisonment. The distribution of functions is not, of course, as clear cut as this. The judiciary, for example, make law as well as adjudicating it, while the civil service have limited rule-making functions.

[1] D. Easton, *The Political System: An Inquiry into the State of Political Science* (1953).
[2] This will be discussed more fully in the section on the political system and culture.
[3] Gabriel A. Almond and James S. Coleman, *The Politics of Developing Areas* (1960). This chapter draws heavily on the introduction by G. A. Almond for its theoretical framework.
[4] G. Almond and J. Coleman, op. cit., p. 7.

But in arriving at decisions and policies governments do not operate in a vacuum. They have to take account of various interests and pressures, and a variety of structures exist in modern industrial societies which feed demands into the political system and provide it with support.[1] Among the most important of the structures which serve to articulate demands and exert pressures are pressure groups, which are organized interest groups seeking to influence political decisions by devices such as lobbying and propaganda. They are not governmental structures, but arise as associations within other sub-systems of society. Within the economic system, for example, there are a variety of associations of manufacturers and employers which include pressure-group functions among their activities. They man the boundary between the political system and the economic system, performing the very important role of providing machinery for relating the economic system to the political system. Similarly, the churches may seek to influence political decisions and in so doing, function as pressure groups. Some associations exist only as pressure groups, such as The Abortion Law Reform Society or the Lord's Day Observance Society. These are parts of the educational system in so far as they exist to change public opinion. Whenever the activities of an organization or association seek to bring pressures to bear on the political process, they function as pressure groups and their activities become a part of the political system.[2]

Unlike pressure groups, political parties are an integral part of the political system. Their emergence in the nineteenth century in the form in which we now know them was a direct result of the extension of the franchise.[3] This made it necessary to establish machinery to organize popular support. They function as vote-getting agencies. As such, political party organizations are located within the political system. But they are not a part of the machinery of government, and like pressure groups, are located at the boundary of the political system serving primarily to link the parliamentary parties (which *are* part of the machinery of government) with the electorate.

There are several different types of parties in modern democracies. To understand such differences, it is necessary to look briefly at the varying circumstances underlying their origins.[4] Parties are relatively recent arrivals on the political scene. In 1850

[1] David Easton, 'An Approach to the Analysis of Political Systems', in A. Pizzorno (ed.), *Political Sociology* (1971).

[2] Gabriel A. Almond *et al.*, op. cit., p. 8. For an account of the variety and functioning of pressure groups in Britain, see J. D. Stewart, *British Pressure Groups* (1958).

[3] R. T. McKenzie, *British Political Parties* (1964), p. 6.

[4] See M. Duverger, *Political Parties* (1959), Introduction.

there were no parties as we know them today. The pattern of their genesis is fairly general. Firstly, there is the emergence of parliamentary groups, followed by the appearance of electoral committees. Finally a permanent connection is established between these two elements. Parliamentary groups have generally antedated universal suffrage. In eighteenth-century Britain, for example, English ministers ensured substantial majorities by buying the votes of MPs. Members received the price of their vote at the desk of the 'Patronage Secretary', who kept an eye on their votes and speeches, functioning also as the 'whip' to maintain discipline. In this way, the organization of the group and authority of the 'whip' emerged before the extension of the franchise, and constituted a rudimentary parliamentary group.

The extension of the franchise of 1832 led to the rapid growth of registration societies to facilitate and encourage the procedure of registration. As the societies grew, they concerned themselves with the nomination of candidates. It was a short step to establishing regular connections between parliamentary groups and electoral committees.

Extra-parliamentary factors have also operated in the genesis of parties. The British Labour Party is a clear example, resulting from a decision of the Trade Union Congress in 1899 to establish an electoral and parliamentary organization by a federation of trade unions and socialist societies to secure the election of working-class representatives to parliament. Parties which originate in this way outside parliament are more centralized, coherent and disciplined, than those arising within parliament. Moreover, the influence of the parliamentary group tends to be greater in parties with parliamentary or electoral origin.[1] It was natural that Labour MPs and the Parliamentary Labour Party were considered to be servants of the movement.[2] The Labour party has traditionally claimed that the Party Conference is the parliament for the party and 'lays down the policy of the party and issues instructions which must be carried out by . . . [Labour] representatives in parliament and on local authorities.'[3] If this were so, then the party caucus would rule, and would usurp the functions of parliament. Robert McKenzie argues, however, that in the major political parties, effective decision-making authority 'resides with the leadership groups thrown up by the parliamentary parties (of whom much the most important individual is the party leader).'[4] In neither case has the mass organization achieved the dominance over the parlia-

[1] M. Duverger, op. cit., pp. xxxiv ff.
[2] R. T. McKenzie, op. cit., p. 13.
[3] Lord Attlee quoted by R. T. McKenzie, op. cit., p. 12.
[4] Ibid., p. 635.

mentary parties which Ostrogorski feared was the trend at the end of the nineteenth century. 'While the Leader of any party is Prime Minister, and his principal colleagues constitute a cabinet, there can be no debate as to where, in principle, final authority in the party lies.'[1]

An important characteristic of political systems is the number of parties. Two-party and multi-party systems provide different mechanisms for expressing and articulating cleavages. In a two-party system, cleavages polarize around one major dimension, and the struggle between factions takes place within each of the major parties. 'If however, the factions become exasperated and can no longer meet on common ground, the basic tendency towards dualism is thwarted and gives way to multi-partism.'[2] In France, the multi-partite division reflects various combinations of a number of dualisms.[3] The Christian Progressives, for example, are pro-clerical and pro-planning but the Socialists are anti-clerical and pro-planning.[4] Duverger shows that the main determinant of the number of parties is the electoral system. 'The simple-majority single-ballot system favours the two-party system.'[5] 'The simple-majority system with second ballot and proportional representation favours multi-partism.'[6]

The political system and culture

Whatever differences there may be between political parties in England, and however bitter the conflict between them may at times be, such conflict is acted out within the framework of agreed rules and procedures. Moreover, it is conflict over a limited range of disagreements, and takes place against a background of substantial consensus over a range of values and beliefs. A high degree of consensus clearly limits the areas of conflict. Moreover, consensus on the norms regulating political activity institutionalizes the modes of conflict. Among the recognized channels of parliamentary procedure are questions, debates and divisions. Further-

[1] Ibid., p. 638. Dr McKenzie also examines Michels 'iron law of oligarchy' which argues that the leadership of organizations becomes stable and irremoveable. Similar tendencies could be argued to exist in trade unions. Such issues, however, are more appropriately examined in the context of the study of organizations in Chapter 8. For a detailed discussion of the relations between the leadership and the parliamentary party, see M. Duverger, op. cit., Book 1, Chapter III.

[2] Ibid., p. 230.

[3] Ibid., pp. 231–4.

[4] The number of parties also has important consequences for the governmental process, influencing the distribution of power between parliament and executive. This is discussed later in the chapter.

[5] M. Duverger, op. cit., p. 217.

[6] Ibid., p. 239.

more, the electoral system structures the struggle for power to take the form of periodic contending for votes at general elections.

There is a whole range of political beliefs and values over which there is substantial social consensus: on the value of liberty, the monarchy, of evolutionary rather than revolutionary change and of English parliamentary and governmental institutions.[1] Differences are more likely to occur over means than over ends. Such consensus is, of course, partly due to political socialization. Respect for the monarchy, for example, is inculcated in the schools, especially through the teaching of history.[2] Moreover, while a few are socialized for leadership roles through attendance at public schools, the majority 'attending secondary-modern schools appear to accept the politically passive roles implicitly stressed by the orientation of the schools.'[3]

Most important for any political system is an acceptance of its legitimacy on the part of the governed. It's not easy to define legitimacy. It is not the same thing as the effectiveness of a government. This is an index of the extent to which its policies have been judged to be successful and is related to the expectations of the electorate. Judgements of legitimacy are affective and evaluative, rather than instrumental.[4] Legitimacy reflects the way in which a society defines the legality of a government and its right or authority to rule. Legitimacy transforms power into authority. This transformation of power into authority is clearly a most important condition for the acceptance of rules and orders. Men may accept authority because it rests upon tradition. In stable societies, authority is legitimized by long usage. In times of crisis and change, traditional authority comes to be questioned. Under such circumstances, *charismatic leaders* may[5] emerge, who are obeyed because they are believed to possess special personal qualities.

In large-scale contemporary societies, the bases of legitimacy are complex. Power is perceived as legitimate if it is exercised accord-

[1] R. Rose, *Politics in England* (1965), Chapter 2. Forty-six per cent in Britain, 85 per cent in America, but only 3 per cent in Italy, are proud of governmental and political institutions. Quoted on p. 52 from G. Almond and S. Verba, *The Civic Culture* (1963).

[2] R. Rose quotes a Liverpool baker who said that his school 'always had the National Anthem on every occasion and scriptures and prayers. Told to love your own country. Always told our country was the best and still believe it' (ibid., p. 64).

[3] Ibid., p. 67.

[4] S. M. Lipset, in R. K. Merton, L. Broom and L. S. Cottrell, *Sociology Today: Problems and Prospects* (1965), pp. 108–9.

[5] This term was used by Max Weber. 'The natural leaders in distress have been holders of specific gifts of the body and spirit; and these gifts have been believed to be supernatural. . . .' H. H. Gerth and C. W. Mills, *From Max Weber: Essays in Sociology* (1947), p. 245.

ing to rules which have been promulgated by a recognized and accepted procedure. A major function of political philosophies is to provide formulae whereby power may be perceived as legitimate. Rapid changes in society, such as those which accompany industrialization, throw up new groups—both entrepreneurs and factory workers—who seek to influence the decision-making machinery. If a government is to retain legitimacy, and avoid revolution, ways must be found to allow such groups access to power by legitimate means. By extending the franchise to such new groups, states have managed to achieve a substantial degree of political integration among sections with diverse interests. The machinery of election, in fact, plays an important part in ensuring the legitimacy of government. It provides interest groups with a legitimate means for achieving their wants.[1] It is also possible that the monarchy plays an important part in providing stability and lending legitimacy to British governments.[2] The monarch may function as an emotional leader and thus ensure the continued legitimacy of governments even if the political leaders fail instrumentally. Indeed, legitimacy may be a more important determinant of stable government than effectiveness.[3]

But although British governments enjoy a high degree of legitimacy, this has been challenged by some minority groups on issues about which they feel strongly. The Committee of 100, for example sought to challenge the government's policy on nuclear defence by calculated violations of the law.[4]

POLITICAL PROCESSES

Political philosophers have long discussed both what are and what ought to be 'the functions of the state'. All but the philosophical anarchists would agree on the need for some organ to ensure the integration of the social system through the maintenance of law and order, relying on the ultimate sanction of force. Whatever differences there may be in views about how far the state ought to go beyond this, the fact remains that the modern state in advanced industrial societies has extended its functions far beyond that of integration. More recently, political scientists have returned to the question of the functions of the state, but from an empirical rather

[1] See S. M. Lipset, op. cit., Chapter 3, 'Social Conflict, Legitimacy and Democracy'.
[2] For a discussion of the monarchy, see E. Shils and M. Young, 'The Meaning of the Coronation', *Soc. Rev.*, Vol. 1, 1953, and the reply by N. Birnbaum, 'Monarch and Sociologists', ibid., Vol. 3, 1955.
[3] S. M. Lipset, op. cit., p. 109.
[4] R. Rose, op. cit. (1965), p. 218.

than a moral perspective. And it is this functionalist perspective which is resulting in a closer convergence between political science and sociology.

There is a variety of functional models, which view the political system as receiving inputs from the social system and processing these inputs in order to arrive at outputs in the shape of decisions and policies. The results of these in turn generate feed-back which provide fresh inputs to the system. Easton differentiates between two main types of inputs; demands and supports. Gabriel Almond has suggested that all political systems perform four input and three output functions. The three output functions—rule-making, rule-application and rule adjudication—have already been mentioned. The political system must also process four main inputs from the social system. Firstly, interest groups must make known their needs and feed them into the political system. This is *interest articulation* and is a function performed by pressure groups. Secondly, political systems must aggregate the various interests and needs of the social system and process these to produce coherent policies which will gain a wide measure of support. *Interest aggregation* is a major function of political parties which act as intermediates between voters and policy-makers. They function to process a wide variety of interest inputs into a relatively small number of policies. Thirdly, *political communication* is crucial to the processes of interest articulation, aggregation and governing. Finally, *political socialization and recruitment* contribute to the perpetuation of prevailing political ideologies, and the allocation of individuals to their roles in the political system.

An alternative approach to the study of politics has focused on the nature and role of elites. These are small groups who occupy key positions in society and exercise influence out of all proportion to their numbers. Indeed, some have argued that such concentrations of power are inevitable. A particularly influential variation of this approach is the theory of the ruling class whose control over the means of production establishes them as a self-perpetuating oligarchy controlling the machinery of the state in the pursuit of its own class interests. Elitist theories can, in fact, be used to support either a consensus or a conflict approach to politics. The conflict perspective stresses the key role of the propertied class and sees political recruitment as the crucial variable. It is the social origins of the leaders which explains political outcomes. The pluralists point to the proliferation of elites in advanced societies and to the distribution of influence among such competing elites.[1]

[1] For a review of elitist theories, see Geraint Parry, *Political Elites* (1969).

Interest articulation and pressure groups

The existence of demands within the social system is not by itself sufficient to ensure that they will be taken into account in the decision-making process. They must first become political issues. Demands may be generated by the experiences of individuals within any of the major sub-systems. Unwanted pregnancies may lead to a demand for changes in the law regulating contraception or abortion, or unhappy marriages to demands for changes in the marriage laws. Unemployment, job insecurity or poverty may generate demands for changes in the economic system, in the laws regulating relations between employers and employees, or in changes in the distribution of incomes. Some demands may originate from within the political system itself,[1] such as the demand for the extension of the francise to women or young voters. In order to become a political issue, such demands must become public and be fed into the political system. Pressure groups are one of the major mechanisms for this politicization process.

The term 'pressure group' is, however, not entirely satisfactory. The process of consultation between the government and the interests which its actions affect is very extensive and complex. As the functions of government have extended to include the regulation and promotion of a wide range of economic and cultural activities, the need for consultation has extended. This takes place through a wide variety of advisory councils specifically established by the government to offer advice on economic, social and cultural issues, such as the National Joint Advisory Council which includes representatives of the Federation of British Industries, and the TUC. In addition to such well-established machinery, other less formal channels of consultation exist whereby ministers and government officials consult the relevant interests involved in seeking information and views relevant to policy or legislation. Moreover, numerous organized interests from the AA to the Lord's Day Observance Society will seek to influence the process of decision-making through the various channels available. It would be preferable, therefore, to refer to 'group pressures' rather than to 'pressure groups, but the latter term is too firmly entrenched to be replaced.[2]

Interest groups may be divided into two main types. *Protective* groups defend some interest in society, such as trade unions and professional associations which protect the interests of their members. *Promotional* groups seek to promote a cause, such as the

[1] Easton suggests the term *withinputs* for such demands.
[2] J. D. Stewart, op. cit., pp. 8–10, outlines the complex network of consultation. This book also includes a detailed account of the various strategies for bringing pressure to bear to influence decisions.

167

Abortion Law Reform Society. Protective groups represent the interests of specific groups in society. By contrast, promotional groups may draw their membership from as wide a cross-section of the population as possible, and their representative character is difficult to establish. Moreover, not all interests are 'represented' by organized groups, and others are so large that they do not need organizations to present their case for them.[1]

It is not easy to assess the influence of such group pressures on government decisions. It is no longer argued, as was once the case, that pressure groups are by-passing parliamentary functions and threaten democratic processes.[2] No government department would now promote legislation or change policy without appropriate consultation with the interests affected. And this can best be done through those organizations which articulate and represent such interests. The party system will normally ensure that major interests are represented in the parliament, and we can expect the parties to reflect important political issues. On major issues, therefore, group pressures will be faced with party policies. The power of the party rests on a much wider basis than that of the pressure group and in arriving at a decision the minister through his party has authority to resist the group.[3] Governments have both the power and the resources to resist group pressures to consider its interests alone. However, over large areas there are no party viewpoints, and on such issues pressure groups may be more influential. A Minister of Agriculture will hear representations from the National Farmers' Union. In the absence of alternative views, there might be a tendency to act as though what was good for the farmers was good for agriculture.[4] But in spite of such dangers, interest groups perform essential functions in articulating interests and providing links between the political and social system. Stewart considers that, in fact, the British system achieves a satisfactory balance between taking account of sectional interests and taking decisions in the wider interests of society.[5]

Interest aggregation—political parties and voting
Pressure groups differ from political parties in that, unlike parties,

[1] See J. Blondel, *Voters, Parties and Leaders* (1963), pp. 160–7, for a discussion of the representative character of interest groups.

[2] On the role of pressure groups in the political process, see R. T. McKenzie, 'Parties, Pressure Groups and the British Political Process', in R. Rose (ed.), *Studies in British Politics* (1966), pp. 255–66.

[3] J. D. Stewart, op. cit., pp. 240–1.

[4] Ibid., p. 242.

[5] Ibid., p. 240. For studies of particular interest groups, see P. Self and H. Storing, *The State and the Farmer* (1962); H. Ekstein, *Pressure Group Politics* (1960); R. Rose (ed.), op. cit. (1966), pp. 220–54.

pressure groups do not exist in order to achieve political power. But parties, like pressure groups, function to ensure that interests are taken into account in the political process. Moreover, they represent a wide range of interests rather than any narrow sectional interest. No mass party could gain support unless it could convince a substantial section of the electorate that it would govern in their interests. In order to do this, it must aggregate as wide a range of interests as possible into broad policy issues. Parties function to aggregate such interests into alternative government policies.

Such cleavages are not necessarily a threat to the cohesion of society. Indeed, Lipset argues that some measure of cleavage is necessary for a stable democratic system in order to ensure 'that there will be a struggle over ruling positions, challenges to parties in power, and shifts of parties in office'.[1] The study of democracy, therefore, argues Lipset, requires us to focus on the sources of both cleavage and consensus. Without cleavages, there would be no struggle for power. But where cleavages run too deeply and divide too sharply, the possibilities of shifts of party preference and alternative governments would be remote. The party system and the electoral process provide the machinery for both the expression of interests and for their aggregation into alternative policies.

Studies of the relation between class membership and support for political parties in Britain provide evidence for the view that the major political parties do not reflect a hard and clear-cut cleavage of interests on class lines, although class factors obviously play an important part in attracting party support. The Conservative party, for example, attracts a sizable proportion of the working-class vote. No Conservative government would, in fact, ever be returned to power without such support, as the working-class vote represents about 70 per cent of the electorate. The Labour vote is more homogeneous, but even this includes about 8 per cent of top business executives. The middle ranges of the social hierarchy, in particular, divide between the two parties. About a quarter of the lower middle-class voting Labour and about one-third of the upper working-class voting Conservative.[2]

On a wide range of issues, there is no marked party cleavage. On humanitarian issues such as corporal punishment, and on foreign affairs such as nuclear disarmament and support for the United Nations, differences between Conservative and Labour voters are small. It is only on economic and social issues that cleavages

[1] S. M. Lipset, 'Political Sociology', in R. K. Merton et al., op. cit. See also S. M. Lipset, Political Man (1960).
[2] J. Blondel, op. cit., p. 57. See also John Bonham and F. M. Martin, 'Two Studies in the Middle-Class Vote', B.J.S., Vol 3, 3 September, 1952.

emerge. There are marked differences between supporters on attitudes towards raising the level of surtax and sympathy with workers on strike. But even here, there are many in the Conservative
party who adopt 'left' attitudes and in the Labour party who adopt
'right' views. Even on the surtax changes in 1961, 32 per cent of
Conservatives were opposed (compared with 67 per cent Labour).[1]
What is remarkable is not the difference but the consensus between
substantial numbers of both parties. It is this which makes possible
the shift of allegiance between parties and which forces parties to
compromise and to make concessions in order either to win or to
retain a majority.

Such evidence suggests that support for a party is not necessarily
support for all the items in its policies. Voting studies indicate that
voters are attracted by the general image of the party. This image
includes class elements. Part of the image of the Labour party
among its supporters is that it is 'for the working class'. But many
Labour supporters disagree with items of its policy, especially on
nationalization. However, issues are related to images. For many
Conservatives, for example, nationalization figures in their image
of the Labour party.[2] Nevertheless, the fact that voters support a
party for its image rather than for any specific item of policy[3] facilitates the task of the party in aggregating a variety of issues into a
coherent policy, and ensures continued support in the face of disagreements on specific issues.

Individuals are members of a variety of groups and occupy a
variety of statuses. Most are consequently subject to at least some
cross-pressures. But where pressures are aggregative, pushing all
in the same direction, they are likely to lead to sharp cleavages incapable of compromise. For many, such is not the case, and they
do not find themselves unequivocally attached to one party unable
to see any merit in the other. Where one issue, such as race or
religion becomes of overriding importance, then cleavage out-
weighs consensus and the social conditions favourable to democracy are absent.

The absence of alternative bases of cleavage in Britain results in
the relations between class and party being much closer than in
other advanced industrial societies, though not so in Ireland where

[1] J. Blondel, op. cit., pp. 75–9. See also Mark Abrams, 'Social Trends and
Electoral Behaviour', *B.J.S.*, Vol. 13, 3 September 1962. Surveys in 1949
showed much more marked cleavage.

[2] See J. Blondel, op. cit., pp. 81–4, and R. S. Milne and H. C. Mackenzie,
Marginal Seat (1958).

[3] A partial explanation of this is the very substantial influence of socialization in determining voting behaviour. Seventy-one per cent of those intending
to vote Conservative in 1960 were the sons of Conservative voters (M. Abrams,
op. cit., 1962, p. 238).

cleavages are on religious rather than class lines.[1] Approximately two-thirds of manual workers vote Labour. Moreover, manual workers who identify with the working class are more likely to vote Labour than those who think of themselves as middle class. And those who belong to trade unions are also stronger Labour voters.

The class-interest theory of voting which assumes such an association between class and party has led to attempts to explain working-class Tories as 'deviant' voters. The solidaristic traditional working class vote labour as an expression of their strong identification with the working class and with socialism. They see politics in class terms, and hold a dichotomous 'conflict' view of society as being divided into 'them' and 'us'. The working-class Tory may be a *deferential* who sees the upper classes as best fitted to rule and accepts an essentially aristocratic view of society and of his place in it. The *seculars*, by contrast, adopt an instrumental attitude towards politics and vote for the party which they think will best serve their interests.[2]

The view that it is the working-class Tory who is deviant has, however, been challenged by Parkin,[3] who argues on the contrary, that it is the working-class socialist who is deviating from the predominant conservative ideology mediated through the dominant institutional orders in British society. It is only where the worker is protected by encapsulating layers of working-class community with its close-knit kinship network and by large concentrations of industrial workers that a contrary ideology can emerge. But if the working-class Tory is problematic, so is the middle-class radical. However, a full examination of the basis of radicalism and dissent and the broader issue of political ideologies and beliefs will be taken up in the next chapter.[4]

Political socialization and communication
Underlying all political behaviour, there are deeply-rooted beliefs about equality, democracy, the monarchy—that is, political ideologies—which are the background against which more specific beliefs about party support are formed. Early political socialization plays a crucial role in shaping such beliefs. Those brought up in

[1] R. Rose, 'Class and Party Divisions: Britain, a Test Case', in *Sociology*, May 1968. For a comprehensive survey of voting behaviour, see D. Butler and D. Stokes, *Political Change in Britain*, 1969.

[2] R. T. McKenzie and A. Silver, *Angels in Marble* (1969); E. A. Nordlinger, *The Working-Class Tories* (1967).

[3] F. Parkin, 'Working-Class Conservatives', *B.J.S.*, September 1967.

[4] The nature of social classes, and theories of class change which have implications for politics will be explored in Chapter 7. In Chapter 5 we are concerned with political behaviour. And although political attitudes and beliefs are important, they cannot provide a total explanation of behaviour.

stable homegeneous working-class communities are much more likely to hold a conflict view of society and support the Labour party. Similarly, experiences during later adolescence, the formative years for crystallizing political beliefs, may have a life-long influence. The effects of political socialization through exposure to distinctive political cultures can be seen most clearly in regional differences in party support[1] and in the existence of distinctive political generations.[2] But we return to a fuller discussion of the factors shaping political beliefs in the next chapter.

Political communication is a two-way process. As we have seen, governments receive a variety of influences from organized interest groups. But since the extension of adult suffrage, governments are also concerned with the views of the less organized and articulate public, on whose electoral support they ultimately depend.

The development of various forms of mass communication have given rise to anxiety about their role in the process of political communication and socialization. As we have seen in Chapter 3 on education, the press is undoubtedly partisan.[3] But the general conclusion of investigations of mass communication in the political sphere confirms the conclusions of our earlier discussion, that the effects of the mass media are less than is frequently supposed. The one intensive study of the influence of television in an election campaign found that its effects were slight.[4] Audience research by the BBC similarly confirms that the impact of political broadcasts is greatly influenced by the predispositions of the viewers, whose evaluation of party broadcasts is closely related to party affiliations. Party identifications are formed by a lengthy process of political socialization rather than by the short-term processes of electoral communications.[5]

Rather less attention has been paid to the question of how far public opinion can influence politics. Modern polling techniques certainly enable governments to keep a finger on the pulse of public opinion. But the concept of 'public opinion' is vague. There is, in fact, a variety of publics and opinions, some informed and some not, and some whose views need to be weighed by governments and others which can be safely ignored. Nevertheless, there is a sense in which there can be said to be a' climate of opinion', which is

[1] S. Cotgrove and C. Vamplew, 'Technology, Class and Politics: The Case of the Process Workers', *Sociology*, May 1972.

[2] D. Butler and D. Stokes, op. cit., Chapter 3.

[3] See also R. Rose (ed.), op. cit. (1966), pp. 161–90, for a discussion of the press and politics.

[4] J. Trenaman and D. McQuail, *Television and the Political Image* (1961).

[5] R. Rose (ed.), op. cit. (1966), 'The 1964 General Election on Television', pp. 191–8.

some indication of what the public will stand for, rather than a pressure for some particular measure to which governments must respond.[1]

Political recruitment, elites, ruling class

The social origins of political leaders has been a major preoccupation of sociologists.[2] Much of this interest stems from Marx's notion of the existence of a ruling class, and assumes a conflict theory of politics. The 'ruling class' perspective assumes that the social origins of political leaders is a primary factor determining their decisions which flow mainly from their self-interests. It follows that fundamental changes in power can only be made by changing the incumbents of power positions.[3] Such a view is challenged by those who emphasize that the important issue is *access* to power rather than the composition of the political elite.

The notion of a *ruling class* implies that an economic class rules politically. For Marx,[4] it was the newly emerging class of capitalists, owning and controlling the productive property of society, who not only controlled the machinery of government, but also shaped the ideas of the times. In other words, one class, the bourgeoisie, dominated the total society, including the state, which it used for its own ends.

This is a view which raises the whole question of the relations between property and power, and, indeed, the sources of power itself. The state monopolizes the coercive means of power by its control of the police and the army. Power may also be exercised by the manipulation of material rewards; by conferring or withholding rights to enjoy incomes, and property of various kinds. The manipulation of material rewards is, in fact, an extremely powerful means of influencing and controlling the conduct of others. To withhold shelter and, above all, adequate food is comparable to physical coercion in achieving compliance.

Those who exercised political power in the nineteenth century were certainly men of property. The political elite was drawn al-

[1] R. Rose (ed.), op. cit. (1966), p. 154, See also R. Rose, *Politics in England* (1958), Chapter 8.

[2] For a summary of the literature, see T. B. Bottomore, *Elites and Society* (1964).

[3] S. M. Lipset, in R. K. Merton *et al.*, op. cit., pp. 106–7.

[4] It is by no means clear either from the writing of Marx or from those who have followed him, precisely who are the members of the ruling class. It has been used to include all those having decision-making powers in society, families and individuals whose control of the means of production allows them to dominate society, those linked by property, kinship and inheritance who also govern, or simply the group of capitalist producers. See S. Keller, *Beyond the Ruling Class* (1963), pp. 47–54.

most entirely from the property-owning class of land-owners.[1] But the view that their power derived from property can be challenged. On the contrary, it can be argued, property depends on power. As we have seen in Chapter 4, property can be defined as a bundle of legally enforceable rights over persons and things.[2] These may include the rights of sale, bequest and exclusive use, or only relatively limited rights may be enjoyed, such as the right to use a post-office telephone or to the labour of an individual between fixed hours. Now only those rights which are ultimately enforceable in the courts can be exercised against opposition. And the decisions of the courts are, in the last analysis, enforceable by the coercive means of the state. Property is, in fact, a bundle of powers. It is force which upholds such powers. Property can be seized by force, by conquest or by political revolution. According to this view, it is power, not property, which is the basic issue.[3]

Nevertheless, studies of the social origins of the political elite demonstrates the close connection in the nineteenth century between property and power (Table 5.1). Men of property used the machinery of government to strengthen the powers of property and to confer substantial rights and protection on the property

TABLE 5.1

CLASS STRUCTURE OF CABINETS 1935–55*

	1886–1916		1935–55	
	Cons.	Lib.	Cons.	Lab.
Aristocracy	26	23	20	1
Middle class	21	28	40	14
Working class	—	2	2	19

* Compiled from W. L. Guttsmann, op. cit., p. 79.

owner. Moreover, the man of property was able to extend his power over things to power over people. The factory owner, for example, was able to exercise extensive power over those who depended on him for work as the sole source of income for the necessities of life. Furthermore, the law protected factory owners from countervailing measures by its restrictions on the rights of workers to organize and to strike. Thus the law served to enforce and under-pin the powers of property, and in this way, political power provided the basis for economic power.

But the gradual extension of the franchise has conferred political power on the property-less and increased the autonomy of the

---

[1] W. Guttsmann, *The British Political Elite* (1963).

[2] 'Things' include intangibles such as patents in inventions, copyright, etc.

[3] This view is supported by R. Dahrendorf, *Class and Class Conflict in Industrial Society* (1959).

political system. Studies of the social origins of the political elites in Britain shows that since the beginning of the nineteenth century, and until the 1950s there has been a gradual increase in the numbers of first, middle-class and then, working-class members of the Cabinet. During the Labour administration of 1929, 67 per cent of the Cabinet were of working-class origin. However, in 1964, only 26 per cent, and in 1967, 9 per cent of the Labour Cabinet had working-class origins[1]—an issue to which we return later. During periods of Conservative rule, it remains true that the majority of

TABLE 5.2

EDUCATION AND OCCUPATION OF THE POLITICAL ELITE: CABINET MINISTERS
1916–55*

	Cons. %	Lab. %
Education		
Elementary	4	51
Grammar	18	18
Eton	32	5
Major public schools	33	15
Other	13	11
	100	100
Occupation		
Land-owning, rentier	35	8
Civil service, professions	43	38
Commerce and industry (entrepreneurs)	14	6
Manual workers and TU officials		46
Others	8	2
	100	100
	(N = 100)	(N = 65)

* Compiled from W. C. Guttsman, op. cit., pp. 106–7.

the Cabinet are drawn from the few exclusive public schools and attended Oxford or Cambridge. In the 1959 House of Commons, 103 Conservative members were directors, manufacturers, landowners and farmers, compared with twelve on the Labour side. The close association between property and Conservative governments in Britain can be interpreted to support the argument that it is power, not property, which is decisive. It is only through the political machinery that the propertied can protect their interests. The loss of political power faces them with the possibility of the restriction of property rights, and the redistribution of wealth and income.

[1] R. Rose, 'Class and Party Divisions: Britain, a Test Case', *Sociology*, May 1968.

The notion of *elites* has been used by many who criticize or reject Marx's theory of a ruling class. It implies the existence of individuals and groups who occupy dominant positions in a particular sphere by virtue of their qualities of excellence relevant to their functioning. In addition to political elites, therefore, there are religious, scientific, intellectual, managerial elites. Indeed, the number of elites will depend on the social system. The growth of division of labour and occupational specialization, and of formal organization will result in the multiplication of elites. They are, that is to say, a function of the increasing structural differentiation of society.

It is such elites, it is argued, particularly those who perform key roles, who are evolving out of earlier core groups, such as aristocracies and ruling classes, as structural alternatives to ruling classes, 'representing a more specialized and advanced form of social leadership'.[1] Their task is to perform the various specialized functions in society, such as production, artistic creation and intellectual advancement. Increasingly, 'the political, economic, scientific, religious, educational, cultural and recreational sectors are organizationally, occupationally and morally autonomous'. And it is the leaders in these spheres who constitute the increasingly differentiated *strategic elites* of advanced societies. The task of the political elite is rather to act as honest broker in a plural society in which there is mutual interaction between elites. Governments, that is to say, are weak rather than strong. The task of political leaders is to steer a hazardous path between conflicting factions.

Different societies, however, will face different problems. In some societies, the primary problem is integration and the achievement of consensus. Such tasks occupy governments in totalitarian societies and are reflected in the strategies they adopt. Advanced industrial societies, however, it is argued, are primarily preoccupied with goal attainment—specifically with maximizing production and with raising the standard of living as rapidly as possible. Such a task requires the co-ordination of the inputs from a number of specialist elite groups. The economic elite are primarily concerned with the application and allocation of means (adaptive function), but in this they depend heavily on the intellectual elite such as scientists and innovators. In addition to elites primarily concerned with instrumental functions such as adaptation and goal attainment, other elites perform primarily expressive and symbolic functions—ecclesiastical dignitaries exhorting drivers not to drink and drive or workers to work harder.

Furthermore, we can observe that such functions may be variously distributed among the elements in a social system. In the

[1] S. Keller, op. cit.

past, they have been performed by single individuals or groups of individuals, such as the priest-king who functions both as warrior and moral leader. In feudal societies, a land-owning stratum both organizes the economy, exercises political functions, and maintains internal order and defence. In advanced societies, such roles become differentiated and specialized, resulting in the emergence of specialized elites who each contribute to the maintenance of the social system.[1]

In a society which emphasizes the maximizing of consumption, elites concerned with the instrumental function of goal attainment and adaptation (i.e. the polity and the economy) occupy strategic positions. But no one elite can occupy a predominant position, uninfluenced by pressures from others. Industrialists are preoccupied with production, but politicians are concerned with allocating resources and products for the achievement of societal goals in response to pressures from consumers and workers.[2] It is politicians who make the ultimate decisions on goals, but they do so in response to electoral pressures, and must achieve the compliance of producers in their plans. In other words, we have a pluralist society in which a number of elites and interests exert influence on the decision-makers.

What is not clear is precisely how these elites are related to the political system. Keller argues that the task of the strategic elites is to 'co-ordinate and harmonize the diversified activities, combat factionalism, and resolve group conflicts. And they try to protect the community from external danger.' It is difficult to see how the elites which, according to her argument, are increasingly autonomous, are able to perform this integrating function. While it is clear that each may exercise influence, and in this sense no one elite is all-powerful, it is still possible to argue that some elites are more powerful than others. However, their political function appears to be mainly that of pressure groups, articulating interests and influencing the political process. Strategic elites have not usurped the functions of government. This would be to confuse influence with government.

[1] S. Keller, op. cit.
[2] The fact that such distribution may be left to market forces does not change the essential argument. This is itself a political decision. According to Parsons, the political system is primarily concerned with goal attainment. It is the political system which must make ultimate decisions on the allocation of resources. For this reason, Parsons includes in the polity banking and finance which exercise control over purchasing power. If such decisions are largely influenced by pressures from industrialists, this does not change the basic argument. The economy is primarily concerned with the adaptive function—with producing means in the form of goods and income. See M. Black, *The Theories of Talcott Parsens* (1961), pp. 124–6.

C. W. Mills[1] is more decisive in attributing a dominant position to three elites who together constitute what he calls the *power elite*. He argues that the power elite comprises a close association between the heads of business corporations, the top military and the political elite. The top men in all three areas, he argues, are drawn from the same predominantly upper stratum in society, share the same values and outlooks and pursue the same interests. Membership of these elites is freely interchanged, with generals becoming members of the political administration and politicians being appointed to top posts in the industrial corporations. There is, that is to say, consensus among the members of the power elite rather than a conspiracy to build structural links between property and politics. It is difficult to see how Mills's[2] use of the concept of a power elite differs greatly from the notion of a ruling class. He stresses the unity of the elite and its common origins from the upper classes. But it is not at all clear why the power elite constitutes one elite and not three.[3] Mills makes an important distinction between levels of power. While politicians deal with intermediate issues, the power elite takes the big decisions, while the masses are powerless.[4] Most, however, who have argued in favour of the idea of elites have rejected the view that the various elites constitute a cohesive group. A recent study,[5] for example, concludes that the various elites in British society constitute a cluster of interlocking circles, each largely preoccupied with its own interests, and each group acting as a check on the others.

These various views on the significance of political recruitment are potentially testable. The cruder forms of a ruling-class model are hardly defensible. What is problematic is the relative influence of various interests under different political systems. And this could be expected to show itself in policy outcomes. All governments, for example, must take some account of pressures towards equality. It is such policy outcomes which could be expected to reflect the class composition of governments—a topic which is taken up in Chapter 7.

Governmental processes
The study of political recruitment has unavoidably involved us in some discussion of governmental processes as distinct from politi-

[1] C. W. Mills, *The Power Elite* (1956).
[2] C. W. Mills, op. cit.
[3] T. B. Bottomore, op. cit.
[4] Some empirical studies which have taken a pluralist position, such as R. Dahl, *Who Governs* (1963), have investigated specific local communities, and are not, therefore, concerned with the level of power discussed by Mills.
[5] A. Sampson, *Anatomy of Britain Today* (1965). See T. B. Bottomore, op. cit., for a summary of the various elitist theories.

cal processes. An examination of the social origins of the political elite has frequently assumed that such data enables us to draw conclusions about the exercise of power—about who takes decisions and enforces them. The pluralists have countered the ruling-class model by arguing that a variety of elites participates in the decision-making process. But by so doing, they have blurred the distinction between the political processes of the articulation of interests, the exercise of influence, and the governmental functions of taking and enforcing decisions. The model adopted in this chapter underlines the importance of distinguishing between influencing political decisions and taking and enforcing them. The presence of industrialists or land-owners in the political elite, therefore, tells us something about the channels of access between social groups and the government and indicates the kind of influences and interests to which the government is particularly exposed. But the model also stresses that in making policy, governments have to process a variety of inputs from a large number of interests. Moreover, where periodic elections determine who makes political decisions, the incumbents of such roles must act in ways which meet the interests of a substantial section of the electorate if they are to continue to enjoy its support.

In democratic societies, the governmental functions of rule-making, rule-application and rule-adjudication are in theory roughly divided among separate agencies. But the separation of functions is not complete. Both the administration and the judiciary have limited rule-making functions. Governmental structures are, to a limited extent, multi-functional. Some societies, such as the United States, have sought to place limits on the concentration of governmental powers by its doctrine of the separation of powers and the incorporation of checks and balances whereby the courts can exercise some control over the rule-making function by declaring acts unconstitutional. This existence of distinctive structures and the distribution of functions among distinct structures matches the differentiation of structure and function in the political system, in which interest articulation is primarily performed by interest groups and parties, and interest aggregation is performed by parties and Parliament.

Duverge[1] shows that the structure of government is profoundly influenced by the party system. In a single-party system, there is marked concentration of powers even where the constitution specifically provides for the separation of powers. In a single-party system, executive and legislative are constitutional facades: the party alone exercises power. Duverger argues that even in a two-party system, as in Great Britain, a similar situation exists. 'In

[1] M. Duverger, op. cit.

179

practice, the existence of majority government transforms the constitutional pattern from top to bottom. The party holds in its own hands the essential prerogatives of the Legislature and the Executive. Government posts are in the hands of its leaders ... draft Bills are prepared by the party's research groups, tabled in its name by a party representative in the House, voted by the party parliamentary group, and applied by the party government. Parliament and government are like two machines driven by the same motor, the party. ... The single-party and the two-party systems differ radically on the limitation of power and the existence of an opposition; they are very close as far as concerns the separation of powers, or rather their concentrations.'[1] Other factors, of course, influence the separation of powers, the concentration being greater in a parliamentary system, such as Great Britain, than in a presidential system, such as the USA, especially when in the latter, congress and the president represent different parties.

The view that in a single-party system the party alone exercises power is somewhat misleading if it implies that the party ignores interests and pressures. In the USSR, for example, it has maintained a dominant position in the political structure, but its relative influence has fluctuated. Under Stalin, the influence of the party declined and that of the state apparatus increased.[2] The dominant role of the party is ensured in part by the diffuse boundaries between the political system and other institutions. The party appoints key posts in the trade unions, cultural and intellectual associations as well as in the state apparatus and thus ensures the interpenetration between the party and key structures. The party in this way functions as the focus for the articulation and aggregation of interests and thus ensures its continuing support. Of course, there are factions and these tend to be more concealed than in Western-type democracies. And with the absence of organized interest groups, the party plays a larger role in interest articulation and aggregation. The greater reliance on coercion for achieving compliance may be an indication of the greater strain to which such a system is subjected.[3]

The internal structure of the parties is a further factor. In Great Britain, discipline, centralization and cohesion are more developed in the Labour party than in the Conservative party, and hence there is a greater concentration of power under a Labour administration. The size of the majority in office also influences the separation of powers. Where the majority is small, parliament regains its importance.[4]

[1] M. Duverger, op. cit., p. 394.
[2] D. Lane, *Politics and Society in the USSR* (1970), Chapters 7 and 8.
[3] Ibid., p. 259.
[4] Duverger, op. cit., p. 400.

Multi-party systems, by contrast, tend towards the separation of powers. The government depends on the stability of alliances and is constantly threatened by a parliamentary vote of no confidence.[1]

It can be seen that societies differ considerably in the distribution of governmental processes. An extreme example is where one or a few structural elements dominate in the performance of not only governmental but also political functions. Pakistan, for example, can be described as a 'modernizing oligarchy', in which the executive and the army together dominate in the performance of both political and governmental processes, and in which parliament does not function. Pakistan is deeply divided by internal cleavages deriving from linguistic, cultural and religious differences. Under such circumstances, it is the executive and the army which aggregate interests and make and enforce rules.[2]

POLITICAL SYSTEMS AND SOCIAL CHANGE

Two main views are currently debated among sociologists about political trends in industrially advanced societies. The first, exemplified by Lipset's 'Political Man', argues that the same convergence of factors produced both democracy and capitalism. Protestantism favoured both the development of capitalism, and the emergence of democratic values through its emphasis on individual responsibility. The growth of a burgher class and its alignment with the monarchy extended the acceptance of democracy among the conservative strata. The second theory, the 'mass society' theme, is concerned rather with trends in fully developed industrial societies. It argues that such societies generate conditions which may lead to the emergence of totalitarian states.[3]

[1] Ibid., pp. 408–9.
[2] G. A. Almond and J. S. Coleman, op. cit., pp. 572–3. See pp. 52–8 for a more detailed discussion of types of governmental and political systems. For an analysis of the role of the military in emerging states, see M. Janowitz, *The Military in the Political Development of New Nations* (1964). The role of the military in the power structure of society has been largely ignored by sociologists partly perhaps because the military in Western societies has been subordinated to civilian control and has not functioned as a contender for power. However, in the newly emerging states, the military is playing a much more decisive role. Its officers are drawn from an educated stratum, are closely in touch with modern technology, and control an efficient organization and communication system. Moreover, in many states, the army provides an opportunity for a new elite to form, recruited mainly from the middle strata of society. It would not be surprising, therefore, to find them aligned against the traditional land-owning stratum and favouring industrialization and more radical land reforms.
[3] See, for example, W. Kornhauser, *The Politics of Mass Society* (1960), for an analysis and critique of this theme.

In a comparative study of a large number of states, Lipset has attempted to isolate those variables which are associated with 'stable democracy'. He finds that the stable democracies include those societies which are industrially advanced and which are characterized by high standards of living and high levels of literacy. They are also societies in which most own radios and large numbers of newspapers are read. Although a number of factors interrelated with industrialization seem to hang together in a cluster, the causal links between such factors and political democracy are more speculative. It is reasonable to suppose that the more affluent societies provide a higher level of satisfaction of needs and do not breed the discontents which are generated by poverty and hunger. Moreover, they possess a more elaborate machinery for producing consensus. The schools, the radio and the press all contribute to the socialization process through the transmission of a common culture. And although minority and deviant opinions may be allowed expression through such media, all societies limit the expression of dissent. For example, in the USA, communist doctrines, and in the USSR capitalist doctrines, are excluded from the normal channels for the dissemination of views and opinions, thus contributing in both societies to a measure of ideological consensus. But it is important to note that some industrially advanced societies such as Germany had not achieved stable democracies during the first half of this century.

The 'mass society' theme argues that industrialization leads to the alienation of individuals from primary group structures, that is, to the atomization of the social structure. Mass society in this sense is particularly vulnerable to totalitarian movements. Kornhauser challenges the view that modern societies all exhibit like tendencies to develop the characteristics of mass society. Moreover, he maintains that mass society is analytically distinct from a totalitarian society.

Both totalitarian and mass societies are characterized by atomized masses. But they differ in the vulnerability of elites to influence. The disruption of primary group ties through sudden and extensive changes in the social structure caused by widespread unemployment or military defeat are among the factors favouring the atomization of populations—one of the ingredients of totalitarianism.

It follows from Kornhauser's analysis that an essential condition for a liberal democracy is the existence of a number of autonomous secondary associations which reduces the vulnerability of individuals to elites. In other words, it is to the pluralist type of society to which Kornhauser turns as a protection against any trend towards totalitarianism. 'In summary, a liberal democracy requires widespread participation in the selection of leaders, and a large amount of self-governing activity on the part of non-elites. It also requires competition among leaders and would-be leaders, and considerably autonomy for those who win positions of leadership.'[1] It follows that Kornhauser believes that a plural society offers the most favourable conditions for democracy. In seventeenth-century England, for example, a variety of class and religious groups were developing. And it is in the highly industrialized and urbanized societies that pluralism and democracy are strongest.

One possible threat to pluralism is the growth of large-scale corporations which transform the middle-class from property-owning independent entrepreneurs to corporation employees. The threat to autonomy is seen in the inclusiveness of the organization which demands the individual's total allegiance.[2] On the other hand, Kornhauser points to the emergence of new middle-class associations such as the professions and their high rates of participation in voluntary associations.

In short, Kornhauser argues that conditions in industrial society make possible both increased alienation and opportunities for the formation of new associational ties. Clearly, these are matters of continuing debate and will be the object of further studies. Moreover, the very knowledge of the vulnerability of industrial society to develop mass society characteristics may lead to countervailing measures. For example, anxiety about the possible consequences of mass communications has led to a substantial volume of research in the USA.[3] One result of these researches, as we saw in Chapter 3, has been in the rediscovery of the primary group and a challenge to the view that mass media operate on atomized individuals. The prevailing view is rather that communication takes place through primary group structures and that the content of mass communication is mediated via opinion leaders in a group context.[4]

There is, however, growing evidence in Britain that the involvement of the working-class in political structures and processes may be declining. We have already referred to the dramatic drop in working-class membership of recent Labour Cabinets. There has also been a decline in working-class Members of Parliament

[1] W. Kornhauser, op. cit.

[2] W. H. Whyte, *Organization Man* (1957).

[3] For a summary of this evidence and a detailed discussion of mass culture and mass society, see Leon Bramson, *The Political Context of Sociology* (1961), Chapters 2, 5 and 6.

[4] One further topic related to political trends is the 'end of ideology' theme. This will be examined in the next chapter.

in the post-war period to only 36 per cent.[1] Furthermore, there is evidence that at the grassroots level, local councillors and party activists are increasingly likely to be middle class. Hindess argues that there has, in fact, been a marked decline in the 1960s in working-class influence and involvement with the result that the policies of the main parties are converging and the working class are becoming politically isolated. This may challenge the legitimacy of political institutions and encourage direct action outside the institutional machinery.[2]

DISCUSSION

The weight of the evidence surveyed in this chapter would at first sight seem to support the functionalist approach with its emphasis on weak governments acting as honest brokers between conflicting interests. It is not possible, for example, to make a very strong case from the data available for the management of consensus through the manipulation of an atomistic mass society. Moreover, a systems model has proved to be useful for analysing political processes in one-party states. Here too, conflicting interests must be taken into account, though perhaps to a lesser degree, in the aggregation of issues into policies. Governments may not achieve consensus, but they seek to minimize conflict.

On the other hand, evidence on voting behaviour gives some support to the view that the emergence of radical perspectives is kept in check by the dominant institutions of society. Moreover, there is some evidence that the composition of governments *does* influence policy outcomes. It will be argued in the next chapter that middle-class radicalism is in fact class-related and does not constitute any fundamental ideogical challenge to the class structure. And in Chapter 7, data will be presented to suggest that the decline of working-class influence in politics has been accompanied by a shift towards greater inequality. Furthermore, the widespread acceptance of status systems legitimizing power and privilege may account for the remarkable persistence of inequality.

A ruling-class model of politics in Western democracies by which a small propertied elite exerts a major influence does not imply the absence of influence and bargaining. But the relative influence of various interests on political outcomes, and the relation of this to such variables as the composition of governments and electoral systems are issues deserving more empirical research.

[1] R. Rose, op. cit. (1968), p. 131.
[2] Barry Hindess, *The Decline of Working-Class Politics* (1971).

G. A. Almond and James S. Coleman, *The Politics of the Developing Areas* (Princeton University Press, 1960), especially the Introduction and Conclusion.

G. A. Almond and S. Verba, *The Civic Culture: Political Attitudes and Democracy in Five Nations* (Princeton University Press, 1963).

W. Barrington-Moore, *The Social Origins of Dictatorship and Democracy* (Beacon Press, 1966).

S. H. Beer, *Modern British Politics: A Study of Parties and Pressure Groups* (Faber, 1965).

J. Blondel, *Voters, Parties and Leaders* (Pelican Books, 1963).

T. B. Bottomore, *Elites and Society* (Watts, 1964).

D. Butler and D. Stokes, *Political Change in Britain* (Macmillan, 1969).

R. E. Dowse and J. A. Hughes, *Political Sociology* (Wiley, 1972).

M. Duverger, *Political Parties* (Allen and Unwin, 1959).

J. H. Goldthorpe, D. Lockwood, F. Bechoffer and J. Platt, *The Affluent Manual Worker: Political Attitudes and Behaviour* (Cambridge University Press, 1968).

W. L. Guttsman, *The British Political Elite* (MacGibbon and Kee, 1963).

B. Hindess, *The Decline of Working-Class Politics* (MacGibbon and Kee, 1971).

H. Hyman, *Political Socialization* (Free Press, 1959).

S. M. Lipset, *Political Man* (Doubleday, 1969).

R. T. McKenzie, *British Political Parties* (Heinemann, 1964).

R. T. McKenzie and A. Silver, *Angels in Marble* (Heinemann, 1968).

W. Kornhauser, *The Politics of Mass Society* (Free Press, 1960).

D. Lane, *Politics and Society in the USSR* (Weidenfeld and Nicolson, 1970).

E. A. Nordlinger, *The Working-Class Tories* (MacGibbon and Kee, 1967).

E. A. Nordlinger (ed.), *Politics and Society: Studies in Comparative Political Sociology* (Prentice-Hall, 1970).

F. Parkin, *Middle-Class Radicalism* (Manchester University Press, 1968).

G. Parry, *Political Elites* (Allen and Unwin, 1969).

A. Pizzorno (ed.), *Political Sociology* (Penguin, 1971).

R. Rose, *Politics in England* (Faber, 1965).

R. Rose, *Studies in British Politics: A Reader in Political Sociology* (Macmillan, 1966).

J. Urry and J. Wakeford, *Power in Britain* (Heinemann, 1973).

Chapter 6

CULTURE AND SOCIETY

Beliefs about how to do things, and what things we ought to do are essential for any action. And most of us need some kind of an answer to the problems that life poses. Such beliefs influence the way in which an individual perceives and defines a situation, its meaning for him, and guide his selection of alternative actions. At the level of society, shared beliefs about which goals are most worth pursuing and how they ought to be pursued may serve to integrate the behaviour of large numbers of individuals.[1] But beliefs such as revolutionary ideologies may also provide new definitions of reality and act as levers of social change.

Whatever differences there may be among sociologists about the integrating functions of beliefs, there would be widespread support for the view that there is a very important sense in which beliefs of all kinds are socially determined. Contributors to the sociology of knowledge would agree that intellectual products, from science to religion, are socially conditioned and transmitted. They would, however, differ in their more detailed explanations of the social determination of knowledge and the functions of belief systems. Those who have followed the Durkheimian tradition have treated knowledge as a symbolic representation of social reality, whereas the Marxist approach has stressed the influence of the interests of various social groups, and in this sense, sees beliefs as a distortion of reality in the interests of a dominant stratum.

Types of intellectual products
How can we differentiate between religion, magic, science and political ideologies? One way in which they differ is the extent to which they are capable of empirical verification.[2] The statement 'Longer prison sentences would soon put a stop to drunkenness on the roads' has reference to empirical things, 'prison sentences' and 'drunkenness', and the relation between them. The proposition

[1] The relation between beliefs and behaviour *is* problematic—as has been frequently stressed. It is being argued only that beliefs are key variables in any explanation of social action.
[2] Such distinctions raise complex philosophical questions about the nature and meaning of propositions. The classification being put forward here claims only to be useful for sociological analysis.

'God is love' does not have such empirical references and is not capable of verification. A second distinction is between beliefs which refer to what things are and how to achieve ends, and beliefs about values. The belief that divorce is wrong is about values. It prescribes how we and others ought to behave. These two distinctions are related. Our belief that divorce is wrong may rest on empirically verifiable propositions, such as its consequences for the welfare of children. Or it may be essentially non-verifiable, such as when a person appeals to conscience and says 'I just know inside me that it is wrong.' We have, then, four main types of belief (Figure 6.1) according to whether they are empirical or non-empirical and cognitive or evaluative.

In practice, belief systems cannot be neatly categorized in this way. Thus a religion may include theological beliefs about the nature of God which cannot be verified, and beliefs about values and morality. It may also include elements of magical and meta-

FIGURE 6.1

TYPES OF BELIEFS

	Cognitive	Evaluative
Empirical	Science Technology	Secular ethics
Non-empirical	Theology Magic	Religious morality

physical beliefs. It may even include beliefs about naturalistic phenomena such as whether the earth is round and the causes of illness. For most purposes of analysis, it is sufficient to arrange belief systems along a continuum according to the extent to which they rest on empirical data. At one end we would have theology and metaphysics, and at the other science and technology.

In many ways it would be more consistent if we spoke of the sociology of culture, since we are interested in all intellectual products including art forms. *Belief systems* are only one component, though a very important one, of culture. The term 'system' stresses the fact that we are now looking at complex wholes, not simply collections of isolated beliefs. Religious beliefs, for example, constitute a system in the sense that they are interrelated. They have a certain internal logical consistency. Indeed, it is this characteristic of closed belief systems which goes some way to explain their resistance to change. No single element stands on its own in isolation but is buttressed by the logical support it receives from other elements. The same can be said of other systems such as political ideologies, or science. The belief in God as creator and architect of the universe, original sin, predestination and hell—all hang together. Remove any element in this system and the fabric of interwoven ideas is weakened.

Recently, interest has extended beyond such more systematized intellectual products to a study of 'everything that passes for knowledge', that is, of the-world-taken-for-granted—the knowledge, axioms and assumptions which are the basis for everyday living. '. . . only a few are concerned with the theoretical interpretation of the world, but everybody lives in a world of some sort.'[1] It is the content and source of this 'social construction of reality' which is the focus of much current study.

Existential bases of knowledge
It is from society, of course, that we derive our construction of reality, and the symbols (language, concepts) which are the vehicles of our understanding. The dominant form of religious belief in England is the Anglican version of Christianity; in the Arab world it is the variety of Islamic faiths. But this does not explain the distribution of beliefs or their origins. It does not explain, for example, why some sections of society support salvationist or millennial religious beliefs. Marx argued that men's beliefs reflected their material conditions and experiences, and these in turn were the result of their roles in society and above all their role in the economic system. But although he took a broadly determinist position, Marx recognized the great complexity of the problem, and that ideologies do not stem in any simple way from a person's objective location in society. He recognized, for example, that some members of the proletariat accept the ideology of the bourgeoisie—a phenomenon that Engels described as 'false class consciousness'. He also recognized that ideas once born have a certain autonomy and may persist in a society long after the material circumstances from which they have derived have changed.

Sociologists such as Mannheim and Merton[2] have developed rather more sophisticated theories of the variables which have to be taken into account in exploring the relations between belief systems and social systems. A possible theoretical approach can be summarized in Figure 6.2. In exploring the beliefs held by any group of individuals in society we can start from the assumption that they are likely to be related to the needs of the individual. That is to say, beliefs enable individuals to adapt to the situation in which they find themselves, providing some kind of an orientation to life by answering such questions as 'Who am I?' 'What

[1] P. L. Berger and T. Luckmann, *The Social Construction of Reality* (1967), p. 27.
[2] R. K. Merton, *Essays in Social Theory and Social Structure* (1957).

ought I to do?' and giving meaning to experiences. We can secondly explore the extent to which the beliefs of individuals are related to their roles in the social structure. Individuals who experience severe deprivations or frustrations, for example, will seek symbolic means of interpreting such a situation in a meaningful way. It would not be surprising to find them supporting beliefs in a life-hereafter, or in the imminent coming of the millennium in which

FIGURE 6.2

BELIEFS AND THE SOCIAL SYSTEM

Social structure	Culture
Economic system	
Political system	
Religious system	Cognitive beliefs
Kinship system	
Educational system	Evaluative beliefs

Types of individuals
Beliefs ⟷ needs

their sufferings would be rewarded. And finally existing beliefs derived from culture will influence the way in which experiences will be perceived, and interpreted. No one starts from scratch in finding answers to life's problems. He can select from the beliefs which are available from those which come closest to his needs and experiences, and will be motivated to search for new beliefs if none enable him to discover meaning and to adapt to his situation.

This model tentatively suggests that individuals are the intervening variable between culture and the social structure. The individual inherits the shared beliefs of his society through the socialization process. He retains those which are congruent with his experiences and searches for others to meet his needs. These include those needs which are organically determined such as those resulting from illness as well as the socially determined needs which derive from his social roles as husband, worker and voter.

RELIGION

Religions are systems of beliefs which include a number of elements. But their essential feature is that these beliefs cluster around a core belief in the supra-natural—in phenomena which cannot be explained in naturalistic (empirical) terms. Usually the supra-natural phenomen is thought of in personal terms, whether as spirits and demons, or the almost metaphysical notion of

189

'personality as the ground and being of existence' held by some contemporary theologians.

It is not surprising that the role of religion in social systems has long occupied the attention of sociologists, and a brief glance at some major theories can help clarify sociological perspectives on this subject.[1] Pareto's contribution represented a particularly important development of the prevailing positivist view which treated the individual actor's orientation to his environment as essentially cognitive and rational. The positivists had been aware of the fact that men might deviate from action guided by facts and logic through ignorance or faulty reasoning.[2] Pareto drew attention to a second important class of non-logical actions—those which were incapable of being tested by scientific procedures. It is precisely this type of orientation which characterizes religious ideas and beliefs. Religious behaviour is essentially non-logical, and expresses deeply rooted sentiments.[3]

A further important development in our understanding of the role of rational (empirically verifiable) and non-rational beliefs emerged in the study of religion and magic among the Trobriand Islanders by Malinowski. He showed that activities such as deep-sea fishing and canoe building were guided by a body of sound empirical knowledge and that behaviour was rationally guided by such knowledge. But side-by-side with such knowledge and action, there existed a second set of magical beliefs and practices. These beliefs related to the occurrence of uncertainty, to outcomes beyond rational control and explanation, such as bad weather, or inexplicable crop failure.

The function of magic is therefore distinct from that of science and technology and should not be treated as a kind of primitive science. Even in advanced industrial societies, 'magical' actions are common. Magic steps in to provide us with a means of adaptation to a situation when empirical means have failed or are inadequate.[4] We cannot be absolutely certain that the pilot will take off successfully, or that we can undertake a journey in safety. We can be even less certain that we can survive a battle. So we carry a talisman for luck, or say a prayer—just in case the servicing of the plane and the take-off drill of the pilot, for example, let us down. Magic, that

[1] See T. Parsons, *Essays in Sociological Theory* (1954), Chapter 10, for a summary.

[2] Pareto referred to such 'pseudo-scientific' actions as *derivations*.

[3] The precise nature of such sentiments is not clear. Pareto was content to classify the variety of non-logical actions into a number of residual categories or residues.

[4] In all societies, the fact of death is something in the face of which we are helpless. And in all societies, as Parsons has pointed out, burial involves actions which go beyond the mere utilitarian disposal of the corpse.

is to say, is essentially an expressive action, providing an outlet for frustrations and pent-up emotions in the face of the failure of empirical means. Magic is the use of non-empirical means directed towards the attainment of empirical ends. Religion is the use of non-empirical means for non-empirical ends.[1]

Various theories have been put forward to account for the origins of religious beliefs and the distinction between the sacred and the profane. The naturalist school sees the sacred as essentially the personification of natural forces. Such beliefs provide answers to the problems of adaptation to man's material environment. Crops fail, rivers burst their banks, pestilence strikes the village. The gods are angry and must be placated. Such beliefs give rise to practices which merge into magic. The Greeks had a pantheon of gods which personified natural forces. Sacrifices, or prayers, may influence the gods to smile more benevolently. The churches fill at times of national crisis or calamity, such as war, and prayers are said for rain or victory in battle.

Durkheim, however, pointed to the weakness of such an explanation. The things that are personified or treated as sacred have no common intrinsic qualities. There is hardly anything which in some society or another has not been treated as sacred. The clue, he argued, was to be found in the symbolic nature of sacred objects. Moreover, the thing that they symbolize must command moral respect. Hence Durkheim was lead to the view that society is always the real object behind the religious symbols. It far transcends the individual, and it is his experience of society which generates in him emotions of awe and respect.[2] We may not accept Durkheim's explanation, but it does draw attention to the important symbolic functions of religion. Religious symbols serve to underline the significance of solemn occasions such as the opening of parliament and the end of term. The school hymn, the dedication of the national flag, are all examples of the reinforcement of secular meanings with religious symbolic meanings.

Weber still further developed these themes by pointing to the distinction between empirical problems of causation and what he called the 'problem of meaning'. Religious systems can provide a variety of 'meanings'—various ways of making sense of everyday life. Moreover, such meanings and explanations have an important relation with the actions men adopt in response to similar situations, and especially in the goals they seek. Specifically, Weber demonstrated the significant differences between Catholics and

[1] A religion may include magical practices, such as prayers for rain, which are linked to the core belief in a deity. But these are peripheral practices, rejected by some.
[2] E. Durkheim, *The Elementary Forms of the Religious Life* (1968 edn.).

Protestants in their economic behaviour, and argued for the substantial influence of Protestantism in generating worldly ascetism (hard work, thrift and abstinence), and its role in the rise of capitalism.[1]

Apart from a need to understand and control the environment, man also has personal needs to adapt, to manage the tensions generated by misfortune and death, and to express deep emotions.[2] In the analysis that follows, we will pay particular attention to the relations between needs and the religious beliefs of social groups.

Social role of religion

Whether we define the persistence or the decline of religion as problematic, depends on a personal point of view. Persistence certainly owes something to socialization. But the association between the beliefs of parents and children is not a determinist one.[3] We may expect the individual to retain those beliefs which are congruent with his experiences and which meet his needs. We may expect, therefore, significant differences between the religious beliefs of different segments in society which reflect their social roles and experiences and the needs which these generate. Thus we find in contemporary society that religious beliefs are more widespread among widows, and among combat troops exposed to the danger of death.[4] They are also more widespread among old people, but this may be because their beliefs perpetuate the stronger religious convictions of earlier generations.

One of the most vivid illustrations of this thesis is the occurrence through history of revolutionary millennial and messianic cults which promised the imminent overthrow of the existing social order and the reign of the dispossessed who would be elevated as saints to positions of power and influence. Such movements took place within the framework of Jewish and Christian doctrine which includes a substantial body of prophetic belief about the final state of the world (eschatology). Christianity teaches, for example, that in the last days, God will return to judge the world. Cohn[5] shows that there were numerous examples of such emotional

[1] M. Weber, *The Protestant Ethic and the Spirit of Capitalism* (1930). For a criticism of Weber, see R. H. Tawney, *Religion and the Rise of Capitalism* (1926).

[2] To recognise that religion meets needs is not necessarily to accept a *functionalist* explanation. For an example of this approach, see T. F. O'Dea, *The Sociology of Religion* (1966).

[3] There is a correlation of 0·65 between the religious beliefs of parents and children. See M. Argyle, op. cit.

[4] Ibid.

[5] N. Cohn, *The Pursuit of the Millennium* (1957).

mass movements in Europe between the eleventh and sixteenth centuries which gained their main support from those exposed to poverty and catastrophe. Such outbreaks occurred during times when society was disrupted by famine, plague and war. They were concentrated, too, in the growing urban communities in which the traditional supportive network of social relations had been disrupted.[1]

Studies of sects in society have similarly demonstrated the association between the social roles and characteristics of supporters and major elements in their teachings. Jehovah's Witnesses, for example, teach that the end of the world is at hand when the wicked will be destroyed and the rule of God established. Studies in the United States show that its membership attracts the underprivileged strata. A detailed study by Bryan Wilson of the Elim, Christadelphian and Christian Science sects in England clearly supports the association between religion and socio-economic conditions.[2]

Both the Elim and Christadelphian movements have drawn in the 'poor, socially neglected and culturally deprived'. God will not only give the saints a heavenly reward, but will also benefit them on earth by their ecstatic experiences and the gift of tongues. In this way, Elim compensates both the economically disinherited, and those disillusioned and embittered by their experience. '... The Elimites are workers, often factory hands, who obtain from religion a transvaluation of life: it reassures them of their ultimate worthiness and provides exciting escape from the dull routine of daily life.'

This functional relationship between the doctrines of sects and the needs of their members faces churches and denominations with a particular problem. In the United States, for example, the predominantly middle-class protestant churches have found difficulty in spreading their liberal doctrines among the lower strata, who wanted ministers who would preach hell-fire and salvation.[3] A church which derives its members from one segment of society is likely to support social policies which alienate those whose social role makes such policies unacceptable. Bishop Wickham[4] shows, for example, that the churches have failed to win support among the industrial working classes of England. Although the Methodists succeeded in winning some support from the well-paid artisans,

[1] Ibid., pp. 21–32. For studies of contemporary messianic cults, see V. Lanternari, *The Religions of the Oppressed* (1965), and P. Worsley, *The Trumpets Shall Sound: A Study of 'Cargo' Cults in Melanesia* (1957). For an alternative approach, see M. Douglas, *Natural Symbols* (1973).

[2] B. R. Wilson, *Sects and Society* (1961), and *Religious Sects* (1970).

[3] S. M. Lipset, *Political Man* (1960).

[4] E. R. Wickham, *Church and People in an Industrial City* (1957).

the bulk of the manual workers remained outside the church. The major factor contributing to this alienation was the social and political policies which the denominations supported and the attitudes of the predominantly middle-class congregations. The churches in the nineteenth century were preoccupied with their own affairs—with disestablishment, ritualism, Sunday observance and the drink question. 'The political composition of the churches . . . precluded any sympathy towards the new working-class political organizations that were being born.'[1]

Secularization

It is not easy to measure the significance of religion in the life of contemporary society. Statistics for church attendance or church membership are only crude indications of belief, although it is reasonable to suppose that they bear some relation to intensity of belief. The broad trend shows a steady rise in church attendances reaching a peak in the 1880s, followed by a steady decline. A religious census of 1851 returned 39 per cent who had attended a place of worship on a particular Sunday. Studies of church attendance in York show a decline from 25 per cent in 1900 to 14 per cent in 1948.[2]

In interpreting these trends, however, we must avoid generalizations from only one industrial society. Comparable figures for the USA show a much higher proportion of weekly church attendance (43 per cent), belief in God (95·5 per cent) and in an after-life (72 per cent). Fewer, however, pray daily (42·5 per cent) and could name the four Gospels (35 per cent compared with 61 per cent).[3]

Wilson argues[4] that such evidence supports the view that industrial society is becoming secularized. In England, this has taken the form of a decline in religious belief and practice. In the USA, it is religion rather than society which has become secularized. The proliferation of sects in the USA has meant that religion is now available in a variety of brand names to meet every taste. But the price of such widespread support is the secularization of religion. It has lost its distinctive religious content and become a part of the American way of life. Martin,[5] however, does not accept this interpretation. He argues that religious belief remains widespread; that the proportion who decisively reject religion is very small, and that the decline in support for various institutional

[1] Ibid., p. 198.
[2] M. Argyle, *Religious Behaviour* (1958). See also D. Martin, *A Sociology of English Religion* (1967), Chapters 2 and 3.
[3] M. Argyle, op. cit.
[4] B. R. Wilson, *Religion in a Secular Society* (1966).
[5] D. Martin, op. cit.

forms of religion is no evidence for widespread secularization. Both are agreed that figures of baptisms, confirmations and church attendance are behavioural indices which tell us little about the meaning, beliefs and attitudes which lie behind the act.[1]

Those who reject a religious view of life must find an alternative mode of adjustment to the inevitability of death, to apparently senseless suffering, and to fortuitous calamity. The Greek philosopher Epicurus, for example, argued that we should not fear death because we ourselves can never in fact meet death: 'when we are, death is absent from us; when death is come, we are no more'.[2] A less sophisticated solution is an acceptance of fate—that we must take what is coming to us—a view which characterizes working-class sub-culture.[3]

How far such non-religious philosophies may eventually replace religion is a matter of speculation. Those who hold such views are at the moment a small and unrepresentative section of society. A study of the British Humanist Association found that its members are mainly drawn from those with above average education. Moreover, they are predominantly from the upper socio-economic categories.[4]

But although death and misfortune have declined in importance as an existential basis for religious belief, there is growing evidence that industrial society generates other problems for the individual for which religion may continue to provide an answer. For example there is increasing awareness of the problem of identity in advanced industrial societies.[5] The increase in mobility, both social and geographical, makes it more difficult for an individual to find an answer to the question, 'Who am I?' The proliferation of cults may be one answer to this problem. And religion may continue to solve an identity crisis for many. Evidence of this comes from Lenski's[6] researches which confirm Herberg's prediction that the disintegration of the old ethnic sub-communities is leading to a religious revival as Americans turn to religion as a source of identity.

Clearly, such conclusions cannot be lifted and applied to the English social system. But Herberg's theory may account for what

[1] For a discussion of the problem of the meaning and criteria of secularization, see K. Thompson and J. Tunstall, *Sociological Perspectives* (1971), Chapter 35 by L. Shiner, 'The Concept of Secularization in Empirical Research'.

[2] Quoted H. Sidgwick, *Outlines of the History of Ethics* (1919).

[3] R. Hoggart, *The Uses of Literacy* (1957).

[4] C. Campbell, 'Membership Composition of the British Humanist Association', *Soc. Rev.*, 1965, pp. 327–36.

[5] O. Klapp, *The Collective Search for Identity* (1969).

[6] G. Lenski, *The Religious Factor* (1961).

appears to be a major difference between England and America—the evidence of a religious revival in the USA compared with a continued decline in Britain. More important, the data on declining church membership in the UK may give a misleading picture of the significance of religion in modern England, since it ignores the possibility that some form of religious sub-communities may exist here as well.

Scientific knowledge is popularly contrasted with religious beliefs by such criteria as empirical verifiability and objectivity. Many would accept Galileo's view that 'the conclusions of natural science are true and necessary and the judgement of man has nothing to do with them'. But many philosophers would challenge the simple positivist view that there is an objective world waiting to be observed and described by law-like statements. And studies of the actual processes of scientific discovery have argued that science, like other forms of knowledge, is socially constructed. It, too, is essentially a human activity—the product of exchanges and interactions between individuals, and of their subjective passions and prejudices.

Public knowledge
The task of science says Ziman, is 'not just to acquire information . . .; its goal is a *consensus* of rational opinion over the widest possible field'.[1] In this sense, science as 'public' knowledge may be contrasted with the 'private' personal knowledge of an artistic or religious experience—the essence of which is not the search for some objective reality, but a personal intellectual or emotional enrichment of experience. No two people necessarily 'see' the same picture or have the same experience of a symphony.

This notion of science as a special kind of knowledge, characterized by openness, objectivity and neutrality, has been encapsulated in the influential paper by Merton[2] in which he spells out the *norms* of science. First and foremost, the most important imperative for the scientist is to publish—the norm of *communism*, since only by publication can the scientific community judge claims to originality and priority. Indeed, such critical scrutiny is the second of Merton's imperatives—*organized scepticism*. Thirdly, the sole criterion for judging a communication is its contribution to science—regardless of the political, religious, ethnic origins or other personal characteristics of its author that

[1] J. Ziman, *Public Knowledge* (1968), p. 9 (italics mine).
[2] R. K. Merton, op. cit.

is, *universalism*. And finally, *disinterestedness* underlines the imperative to pursue knowledge for its own sake, uninfluenced by personal gain or profit.

It must be remembered that Merton's paper was written in the early stages of World War II. It can in this sense be seen as an ideological defence of the autonomy of science against political interference and as a reaffirmation of the universalism of science, against a background of the secrecy imposed by war which severed communications between the scientists of the warring states. For Merton, therefore, the norms were the necessary conditions (functional prerequisites) without which science could not function properly. They were a statement not only of how science functions as a social institution, but of how it ought to function.

This picture of science has been subject to increasing criticism. Merton has recognized that the pattern of recognition is skewed in favour of the more distinguished scientists, so that in cases of multiple discoveries it is the more famous scientist who gets the most credit—what he calls the 'Matthew Effect'; to him that has shall be given.[1] There are various difficulties, too, in reconciling the evidence of fierce disputes over priorities in discovery with the picture of open-minded disinterestedness which Merton paints. But more serious is the empirical evidence that many scientists do not in fact subscribe to the Mertonian norms; only a minority in fact attach importance to publication.[2] In short, the Mertonian norms are of little help when we look beyond the cloistered and monastic *academic* science of the university to the 'real' world of science, harnessed to defence and industry.[3]

The process of discovery

But there is other evidence which challenges the Mertonian picture of open-minded, detached and neutral scientists. And this takes us to the centre of the controversy currently raging among the philosophers, historians and sociologists of science. In a nut-shell, Popper argues that what distinguishes between scientific and non-scientific theories is that the former are open to empirical *falsification*.[4] In short, the imperative of critical scepticism, which the neophyte acquires through the seat of his pants as the result of his lengthy apprenticeship, is raised to a principle of philosophical proof. The task of the scientist is to dedicate himself not to proving his theory, but to disproving it. So, according to Popper, as soon

[1] R. K. Merton, 'The Matthew Effect', *Science*, 159 (1968), pp. 56–63.
[2] S. Cotgrove and S. Box, *Science, Industry and Society* (1970).
[3] For a critical discussion of the 'norms' of science, see Leslie Sklair, *Organized Knowledge* (1973), Chapters 4 and 5.
[4] K. Popper, *Conjectures and Refutations* (1963).

as observations disagree with theory, then the theory must be discarded.

Now, however philosophically attractive such a logically rigorous stance may be, there are a number of objections. It is certainly far from being a description of the way in which scientists in fact behave. Nor is it clear that it is the way in which they *ought* to behave. It is doubtful if science could progress if scientists were *so* open-minded that they were willing to drop an exciting theory at the first sign of trouble. On the evidence, it may be the opposite —that they are tenacious to a fault. Indeed, Max Planck, after continued resistance from Helmholtz to his ideas on the second law of thermodynamics, concluded: 'This experience gave me also an opportunity to learn a new fact—a remarkable one, in my opinion: a new scientific truth does not triumph by convincing its opponents and making them see the light, but rather because its opponents eventually die and a new generation grows up that is familiar with it.'[1]

It is such observations which have led Kuhn to formulate his influential and controversial theory of scientific revolutions.[2] Far from being an open-minded activity, Kuhn stresses the role of what he calls *paradigms* in guiding the observations and explanations of scientists. Indeed, it is only by such commitment to shared theories, concepts and methods that science is possible at all. Such sets of directives provide the framework for the day-to-day work of the scientist, guiding him in the selection and evaluation of data: 'Normal science, the activity in which most scientists inevitably spend almost all their time, is predicated on the assumption that the scientific community knows what the world is like. . . . Normal science, for example, often suppresses fundamental novelties because they are necessarily subversive of its basic commitments.'

But periodically normal science breaks down. Known rules and procedures prove to be inadequate. Observations accumulate (what Kuhn calls anomalies) which cannot be explained within the prevailing paradigms: 'then begin the extraordinary investigations that lead the profession at last to a new set of commitments, a new basis for the practice of science. The extraordinary episodes in

---

[1] Quoted in B. Barber and W. Hirsch, *Sociology of Science* (1962), pp. 542–3. For a discussion of more recent resistances to discovery, see M. Mulkay, 'Cultural Growth in Science', in B. Barnes (ed.), *The Sociology of Science* (1972).

[2] T. S. Kuhn, *The Structure of Scientific Revolutions* (1970). For a discussion and critique, see I. Lakatos and A. Musgrave (eds), *Criticism and the Growth of Knowledge* (1970); and D. Bloor, 'Two Paradigms for Scientific Knowledge', *Science Studies*, Vol. 1, No. 1 (1971).

which that shift of professional commitments occurs are the ones known in this essay as scientific revolutions.'

By contrast with Popper, Kuhn paints a picture of science as much less open, dominated by prevailing orthodoxies, looking much more like a religion with its doctrines and high priesthood. But this is not necessarily a charge of irrationality. It is precisely such commitment to an exciting theory which explains the enthusiasms and passions of science, which in its higher reaches is more akin to artistic creativity.[1] Only by holding tenaciously to a theory in the face of opposition are scientific revolutions possible. Indeed, the process of discovery *is* much more like a theological dispute, in which competing schools of thought contend for mastery. And even at the more mundane level of normal science, there is a process of striving for consensus through the mechanisms of communication, criticism and negotiation. 'The validity of new concepts is usually established ultimately by processes not dissimilar to those involved in the determination of guilt or innocence in a court of law.'[2] This is indeed a long way from Galileo's notion of scientific knowledge as independent of the judgement of man.

Science and ideology

In short, scientific knowledge like other forms of knowledge, is socially constructed. And in this process, subjectively held theories mediate between the individual and the 'real' world, structuring his perceptions and influencing the meanings which he attaches to the readings on the dial.[3] This is not necessarily to detract from the claims of science to be a special kind of knowledge. Indeed, it can claim to have been spectacularly successful in building a consensus of certified knowledge, which goes beyond the subjective judgement of any one individual. Whatever may be the human failings and passions of individual scientists,[4] and whatever the enthusiasms of the individual for his own theory, the success of science may lie in the way in which it has collectively regulated and harnessed the passions of such individuals to the shared enterprise of advancing public knowledge without deadening the enthusiasm necessary to sustain the often intense commitment to a theory. What keeps the individual creative scientist from being

[1] For a convincing statement of this view, see Michael Polanyi, *Personal Knowledge* (1958), Chapters 1 and 6.

[2] 'What to Say About Scientific Evidence', *Nature*, 8, 497 (Oct. 1973).

[3] For historical evidence on this essentially phenomenological position, see G. Holton, *Thematic Origins of Scientific Thought: Kepler to Einstein* (1973).

[4] For a critical perspective on this see A. Koestler, *The Sleepwalkers* (1959).

swept away by his own enthusiasm is the institutionalized 'code of conduct', which ensures that his work is subject to the critical scrutiny of his peers. It is this 'quality' of scientific knowledge which commands respect.

Nevertheless, there have been mounting criticisms[1] of science in recent years, which stem in part from the claims of some scientists for scientific knowledge to be *the* contemporary culture which will eventually usurp other ways of knowing. By contrast, the critics fear that the penetration of science into contemporary culture constitutes a major threat to human values and human freedom. In brief, it is argued, modern science reduces man to mechanism. Post-Newtonian physics has all too successfully exorcised the ghost in the machine. In place of the 'primary' human experiences of taste, touch, sight, sound and smell, nature is now explicable to modern science only in terms of matter in motion, or more recently, forces and fields. So, the Baconian dream of mastery over nature for the 'relief of man's estate' has been turned into a nightmare in which science becomes the basis for the de-naturing not only of nature but also of man. In the last analysis, mind and human personality; purposes and values, freedom and dignity—all are reducible to matter in motion.[2] Man, too, as a part of nature, thus becomes the object of manipulation and control. The mastery of nature becomes the basis for the oppression and repression of all that is human.[3] The use of science in this way to justify and legitimize particular economic and political doctrines (scientism) has a long history. There is a long tradition, for example, of justifying inequality, conflict, hierarchy, domination and competition through crude applications of biological notions to societal dynamics (Malthus, Spencer and the social Darwinists).[4] Such scientism has entered a new lease of life with the current intellectual revival of ethology, and its popularization through such best-sellers as Desmond Morris's *Naked Ape*, and the earlier work of Lorenz. But the gap between genetic codes and such complex behaviour as religion, aggression or monogamy is so wide as to require a remarkable leap of faith to discover the bases of social relations and religious beliefs in the macro-mole-

[1] For a more detailed discussion, see S. Cotgrove, 'Objections to Science', *Nature* (1974); and 'Anti-Science', *New Scientist* (12 July 1973).

[2] See, for example, B. F. Skinner, *Beyond Freedom and Dignity* (1972); and J. Monod, *Chance and Necessity* (1972).

[3] For a powerful statement of such views, see Brian Easlea, *Liberation and the Aims of Science* (1973).

[4] For a review of the influence of Darwinism on social thought, see Donald MacRae, *Ideology and Society* (1961), Chapters XI and XII. For other examples (e.g. Crick and Wooldridge), see Easlea, op. cit., pp. 259–63.

cules of the DNA code.[1] Moreover, the lessons from biology are ambiguous. Kropotkin, for example, argued that mutual aid and co-operation were as important in evolution as conflict and struggle. Similarly, the contemporary ecology movement draws on 'scientific' evidence about environmental dangers to justify small-scale co-operative communities which seek to work .with nature rather than to exploit and dominate it.

There is one further sense in which science is seen to be the contemporary ideology. The application of 'science' to human affairs extends far beyond the natural sciences to techniques of control and decision-making, such as systems analysis and cybernetics. Habermas maintains that 'the scientization of politics', in which political decisions are made on the basis of 'objective necessity', will reduce 'the process of democratic decision-making to a regulated acclamation procedure for elites alternatively appointed to exercise power'.[2] It is in this sense then that the critics of science see it as a subtle source of domination. These are issues to which we return in the discussion in the final chapter on post-industrial society.

POLITICAL BELIEFS

Ideologies and beliefs

The search for meanings, legitimations and guides to conduct may take non-religious or secular forms. But an *ideology* is more than simply a system of ideas and beliefs. It is essentially a simplification or falsification of beliefs which arises when beliefs are related to actions. As Bell has put it, 'ideology is the conversion of ideas into social levers'.[3] In order to win the widest possible support, they are couched in simple terms, reducing the complexities of social reality to ideological definitions. Moreover, they reflect the needs of specific groups for a guide to action and a legitimation of their claims. Mannheim has drawn a useful distinction between those ideas which defend existing interests, namely *ideologies*, and those which seek to change the social order, which he calls *utopias*.

There is some evidence for the view that secular ideologies can function as alternatives to religion. Support for the more extreme political ideologies appears to come from the same strata which also provide recruits for chiliastic movements. Trotsky recruited the first members of the South Russian Workers' Union from

[1] For a critique of reductionist theories, see A. Koestler and J. R. Smythies, *Beyond Reductionism: New Perspectives on the Life Sciences* (1969); and H. and S. Rose, in Richard Whitley (ed.), *Social Processes of Scientific Development* (1974), pp. 154–69.

[2] J. Habermas, *Toward a Rational Society* (1971), Chapters 5 and 6.

[3] See D. Bell, *op. cit.* (1961) p. 400.

members of religious sects.[1] As Cohn points out,[2] revolutionary political ideologies have certain resemblances to their religious counterparts. In both, a final solution is envisaged which by a single revolutionary event (the proletarian revolution) will usher in the millennium. Hitler, for example, spoke of the Third Reich lasting for a thousand years. Cohn argues that when the existing structure of society is undermined, members of that society become less able to face calamity. When some major catastrophe strikes the lower and more exposed strata, the way is open for chiliastic social movements, couched in either religious or secular terms. Thus defeat in war, and unemployment, paved the way for the support of fascism by those whose social world had been most disrupted and who were then exposed to the catastrophic inflation of the late 1920s. It was from the lower middle class of small proprietors in particular, that Hitler gained much of his support.[3]

Political ideologies, then, can be functional alternatives to religions. They offer alternative modes of adaptation to cope with situations of strain and conflict. Studies in Holland and Sweden show that communism is strongest in regions which were once centres of fundamentalist religion.[4] Moreover, some ideologies such as nationalism, by providing a shared goal, would appear highly successful in integrating diverse religious and tribal units. Once independence is achieved, the integrating function of nationalism becomes less effective and the underlying conflicts reassert themselves.

Bell has argued that the old ideologies are exhausted, and nothing has emerged to take their place. Events such as concentration camps and the suppression of the Hungarian workers have resulted in a disenchantment with utopias, and blueprints for social engineering, while the rise of the Welfare State has removed the existential basis for protest movements. Moreover, there is considerable convergence of ideas, and the old extreme positions on the role of the state are no longer held. Only in the newly emerging states of Africa and Asia are ideologies still alive, but they arise out of different social contexts and are ideologies of industrialization, modernization and nationalism, distinctively different from the ideologies of equality and freedom of the nineteenth century. There is a rejection of the older chiliastic vision of a 'new society'. The very absence of modern causes is reflected, he argues, in the anger of recent left-wing writing,[5] which

[1] S. M. Lipset, op. cit., p. 108.
[2] N. Cohn, op. cit.
[3] S. M. Lipset, op. cit., pp. 140–8.
[4] Ibid., p. 108.
[5] D. Bell, op. cit., pp. 402–7.

is remarkable for its failure to define the 'cause' which they seek.

It could be argued that events have overtaken the proponents of the 'end of ideology' thesis. Race, poverty, war, sex, have all emerged in recent years as foci for political protest. How can we explain the emergence of the radical protest expressed, for example, by the CND movement in the 1960s, the upsurge of student protest, women's liberation and the like?[1] On the other hand, it would appear that such beliefs are held by only a small minority, and are no evidence for the widespread existence of political ideologies among the majority of voters. It is to the patterns of political beliefs and attitudes general among the electorate that we now turn.

A dominant view of politics seeks to explain political beliefs and behaviour as an expression of class (economic) interests. The way people vote is not, of course, any very clear indication of their political beliefs. As we saw in Chapter 5, the Labour vote may express the deep-seated ideology of the 'solidaristic' supporter, or a calculative 'instrumental' involvement in politics. We need, therefore, to study political attitudes and beliefs at first hand and cannot infer these from voting behaviour.

The class interest approach to politics has led to the view that political attitudes and beliefs can be located along a continuum from 'left' to 'right'. Thus, we would expect to find patterns of beliefs about specific issues clustering together, reflecting some coherent political ideology. For example, we would anticipate that those on the 'left' support a cluster of issues including the nationalization of industry, trade union power, a more equitable distribution of income and property, opposition to the death penalty, to corporal punishment and to nuclear weapons.

Surprisingly, this is not the case. Although it is possible to find some clustering around economic and social issues, there is practically no connection between support for such items as nationalization, and support for humanitarian and moral issues such as capital punishment and the 'Bomb'.[2] However, some who take a position on one humanitarian issue are likely to take a related stand on others—to be opposed to both the 'Bomb' and capital punishment, and to favour more liberal divorce laws. In other words, we can detect not one, but two dimensions of political belief. The first corresponds to the notion of 'left' and 'right', but the second cuts across this dimension. This second cluster of

[1] In this section, we are concerned only to explore the social bases of ideas and beliefs, not behaviour. Political action (such as voting, protest marches, etc.) is clearly related to beliefs, but the precise relation is problematic. Such issues will be discussed in the final chapter.

[2] D. Butler and D. Stokes, *Political Change in Britain* (1969), p. 199.

beliefs could be characterized as 'liberalism' or 'tender-mindedness' by contrast with its opposite 'authoritarianism' or 'tough-mindedness'.[1]

This is not, however, evidence for the existence of enduring clusters of attitudes indicating the existence of strongly-held political ideologies. Firstly, beliefs on such issues are not stable. A high proportion change their views. Moreover, relatively few (21 per cent) of the electorate think of the parties as being to the left or the right in politics. And if we go further and seek to discover the meaning which these terms have, very few indeed (16 per cent) are able to express anything which can be recognized as a coherent political philosophy. And it is only among this small minority that there is any clustering of attitudes held towards specific issues. That is to say, it is only among those few who are able to express a coherent political ideology of the left that there is support for a cluster of issues such as nationalization and extensions of the social services.[2] In short, there is little evidence for the existence of class ideologies reflecting economic interests except among a relatively small section of the electorate.[3]

Political radicalism

Even more challenging to the class-interest approach to politics is the existence of radicalism among middle-class voters, whose class interests would appear to push them to the right in politics. An example of a radical protest movement whose supporters were mainly middle class was the Campaign for Nuclear Disarmament.[4]

The clue to this apparently anomalous situation is to be found in the distinction between an *instrumental* and an *expressive* involvement in politics.[5] Middle-class support for CND can be seen as an *expressive* activity—geared to the expression of values and ideals. 'It is argued that the main pay-off for middle-class radicals is that of a psychological or emotional kind—in satisfactions derived from expressing personal values in action. . . . Identification with CND could be taken to be a capsule statement of a distinctive moral and political outlook, and support for its activities

---

[1] H. J. Eysenck, *The Psychology of Politics* (1954). It is this distinction which accounts for the apparently anomalous support for Enoch Powell among the dock workers.

[2] D. Butler and D. Stokes, op. cit., Chapter 9.

[3] Butler and Stokes argue that for most, ideology follows partisan support for a party rather than ideology being the basis for support.

[4] Frank Parkin, *Middle-Class Radicalism* (1968). The marchers tended to have experienced an extended education, and to be predominantly employed in welfare and creative occupations. See Chapter 8.

[5] Ibid.

a means of affirming this outlook through symbolic acts.'[1] This expressive orientation to politics is exemplified by the overwhelming support (80 per cent) for propositions such as 'The Labour party should put principles before power.' In other words, the radicalism of the middle class expresses the liberal 'tender-minded' humanitarian dimension of political belief rather than the left–right dimension.

By contrast, working-class radicalism aims at material goals, for example economic redistribution, improved working conditions and the like, and frequently involves the support for the replacement of the existing social order by one based on different property and authority relations.[2] The form which radicalism takes, therefore, reflects the social base of its exponents. And although the majority of the marchers were middle class, class differences were marked. The working-class marchers stressed the importance of economic issues, such as unemployment benefits, nationalization and legal protection for trade unions, while the middle-class marchers attached most importance to moral issues, such as immigration laws and reform of homosexual legislation. Moreover, the middle-class radicals held an overall view of society which emphasized opportunity and the absence of class antagonisms.[3] Hence, there is little inconsistency between middle-class radicalism and the high socio-economic status of the marchers.[4] Their radicalism does not involve any fundamental challenge to the basic structure of society. Nor does it demand adherence to any comprehensive political ideology. 'The end of ideology, then, does not necessarily herald the end of radicalism . . . but rather casts it in a different, somewhat less ambitious, political mould.'[5]

The Women's Liberation movement can similarly be seen as an example of middle-class radicalism. It shares with the counter-culture and some of the more radical youth movements discussed later in this chapter an overriding concern with liberation and opposition to structured social forms, including leadership and hierarchies. Despite the revolutionary fervour of some of its members against the capitalist system, and their definition of women as an oppressed class, its supporters are predominantly

[1] Ibid., pp. 2–3. For a discussion of the distinction between instrumental and expressive politics, see pp. 34–40.

[2] Ibid., p. 40.

[3] Ibid., pp. 42–7.

[4] Whether the typical occupations of the marchers are the cause or consequence of their values is problematic. But the most plausible explanation is that the marchers have tended to choose occupations which avoid deep implication in a capital system. Ibid., p. 187.

[5] Ibid., p. 57.

well-educated middle-class women and its main activity is moral protest and 'consciousness raising'.[1]

THE CULTURE OF DEPRIVATION

Class sub-cultures

Social classes are groups whose differences in experience could be expected to give rise to distinctive outlooks and beliefs. As we shall see in the next chapter, manual workers typically earn less than non-manual, own less, are less secure in their jobs, have less autonomy in their work, are less influential in politics and do not provide their children with the same opportunities for education and social advancement.

Manual workers are not, of course, a homogeneous group. Klein[2] draws a distinction between the traditional and the mobile among both manual and non-manual workers, which helps to throw light on the extent to which such differences are related to class identity and consciousness. The sub-cultural orientations of manual workers will be taken as an example.

Traditional manual workers live in relatively stable communities, characterized by a close-knit social network.[3] These are conditions which favour consensus on norms and the perpetuation of tradition. Neighbourliness, a sense of community and mutual self-help are highly valued. There are permissive and indulgent attitudes towards children and adolescents—'you're only young once'. There is a deep emotional attachment to home, and a reluctance to move far away. Pleasures are taken as they come (short-term hedonism)—there is little long-term saving, and the periodic 'splash' on the occasion of a wedding, Christmas, holidays or similar events absorbs a large part of the budget. But at the same time, there is an emphasis among the 'respectable' stratum on cleanliness, thrift and self-respect. The 'splash' is an institutionalized and regulated extravagance which co-exists with an anxiety to avoid being submerged by poverty and circumstances. Above all, the traditional working man seeks to make 'them' appreciate his respectability. The world is seen in terms of 'them' and 'us'—'they' are the bosses, the people at the top, tell you what to do 'treat y' like muck'.[4]

It has been suggested in Chapter 3 that there are class differences in the use of language, which arise out of the nature of social

[1] J. Mitchell, *Women's Estate* (1971), pp. 175–82. For a discussion of social movements, see Chapter 9.

[2] J. Klein, *Samples from English Culture* (1965), Vol. 1.

[3] See Chapter 2 for a more detailed discussion of this concept.

[4] Summarized from J. Klein, op. cit., Chapter 4.

relationships within the working-class family. In a somewhat similar way, it has been argued that working-class notions of justice and privacy differ. Briefly, working-class culture is of a 'received' type. And this in turn, it is argued, springs from the chronic shortage of material resources. As a result, distribution is rationed, according to ascribed statuses of age and sex. Thus the older working males will receive a bigger share of meat. Such rules do not spring from an 'interpretation' of a situation, but are 'received'. Working-class culture is in this sense rule-governed: there is no room for the exercise of discretion.[1] 'Thus the child learns a model of justice as a self-evident order, as something which is "right and proper" . . .'[2] Since the child has learned to differentiate between people only in terms of broad status categories of age and sex, such criteria become the basis of other relations such as friendship. Thus friendships are entered into totally. By contrast, a middle-class friendship may be segmental—a limited interaction based on, say, a shared interest in golf. Hence, too, the notion of privacy will be absent, since relations are total—nothing is held back in private.

Many aspects of this traditional culture are undergoing change. With the decline in the close-knit social network, there is more emphasis on individual self-reliance. There is a new attitude towards saving, with a shift of expenditure towards household furnishings and consumer durables, with much time spent on redecorating—the growth of home-centredness. Borrowing and popping in and out are no longer approved. But a more complete analysis of changes would raise the question whether the working class are becoming middle class, which must be postponed until a later chapter.

The culture of poverty
We can expect to find clearest evidence on the social conditioning of beliefs among those whose experiences differ most markedly from the norm. For example the poor, particularly those groups in society which have experienced the extremes of poverty.

It is not easy to draw a clear line between the debate on the culture of poverty, and the less controversial issue of the existence of distinctive beliefs and values among the working class, examined in the previous section. The culture of poverty protagonists, however, presents a picture which indicates a qualitative difference, not simply the end point on a continuum of various dimensions of

[1] This also has implications for role-playing, which will be discussed in Chapter 8.
[2] J. Ford, D. Young and S. Box, 'Functional Autonomy, Role Distance and Social Class, *B.J.S.* (1967), in B. R. Cosin, op. cit. (1971), p. 68.

beliefs and attitudes. 'There is, in short, a language of the poor, a psychology of the poor, a world view of the poor. To be impoverished is to be an internal alien, to grow up in a culture that is radically different from the one that dominates the society.'[1]

A particularly influential statement of the concept is that formulated by the anthropologist Oscar Lewis. For him, the term is used more broadly than is general among sociologists to embrace behavioural aspects as well as attitudes and beliefs. 'On the level of the individual the major characteristics are a strong feeling of marginality, of helplessness, of dependence and of inferiority . . . a strong present-time orientation with relatively little ability to defer gratification . . . a sense of resignation and fatalism, and a widespread belief in male superiority. . . . People with a culture of poverty are provincially and locally oriented and have very little sense of history . . . they do not have the knowledge, vision or the ideology to see the similarities between their problems and those of their counterparts elsewhere in the world. They are not class conscious, although they are very sensitive indeed to status distinctions.'[2]

Lewis argues that the culture of poverty transcends rational and ethnic differences, and explains this as a common adaptation to common problems. That is, he sees the culture of poverty as a 'reaction of the poor to their marginal position in a class-stratified and highly individualistic society. It represents an effort to cope with feelings of hopelessness and despair which develop from the realization of the improbability of achieving success in terms of the values and goals of the larger society.'[3] But it is not simply an adaptive response. It is also perpetuated from generation to generation, so that the young 'are not psychologically geared to take full advantage of . . . increased opportunities.'[4]

It is not easy to unravel Lewis's explanation of the precise ways in which the conditions of poverty generate the adaptive culture.[5] It flourishes in societies with a cash economy, wage labour, and production for profit, high levels of unemployment, low wages, the failure to provide organization for the low incomes. Indeed, a major characteristic of the poor is this lack of effective participation and integration. It is this to which Lewis attaches particular importance as a source of their sense of powerlessness and resignation. But Lewis also lists briefly several family characteristics which indicate a psycho-dynamic explanation of the personality

[1] Michael Harrington, *The Other America: Poverty in the United States* (1963).
[2] Oscar Lewis, *La Vida: A Puerto Rican Family in the Culture of Poverty* (1967), p. xlvii.   [3] Ibid.   [4] Ibid.
[5] For a critique, see C. A. Valentine, *Culture and Poverty: Critique and Counter-Proposals* (1968), pp. 114–20.

characteristics of the poor, including maternal deprivation, weak ego structure, confusion of sexual identification, and a high tolerance for psychological pathology.

It is clear that the whole concept has a high potential for ideological debate. This, plus the relative poverty of research data, makes objective discussion difficult. For example, the stress on the strong element of socialization, which prevents the young from taking advantage of the opportunities available in society has had a particularly powerful impact in the American poverty programme. On the basis of this diagnosis, the emphasis has been on the need for compensatory education, to give the children of the poor a better chance (the Head Start programme).[1] Not surprisingly, the concept has been attacked by radicals as being a labelling device for blaming poverty on the poor—a re-statement of the puritan ethic which sees riches as a reward for hard work, thrift and abstinence, and poverty as an indication of a lack of moral fibre.[2] Furthermore, it could be argued, if the culture of poverty is an adaptive response to the conditions of poverty then the situation could be changed by the actions of the non-poor who perpetuate a social system which generates poverty.[3] In short, is it poverty which generates the adaptive culture, or is it culture which perpetuates poverty?

A study of the poor in Nottingham found some evidence for differences in attitudes and beliefs among the very poor. 'Certainly we observed the hopelessness and despair, saw that our respondents did not participate to any significant degree in the "major institutions" of the larger society . . .'[4] The aspirations of the very poor were also low, in terms of what they would define as becoming well-off. An aggressive dissatisfaction with levels of earnings, however, was found only among the better-paid trade-unionists but not among the poor. In most respects, there is little here that could be labelled a distinctive culture of poverty. Many of these values and attitudes have been reported to be found in varying degrees in traditional working-class communities. The only group which was distinctive was a small group of multi-problem families,

[1] S. A. Levitan, 'Is Head Start a Slow Start', in R. E. Will and H. G. Vatter, *Poverty in Affluence* (1970).
[2] There has been little attempt to explore the 'ideology of poverty'—the attempt by the 'haves' to provide meanings and justifications for the existence of the 'have-nots'. There may be a rich harvest here. See, for example, A. Carnegie, *The Gospel of Wealth and Other Essays* (1901), 'the greatest and best of our race have necessarily been nurtured in the bracing school of poverty—the only school capable of producing the supremely great, the genius.' (Quoted in Will and Vatter, op. cit.)
[3] C. A. Valentine, op. cit., p. 137.
[4] K. Coates and R. Silburn, *Poverty: The Forgotten Englishmen* (1970).

who lived from one crisis to another. Any differences in beliefs and attitudes could be argued to be realistic appraisals made by those who are well aware of the limited chances that life has to offer those with little skill, or potential for organization, and the virtual impossibility of earning more than a minimum wage.

In short, far from being an adaptive mechanism, the so-called 'culture of poverty' could be explained as the behavioural response to low wages, malnutrition and overcrowding, which generate apathy, lethargy and the lack of parental control.[1] Alternatively, it could be argued that a more useful model would be to stress the interaction between poverty and culture, rather than to emphasize a one-sided causal relationship.

AGE GROUPS AND YOUTH CULTURE

One further social basis for the development of distinctive beliefs is age. Young people have particular problems, generated by the transitional and ambiguous nature of their role in industrial societies,[2] hovering uncertainly between childhood and adult status. Whereas for the child in the family, status is ascribed, in the adult society it is achieved, and judged by universalistic criteria, mainly performance.[3] There is, that is to say, a sharp discontinuity between the emotionally secure world of children and the impersonal world of adults. The school, however, does little to bridge this gap. It reflects rather the achievement-oriented, universalistic, affectively neutral values of adult society. The emphasis is on the instrumental activities of mastering educational skills. Moreover, the great difference in power and authority between teacher and pupil still further emphasizes the discontinuities between the world of the child and that of the adult.[4] Furthermore, the extension of education delays social maturity until well beyond the attainment of sexual and physiological maturity, generating fresh problems for the older adolescent.

It is under such conditions that young people develop a need to join youth groups. Here the emphasis is on solidarity, on belonging to a group, in which status is ascribed. The criterion for acceptance

[1] A. Schorr, 'The Non-Culture of Poverty', *Am. J. of Orthopsychiatry*, October 1964 (quoted in K. Coates and R. Silburn, op. cit., p. 140).

[2] For an early and readable discussion of this view, see M. Mead, *Coming of Age in Samoa* (1971 edn).

[3] S. N. Eisenstadt, *From Generation to Generation* (1956), especially pp. 159–85.

[4] M. P. Carter, *Home, School and Work* (1962), documents the strong resentment against the authority relations of the classroom, where adolescents are treated like children and contrasts this with the adult status of the young worker in the factory. These considerations raise serious doubts about the recommendations of the Newsom Report to extend the school day.

is age. The emphasis is on expressive activities (sports, dancing, wearing fashionable 'gear', special language), participation in which symbolizes membership and solidarity. There is strong emphasis on common experience, and mutual identification.[1] The age group functions, that is to say, to help the adolescent to achieve an identity, with an accepted status in a group, in a society in which he has not yet achieved an adult status, and in which his ascribed family status is no longer adequate. The very insecurity of his status in the changing peer group emphasizes the need for conformity and the intolerance of conconformity.[2] It is the discontinuities between childhood and adulthood which explain the adolescent's need for the membership of an age group.

The existence of age groups does not necessarily justify the conclusion that these are also characterized by distinctive sub-cultures. There is, in fact, some terminological confusion as to the precise meaning to be attached to the notion of a youth culture. Hess argues, that if we mean by this 'a set of values that are independent of the values of adult society, and . . . are transmitted from one generation to another',[3] then it would be difficult to argue that youth culture in this sense exists. More usually, however, the term is used to indicate patterns of behaviour among young people which differ from, and are sometimes in conflict with, those of their parents. Parsons, for example, characterizes youth culture as emphasizing athletic prowess, and evaluating individuals by non-utilitarian qualities such as glamour and irresponsibility.[4] It is important to establish that such sub-cultural differences are not, in fact, a reflection of differing adult sub-cultures; that is, that they reflect class sub-cultures. Moreover, the degree of difference may be relatively mild. Where the differences involve marked conflict with adult values, Yinger suggests the term contra-culture.[5]

Empirical researches in America, however, have failed to find support for the existence of a contra-culture.[6] A recent study of political attitudes among young voters in Britain[7] also fails to find any distinctive characteristics. Moreover, a study of the aspirations of school-leavers found that in their beliefs about the place of hard

---

[1] S. N. Eisenstadt, op. cit., p. 184. This is also the conclusion of a study by Ralph Turner, *The Social Context of Ambition* (1964).

[2] Ralph Turner, op. cit.

[3] D. Gottlieb and J. Reeves, *Adolescent Behaviour in Urban Areas* (1963).

[4] T. Parsons, op. cit., Chapter 5.

[5] J. M. Yinger, 'Contra-culture and Sub-culture', *A.S.R.*, 25 October 1960, pp. 625–35. See also D. M. Downes, *The Delinquent Solution* (1966), Chapter 1 for a discussion of the concept of delinquent sub-culture.

[6] Ralph Turner, op. cit.

[7] P. Abrams and A. Little, 'The Younger Voter in British Politics', *B.J.S.*, June 1965.

work in getting-on, and in their ambitions, 'young people do seem to be remarkably like us'.[1]

Turner provides a clue when he stresses the segmental and ritualistic character of youth culture.[2] It does not embrace a set of values and beliefs about all the major areas of life, but is primarily related to peer-group activities. Moreover, its symbolic functions as a means of expressing solidarity gives it a ritualistic flavour: it may be subscribed to without any inner conviction or internalization. It follows that youth culture does not necessarily involve the devaluation of academic and occupational achievement. In particular, it does not necessarily eradicate differences in attitudes towards education and occupation derived from class backgrounds, and has less of an equalizing effect than might be supposed. A study of English grammar-school boys supports such a conclusion. Criteria for choosing friends included among favoured characteristics putting homework first, reading and talking about books, and a preference for those who spend half rather than most of their time in playing games. There were, however, significant differences in the preferences of working-class boys, indicating the persistence of sub-cultural differences in the grammar school, with middle-class boys showing a higher regard for scholastic attainments and greater willingness to postpone gratifications.[3]

If this view is correct, it suggests that the role of the mass media in determining youth culture is less crucial than is often supposed. The teenager has certainly become an industry. His substantially increased earnings have attracted the interests of the mass media, advertizing and the entertainments industry.[4] These have provided him with the symbols which he needs—'pop' music, 'pop' art, 'gear' as expressions of peer-group identity and symbolic ritual activities. But in doing so they are meeting needs generated by the ambiguous status of the adolescent in society, and the discontinuities, between childhood and adult status which the family fails to meet, and the extended schooling exacerbates.

There is little evidence, then, for the existence of marked generational differences. Nevertheless, it is among the young that radical views are particularly likely to gain support, and indeed it is from the ranks of the young that much of the radical protest has come in recent years. This is not to say, of course, that the young are radical, but rather that the radical are typically young. The question we have to ask is what are the characteristics of the radical young that distinguish them from the great majority who

[1] T. Veness, *School Leavers* (1961), p. 165.
[2] R. Turner, op. cit., p. 144–6.
[3] A. N. Oppenheim, 'Social Status among Grammar School Boys', *B.J.S.*, September 1955. [4] M. Abrams, *Teenage Consumer Spending in 1959* (1961).

are remarkably like their parents? And is the radical group likely to increase in size?

The concept of a distinctive political generation is not very helpful. As we have seen, there is some evidence that individuals are likely to be influenced by exposure to dramatic social or political experiences in their formative years. But the evidence shows that the great majority who grew up in the years of the Bomb, Suez and Cuba, were not in any way 'radicalized'.[1]

A plausible explanation is the influence of political socialization. Parkin found that the young marchers were likely to have at least one parent who was a CND supporter, was a political activist, to be to the left in politics, and to come from mother-centred families.[2] It is particularly notable that more than half the marchers between 18 and 25 were students in full-time education, and thus would have been more strongly exposed to high social ideals and values, and to the liberalizing influence of university. Such young people would be particularly aware of the discrepancy between ideals and the actualities of social life. Moreover, as students they also experience *status discrepancies*.[3] That is to say, by criteria such as education they enjoy high status, but their economic status is low. This, together with their distance from the levers of power, may encourage not only radical beliefs, but also actions outside the formal institutional channels.[4]

Finally, there is evidence that for some, the appeal of the marchers reflected 'the anti-adult, anti-authoritarian character' of the CND. 'The Bomb could be, and was easily held up as a symbol of the older generation's moral and political bankruptcy.' For many, nominal support for CND, like wearing outlandish clothes, was symbolic of a more 'diffuse adolescent anger against authority'.[5] In short, not all who marched were convinced believers. Beliefs cannot be deduced from behaviour. Nor is co-ordinated action necessarily an expression of consensus. And the aetiology of the beliefs of this anti-authority group is likely to differ somewhat from those whose marching expressed a moral protest against the Bomb.[6]

The more recent emergence of the so-called 'underground' and the notion of an 'alternative society' has many similarities with the

[1] F. Parkin, op. cit., p. 142.
[2] Compare the association between authoritarianism and 'father-dominated' families.
[3] This concept is examined more fully in Chapter 7.
[4] R. Jenkins, 'Who Are the Marchers?', *Journal of Peace Research*. See also Edward Shils, 'Centre and Periphery', in P. Worsley (ed.), *Readings* (1970), Chapter 65.   [5] F. Parkin, op. cit, pp. 157–8.
[6] See Kenneth Keniston, 'The Psychology of Alienated Students', in C. Gordon and K. J. Gergen, *The Self in Social Interaction* (1968), pp. 405–14.

CND movement and may be seen as its successor.[1] It shows the same opposition to authority, and in its attack on the 'technocratic' society,[2] mounts a moral protest against the dehumanizing aspects of a society[3] dedicated to material objectives and efficiency. 'They seek to invent a cultural base for New Left politics, to discover new types of community, new family patterns, new sexual mores, new kinds of livelihood, new aesthetic forms, new personal identities on the far side of power politics, the bourgeois home, and the consumer society.'[4] It is expressive politics, dedicated to advancing the extreme liberalism of the tough-tenderminded dimension in politics, very different from the radical attack on the class structure of the traditional political left. And, not surprisingly, its supporters are primarily the children of the comfortably-off middle class. 'The bourgeoisie, instead of discovering the class enemy in its factories, finds it across the breakfast table in the person of its own pampered children.'[5]

It would seem, then, that the notion of a youth culture as a pervasive feature of the beliefs of young people is misleading. Much of the behaviour is age-related, and not indicative of any marked generational differences in basic beliefs. It is in this sense symbolic, segmental and ritualistic. But within this general pattern of conformity, there are small groups whose beliefs are a reflection of the radical element in adult society. And within this group again, there are those whose opposition to authority of all kinds may be indicative of an alienated personality. It is this last group which comes closest to the idea of a generation gap with its general opposition to adults as the upholders and embodiment of authority.

DISCUSSION

What, then, can we say about the relationship between consciousness and society? There is ample evidence that there *is* such a relationship between the social world which the individual occupies, and his consciousness. Beliefs, meanings, legitimations about politics, class, values—can all be shown to bear some relation to the experienced world.

But the relation is complex. Experience itself is mediated through perceptions structured by beliefs already formed. For example, political meanings acquired through socialization interact with experience and result in interpretations which for some confirm

[1] In some cases, the connection is explicit, e.g. Jeff Nuttal, *Bomb Culture* (1970).

[2] T. Roszak, *The Making of a Counter-Culture: Reflections on the Technocratic Society and Its Youthful Opposition* (1970).

[3] In this it has more affinity with the early Marx's preoccupation with alienation.   [4] Ibid., p. 66.   [5] Ibid., p. 34.

a view of society as divided into 'them' and 'us', or alternatively, for others, confirm the belief that success for those who climb the social ladder is the reward for effort and ability. It is in this sense that we can agree with the view that reality is a 'social construction.'

Such an approach can help to make sense, too, of the more long-term trends in beliefs. It has been shown that the impact of secularization is uneven. For some groups, religion continues to provide meanings, especially at the individual level. For example, for those who cannot find a satisfactory confirmation of the self through meaningful work, and for those with stigmatized identities, religion may provide a sense of personal worth. But industrialization has destroyed the monopoly of religion as a total explanation. It is in the economic sphere above all, that religion has become de-throned, although religious symbols continue to play a part in the institutions of the family and the state.[1] Individuals occupy roles in a variety of structures. And whereas religious meanings persist in some, religion is 'left behind at the factory gates'. Thus in a pluralist society, religion loses it 'objective' reality as part of world-taken-for-granted, and its beliefs are no longer pervasive throughout the social fabric. Religion thus becomes a private affair, rooted in the consciousness of the individual.[2]

We have focused mainly on those systems of belief where the evidence is capable of a variety of interpretations. But if we turn to the opposite end of a continuum from religion and political ideologies to science, the differences would appear to be of degree rather than kind. The 'hard' sciences such as physics involve the rigorous testing of theories and models by reference to observable sensory data. However, here too the observations are interpreted and given meaning in terms of the prevailing paradigms.[3] Further, a scientific paper, to be built into the edifice of knowledge, must first be read and cited by other members of the scientific community. In this sense, too, science is a social construct. But whereas in the harder sciences there is substantial consensus, unanimity decreases as we move through the social sciences to the areas of political and religious belief. And this is due in part to the fact that such differences in belief reflect the different social worlds which are occupied by various groups in society as well as the absence of readily accepted paradigms.

[1] Peter L. Berger, 'Secularization and the Problem of Plausibility', in K. Thompson and J. Tunstall, op. cit.

[2] Peter L. Berger, op. cit., p. 456. Institutional orders are external to the individual and were there before he was born. It is in this sense that the beliefs which they embody are objective, external, taken-for-granted.

[3] For discussion and references, see Chapter 1.

It must be stressed that this chapter is illustrative, and not exhaustive. There has not been any attempt to explore in any systematic way the influence of beliefs on society. Previous chapters have paid some attention to this, for example to ideologies of work and family life. Thus we have not explored the way in which religion contributes to social control—a topic which fits more logically into the final chapter. The perspective throughout has focused on the social structuring of beliefs—on the influence of society on consciousness.

One final point. After having surveyed the influence of social experiences (including socialization) in the formation of beliefs, the relatively small impact of the mass media [1] is hardly surprising. Our view of the world is deeply rooted in everyday experience, past and present, in which TV and newspapers play only a small part in constructing our picture of reality.[2]

READING

B. Barnes (ed.), *Sociology of Science* (Penguin, 1972).
D. Bell, *The End of Ideology* (Collier-Macmillan, 1962), especially Part 3, 'The Exhaustion of Utopia'.
P. L. Berger and T. Luckman, *The Social Construction of Reality* (Penguin, 1967).
N. Cohn, *The Pursuit of the Millennium* (Secker and Warburg, 1957).
T. S. Kuhn, *The Structure of Scientific Revolutions* (Chicago, 1970).
I. Lakatos and A. Musgrave (eds), *Criticism and the Growth of Knowledge* (Cambridge University Press, 1970).
V. Lanternari, *The Religions of the Oppressed* (Mentor Books, 1965).
G. Lenski, *The Religious Factor* (Doubleday, 1961).
O. Lewis, *La Vida: A Puerto Rican Family in the Culture of Poverty* (Secker and Warburg, 1967).
S. M. Lipset, *Political Man* (Heinemann, 1960), Chapters 4 and 5.
D. Martin, *A Sociology of English Religion* (Heinemann, 1967).
R. K. Merton, *Social Theory and Social Structure* (Free Press, 1957).
M. J. Mulkay, *The Social Process of Innovation* (Macmillan, 1972).
T. F. O'Dea, *The Sociology of Religion* (Prentice-Hall, 1966).
R. Robertson (ed.), *Sociology of Religion* (Penguin, 1969).
L. Sklair, *Organised Knowledge* (Hart-Davis, 1973).
C. A. Valentine, *Culture and Poverty: Critique and Counter Proposals* (University of Chicago Press, 1968).
B. R. Wilson, *Sects and Society* (Heinemann, 1961).
——*Religion in a Secular Society* (Watts, 1966).
——*Religious Sects* (Weidenfeld and Nicolson, 1970).
——(ed.), *Rationality* (Blackwell, 1974).

[1] See Chapter 4.
[2] This point was made at some length by R. Hoggart in his *Uses of Literacy* (1957).

SOCIAL PROCESSES

Chapter 7

SOCIAL DIFFERENTIATION AND STRATIFICATION

Rich and poor, powerful and weak, honoured and despised—such dichotomies are widely characteristic of human societies. Prophets have denounced the exploitation of the poor, idealists have sought to establish utopian communities in which all are equal, and political reformers have set their feet on the road to a classless society. And yet differences in wealth, in power, and in prestige stubbornly persist. Are such differences necessary for the functioning of any social system? Or are we, in fact, moving towards a more equalitarian society?

But it is not only power and material goods which are differentially distributed. In most societies the rich and the powerful are also deemed worthy of honour and prestige. In other words, we are concerned not merely with the facts of social differences but also with their social evaluation. Status hierarchies confer honour on some (and dishonour on others), but in so doing, they legitimize differences and authorize inequality. Those whom society honours, 'ought' to be rewarded, while poverty may be attributed to the lack of moral fibre of the poor and in this sense 'deserved'. In such ways, societies moderate and try to contain the disruptive potential of power and privilege. And where such methods of control fail, power in its various forms, naked and disguised, stands in the wings, as the ultimate means of social control. Where societies differ is largely in the balance between consensus and coercion.

Types of stratification

We are confronted at the outset by a considerable semantic confusion. The word 'class', for example, is frequently used in everyday speech and writing with a variety of meanings. The lack of consensus among social scientists still further complicates the matter. We must distinguish, for example, between the facts of

217

objective differences in income, prestige and power and the existence of *classes*, which are more than mere statistical aggregates of individuals, differentiated according to some such criterion. Class refers to the existence of solidary groupings which arise on the basis of such differences. Furthermore, we must distinguish between *class* and *stratification*. The latter term refers to the existence in a society of a hierarchy of layers marked off by differences in status. Thus, the nobility in feudal Europe constituted a *stratum*. Strata emerge, therefore, where there are clear-cut and consistent differences in the distribution of status which make it possible to allocate individuals to a particular layer in the hierarchy.

There is, in fact, a variety of types of stratification, of which social classes are only one. These types can be distinguished according to the rigidity of the grades and the possibility of mobility between them, the nature of the sanctions by which the divisions are enforced, and the degree of functional specialization.[1] The estate system of feudal society was characterized by very restricted mobility, the divisions were enforced by legal sanctions, and each estate performed characteristic functions. The noble strata performed the political and military functions while the peasantry and serfs carried out menial tasks. Somewhat similar functional distinctions between prayers, fighters and workers exist in the caste system of India, but here there is no possibility of movement between the rigid caste grades. Birth determines caste, and the distinctions are upheld by strong social and religious taboos which enforce rules of commensality and endogamy.

By contrast, in a social class system of stratification, there are no legal distinctions between classes—all are subject to the same laws and all have equal citizen rights.[2] The barriers to mobility are largely those of opportunity. How far differences in income, property, status and power underlie the existence of distinctive classes, is a matter to which we shall now turn.

THE DISTRIBUTION OF DIFFERENCES

Differentiation and the economic system
Sociological researches have now provided us with a very substantial amount of empirical data on the differential distribution of property and income, power and prestige. But such material is largely descriptive. There has been less success in relating the facts of social differentiation to any satisfactory body of theory which provides a coherent explanatory framework. Much of the research

[1] M. Ginsberg, *Sociology* (1934).
[2] For a discussion of the extension of citizenship, see T. H. Marshall, *Citizenship and Social Class* (1950).

on social differences has not, of course, been directed to any such attempt to understand the workings of social systems. In Britain, for example, much of our data has been collected as a basis for administrative policies to solve the problems of poverty. Booth's survey of poverty in London provided authoritative data on the size of the problem by demonstrating that one-third of the population of London in the 1890s was living in poverty.[1] He also showed that over half this poverty was the result of irregular employment and low wages, while a further substantial fraction (about a quarter) was due to circumstances largely outside the control of the individual, such as illness, infirmity, and large families. In the light of such data, it could no longer be argued that poverty was mainly a question of thriftlessness, or drink, and the case for state action in the form of unemployment insurance, labour exchanges, health insurance, and family allowances was greatly strengthened.[2]

Subsequent researches, such as Bowley's survey of five towns, showed a substantial reduction in the incidence of poverty in 1923–34 to only one-third of that in 1913, due to two main causes—the decrease in the size of families plus higher wages.[3] In the inter-war years, unemployment became a primary cause of poverty, especially in the depression around 1930.

By the 1950s and early 1960s, it was confidently believed by most that poverty had been largely abolished. Surveys of York in 1936 and 1950 showed a decline from 18 per cent to 1·5 per cent living in poverty. But a series of studies in the 1960s challenged this view. Taking national assistance scales as the criterion, it was shown that the proportion of the population in poverty had risen from 7·8 per cent in 1953 to 14·2 per cent in 1960.[4] And there is evidence that the proportion has continued to rise in the 1960s.

Not only has the incidence changed, but the relative contribution of factors causing poverty has fluctuated (Table 7.1). Compared with 1950, there has been a return to a pattern of poverty similar to that in 1936 and 1899, with inadequate wages as a major cause.

Controversy about the extent of poverty is in part the difficulty of definition and agreeing criteria. Rowntree calculated the minimum income necessary to 'secure the necessaries of a healthy life', assuming that the housewife had a knowledge of the cheapest way to obtain the best nutritional value. Apart from such unrealistic

---

[1] C. Booth et al., Life and Labour of the People in London, (1902), 17 vols.
[2] M. Abrams, Social Surveys and Social Action (1951).
[3] A. L. Bowley, Has Poverty Diminished? (1925).
[4] Ken Coates and Richard Silburn, Poverty: the Forgotten Englishman (1970), Part 1; A. Atkinson, Unequal Shares (1972).

assumptions, and the monotony of a diet which includes 6 lbs of swedes, the whole notion of what is necessary is clearly problematic. 'If clothing, money for travel to work and newspapers are considered to be "necessaries" ... why not tea, handkerchiefs, laundry, contraceptives, cosmetics, hairdressing and shaving and life-insurance payments?'[1] Moreover, by focusing on income, such an approach does not take account of the other dimensions of deprivation which the poor experience, especially their powerlessness and lack of influence, and their cultural deprivation.

TABLE 7.1

CAUSES OF POVERTY

	Percentage of those in poverty			
	1899	1936*	1950*	1960†
Inadequate wages	52	42	⎰ 4	40
Miscellaneous, including large families	25	3	⎱	
Fatherless families	16	8	6	10
Old age ⎱	5	15	68	33
Sickness ⎰		4	21	10
Unemployment	2	29	—	7

* Surveys by Rowntree and Lavers.

† Abel Smith and P. Townsend. Based on K. Coates and R. Silburn, op. cit., pp. 34 and 35.

Judgements as to what are necessities are bound to be relative to the generally prevailing standards. Instead of searching for some absolute criterion, therefore, we may define poverty in terms of *relative deprivation*. Harrington[2] goes further than this and argues that poverty should be defined absolutely in terms of what man and society could be. While there are those below this optimum, there is poverty. 'Placed in this context, the stringently calculated subsistence-level poverty line is seen to be an aberration on the part of those whose yearning for precision and parsimony exceeds not only their common humanity, but also their desire for sociological sophistication.'[3]

At the other end of the income distribution scale, a relatively small number (1 per cent) of incomes of over £5,000 after tax now take 7 per cent of the national income, compared with 5 per cent in the early 1960s. Although taxation has reduced the differences in net incomes, there are still 66,000 incomes of over £5,000 net.[4] Moreover, it is probable that official statistics underestimate the

[1] P. Townsend, 'Measuring Poverty', *B.J.S.*, 1954.
[2] M. Harrington, *The Other America* (1963), pp. 173–5.
[3] K. Coates and R. Silburn, op. cit.
[4] Inland Revenue Statistics, 1971, Tables 57 and 79.

size of real incomes enjoyed by the well-to-do, as they fail to take account of incomes in kind and other emoluments.[1]

Differences in the distribution of property are even more marked. The top 10 per cent of incomes own 43 per cent of the total liquid assets.[2] Less than 6 per cent of income units own stocks and shares, while these are heavily concentrated (52 per cent) in the top income groups. Twenty-two per cent own houses, but 10 per cent still have mortgages to pay off.

Such differences are clearly related to the position occupied by individuals and groups in the economic order. For Marx, for example, the key is to be found in the relation to property. Those who own productive resources such as factories, capital and land are contrasted with those who have only their labour to sell. The incomes derived from these sources (profits, interest, rent and wages) differ greatly in size and security. A relatively small group of individuals takes a disproportionately large share of the national product in the form of rent, interest and profits, although the marked decline in the share taken by property after the Second World War is notable.

Marx's approach, however, does not help us to explain the substantial differences in income among the property-less. For Weber, the key to class differences is to be found in the market situation, which he defined as '. . . the typical chance for a supply of goods, external living conditions, and personal life experiences, in so far as this chance is determined by the amount and kind of power . . . to dispose of goods or skills for the sake of income in a given economic order'.[3] Such an approach directs our attention to the factors which influence the 'amount and kind of power' in the market, such as skill and security. We have already seen in Chapter 4 that occupations adopt a variety of strategies to strengthen their market situations. There is little doubt that such techniques can have a considerable influence on the relative income of an occupation, particularly where (as in the printing trades) the union is able to exercise close control on recruitment through apprenticeship. But it is a matter of controversy whether the shift in the share of the national income going to wage-earners since 1938 is due to union action or to scarcity of labour.[4] In other words, income differentials can be seen partly as a function of the efforts of an occupational group to increase its share of the cake and partly as a function of the use of differentials by employers to stimulate the

---

[1] R. Titmuss, *Income Distribution and Social Change* (1962).
[2] H. F. Lydall, *British Incomes and Savings* (1955).
[3] H. H. Gerth and C. W. Mills, *From Max Weber* (1970), p. 181.
[4] Full-employment and the increasing employment of married women have also contributed substantially to rising prosperity of manual workers.

supply of both the quantity and quality of labour power. And since the division of labour results in differential skills, it can be argued that differential rewards are necessary to call them forth in the required amounts—a question to which we shall return later.

Finally, a form of social differentiation of increasing significance is 'racial' discrimination based on skin colour and ethnic differences. In the field of employment, Indians are slightly over-represented[1] in white-collar occupations, but only 5 per cent of Jamaicans in the London area, compared with 33 per cent of the total population, are in such jobs. Moreover, coloured immigrants form a higher proportion of the unemployed particularly during rising unemployment. Such discrimination also extends to housing and the provision of services (hotel and holiday accommodation, etc.). There is little doubt 'that the major component in the discrimination is colour'.[2]

Differentiation and culture: the status system

Utopians frequently envisage an ideal society in which all men are judged to be equal. But with few exceptions, 'the differential evaluation of men as individuals and as members of social categories is a universal, formal property of social systems'.[3] The fact that there are differences in skin colour, income, position, age, sex, intelligence, does not by itself result in *social stratification*. This depends on the meaning which society gives to the objective differences. It is the cultural definitions and meanings of wealth, skin colour, sex or age which gives them social significance. The differences can persist, but the cultural definitions change. Money or birth can become more or less important as bases for social stratification.

It is this fact which Max Weber stresses when he insists that status differentiation is analytically distinct from economically determined differences in class situation.[4] Status is the social evaluation of the individual—the degree of honour which society confers on him. Income and property do not by themselves ensure the conferment of high status although, in the long run, they are closely related to it. Titles are examples of status in our society. Wealth by itself does not carry the automatic right to a title, nor does its absence debar a title. Empirical studies of the prestige of

[1] That is, the percentage of Indians is higher than that for the total population. See N. Deakin, *Colour, Citizenship and British Society* (1970), pp. 79–81.
[2] W. W. Daniel, *Racial Discrimination in England* (1968), p. 209.
[3] R. Williams, *American Society* (1961), p. 88.
[4] H. H. Gerth and C. W. Mills, op. cit., pp. 186–7.

occupations confirm that the criteria by which an occupation is allocated to a position in the prestige hierarchy are complex. The ranking of occupations in terms of prestige does not correspond exactly to their ranking in terms of income, although there is normally a significant correlation between the two rankings. Other factors may enter into the ranking process. Status may be *ascribed* or conferred on the basis of the possession of some quality. Birth, for example, or inborn personal qualities, such as skin colour, may be the criterion for status ascription. Or status may be *achieved* by personal effort, such as the passing of examinations and the conferment of degrees or titles. Parsons[1] has identified six main criteria: (1) birth, (2) possessions, (3) personal qualities, (4) personal achievement, (5) authority, (6) power.

The relation between an individual's ranking on a number of criteria, such as occupation, income, education, and ethnic group, can be close, or there may be a lack of congruence between such rankings. If there is a good 'fit' between a person's position in each of the major rankings, then this indicates a high degree of *status consistency* (or status crystallization).[2] A person may, for example, be highly qualified edcationally, but be a member of an ethnic group or occupation with a relatively low status. Where there is a high degree of status consistency, we may refer to the individual's status profile as flat, compared with the irregular profile of status inconsistency.

There is a considerable volume of empirical research which demonstrates general agreement on the social grading of occupations, and shows that there is substantial congruence between the rank order of different industrial countries.[3] But this does not necessarily indicate a moral consensus about the way occupations *ought* to be ranked. Such studies may simply be 'tapping the general awareness of an existing state of affairs'.[4] Nor is it plausible to argue that the status system derives from the popular evaluation of positions. Indeed, there is evidence that the consensus is not as widespread as some studies suggest. Perhaps the most significant inquiry is that of Young and Willmott[5] among a working-class sample in East London. They found that about one-quarter of

[1] T. Parsons, 'An Analytical Approach to the Theory of Social Stratification', *A.J.S.*, May 1940, pp. 848–9.

[2] See L. Broom, 'Social Differentiation and Stratification', in R. K. Merton, L. Broom and L. S. Cottrell, Jr, *Sociology Today: Problems and Prospects* (1965).

[3] J. R. Hall and C. A. Moser, 'The Social Grading of Occupations', in D. Glass (ed.), *Social Mobility in Britain* (1954), Chapter 2.

[4] Frank Parkin, *Class, Inequality and Political Order* (1971).

[5] M. Young and P. Willmott, 'Social Grading by Manual Workers', *B.J.S.*, December 1956.

their respondents differed significantly in their ranking. Skilled manual jobs were elevated while non-manual occupations such as insurance agent, clerk and shop assistant were lowered. The 'deviants' differed greatly from the 'normal' in their criteria for judgement, all but one giving 'social contribution' as the basis for elevating or depressing the prestige of an occupation.

It is more plausible to argue that it is those who occupy the dominant positions in society who are in a position to determine the system of social evaluation and to manipulate and distribute the symbols of honour and prestige. And if property and income are highly valued, material rewards will also function as symbols of social honour, while those who are honoured will be defined as entitled to wealth and privilege.

Status rankings function to legitimize differences in the distribution of wealth and power. Those who have power are honoured, and their status underpins their exercise of power. The enjoyment of deference and privileges, such as exemption from unpleasant tasks, special immunities (from taxes, military service, prosecution by the common courts), is tolerated while it is accepted that rank confers a title to such privileges. An example of this is the view often expressed by non-manual workers that they 'ought' to be better paid than manual workers, even though their work may be less skilled.

In short, it is precisely because the distribution of honour so closely matches the distribution of reward that inequality enjoys normative support. The prestige order 'serves to stabilize and legitimize inequalities by harnessing notions of social justice in defence of existing class privileges'.[1] We must, therefore, question Weber's claim that status is a distinct dimension of stratification. It is more 'plausible to regard social honour as an emergent property generated by the class system'.[2]

This is simply another way of saying that in a stable social system, we can expect congruence between the values of society and other aspects of the social structure. It is not surprising, for example, to find churches supporting the values of the societies of which they are a part. Thus, the encyclical 'Rerum Novarum' (Leo XIII) of 1891 is a powerful plea for private property, a condemnation of socialism, and a defence of *laissez-faire*. A chief function of the state '. . . is the duty of safeguarding private property by legal enactment and protection. Most of all, it is essential, where the passion of greed is strong, to keep the people within the line of duty; for if all may justly strive to better their condition, neither justice nor the common good allows any individual to seize upon that which belongs to another, or, under the futile and shallow

[1] Frank Parkin, op. cit.   [2] Ibid., pp. 41–2.

pretext of equality, to lay violent hands on other people's possessions.'[1]

The normative support for inequality extends to justifications for poverty and for sexual and racial discrimination. A widely-held view sees poverty as a condition which is deserved: the poor are said to be lacking in those moral qualities of hard work, thrift and abstinence, which would enable them to rise above their condition: or in contemporary phraseology, they are feckless and work-shy. An alternative justification is to see poverty as a virtue. 'Poor boys reared directly by their parents possess such advantages over those watched and taught by hired strangers, and exposed to the temptations of wealth and position, that it is not surprising they become the leaders in every branch of human action.'[2] Finally, there is the variety of more pragmatic justifications which see, poverty, or certainly relative poverty, as a necessary spur to effort. Such views are countered by those who locate the sources of poverty not in the inadequacies of the poor but in their position in a stratified society.[3]

Somewhat similar justifications are advanced to explain racial and sexual discrimination. Lack of qualifications, frequent job changes, and personal qualities such as idleness and unwillingness to learn are frequently given as reasons for not employing coloured citizens. Or, it is argued, that customers, other employees, or neighbouring householders or tenants hold such unfavourable views.[4]

Such justifications for power and privilege, riches and poverty, can be located within broader ideologies of social justice. Ultimately, it is what society (or sections within society) accept as fair and just which authorizes the differential distribution of rewards. And although such issues have been explored by philosophers, we know little about the views on social justice which are held by various sections of society.

Differentiation and the political system
The analysis so far implies that economic differentiation is entirely a function of the economic system. But, as previous chapters have shown, the economy is not autonomous, being particularly closely related to the political system. It could also be argued that the political system plays a major role in determining the distribution of rewards. It is political laws which confer powers in the market

[1] Catholic Truth Society, *The Pope and the People* (1943), p. 154.

[2] Andrew Carnegie, *The Gospel of Wealth and Other Essays* (1901), quoted in R. E. Will and H. G. Vatter, *Poverty in Affluence* (1970).

[3] For a more detailed discussion of ideologies of poverty, see ibid., pp. 27–45.

[4] W. W. Daniel, op. cit., Chapters 4 and 13; J. Mitchell, *Women's Estate* (1971).

and over property. And political action can abolish the whole class of factory owners and businessmen. Moreover, political action has influenced the distribution of the national product through taxation. The bargaining power of labour has been strengthened by the right to strike, unemployment insurance and full-employment policies. How far social benefits have redistributed incomes is more problematic. Vaizey has calculated that although the middle class contribute a higher proportion to the costs of education, they also consume more, and on balance enjoy a net gain.[1] Martin[2] has demonstrated the differential consumption of health services; prescriptions for middle-class patients involving significantly greater cost than those for working-class patients.

But the relations between social differentiation and the political system are more fundamental than simply the effect of politics on economic rewards. The differential distribution of power and authority is as much a characteristic feature of societies as economic differences. Indeed, since organization is an essential feature of large-scale societies, it can be argued that differences in power are a functional necessity. We have already seen in Chapter 5 that there is a substantial concentration of political power, and that there is a close association between the economically and politically dominant strata. But whether social differentiation is best understood as a function of the political system or of the economic system and the relative importance to be attached to each, is still a matter for controversy.

Recent comparative studies of socialist societies throw some light on this issue. Studies of countries such as Sweden, Norway, Denmark and, to a lesser extent, Britain, which experienced periods of socialist government, indicate that the influence of politics on equality in capitalist societies is slight but detectable. Such countries show slightly greater chances of upward mobility from non-manual to manual, and a higher proportion of university students of working-class origins. But there is no evidence that socialist governments have succeeded in achieving any significant redistribution of material rewards. More egalitarian trends in the post-war period occurred in all industrial societies. And more recently in the 1960s, there has been a similar reversal of such trends, including the period of the Labour administration in Britain from 1964.[3] In short, social democratic parties are more successful in broadening the basis of recruitment to more highly rewarded positions than they are in achieving greater equality of rewards.

[1] J. Vaizey, *The Costs of Education* (1958).
[2] J. P. Martin, *Social Aspects of Prescribing* (1957).
[3] Frank Parkin, op. cit., Chapter 4.

In the communist states of Europe, a somewhat different picture emerges. The early post-revolutionary phase has everywhere been characterized by a marked equalization of income. But this has been followed by a substantial widening of differentials, particularly for the highly qualified. And although recruitment to privileged positions, particularly elites, remains much more broadly-based, inequalities of income have re-emerged which in some cases approximate to those in capitalist societies. 'These facts suggest that the political elites have been unable in some respects to shape the system of stratification to their own specifications, and that they have been confronted with other social forces. . . .'[1] Just what these forces are, we examine in more detail later.

CLASS SOLIDARITY

So far, this discussion has deliberately avoided using words like 'middle class' and 'working class' wherever possible. Such words in the vocabulary of social differentiation are ambiguous in meaning and present considerable difficulty. They imply the existence of a group of individuals which is more than simply a statistical aggregate like 'tall men'. Indeed, some textbooks of sociology include a discussion of social classes as part of the analysis of the organization of society.

Now we need to tread cautiously in moving from a description of the distribution of differences in income, property or prestige to the assumption that actual groupings have evolved on the basis of such differences. Marx, for example, was aware of the fact that the common experiences of those occupying similar roles in the production process did not necessarily result in the formation of a class. It is only when such individuals become aware of their common fate and come together for collective action that they are transformed from a 'class in itself' to a 'class for itself'. The facts of class, as Tawney[2] has reminded us, are not the same thing as the consciousness of class.

We need further to distinguish between a *class* and a *stratum*. A social stratum is an aggregate of individuals with similar social status. A stratum is a statistical construct. But where a stratum is relatively homogeneous, composed of individuals with flat status profiles, there is more likelihood that its members will become aware of the stratum as a distinct entity, and its relation to others in the hierarchy of strata. Such shared perceptions and awareness

[1] David Lane, *The End of Inequality?* (1971), p. 132. See also F. Parkin, op. cit., Chapter 6.
[2] R. H. Tawney, *Equality* (1952).

of shared interests can become the basis for the transformation of a stratum into a class.[1]

We can then distinguish four main elements in the process of increasing crystallization of classes on the basis of the differential distribution of rewards.[2] Firstly, there is the consciousness of identity, of belonging to a group with common characteristics and a common fate. Secondly, there is the emergence of shared beliefs, attitudes and values (culture).[3] Thirdly, there is the increasing interaction between members of such emerging groups. And finally, there is concerted action for the pursuit of common interests through the formation of class associations such as political parties.

Class identity and class consciousness

In a study by F. M. Martin,[4] subjects in Greenwich and Hertford were asked: 'How many social classes would you say there are in this country?' 'Can you name them?' 'Which of these classes do you belong to?' Ninety-six per cent of the sample saw society as being divided into three main classes, upper, middle and working, 36·6 per cent replying that they were 'working class' and 42·5 per cent 'middle class'. A further 9 per cent replied 'lower class' or 'poor'. Most, therefore, think of society as being divided into two main classes and are able to allocate themselves to one of these categories. The relation between occupation and class identity can be seen in Table 7.2. Two-thirds of non-manual workers thought of themselves as middle class, compared with one-quarter of manual workers.

TABLE 7.2

	Occupation	Class identity	%
A.	Professional, managerial	Middle class	93
B.	Other non-manual	Middle class	65
C.	,, ,,	Working class	32
D.	Manual	Middle class	26
E.	,,	Working class	70

To know that a person thinks of himself as middle class tells us little unless we also know the meaning which he gives to the term. The 'deviant' groups 'C' and 'E' in Table 7.2 are of particular interest in this context, that is to say, non-manual workers who identify with the working class and manual workers calling themselves 'middle class'. Martin found that these two groups in fact gave rather different answers to the questions, 'What sort of

[1] L. Broom, op. cit.
[2] R. Williams, op. cit., p. 92.
[3] This has already been discussed in Chapter 6.
[4] In D. V. Glass (ed.), op. cit., Chapter 3.

people belong to the same class as yourself?' Most respondents defined the working class in occupational terms as manual workers factory workers, or artisans. But group 'D' who defined themselves as middle class, also had a different frame of reference by which they assessed membership of the working class. They were much more likely to define working class in terms of low income and standard of living and in moral and evaluative terms such as laziness and lack of ambition. Similarly, group 'C' defined 'working class' as 'everyone who works for a living' and extended the working class to embrace minor non-manual occupations. It is not surprising, too, to find that respondents differed in their allocation of occupations to class categories. Group 'C', the salaried working class, tended to extend the description 'working class' to workers in occupations similar to their own.

Such data confirm that although the notion that society is divided into classes is widely accepted, there is a considerable confusion as to what constitutes the basis for inclusion, in either main category. It is difficult, however, to know what significance to attach to these findings. Existing researches do not tell us the degree of importance which respondents attach to their class identity. For some, being 'working class' may be a most significant element in their identity which influences their behaviour in a number of ways, especially voting behaviour. For others, it may be a largely meaningless label. We will therefore turn to such evidence in a later section. One other tentative conclusion can be drawn. Those who are not rewarded by the existing social system with income and prestige, can adopt a number of strategies. One, we have already seen, is to reject the prevailing social norms which fail to attach sufficient value to their particular role. Another is to redefine the norms themselves in such a way that the prestigious categories are extended to include them. This is apparently the strategy of many manual workers who are rejecting the label, 'working class'.

Interaction and association
Reference has already been made to the distinctive interaction patterns which characterize the traditional manual workers' community. The close-knit community leads to informal relations but notions of privacy exclude strangers who are not close friends or kin. Under such circumstances, there may be less need for membership of formal associations and consequently there is considerably less joining of clubs and voluntary associations. The associations joined, such as darts clubs, require relatively little organization and will largely exclude non-manual workers. In other words, for many the pub is also the club, providing a locus for whatever

association is needed outside the informal relations of the social network. There is, in other words, a full associational life, but it takes place largely outside formal organizations.

There appear to be a number of factors underlying this reluctance of working men to join formally organized associations. Among these is a fear of commitment which inhibits entering into any obligation which looks like a contract, together with a dislike of being pushed around. Problems of communication between different strata are also contributory factors. Bernstein[1] has drawn attention to the restricted language forms characteristic of a close-knit kinship system which hinder verbal expression and therefore social interaction outside the network. Working-men's teams and clubs are differentiated from the more formal associations by what Klein[2] calls 'effortless sociability'. Notification is casual, and nobody worries if he is absent. Middle-class associations require more formal commitment, and activities are planned further ahead. But there is no doubt that 'there are strong influences towards segregation in accordance with occupational status'.[3]

Other evidence of the restricted interaction between strata comes from data on marriage. There is a particularly high degree of association between the social origins of brides and grooms at the top and bottom of the social ladder, although there has been a slight decline over the last fifty years.[4] There is also a tendency for grooms to marry brides with a similar educational background—this is particularly strong among those with secondary or further education.

SOCIAL MOBILITY

One factor influencing the extent to which strata coalesce into solidary groupings is the degree to which they are self-recruiting. Restricted mobility facilitates the protection of privileges by a stratum and the development and persistence of a unitary culture. It is widely believed, particularly in America, that modern industrial societies in fact make possible a substantial degree of mobility and are in this sense 'open' societies, in which there is a reasonably close relation between a person's ability and his position in society. Status is achieved on the basis of merit rather than ascribed by birth. Before examining the relevant evidence, it is first necessary to look more closely at what we mean by social mobility, how it is measured, and the factors which offset it.

In investigating mobility, we want to know how the position

[1] B. Bernstein, in A. H. Halsey *et al.*, op. cit. (1961).
[2] J. Klein, *Samples from English Culture* (1965), p. 212.
[3] Ibid.   [4] D. V. Glass (ed.), op. cit.

which individuals achieve in society differs from that of their family of origin. The method widely used by sociologists is to compare the status of fathers and sons, using occupation as the index of status. The same status scale is used for classifying both fathers and sons and it is assumed therefore, that there have been no marked changes in occupational status. Such an approach measures mobility by using only one dimension of stratification— *status*—and ignores others such as *power* and *class*. It also faces the practical difficulty that at the time of the inquiry, sons may not have reached the height of their careers. However, movement within a generation is very much less than between generations.[1] Seventy-nine per cent of those who begin as manual workers remain in this category.[2]

Even when we know how the statuses of fathers and sons compare, there is still a considerable problem of interpretation. Industrialization has resulted in a very considerable change in the occupational structure. There has been a relative decline in the primary extractive industries such as agriculture, and an increase, especially in the later stages, of tertiary service industries, including clerical work, and professional and technical occupations.[3] In other words, there has been an increase in the proportion of higher status non-manual occupations. This alone will account for some improvement in the statuses of sons compared with fathers. In 1881, for example, 21·5 per cent of occupied males in England were non-manual workers, compared with 27 per cent in 1951.

A second factor influencing comparisons of intergenerational status is a demographic one—the relative fertility rates of different strata.[4] Since non-manual workers have smaller families, some non-manual jobs will have to be recruited from the sons of manual workers, even if the proportion of such jobs remains constant.

The comparison of statuses between generations raises a further difficulty. In a society in which 80 per cent of the population are peasants and agricultural labourers, we could expect 80 per cent of their sons to remain peasants and labourers, assuming a perfectly random distribution of occupations among sons, with no bias whatever. In other words, we have to take account of the size of various occupational groups in our attempts to measure the degree of mobility.[5] The more closely the numbers recruited to any status

---

[1] D. V. Glass, op. cit.

[2] G. Thomas, *The Social Survey: Labour Mobility in Britain 1945–9*. With the increase in the importance of education as the determinant of occupation, there are signs of a *decrease* in career mobility. See Acton Society Trust, *Management Succession* (1956).

[3] See Chapter 4.   [4] See Chapter 2.

[5] See D. V. Glass, op. cit., Chapter 8, for a discussion of statistical methods of calculating an index of mobility.

category are proportionate to their numbers in the population, the nearer we are to 'perfect' mobility.[1]

The extent of mobility

Studies of the extent of social mobility in Britain indicate that about 40 per cent of sons are upwardly mobile. Moreover, this proportion appears to be family stable. Precise international comparisons are not possible since surveys in other countries are not strictly comparable. But the proportion of non-manual sons of manual fathers varies from 29 per cent in Germany to 33 per cent in the United States and 45 per cent in Switzerland.[2] It is interesting to note that the perception which individuals have of the opportunity structure does not necessarily correspond to the facts; notably, the view that mobility is high in the United States and low in Europe. Such data does not indicate the relative opportunities open to sons of manual and non-manual fathers. Miller[3] has constructed an 'index of openness', which compares the chances of the children of non-manual and manual workers remaining in or attaining non-manual jobs. This again shows some differences, with countries such as Great Britain, Denmark, France and Sweden being most open (indices of 234, 262, 264, 284) and West Germany and Italy the least open (355, 747). But again the differences are not generally marked.

Two points need to be made to qualify this picture. Firstly, the amount of movement is limited—typically one or two status categories. Secondly, such data fails to bring out the high degree of self-recruitment in the higher strata. That is to say, if we take account of the relatively small numbers of sons in status category 1, the proportion who end up in the same status is quite disproportionate. Nearly half of those in this category are the sons of a small group comprising less than 4 per cent of the population.[4] In other words, their chances of staying at the 'top of the ladder' are many times greater than we could expect if such chances were fairly equally distributed throughout the population.

In summary, although rather more than one-third of sons have a higher status than their fathers, the shift is seldom more than one category, and takes place mainly in the middle ranges of the status hierarchy. Moreover, mobility to the highest stratum is relatively small.

[1] This phrase does not imply that such a degree of mobility is desirable.
[2] S. M. Lipset and R. Bendix, *Social Mobility in Industrial Society* (1959), p. 24.
[3] S. M. Miller, 'Comparative Social Mobility', *Current Sociology*, 1960, No. 1, Table 4a.
[4] D. V. Glass, op. cit.

Elite mobility

Studies of the recruitment of particular elites provide more detailed and precise information on elite self-recruitment. About 60 per cent of the businessmen in Britain[1] and the United States are the sons of businessmen. Studies of the higher civil service show that 48 per cent attended public schools while 30 per cent came from families of property owners and professionals which comprise only 3 per cent of the population.[2] Studies of high court judges, bishops and Cabinet ministers show a similar preponderance of those drawn from the upper echelons of society. Such evidence supports the view that industrial societies are characterized by a high degree of mobility only if mobility is conceived in a somewhat restricted sense. It also suggests that mobility to positions of power is even more restricted and, in this sense, there is still relatively little mobility in contemporary societies. Members of the elite strata have, that is to say, a number of strategies, such as the public schools, which enable them to preserve their positions for their sons. But although the movement between one generation and the next may be less than supposed, the cumulative effect of changes over a number of generations could be expected to be considerably greater.

The process of social mobility

Most research on mobility has concentrated on the amount of movement between generations. Less is known about the mobility process, and the actual mechanisms by which individuals move up or down the social ladder, and the consequences of such movement.

The chance of movement between generations depends not only on variables such as differential fertility and occupational change. It depends, too, on the avenues which exist for upward or downward mobility and the existence of barriers hindering mobility. One major reason for expecting an increase in mobility in industrial societies is the growth in the number of occupations requiring educational qualifications, and in the expanding role of bureaucratic organizations such as central government and large-scale industrial and commercial undertakings using formal criteria for recruitment and promotion. There has been a corresponding decline in the number of inheritable positions. But although these changes have opened up fresh avenues of mobility, it must also be remembered that other avenues have become more restricted. The increasing capitalization of production has made successful entrepreneurship more difficult. Moreover, it is becoming increasingly

[1] G. H. Copeman, *Leaders of British Industry* (1955); Acton Society Trust, op. cit.

[2] R. K. Kelsall, *Higher Civil Servants in Britain* (1955).

233

hard for the small shopkeeper to survive, whereas in the latter part of the nineteenth century, rapid population growth, urbanization, and rising levels of living had resulted in retail trade providing a significant avenue for mobility.

There is considerable evidence on the role of education in mobility and on the relation between ability and occupational achievement. Studies in Britain show that the type of schooling significantly affects the association between the status of father and son. The grammar school is the decisive stage. But as we have seen,[1] both access to education and educational achievement are heavily influenced by parental background. Consequently, the influence of education modifies but does not destroy the association between the status of father and son. Thus in the British mobility survey, 40 per cent of the sons of status category 5 (43 per cent of the sample) who attended independent schools achieved categories 1 and 2, compared with only 2·3 per cent of those attending elementary schools.[2] By contrast, 66 per cent of the sons of categories 1 and 2 (8 per cent of the sample) attending independent schools achieved categories 1 and 2, but so did 26 per cent of those who had not attended grammar school.[3] In other words, not only are the chances of attending a grammar school less for able children in working-class homes, but the chance that a grammar-school education will lead to the higher rungs of the occupational ladder are also considerably reduced for the sons of manual workers. That is to say, education is a factor in social mobility, but it is by no means the only one. Not only is educational opportunity restricted for those from working-class homes, but so are the occupational opportunities of those who have reached similar levels in the educational system.

But mobility is not only a function of the opportunity structure and the ability of the individual. It is related also to the extent to which the individual is motivated to climb the social ladder. And this in turn will be determined in part by the culture of society, specifically the prevailing mobility norms which may value or discourage upward striving, and the extent to which society is defined as providing opportunities for mobility. But there is also evidence to suggest that quite complex personality differences exist which help to explain why individuals with similar levels of ability experience differing degrees of mobility.[4] Studies suggest that the

[1] Chapter 3.

[2] This term refers to the non-grammar schools pre-1945 in which education normally ceased at fourteen.

[3] D. V. Glass, op. cit., Chapter 10.

[4] For a survey of the literature, see D. F. Swift, 'Social Class and Achievement Motivation', *Educational Research*, February 1966.

upwardly mobile have received earlier training for independence, have had more opportunities for interaction with adults, have the capacity to deal with others instrumentally rather than emotionally, have learned to defer present gratifications, and have higher rates of mental disturbances. Researches also indicate that such differences are related to sociological variables such as parent-child relationships. It suggests, for example, that upwardly-mobile children are likely to come from homes where parents have adopted higher status groups as reference groups and have subjected their children to anticipatory socialization into middle-class norms, and in which parental approval is conditional upon the mastery of tasks.[1]

Further evidence on the mobility process comes from studies of the factors influencing the choice of, and entry into, occupations. Children from working-class homes have a restricted knowledge of the range of occupations open to them. They are unlikely to have relatives who are accountants, solicitors, or businessmen. They are far more likely to be influenced in their occupational choice by *significant others*, such as father, elder brother or uncle, and for this reason, many will follow in the footsteps of an admired relative.[2] It is first occupation which is the crucial choice. Once a manual job has been taken, there is little chance of mobility. In short, the boy whose father is semi- or unskilled is handicapped in a variety of ways. Early socialization is unlikely to have developed the personality characteristics of the upwardly mobile, such as deferred gratification and strong achievement motivation; he is likely to be an under-achiever at school and to acquire a distaste for his studies; his range of occupational choice will be restricted by inadequate educational qualifications, and by lack of knowledge of the requirements and strategies for occupational mobility. His subsequent choice is likely to be strongly influenced by admired individuals within his own immediate social sphere, and once chosen at fifteen or sixteen, his future career is more or less determined.

In short, for many, the cards are so stacked that upward mobility is the exception. The mechanisms at work are complex and subtle, and unlikely to be solved by simple administrative solutions such as improvements in the Youth Employment Service or better student grants, however necessary such changes may be. There is little evidence to support the view that industrial societies have become 'meritocracies' in which rewards reflect the merits of the individual.

[1] See S. M. Lipset and R. Bendix, op. cit., for a summary of such researches.
[2] R. F. L. Logan and E. M. Goldberg, 'Rising Eighteen in a London Suburb', *B.J.S.*, Vol. 4, pp. 323–45; M. Carter, *Home, School and Work* (1962), and *Into Work* (1966).

Social mobility and the social system

Social mobility is not only a function of the occupational structure, differential fertility, and cultural variables. It also has consequences for the social system. A society which rewards success raises problems for those who fail. Upward mobility, it must be remembered, also implies related degrees of downward mobility. Underlying much research and writing on mobility, there is the assumption that it is a 'good thing' and that a high rate of mobility is both socially and morally desirable. Such judgements can only be sustained on the basis of factual knowledge as to the actual consequences of high and low rates of mobility.

Some indication of the possible strains generated by mobility comes from evidence on the incidence of suicide and mental disorder, which is higher among the mobile than the non-mobile. A possible explanation is that mobility removes the individual from the primary-group support which results from the disruption of family and friendship cliques.[1] But the possibility that a degree of mental disorder is a cause rather than a consequence of mobility must not be overlooked.

Cultures such as America which stress the value of success raise particular problems of adjustment for failure. One possible mode of adjustment for those who fail to achieve success by legitimate means is to seek illegitimate and deviant avenues. Another possible adjustment is support for transvaluational religions or radical politics.[2] A third is to become child-centred and to seek vicarious satisfaction in high aspirations for one's children. All such evidence suggests that high rates of mobility are to some extent disruptive. But they do not by themselves result in social instability as there are examples of stable societies such as Britain in which mobility is relatively high. By contrast, the acquisition of wealth by the eighteenth-century French bourgeoisie generated status discrepancies and revolutionary zeal among those who felt that they were being denied status and power commensurate with their wealth—a further reminder that it is not enough to study mobility along one dimension only.

CLASS CONFLICT

Although the evidence is far from complete, there seems little doubt that classes exist in a more solidary form than mere statistical aggregates of individuals of similar income, occupation, or prestige. There is a consciousness of kind, of belonging to per-

[1] S. M. Lipset and R. Bendix, op. cit., pp. 66–7.
[2] The evidence for this was examined in Chapter 6. See also F. Parkin, op. cit., Chapter 2.

ceived and definable groups, marked off by differences in beliefs, values and styles of life. Visiting, eating together (commensality), intermarriage, membership of clubs—all of these interactions are structured by an awareness of status differences. It is the status groups, differentiated by occupation and styles of life, which are the basis of such distinctions. Above all, it is the divide between banausic manual work and higher status white-collar jobs which is particularly significant. And it is the emphasis on consumption rather than on role in the production process which is crucial. Such 'estates' are particularly clear-cut at the top, where membership of 'society' is a matter of acceptance. Here, a small elite of wealth and power are united by multiple bonds of association, intermarriage, and membership of exclusive clubs.[1]

It is some index of the effectiveness of the status system in legitimizing power and privilege that the disruptive potential of social differentiation does not in general erupt into overt class conflict. The existence of class conflict is to some extent a matter of definition. For Marx, conflicts derive essentially from the ownership and non-ownership of the means of production. Marx believed that the increasing concentration of ownership and the resulting increasing impoverishment of the masses would lead to the growing polarization of society into warring classes, and the eventual overthrow of capitalist owners by the proletarian revolution. Indeed, it was in the class struggle that Marx located the dynamics of social change; 'The history of all hitherto existing society is the history of the class struggle.' But this does not mean that every strike over wages is part of the class struggle. Only if workers define themselves as members of a common class with a common fate and are seeking to change the position of their class by achieving power can such a conflict be defined as a class conflict in Marx's sense.

In fact, industrialization and the growth of *per capita* income is directly related to weak support for such revolutionary class movements. But it is not poverty alone which generates radicalism. On the contrary, stable poverty tends to be associated with conservatism. It is the awareness of the possibilities of the betterment which accompanies industrialization, which is explosive. It is relative deprivation,[2] not absolute poverty, which generates discontent. Where industrialization has been accompanied by the extension of the franchise and a party system, it has provided legitimate channels for the expression of discontent.[3] Indeed, as we saw in Chap-

[1] A. Sampson, *Anatomy of Britain Today* (1962).
[2] For a recent discussion of this concept, see W. G. Runciman, *Relative Deprivation and Social Justice* (1966).
[3] S. M. Lipset, op. cit. (1959), pp. 61–7, 'Economic Development and the Class Struggle'.

ters 5 and 6, it is a relatively small minority who support a political ideology of the left, and see politics in class terms.

Dahrendorf, however, argues that class is essentially a question of power. All associations are co-ordinated by means of an authority structure, and it is the resulting differential distribution of authority which dichotomizes society into those who have and have not power. The class struggle is the struggle for power—including power to dispose of material resources, and to regulate conditions of work. Thus, even in a fully socialized society, the struggle to gain material resources and to control aspects of the work situation would remain. The 'new class' would be the managers and party officials who exercised control. According to this view, the class struggle is a permanent feature of all organized societies. Its severity can be mitigated and controlled by the reduction of objective differences and by the 'institutionalization' of conflict, but it cannot be entirely abolished.

STRATIFICATION AND SOCIAL CHANGE

Two main debates provide clues on the possible long-term trends in stratification in industrial societies. In America, a paper by Davis and Moore in 1945[1] started one of the most long-lived discussions in contemporary sociology. Moore explained the universality of stratification in functional terms, arguing that differentiation is a necessity in any society. It functions to motivate individuals to fill the various positions required by the division of labour and to carry out the necessary duties. It follows, therefore, that there are limits to any trend towards equality. On the other hand, it has been argued that industrialization is resulting in substantial convergence between the stratification systems of advanced societies in which all are moving towards a minimizing of differences and towards a greater consistency between income, education, and prestige. In Britain, considerable debate has centred around the view that affluence and mobility are eroding the traditional working class with its support for working-class associations such as the Labour party and trade unions.[2]

The embourgeoisement of the working class
Many in both the United States and in Europe have claimed to detect a trend towards the blurring of class lines, and the disappearance of cleavage between manual and non-manual. The

[1] Kingsley Davis and Wilbert E. Moore, 'Some Principles of Stratification', *A.S.R.*, Vol. 10, 1945.
[2] This debate has largely centred round the electoral position of the Labour party. See Mark Abrams and Richard Rose, *Must Labour Lose?* (1960).

argument rests on the assertion that income differentials have declined and that the achievement of middle-class incomes by many manual workers is accompanied by the adoption of middle-class styles of life.

A careful study of the empirical evidence, however, does not support this view. American data shows that the apparent overlap between clerical and skilled manual median incomes ignores the influence of sex and age. Clerical work employs large numbers of women, while for many men, it is a stepping stone to managerial positions which are reached in middle age. When these two factors are controlled, clerical incomes are considerably above those of craftsmen and foremen except for the over-45s, which includes mainly those males who have been unsuccessful in achieving promotion. If foremen are excluded from the manual group, the differences increase.[1] Studies in Germany suggest that there has, in fact, been a widening of the gap between middle and working class judged by the percentage owning consumer durables in 1953 and 1959.

But the achievement of comparable incomes does not in any case justify the assumption that these will be spent on similar 'life-styles'. German evidence shows marked differences between manual and non-manual workers in the ownership of durable consumer goods, even when income is controlled.[2] Middle class homes have more luxury goods and expensive household aids. Working class homes are superior to the homes of the equivalent middle class income group mainly in the presence of more expensive television sets and record-players; that is, in items of home entertainment. There also are marked differences in attitudes toward liquidity and savings. In a more impressionistic study, Zweig[3] found similar attitudes and patterns of expenditure among British workers.

But even if it could be demonstrated that some manual workers aspire to middle class styles of life, this is not evidence of assimilation. It must also be shown that such manual workers take the middle class as a reference group and desire to be accepted as members of the middle class. Goldthorpe and Lockwood doubt whether in fact the evidence supports the view that any such substantial embourgeoisement of the working class in this sense has

[1] Richard Hamilton, 'The Income Differences between Skilled and White-Collar Workers', *B.J.S.*, Vol. 14, December 1963. Much of the improvement in the relative position of manual workers derives from full-employment and the increasing employment of their wives. J. H. Goldthorpe, 'Stratification in Industrial Society', *Soc. Rev. Monograph, No. 8*, 1964.

[2] Richard F. Hamilton, 'Affluence and the Worker: The West German Case', *A.J.S.*, Vol. 71, September 1965.

[3] F. Zweig, *The British Worker* (1952).

occurred.[1] Despite the fact that many now own cars, television sets, and refrigerators, this has not led to their acceptance by their white-collar neighbours on equal terms. Willmott and Young report marked status segregation in the middle-class suburbs to which the more affluent workers are moving.[2] Goldthorpe and Lockwood suggest that the subordinate status of the manual worker in the work situation spills over into community and associational context. They question whether similarities of income and life-style can iron out barriers to social intercourse which derive from different positions in the authority structure of industry.[3] They doubt, too, whether the attitudinal changes are as dramatic and far-reaching as some writers have supposed. True, there has been a decline in the cohesion of the working class community as families move to new housing estates, and the emergence of home and family centredness.[4] There is more preoccupation with money, a decline in short-term hedonism and the emergence of a longer view. But the working class has never been homogeneous and has always included a 'labour aristocracy' of highly-paid craftsmen who have in many ways been similar to the middle class in outlook and values.

Goldthorpe and Lockwood suggest three stages in the embourgeosiement of the worker. Firstly, there is a decline in involvement in the traditional working class community and in the acceptance of its norms. At this stage the worker does not aspire to acceptance of membership of the middle class. He has become 'privatized', withdrawn into a private world of home-centredness. It is this which Goldthorpe and Lockwood believe to be the condition of the affluent worker. In the next phase, the socially-aspiring worker identifies with the middle class, accepts their norms, and wishes to be accepted by them. Only when such a worker is fully accepted by the middle class can embourgeoisement be said to have taken place And from the evidence, this does not appear to be the case. Nor is there much evidence to suggest that such a trend is likely to occur. The limited chances for promotion, and the subordinate position of the manual worker remain distinctive characteristics of the working class situation. Under such circumstances, it is difficult to see how manual workers will shift their social perspectives from

[1] For a discussion of this thesis, see J. Goldthorpe and D. Lockwood, 'Affluence and British Class Structure', *Soc. Rev.*, Vol. 11, July 1963, and W. G. Runciman, '"Embourgeoisement", Self-Rated Class and Party Preference', *Soc. Rev.*, July 1964.

[2] P. Willmott and M. Young, *Family and Class in a London Suburb* (1960), Zweig, *The Worker in an Affluent Society* (1961), quotes one respondent: 'I am working class only in the works, but outside I am like everyone else.'

[3] J. H. Goldthorpe and D. Lockwood, op. cit.

[4] These trends were discussed in Chapter 2.

the traditional working class 'power' model, which sees society dichotomized into 'them' and 'us', to the middle class 'status' model of society as a hierarchy of open strata up which the individual can climb by his own efforts.

The fact that an increasing number of manual workers are calling themselves middle class is not, by itself, evidence of embourgeoisement, as this would require that they were also accepted by the middle class. Runciman argues that the evidence on class identification supports the 'privatization' hypothesis. The fact that many manual workers who call themselves middle-class reject working-class identity on evaluative or income grounds supports privatization. However, it can also be argued that the many who call themselves middle class define the middle class in terms of approval, thus suggesting that they may be aspiring to membership. They are not merely status-dissenters but are positively adopting the middle class as their reference group; they are socially aspiring. Evidence for this view is the fact that manual workers in Woodford who call themselves middle class, show a shift towards middle class values and behaviour in other ways. Fifty-two per cent (compared with 36 per cent) go to church, and 42 per cent (compared with 27 per cent) go to social clubs. This is more than simply an enjoyment of middle class material standards. All that can be said at this stage is that the evidence is neither unambiguously for or against the embourgeoisement hypothesis.

The functional theory of differentiation
The Davis-Moore position stated in its simplest terms stresses the functional necessity of social differentiation and therefore the limits to any trend towards equality. Social inequality is the device '... by which societies ensure that the most important positions are filled by the most qualified persons. Hence every society, no matter how simple or complex, must differentiate persons in terms of both prestige and esteem, and must therefore possess a certain amount of institutionalized inequality.'[1]

The early stages of the debate were marked by semantic confusion, which has since been clarified. As Buckley[2] has pointed out, Davis and Moore failed to differentiate between social differentiation and stratification. The existence of social differences does not necessarily give rise to strata. What Davis and Moore have argued is that social differences are a functional necessity. But as Tumin insists, differences in income need not be taken up into the stratifi-

---

[1] Davis and Moore, op. cit. This and the articles referred to below are to be found in M. V. Tumin, *Readings on Social Stratification* (1970).
[2] W. Buckley, 'Social Stratification and the Functional Theory of Social Differentiation', *A.S.R.*, Vol. 23, 1958.

cation system and become the basis for invidious distinctions in social ranking. And it is in this sense that the principal protagonists have defined the notion of stratification as 'the presence in any society of a system by which various social units are ranked as inferior and superior to each other on a scale of social worth . . .'[1] Strata emerge then when clear-cut and consistent statuses attributable to individuals are generalized into categories for individuals of 'similar' status, and the categories ranked as 'strata'.[2]

It would be possible, therefore, to have a stratified society, reflecting social differences in rewards, which was not a 'class' society. In such a society, a person's social position would be determined entirely by his abilities and efforts. That is, it would constitute a 'meritocracy'.[3] But the possibility of achieving a classless society in this sense has not been examined by the functionalists. It would be necessary to explore the possibility of ensuring equality of access to positions, a subject which the functionalists have only touched on. Their main concern, it now becomes clear, has been to argue the necessity for unequal rewards for positions of unequal importance.[4]

The core problem, as Tumin[5] has pointed out, is how to judge functional importance in order to avoid the purely circular argument that the most important positions are the most highly rewarded because they are the most important. Moreover, the precise amount of differentiation is indeterminate. Furthermore, the functionalists appear to be arguing that most of the differences can be explained as functional. Thus the magnitude of the differences will reflect the scarcity of talent and the sacrifices involved in training. This involves a logical confusion. To argue that differences in function lead to the necessity for differences in reward does not justify the conclusion that all differences in reward are due to differences in function. It is on this point that the functionalist case appears naïve. There are only the most occasional hints that other mechanisms may be at work contributing to differentia-

[1] M. Tumin, 'On Inequality', A.S.R., Vol. 28, 1963. The controversy had failed to distinguish, as Weber had done, between market and status situations.
[2] W. E. Moore, 'But Some Are More Equal than Others', A.S.R., Vol. 28, 1963. This notion of strata takes no account of the literature on status consistency from Lenski (1954) onwards.
[3] M. Young, The Rise of the Meritocracy (1961).
[4] W. E. Moore, op. cit. This article shows a considerable shift from the original which sought to explain the universality of stratification in functional terms. It recognizes, for example, the possibility of status inconsistency.
[5] M. W. Tumin, 'Some Principles of Stratification: A Critical Analysis', A.S.R., Vol. 18, 1953.

tion.[1] Most notable is an absence of any discussion of the strategies which are used to increase differences in rewards, such as the strategies adopted by trade unions and professions for limiting entry to an occupation and thus strengthening their market positions. The income differences which result can hardly be described as functional requisites.

The functional argument assumes that there are no barriers to the mobilization of talent. But, as mobility studies show, such barriers do exist. There is little reference to the 'contrivances of various elites who find the social situation to their liking and wish to preserve it'.[2] Indeed, stratification systems which have coalesced into classes are in many ways dysfunctional. The discovery of talents is limited by unequal access to motivation, recruitment and training. Class systems, therefore, set limits to the expansion in the supply of talent.[3]

To sum up, the functionalist debate has to a considerable extent developed out of a semantic confusion between social differences, social strata, and classes. It has failed to establish that differences of any specific magnitude are essential, or to identify clearly what are the positions of most importance. Nor has it shown that all differences can be explained as reflections of a society's efforts to mobilize talent. It has neglected to explore the sources of inequality which derive from the organized efforts of groups to increase their shares, and from the intervention of the political system in the distribution of rewards. While it now recognizes the dysfunctional aspects of differentiation, it continues to stress its functional necessity.

While the functionalists have argued that some degree of differentiation is necessary, others claim to have detected a substantial convergence between the stratification systems of advanced societies in which all are moving towards a minimizing of differences to a greater consistency between income, education and prestige. Such an argument assumes that the economic system is the main determinant of stratification and ignores the influence of the political system and of culture. As Goldthorpe[3] has pointed out, there are considerable differences in the stratification systems of societies at similar levels of development. In totalitarian societies such as the USSR, the political system dominates the economic

[1] Davis and Moore, op. cit., recognize that where a priestly guild controls membership, this may prevent competition. Moreover, they recognize that property ownership introduces a compulsive element into contractual relations. Yet the profound implications which this has for the theory are not discussed.

[2] M. Tumin (1963).

[3] J. H. Goldthorpe, 'Social Stratification in Industrial Society', *Soc. Rev. Mon. No. 8*, 1964.

system and deliberately manipulates the distribution of incomes and prestige to ensure loyalty to the regime and compliance with its policies. Stratification systems are influenced, too, by ideologies, which generate purposive social action. Thus in the USA, the gap between rich and poor appears to be diverging, especially with the growth of unemployment among the unskilled,[1] whereas in Sweden deliberate social policies have helped to maintain a high general level of employment and welfare.

The data necessary for the empirical testing of these various theories is still scanty, but recent comparative studies make it possible to detect some broad patterns. There is now considerable evidence from socialist societies to show that the marked degree of egalitarianism which characterized the early phase of socialist reconstruction has given way to a considerable increase in differentials. Incomes of the highly-educated experts have shown a marked rise. This has been accompanied, and indeed made possible, by the de-proletarianization of the party and the political elite with a rapid increase in the recruitment of technicians, engineers, economists, lawyers and other experts. In short, as the emphasis has shifted from political stabilization to industrial efficiency, a conflict emerges between the ideology of equality and the demands of economic growth. And as the highly educated, whose contribution is essential for increased efficiency, grow in influence, the balance of rewards shifts in their favour so that a pattern of inequality emerges which is closer to (though not identical with) that in Western industrialized societies. The roots of such inequality are to be found in the requirement of industrial society for a high degree of division of labour, resulting in the differential distribution of skill, material rewards, power, prestige and privilege.[2]

DISCUSSION

Inequality is a persistent feature of societies with the private ownership of productive resources and market economies. And after a period of substantial equality a marked trend towards inequality of power and privilege has reasserted itself in socialist societies, in which productive resources are owned by the state and a command economy is controlled by the party apparatus. Such evidence lends some support to the more moderate functionalist argument that *some* measure of inequality is necessary for economic efficiency. It lends some support to the logic of industrializa-

[1] Michael Harrington, *The Other America: Poverty in the United States* (1963).
[2] David Lane, op. cit., Chapters 4, 5 and 6. Frank Parkin, op. cit., Chapters 5 and 6, and 'Class Stratification in Socialist Societies', *B.J.S.*, December 1969.

tion thesis of convergency. But only some. Political and ideological forces can and do shape the reward. And the degree of inequality *is* significantly different. Nor can the similarities or the differences be explained in terms of the logic of industrialization. Just how small the differences can be, compatible with efficiency, must await further evidence. That the magnitude of differences exists in the West is functionally necessary is open to serious doubt. That the abolition of differences hinders efficiency has strong supporting evidence.[1] The conflict would appear to be between the pursuit of some notion of social justice and economic efficiency. Its resolution is essentially a political decision, though the remarkable stability of stratification systems in advanced industrial societies throws doubt on the possibility of achieving any marked shift towards egalitarianism. The main thrust of change has been towards some opening up of recruitment, mainly through a small increase in educational opportunity and most markedly in socialist societies. The chances of becoming unequal have become slightly more equal. But poverty in the sense of relative deprivation would seem to be endemic in advanced industrial societies.

The remarkable stability of inequality is in part a reflection of the success with which most industrial societies have legitimized differential rewards through status hierarchies and the differential distribution of honour. This plays a major part in shaping the definition of social justice. For most, social justice means the achievement of a meritocracy—equal chances to be unequal— rather than an egalitarian society, though there are signs of a steady erosion in the legitimacy accorded to social inequality.[2] Class conflict, in other words, has not in general threatened the stability of society.

On such evidence, we may comment more speculatively on the perennial debate about the relations between man and society. To be born into the lower strata of society tells us something about being and becoming. More than anything else, birth influences 'life chances'—the chances for education, employment in work which gives opportunities for self-expression and development, and the receipt of honour from our fellow-men. We cannot separate what we do, what we achieve, and what we are. In this sense, birth still plays a part in determining what a man is capable of becoming, and the realization of human potential. The accident of birth, in short, more than any single factor, shapes the nature of the man.

[1] There was a tendency for university graduates in Czechoslovakia to enter factory work in the late 1950s. (F. Parkin, op. cit. (1969), p. 363.)
[2] A. Beteille, 'The Decline of Social Inequality?', in A. Beteille (ed.), *Social Inequality* (1969).

R. Anderson and R. Blackburn, *Towards Socialism* (Fontana, 1965).

R. Bendix and S. M. Lipset, *Class, Status and Power* (Routledge, 1967).

André Beteille (ed.), *Social Inequality* (Penguin, 1969).

T. B. Bottomore, *Classes in Modern Society* (Ampersand, 1955).

Ken Coates and Richard Silburn, *Poverty: The Forgotten Englishman* (Penguin, 1970).

L. A. Coser and B. M. Rosenburg, *Sociological Theory* (Collier-Macmillan, 1964).

C. A. R. Crosland, *The Future of Socialism* (Cape, 1964).

W. W. Daniel, *Racial Discrimination in England* (Penguin, 1968).

N. Deakin, *Colour, Citizenship and British Society* (Panther, 1970).

D. V. Glass (ed.), *Social Mobility in Britain* (Routledge, 1954).

J. H. Goldthorpe *et al.*, *The Affluent Worker in the Class Structure* (Cambridge University Press, 1969).

W. Guttsman, *The British Political Elite* (MacGibbon and Kee, 1964).

M. Harrington, *The Other America* (Penguin, 1963).

J. A. Jackson (ed.), *Social Stratification* (Cambridge University Press, 1968).

J. Klein, *Samples from English Culture* (Routlege, 1965).

David Lane, *The End of Inequality?* (Penguin, 1971).

G. E. Lenski, *Power and Privilege: A New Theory of Stratification* (McGraw-Hill, 1966).

S. M. Lipset and R. Bendix, *Social Mobility in Industrial Society* (Heinemann, 1959).

R. K. Merton, L. Broom and L. S. Cottrell, *Sociology Today: Problems and Prospects* (Harper and Row, 1965), Chapter 19.

J. Mitchell, *Women's Estate* (Penguin, 1971).

S. Ossowski, *Class Structure in the Social Consciousness* (Routledge, 1963).

Frank Parkin, *Class, Inequality and Political Order* (MacGibbon and Kee, 1971).

J. Rex, *Race Relations in Sociological Theory* (Weidenfeld and Nicolson, 1970).

J. Rex and R. Moore (eds), *Race, Community and Conflict* (Oxford University Press).

J. L. Roach and J. K. Roach, *Poverty* (Penguin, 1972).

W. G. Runciman, *Relative Deprivation and Social Justice* (Routledge, 1966).

M. V. Tumin, *Readings on Social Stratification* (Prentice-Hall, 1970).

R. E. Will and H. G. Vatter, *Poverty in Affluence* (Harcourt, 1970).

Chapter 8

INTERACTION AND ORGANIZATION

At a number of points in our analysis of society, the polarity between the self and society has become apparent. In this chapter, this issue is central. Functionalism, especially, paints a picture of man as the prisoner of society, socialized to act the part which society has allotted him, and constrained by social pressure to conform. More recently, the social action approach reintroduces a voluntaristic perspective. It focuses on the individual actors in interaction through the use of concepts of 'self', 'identity', 'social exchange', and 'negotiated orders'.

In the analysis of interaction and organization, society is dissected through a dimension which cuts across the various sub-systems explored in earlier chapters. Interaction and organization are processes which occur within the family, schools, factories and churches. We focus especially on the sensitive points of interaction between the individual and others in a variety of unstructured and structured situations—factories, schools, hospitals, prisons. We look at the various theories about how to integrate the behaviour of collectives of individuals, and most important, how individuals respond to such attempts to control and direct. But first, it is necessary to explore the concepts used in the analysis of the self in interaction.

IDENTITIES AND INTERACTIONS

Roles

The concept of role is central to the study of the interaction process. It provides the bridge between the individual and others—the self and society. And at first sight (and in some of its usages), it *is* deterministic in its implications.[1] The concept of the role of father or husband or teacher stresses the idea that the individual is expected to play a part, to conform to society's expectation of what it is to be a husband or a teacher. This essentially structuralist approach emphasizes the pressure of society and the conformity of the individual to its norms.

---

[1] For a discussion of the variety of meanings and the development of role theory, see M. Banton, *Roles* (1965), Chapters 1 and 2.

But the picture is over-drawn in a variety of ways. Firstly, it assumes that the behaviour implied by a role is a rigid set of prescriptions, spelt out in great detail. Such is not the case, even in highly-structured situations.[1] And much social interaction takes place in situations which are unstructured or only loosely structured. So, for example, behaviour in morning assembly in a school is highly-structured, but that in the classroom much less so. Secondly, it ignores the fact that individuals both take and make roles in interaction with others. When an individual, *ego*, interacts with another, *alter*, he tries to discover what the other expects of him—to test the other's role and his expectations. 'The idea of role-taking shifts the emphasis away from the simple process of enacting a prescribed role to devising a performance on the basis of an imputed other-role.'[2] This interactionist approach enables us to see role behaviour in structured situations as a compromise between formalized role prescriptions and the more flexible interaction between individuals.[3] The fact that each is able to execute some plan of action does not mean that there is consensus between them, but only that there is 'a sufficient lack of disagreement about one another for each to proceed . . .'.[4]

In other words, it is sometimes useful to employ the notions of *transaction* or *negotiation* in the interaction process. Although the roles of husband and wife are broadly defined, the precise nature of their interaction will depend not only on each exploring the more explicit expectations of the other, but also on some element of negotiation where there are differences. Even in highly-structured situations, such negotiation occurs. Psychiatric hospitals, for example, are highly organized. Physicians, psychiatrists, nurses, inmates—each have roles governed by the rules of the organization. But the rules are 'far from extensive, or clearly stated or clearly binding'.[5] Consequently, rules can be used, stretched, or conveniently forgotten when it suits any particular individual or group. The non-professional staff, for example, will wish to control the conditions of their work as much as possible. 'Illustrating from one area only, that of controlling superiors—aides have various means of such control. These include withholding information and displaying varying degrees of co-operation in charting or in

---

[1] Military roles and games are limiting cases, not typical.

[2] Ralph H. Turner, 'Role-Taking: Process Versus Conformity', in A. M. Rose (ed.), *Human Behaviour and Social Processes* (1962), p. 23.

[3] Ibid., p. 38.

[4] G. J. McCall and J. L. Simmons, *Identities and Interactions* (1966), p. 127.

[5] A. Strauss, L. Schatzman, D. Erlich, R. Bucher and M. Sabshim, 'The Hospital and Its Negotiated Order', in F. G. Castles (ed.), *Decisions, Organizations and Society* (1971).

attending meetings.'[1] Similarly, patients will negotiate for privileges and information. In short, the existence of a formal structure and a hierarchy of roles does not prevent individuals and groups negotiating to accomplish their various purposes.

Roles frequently bring an individual into interaction with a number of other roles, and consequently subject the individual to a variety of demands and expectations from members of his *role-set*.[2] Teachers, for example, may be subject to varying and conflicting expectations from heads, parents, and the education authority. Occupying a multiplicity of roles also generates problems of conflicting demands and budgeting one's time and energy between the demands of the various roles.[3] Working wives, for example, will experience *role strain* generated by the conflicting demands of their roles as workers, wives and mothers.

The incumbency of a number of roles means that an individual also has a number of social selves. When acting the role of, say, scientist, the identity of devoted father and husband is, as it were, in the background as a *latent identity*.[4] Sexual roles, for example, and the identities with which they are associated, are latent in many situations. Thus, in many work situations, sexual roles and identities are left outside the factory gates, and interaction takes place within the context of work roles. But not entirely. Thus tensions may arise if a young woman is put in charge of an older man.

Identities and interaction

So far, the discussion has focused on the parts which the actor plays. We need also to explore the characteristics of the 'self' as distinct from the various roles played by the self. Some roles, such as work roles, may involve only a part of the self. Others, such as the roles of an artist or priest, may be seen as *total roles*, in the sense that they provide a means for a total expression or acting-out of the self. It is to this notion of the 'self' to which we now turn.

Acting a role involves presenting some aspect of the self. A student sweeping railway platforms as a holiday job will be anxious to maintain his identity as a student: he is not 'really' a porter. In taking and negotiating roles, we are also negotiating *identities*. And the range of roles we play provides us with a range of iden-

[1] Ibid., p. 114. See also P. Blau, 'Social Exchange', in K. Thompson and J. Tunstall, *Sociological Perspectives* (1971), pp. 220–33.
[2] R. K. Merton, 'Role Sets', in ibid., pp. 209–19.
[3] W. J. Goode, 'A Theory of Role Strain', *A.S.R.*, 1960, pp. 483–96.
[4] A. W. Gouldner, 'Cosmopolitans and Locals: Towards an Analysis of Latent Social Roles', *Admin. Sc. Qu.*, Vol. 2, 1957, pp. 281–306, 444–80.

tities—as generous, intelligent, athletic, beautiful—whatever our *self-concept* may be.

It is clearly not enough simply to have a private self-concept: it must also be accepted and reinforced by others. Hence Cooley's concept of the *looking-glass self*, the self which we see reflected in the reactions of others towards us. This interactionist approach to the development of self-concepts has generated a substantial literature on the strategies which the individual adopts to present the self in as favourable a light as possible. Goffman's exploration of such performances draws heavily on dramaturgical analogies. The self which a waiter presents to the customer, for example, may be very different from that which emerges *back-stage* in the kitchen.[1] For some, the achievement of a satisfactory identity presents special problems. Those with physical defects or those on whom society has conferred stigmatized labels (eleven-plus failures, criminals) have special problems in the 'management of spoiled identities'.[2] There are also some situations, such as sexual encounters, which present risks to identity where face may need to be saved, or where we need to drive a 'wedge between doing and being'. Where an activity implies a 'self' which the individual is loathe to accept, he will attempt to display *role distance*.[3]

Recently, however, doubts have been raised about the dramaturgical options available to those socialized within a working-class culture. If, as has been suggested, this is a rule-governed 'received' culture, then its members have had no opportunity to *play at* roles; only to play them. This will place severe limitations on their ability to exercise the kinds of options which have been discussed above, and, in this sense, to *create* structures and thus to escape from society as a prison.[4]

Socialization

It will be obvious by now that the symbolic interactionist school whose work has been discussed is interested not only in the inter-action between the self and society but also in the ways in which the self is a product of such interaction. Identities or self-concepts are formed and sustained by the actions of other towards us. It is this emphasis on social interaction which is the specific contribu-

[1] E. Goffman, *The Presentation of Self in Everyday Life* (1969).
[2] E. Goffman, *Stigma: Notes on The Management of Spoiled Identities* (1970).
[3] E. Goffman, *Where the Action Is* (1969). Role distance may also function to facilitate interaction. Thus a teacher may joke and use slang, implying that he is 'coming down' to the pupils' level. On the functions of role distance in surgery, see ibid., pp. 73–84.
[4] J. Ford, D. Young and S. Box, op. cit. (1967).

tion of sociology to an understanding of the socialization process.

A particular emphasis of the interactionist approach is the crucial role of symbols, especially language. Such symbols convey meanings and values. It is this distinctive capacity for communication through symbols which differentiates men from animals. Symbols enable the individual to stimulate behaviour in others as well as himself, and to exercise some control over others. Symbols encapsulate huge amounts of experience in the form of meanings and values which, when shared, constitute the culture of a society. It is through the acquisition of such a storehouse of meanings that the distinctively human process of socialization takes place. Such learning is very rapid, and in this way quite different from animal learning through trial and error and conditioning, although such learning plays a part in the early stages of the socialization process.[1]

A central core of the socialization process is learning to play roles. But even more crucial is the learning to differentiate between the self and the external world—partly as a result of experiencing a series of 'shocks'—including weaning and toilet training—by which the individual becomes aware of the 'rough contours of the external world'.[2] By the age of 5 or 6, the child will begin to develop a 'self-image', as, for example, a 'good boy'. In short, he comes to see himself as others see him. During adolescence, as he moves out into a stream of new worlds, and experiences a new range of interactions, he may become less sure of his identity, or become dissatisfied with what he considers to be a stigmatized identity (for example 'C'-steam failure).

Learning to play roles is an important source of a self-concept. It is in this way, for example, that a sexual identity is formed. Future occupational roles may also provide a major component of the individual's identity. A prestigious role, such as that of a doctor, which requires a substantial investment of the self and opportunity for self expression can function in this way. Indeed, some have gone so far as to argue that 'in choosing an occupation one is, in effect, choosing a means of implementing a self-concept'.[3] The choice of an occupation may thus exercise an important formative influence on the development of identity, through the process of anticipatory socialization[4] discussed in Chapter 4. Thus,

[1] For a brief account, see A. M. Rose, op. cit., pp. 3–18.

[2] G. J. McCall and J. L. Simmonds, op. cit., p. 207. For an account of the emergence of the self-concept or identity, see ibid., pp. 207–10.

[3] D. E. Super, 'Vocational Adjustment: Implementing a Self-Concept', *Occupations* (1951).

[4] S. Cotgrove and M. Fuller, 'Occupational Socialization and Choice', *Sociology*, January 1972.

the medical student *becomes* a doctor. But for the great majority for whom occupation provides little opportunity for implementing a self-concept, the search for roles which can help establish and confirm an acceptable identity must take other forms. Moreover, changes in roles, such as unemployment, widowhood and old age, can generate crises of identity. Thus, middle-aged people may try to 're-activate glamorous roles that they have more or less used up or passed by . . .'[1] We return to this search for identity in the final chapter.

Roles, then, are closely related to identities. There is a sense in which by acting the role of husband/wife we are *being* a husband/wife. Is the self then nothing more than the sum of the roles which the individual plays? We can certainly distinguish between roles which have varying degrees of saliency for the self. Some roles are more closely related to the values of the self than others. Thus some value the role of husband as more central to and expressive of the self-concept than that of worker. We may, therefore, distinguish between what Mead calls the 'I' that is, a person's definition of himself (his self-concept), and the 'me', which is the individual's perception of the attitudes of others reflected in the various roles which he plays.[2] Thus, the 'I' is more than the sum of the roles; and the individual is conscious of the self as an object; and of the fact that any particular role expresses only a part of his 'self'.

One final point. The sociological perspective on the development of the self through interaction indicates that there is no final completed and crystallized self. As indicated above, phases in the life-cycle lead to re-definitions of the self. But the interactionist approach also throws light on the mechanisms for the transformation of identities. Some transformations are institutionalized through *rites de passage* which mark movement from one status to another, such as graduation ceremonies which provide a symbolic confirmation of a change of identity.[3] Society has also evolved strategies for changing selves, including public schools, psychiatric hospitals, prisons, and military academies.[4] Such *total institutions*, to use Goffman's[5] term, are marked by a high degree of what Etzioni calls *scope* and *pervasiveness*. The scope of the organization refers to the number of activities carried out jointly by the

[1] G. J. McCall and J. L. Simmons, op. cit., p. 228.

[2] See K. Thompson and J. Tunstall, op. cit., pp. 144–58.

[3] Anselm Strauss, 'Transformation of Identity', in A. M. Rose, op. cit., Chapter 4.

[4] M. Stein, A. J. Vidich and D. M. White, *Identity and Anxiety* (1960), Part 2, Section E, 'The Dissolution of Identities'.

[5] E. Goffman, *Asylums* (1961).

participants, while pervasiveness refers to the extent to which the organization seeks to control the life of the individual. Churches, for example, seek to regulate the conduct of members not only in the performance of specifically religious activities, but in a wide range of activities carried on outside.

Total institution can bring about profound modifications in the personality of the individual. At the outset, the neophyte is subjected to what Goffman calls a 'mortification' process in which elements of his personality are stripped off. The cadet at the American military academy, for example, is completely socially and geographically isolated. Uniforms are issued which remove distinctive styles of dress, and discussions of family background are taboo. The cadet is stripped of all clues which would enable him to retain his original identity. His personality may be further attacked by degrading initiation ceremonies and an inferior status conferred by the use of terms such as 'swab'.[1] Similarly, in prisons all supports for individual identity are abruptly chopped off. Family, occupational and educational status are completely excluded and the prisoner is stigmatized by the anonymous status of a number.

While this breaking-down of identity is in progress, the inmate is exposed to the incentives and rewards of the privilege system. It is around these that some re-building of the self takes place. Because there is no escape from the institution, and because it is total in its scope, such rewards and punishments take on a disproportionate significance. A few cigarettes, or the threat of losing a minor privilege, constitute severe pressures to conform.

A variety of responses are adopted to these attacks on identity and pressures to conform. Some inmates withdraw attention from everything except immediate events. A second adjustment is the complete acceptance of the inmate world in an attempt to extract the maximum satisfactions which are available. In mental hospitals, such individuals have become completely institutionalized and do not wish to leave.[2] A more extreme form of adjustment is conversion in which the inmate accepts the perspectives of the staff and tries to act the role of the perfect inmate. In concentration camps, inmates sometimes go so far as to talk and behave as camp guards, fully identifying themselves with their role.

The breakdown and restructuring of personality that can occur in total institutions (including mental hospitals) seldom appear to have a permanent effect. Return to the original environment provides all the familiar supports for the old identity and the experience may have only relatively short-term consequences.

[1] M. Janowitz, *The Professional Soldier* (1960).
[2] E. Goffman, op. cit. (1961).

253

Much human interaction takes place within structured situations. During the course of a typical day, we go to school or college, office or factory. Less frequently, we may go to church, hospital or prison. We may belong to a trade union or frequent a bingo club. Each and all of these activities involves an organization. We work, study, and play in them. They are present when we are born and they undertake the disposal of our mortal remains. They touch our lives at countless points; their influence is pervasive.

Specialization and division of labour is the key to organizations. Men form associations in order to pursue goals more effectively. Trade unions enable workers to achieve goals through collective action. Associations, then, are a form of social division of labour. Of course, an organization may exist to pursue more than one goal. Some trade unions, for example, provide friendly society benefits, and churches arrange social activities. But they differ from a community, which is inclusive rather than exclusive in the goals it pursues. By contrast with an association, a community functions to meet a more or less inclusive range of needs.

We are members of many groups which are not organizations, such as friendship cliques. Such groupings are more than random associations of individuals. The behaviour of members is structured in the sense that there are regularities in the shared ways of acting, thinking and feeling. These pattern the interactions of members. A group of friends may meet to discuss a common interest. Students, for example, may meet to discuss their subject. The shared value in the importance of, say, sociology structures their activities (place, time, and frequency of meeting) and their interactions (content of discussion; deference paid to the more knowledgeable members). But such a group is not an organization. Organizations are groups, but in addition to possessing a structure and culture they are characterized by having a decision-making and enforcing machinery, deliberately set up and constituted for the pursuit of their common goals. A group of students may form themselves into an organization by electing a committee, drawing up terms of reference (a *charter*, or statement of formal aims), and a machinery for admitting members. They may do this because they find the informal meetings unsatisfactory. Discussion is unplanned and uncontrolled, and there are differences of opinion about priorities in discussion. Once a committee is set up, machinery is established for taking decisions and executing them.

In the past sociologists have tended to look at organizations from the top down, from the perspectives of those whose job it is to direct and control. Managerial sociology, in particular, has been preoccupied with prescriptions for the effective control of industrial workers. The inadequacies of this approach will become apparent as we proceed. But first, Weber's classic analysis of bureaucracy will be examined as an example of this perspective.

Bureaucracy
It must be remembered that Weber was attempting to construct a model of the typical characteristics of a bureaucracy. In his own terminology he was constructing an *ideal type*,[1] that is to say, the 'idea' of bureaucracy. In constructing his model he derived his concepts from an examination of the administrative machinery of modern governments and large-scale business organizations. Bureaucracy, as he understood it, is in fact only to be found in its fully developed forms in the modern state, in which rational techniques of administration have reached their highest forms of development.[2]

FIGURE 8.1

A TYPICAL ORGANIZATION CHART

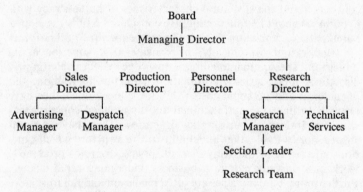

The two main characteristics of bureaucracy, according to Weber, are division of labour and a hierarchical structure of officials. The organization chart of a large company, army unit, or civil service section, is a typical example. Each official in the hierarchy is allocated specific tasks. Moreover, he is responsible to, and is controlled by, the official next above him in the hierarchy, and in turn controls those next below him. The hierarchy of officials thus ensures the co-ordination of the various functions and provides formal channels of communication from the board

[1] Weber did not mean the term to be prescriptive. He was not describing the 'best' type of bureaucracy, although he did, in fact, believe bureaucracy as he described it to be the most efficient form of administration.

[2] H. H. Gerth and C. W. Mills, *From Max Weber: Essays in Sociology* (1947).

down to the operatives through directors, managers, supervisors, foremen, and chargehands.

Weber believed that such a structure was not only the most rational but also the most efficient form of administration. The tasks of the organization are distributed in a rational way; each official has defined duties, and his activities and interactions with others are governed by the formal rules of the bureaucracy. The official does not act arbitrarily, nor are his actions influenced by personal considerations. A student applying for a grant, for example, completes a form which is then sent to the appropriate official in his local authority for a decision. If he comes within the categories to which grants are allowed he receives one, even if he has offended the official by a rude telephone call. If his case is not allowed by the rules, then no grant is given, even if the official is his uncle. The rules ensure uniformity, rational decision-making, and efficiency. They co-ordinate the actions of officials and promote continuity (since any qualified individual can take over the tasks of an official after appropriate training).

A major criticism of Weber's theory is that he has confused concepts about the structural characteristics of bureaucracy with hypotheses about its functioning. He considered a fully developed bureacratic organization to be technically superior to other forms of organization. Specifically, he considered it superior in its 'Precision, speed, unambiguity, knowledge of files, continuity, discretion, unity, strict subordination, reduction of friction, and of material and personal costs . . .'[1] Subsequent researches have brought to light the dysfunctional and unintended consequences which characterize bureacratic structures. They have demonstrated, for example, that an administrative structure which functions effectively in the army or civil service, does not necessarily work in a university or in a business undergoing rapid change. Furthermore, bureaucracies are often inefficient and fail to achieve their intended goals. Both Merton and Gouldner[2] have pointed to the dysfunctions of bureaucracy. These include a tendency towards over-rigid adherence to the rules, timidity, secrecy, red-tape, jealousy of other departments, and inflexibility under changed conditions.

Argyris[3] has also criticized Weber's hypotheses. He found that extreme specialization leads to psychological difficulties at the lower levels which prevent individuals from becoming more expert in their field. Moreover, bureaucratic detachment among top

[1] H. H. Gerth and C. W. Mills, op. cit., p. 214.

[2] R. K. Merton (ed.) *et al.*, *Reader in Bureaucracy* (1952); A. W. Gouldner, *Patterns of Industrial Bureaucracy* (1955).

[3] C. Argyris, *Integrating the Individual and the Organization* (1964).

management has led to mistrust, lack of confidence, and lack of understanding between individuals and groups. But it is useful to start with the Weberian model because it is relatively simple and logical.

One of the most influential theories in the classical tradition was the work of Frederick Taylor, which has come to be known as Scientific Management. Taylor was mainly interested in industrial management. His model of the structure of administration was basically the classical model put forward by Weber. But his interest in the behaviour of workers rather than managers led him to formulate a different theory of compliance. Researches had shown that fatigue was an important factor influencing the output of the worker. By changing the physical conditions of work (e.g. shortening the length of the working day) fatigue could be reduced and output increased. Taylor linked this with the view that the individual is mainly driven by the search for profit. In order to maximize output, therefore, what is needed is to link work done as closely as possible with payment made, and to minimize fatigue by making sure that the operations are carried out in the most efficient way possible. The results of Taylor's recommendations, then, were piece-work and time and motion studies.

The basically Weberian approach has been developed and elaborated by more recent researches. March and Simon, for example, continue to view administrative organizations as formal decision-making structures. But unlike Weber who prescribed the 'right' structure, the more recent approach has been to investigate empirically ways in which the goals of an organization are achieved. Weber, for example, ignored the possibility of conflict within the organization and assumed that the rules of the organization would ensure the smooth co-ordination of the various levels. The more recent approach has been to investigate the various ways in which organizations, in fact, resolve conflict. Another recent trend arises out of the classical emphasis on rational decision-making. This has led to the development of decision-making theory which aims to analyse logically the steps which a decision-maker should follow. Although largely theoretical and prescriptive, such recent efforts have attempted to analyse actual decision-making and the conditions under which rational decisions are likely to be made,[1] and to discover the factors which restrict rationality.

[1] H. A. Simon, *Administrative Behaviour* (1950); J. G. March and H. A. Simon, *Organizations* (1958). For a summary and discussion, see P. M. Blau and W. R. Scott, *Formal Organizations* (1963). There is also a large literature on the 'principles of management' and 'administrative science' which has grown out of the classical Weberian approach and which is basically prescriptive.

Human relations

Reactions against classical organization theories arose on two main counts. Firstly, they were based on a false image of man. Taylorism, for example, rested on an inadequate theory of motivation and accepted the classical economists' view of economic man, responsive primarily to monetary incentives. Secondly, there were serious discrepancies between the model of rational organization and the realities of organizations.[1]

The breakthrough came as the result of the now famous series of researches in 1927–32 at the Hawthorne Works of the Western Electric Company—probably one of the most written about and most influential of all social investigations. The researches were in the 'scientific management' tradition and were aiming to measure the effect of illumination on production. Contrary to expectations, the productivity of workers in the experimental room continued to increase not only when illumination was improved, but also when it was decreased to a very low level. Other experiments with rest pauses confirmed that there was no simple connection between fatigue and output. Further inquiries at the same plant proved that workers had deliberately restricted their output to a level far below that which they were capable of reaching, even though this meant that they failed to earn a production bonus. The simple assumptions of scientific management had been decisively challenged. The reduction of fatigue and the linking of payment to output did not necessarily maximize output. And workers did not work as hard as they could to maximize their income.[2]

The Hawthorne inquiries brought to light two main discoveries. Firstly, that the classical view of organizations ignored the existence of informal groupings which play an important part in influencing the achievement of organizational goals. Secondly, that workers respond to non-economic rewards and sanctions. Workers, it was found, formed informal groups which were not part of the official organization of the plant. This organization within an organization had evolved its own culture comprising beliefs about what would happen if they worked harder (their pay would be reduced) and a set of norms about what constituted a fair day's work. Both 'rate busters' who exceed the norm and 'chisellers' who failed to reach it, were subject to punishment ranging from 'symbolic' sanctions in the shape of losing the

[1] For a critique of theories and bibliography, see Renate Mayntz, 'The Study of Organizations', *Current Sociology*, Vol. 13, 1964, No. 3. See also W. G. Scott, 'Organization Theory: An Overview and Appraisal', in J. A. Litterer, *Organizations: Structure and Behaviour* (1964), pp. 13–26.

[2] H. A. Landsberger, *Hawthorne Revisited* (1958).

respect and affection of the group, to physical sanctions in the form of mild punch-ups during horseplay.[1]

Classical theory then had failed to recognize the importance of *informal organization* and of informal leaders. The *human relations* school had demonstrated the great influence which informal leaders of work groups exercised—far more effective than the formal leadership of foremen and inspectors in setting the level of output. The human relations school therefore came to stress the importance of the foreman and supervisor as the last link in the chain between management and men, and of leadership styles. 'Democratic' styles which sought to gain the participation of followers were demonstrated to be more effective in achieving goals, while democratic leadership is more likely to overcome resistance to change. Moreover, in order to maximize the participation of the lower ranks in striving for organizational goals, good communication is essential. If the reasons for courses of action are explained and communicated, and if the active involvement of the lower ranks is sought by democratic styles of leadership, then the result, it is argued, will be the co-ordination of efforts towards the achievement of organizational goals. Conflicts and non-cooperation, it was believed, are the result of the neglect of these maxims.

In this description of the work of the human relations school, it has been difficult to separate an account of the findings of empirical inquiries, the interpretation placed upon them, and the prescriptions for action derived from such interpretations. Management wanted answers to administrative problems. It is difficult for those who have to take decisions to maintain the attitude of scepticism and suspended judgement of the scientist. The human relations school, therefore, found itself involved in advising management on solutions to administrative problems, and its findings were incorporated in the teaching at schools of management which grew up first in America and, after the Second World War, in this country. The perspective of such studies was essentially slanted towards management—concerned with devising administrative techniques which would assist management in achieving the compliance of workers with organizational goals. It is not surprising that it has earned the epithet 'Cow sociology', or how to produce happy and contented workers. But this should not blind us to the fact that it has resulted in significant advances in our knowledge of organized behaviour.

[1] This is another example of the strategies available to workers to control aspects of their work and market situations, discussed in Chapter 4.

Further understanding of the structure and functioning of complex organizations has come as a result of the extension of researches to the study of a variety of organizations. Whereas earlier studies had concentrated mainly on industrial bureaucracies, recent inquiries have looked at prisons, mental hospitals, research laboratories and colleges. As a result, the various 'schools' are moving closer together, and a more inclusive body of theory and research is emerging. It is now becoming clear that there is not one administrative structure which is always superior, nor one best way of achieving compliance. Rather there is a complex interrelation between types of organizations and forms of leadership and control. What works in a business or an army won't work in a college. The administration of prisons, hospitals, and social work agencies cannot be the same. Nor can we manage scientists and college lecturers in the same way that we would manage clerks or production workers.

Recent developments in organization theory have been along two main lines. Firstly, it has been recognized that there are a number of possible models for organizations, unlike the classical view of one model of rational bureaucracy. Secondly, organizations have been conceptualized as systems, and this has lead to a search for significant organizational variables. Among the main variables examined have been socialization and selection, organizational goals, rewards and sanctions, communication, adaptation to the external system, and boundary maintenance. But so far there has not been much success in demonstrating the interdependence between such variables. If organizations are systems, we can expect key variables to exercise constraint on others. Among the more interesting attempts in this field has been the classification of organizations according to rewards and sanctions (modes of compliance) by Etzioni.[1]

Models of organizations

There is still some controversy as to whether one basic model can be used for the study of all organizations, or whether different models are appropriate for different circumstances. Gouldner[2] exemplifies the first of these positions. He argues that two opposing theories have dominated the literature, neither of which is adequate, but which can provide the basis for a single synthesized model. The *rational model* is exemplified in the work of Weber and

---

[1] A. Etzioni, *A Comparative Analysis of Complex Organizations* (1961).

[2] A. W. Gouldner, 'Organizational Analysis', in R. K. Merton, L. Broom and L. S. Cottrell, *Sociology Today* (1965).

the classical school which has already been discussed. Here the organization with its division of labour and hierarchy of offices is the rationally devised means for the efficient attainment of given organizational goals. 'Fundamentally, the rational model implies a "mechanical" model, in that it views the organization as a structure of manipulable parts. . . .'[1] By contrast, the *natural-system model* regards the organization as a natural whole or system, which strives to survive and to maintain its equilibrium, even though this may lead to the distortion of the organization's goals (goal displacement). This model focuses attention on the unplanned and informal aspects which contribute to survival.[2] But it tends to neglect planned and rational administration.

As a result of empirical studies, Burns and Stalker[3] have arrived at a somewhat similar distinction between what they call *mechanistic* and *organic* structures. The former corresponds to the classical model in which communication and authority flow vertically, mainly from top to bottom. In the organic model, authority and communication flow laterally as well as vertically. There is a complex network of control and communication. But unlike Gouldner, Burns and Stalker see these two types as descriptions of empirical reality, each of which is appropriate for different circumstances. The mechanistic structure is more suitable for the execution of policies in relatively stable organizations where the goals are fixed and where there is little innovation of either means or ends. The organic model is more relevant for organizations undergoing change. Responsibility and knowledge are more widely distributed, there is more horizontal interaction, and compliance is achieved through the commitment and involvement of individuals rather than through commands.

Likert's[4] model is rather more elaborate since it involves two dimensions: the amount of control exercised over individuals and the motives used to control and co-ordinate. This yields two main types (authoritative and participative) and two sub-types. The *exploitative authoritative* uses both physical and economic sanctions and exploits the need for security. It uses mainly threats and punishment, decisions are made at the top, and there is little communication. There is little interaction and an attitude of hostility towards the goals of the organization. The *benevolent authoritative* appeals mainly to economic motives, and uses rewards as well as

[1] Ibid., p. 405.
[2] The informal groups described by the Hawthorne studies, for example, pursued policies aimed to ensure their survival rather than the company's goal of maximizing production. This model has been influenced by cybernetics and has incorporated concepts such as feedback, and homeostasis.
[3] T. Burns and G. Stalker, *The Management of Innovation* (1960).
[4] R. Likert, *New Patterns of Management* (1961), Chapter 14.

punishment. The *consultative participative* offers satisfaction of a wider range of needs, there is two-way communication, and decision-making is more widely distributed. In the *group participative* model, compliance is achieved through a high level of group participation in decision-making, with high levels of communication and the absence of suspicion in interactions.[1]

Organizational variables[2]

It can be seen that these typologies select a number of different variables as bases for differentiation. Moreover, they hypothesize that the differences between the variables are not random, but fall into a number of patterns. Thus the distribution of authority is related to communication, interaction, sanctions, and goals. This line of reasoning suggests an alternative approach. It can be argued that the above models try to tell us too much. They not only seek to discover significant variables but also to state the relations between them. A more modest approach would be to seek to discover significant organizational variables which would provide a systematic approach for organizational research, and attempt to discover empirically the main modes of relations between variables. Such data would then provide the basis for constructing generalized models of various types of organization. These variables will include both structural variables, such as authority structures and sanctions, and functional variables (processes), such as selection, control, communication, goal-attainment and boundary maintenance.

A recent attempt to construct 'profiles' of organizations along these lines is the work of Lupton and his associates.[3] Their first step has been to attempt to isolate and conceptualize a number of structural dimensions. They hypothesize six primary dimensions of organizational structure; (1) specialization (the number of specialisms and the degree of role specialization), (2) standardization (for example, of decision-making and communication procedures), (3) formalization (how far communications and procedures are written down and filed), (4) centralization (the location of decision-making at particular points in the authority structure), (5) configuration (exemplified primarily by the organition chart, and including height, width, spans of control), (6)

---

[1] These types are similar to Gouldner's 'punishment-centred' and 'representative' bureaucracies in *Patterns of Industrial Bureaucracy* (1955). In the latter, authority is based on expertise, there is collaboration in the initiation of rules, and persuasion and education are used to obtain compliance.

[2] See W. G. Scott, 'Organization Theory: An Overview and Appraisal', op. cit., 1964, pp. 19–24.

[3] D. S. Pugh *et al.*, 'A Conceptual Scheme for Organizational Analysis', *Admin. Sc. Qu.*, Vol. 3, 1963, pp. 289–315.

flexibility (changes in the organizational structure). The great advantage of this approach, they claim, is that it provides a conceptual scheme for the empirical investigation of organizations, and facilitates the generation of hypotheses.

The analysis of the structure of organizations cannot be separated from a study of their functioning. It is to studies of organizational functions and processes that we now turn.

Selection and socialization

Most organizations are faced with the problem of selecting individuals who possess the characteristics appropriate to the performance of organizational tasks. The selection process includes both self-selection by individuals and selection by organizations. Selection functions to help maximize the congruence between the expectations of the individual about role requirements, the demands of the organization[1] for role performance, and the possession of the requisite personal skills and qualities. A high degree of congruence minimizes the need for organizational controls. A research laboratory, for example, will seek to recruit scientists who are not only qualified scientifically but who are also willing to pursue the research interests of the company, and will not object to the restraints on publication which industrial research involves. Scientists will similarly seek jobs which are congruent with their interests and expectations.[2] Similarly grammar schools seek to select pupils with both the interest and capacity for academic achievement. By contrast, secondary-modern schools are unselective and therefore face more difficult problems in achieving the compliance of pupils with the aims of the school. Clearly, organizations such as prisons whose inmates have not chosen to enter, face even more difficult problems.

Under some circumstances, socialization may become dysfunctional for the organization. Merton[3] discusses the tendency in bureaucracies for officials to become over-conformists, to adhere rigidly to the rules and regulations for their own sake. A major structural pressure to behave in this way stems from the fact that

[1] It is, of course, recognized that the term 'demands of organizations' involves reification. In the last analysis, there are only *individuals*, and organizational demands are made by definable individuals. We return to the role of the individual in a later section.
[2] S. Box and S. Cotgrove, 'Scientific Identity, Occupational Selection and Role Strain', *B.J.S.*, March 1966.
[3] R. K. Merton, 'Bureaucratic Structure and Personality', in *Social Theory and Social Structure* (1957). L. Reissman has suggested a more elaborate classification of types of bureaucrat: functional, specialist, service and job ('A Study of Role Conceptions in Bureaucracy', *Social Forces*, Vol. 27, March 1949).

the official's life is planned for him in terms of a graded career. The rewards for conformity are promotion, security, and eventually a pension. These pressures to conform induce timidity, and conservatism. Moreover, strict conformity to the rules protects the individual against criticism, and may be a device sought by the timid. The result is that importance comes to be displaced from ends to means; from organizational goals to rules. How far this process is the result of the socialization of the official and how far it is due to a tendency for bureaucracies to attract less adventurous types of personality, is difficult to say.

Achieving compliance

One major problem which faces any organization is how to ensure the compliance of its members. Now we have seen that not only was Weber's model of bureaucracy inadequate as an account of the structure of organizations, but it also failed to discuss the means by which they achieve the compliance of individuals other than officials with organizational demands. Both the Scientific Management and Human Relations theories have suggested that the mechanisms are in fact complex. The incentives which lead the official in a public bureaucracy to conform are hardly likely to be effective with the assembly-line worker or the prison inmate. Moreover, Gouldner[1] has distinguished punishment-centred and representative bureaucracies according to the means of control, while Likert[2] has examined the variety of sanctions used to achieve compliance in different types of organizations.

Etzioni[3] has suggested that there are, in fact, three main types of power available (physical, material and symbolic), and each typically produces a different form of compliance. In prisons, for example, coercion is the main means of power; in factories, material rewards such as wages and bonuses are offered; while colleges and churches use moral power.

The use of different means of control has consequences for the responses elicited. Moral power uses symbols to manipulate behaviour, particularly verbal expressions like: 'You've done well.' Individuals are rewarded by prestige, approval or affection. The use of moral power is more likely to result in normative compliance, that is to say, compliance because, as with Weber's officials, it is believed to be right. By contrast, coercion is unlikely to generate any commitment; it is, that is to say, more alienative. The individual feels powerless but is forced to comply with orders to which he attaches no value and which he does not define as

[1] A. W. Gouldner, op. cit.   [2] R. Likert, op. cit.
[3] See A. Etzioni, *Modern Organizations* (1964), for a simplified analysis of types of power and compliance.

right. The use of utilitarian power, such as wage incentives, results in *calculative involvement* in which actions are performed on the basis of calculated self-interest.[1] In practice, of course, control is seldom exercised by one means alone, and compliance may involve elements of all three types. All that Etzioni is saying is that the dominant element in the method of control is likely to result in the predominance of one type of compliance.

A prison is an example of an organization where the problems of achieving the compliance of inmates are extreme. Inmates neither identify themselves with the goals of the organization nor accept them as either desirable or legitimate. The sources of power available for control, therefore, are extremely limited. Utilitarian power can be used to a small extent by granting privileges and remission of sentence for good conduct. But coercion is of necessity the main source of power, and since its use is strictly regulated, it proves to be an inadequate means of control.

The lack of support among the inmates for the goals of the organization and the desire to protect themselves as far as possible from the rigours and isolation of prison life favour the development of a strong informal organization with its own leaders, communication network and culture. There is a more extreme form of the informal organization and culture which sometimes develops in industry where, as we have seen, the workers wish to pursue goals contrary to the official aims of the organization. The aim of the inmate code is to provide support for other inmates, to avoid trouble and to maintain a sharp distinction between inmates and officials.

In this context it can be appreciated that therapeutic activities such as psychiatric work are of limited success in traditional prisons. Their coercive nature generates a protective inmate culture which, to some extent, isolates the prisoners from any kind of personal relationship with the staff. Therapeutic and custodial goals require different systems of control, and the attempt to increase the therapeutic functions of prisons is presenting difficult problems. Similar difficulties also face borstals, approved schools and mental hospitals.

Control, participation and communication
A debating society is run for the benefit of its members. An army serves to protect society. It is reasonable to suppose that such different organizations will adopt different solutions to the problems of control, and will devise different structures. In order to

[1] Etzioni stresses that the responses to types of power will depend in part on the characteristics of the participants. The contemporary worker will react differently to physical violence from his nineteenth-century counterpart.

explore such differences, we may take as a starting point Blau and Scott's[1] classification of organizations based on prime beneficiary. They suggest four main types; (1) mutual benefit associations (e.g. trade unions), (2) business concerns (where the owner is the prime beneficiary), (3) service organizations (where the client is prime beneficiary, e.g. hospitals and schools) and (4) commonwealth organizations (where the prime beneficiary is the public at large, such as the army, and prisons).

A Trade union is an example of an organization in which the prime beneficiary is the membership, and in which the participation of members and their control over its policies could be expected to be high. The evidence, however, shows that active participation in union affairs by the rank and file is generally low. Voting typically involves 15–25 per cent of the membership and in some unions can be as low as 2 per cent. However, in others, such as printing, a much higher proportion vote—nearer 70 per cent. In part, this is because attendance at some meetings is compulsory, and the meetings occur at the place of work. But the nature of the work (and especially the amount of interaction it generates both on and off the job) seems to be an important variable. Thus miners, who develop a strong *occupational community*, have a higher rate of participation.

Another aspect of the failure of internal democracy is the tendency for the leadership once established to become stable and irremovable, whether elected or not. This tendency towards the concentration of power in the hands of a few has been observed to occur in a wide range of organizations, including political parties. In fact, Michels considered this to be an inevitable tendency in all such organizations and referred to it as the *iron law of oligarchy*.[2] Weber made somewhat similar observations about officials in government bureaucracies.

According to both Michels and Weber, a major reason for this tendency to oligarchy is the fact that the officials develop vested interests in maintaining their positions. For trade unionists, for example, the loss of paid office may mean return to the bench.[3] When this happens, there may be a tendency for the union to become a business concern, run partly for the benefit of the officials.

English students of trade union structure, however, have argued that the unions have chosen to sacrifice democracy to the

[1] R. M. Blau and W. R. Scott, op. cit. (1963).
[2] R. Michels, *Political Parties* (1959). For a summary, see L. Broom and P. Selznick, *Sociology* (1955), pp. 247–50.
[3] The 'professionalization' of leadership by recruiting graduates or others who had not worked their way up might reduce this tendency.

need for efficiency. Allen argues that as the unions have grown in size, and their tasks increased in complexity, officials have been forced to take decisions with a minimum of recourse to the cumbersome machinery of democracy. Moreover, the complexity of the issues has made democratic participation more difficult. A result has been the drying up of branch democracy.[1]

This discussion, of course, assumes that a high level of active participation by the rank and file is necessary if the union is to meet the needs of its members. Allen[2] challenges this assumption and questions whether organizations such as trade unions need to provide exercises in self-government. The membership supports the actions of its leaders by belonging and paying its dues. Once the leaders lose the support of the rank and file, they will vote with their feet, and the officials will be faced with declining membership. This mechanism, Allen argues, is sufficient to ensure the responsiveness of the leaders to the members, where membership is voluntary.

Roberts,[3] however, places a different interpretation on the evidence. He agrees that unions have tended towards bureaucracy, and have developed routine office administration and impersonal control. But, he argues, that there are powerful forces at work keeping the officials under the control of the rank and file. He cites as evidence the relatively low ratio of officials to members, and the low salaries paid to top officials who are also overworked —evidence he believes of the sacrifice of efficiency to democracy.

The administration and control of functions, such as research or teaching, present quite different problems. The study of the organization of hospitals, colleges and research departments brings to light an ambiguity in Weber's analysis of bureaucratic authority. What kind of an expert is the official? Is Weber referring to his expert knowledge of the files of the bureaucracy? Or to the special knowledge derived from the official's formal education? If we look at a college, for example, or at a hospital, the difference between these two kinds of expertise becomes clearly apparent. The expert knowledge of the professor of physics is quite different from that of the registrar. In industry, knowledge and qualifications are more likely to be concentrated at the middle levels in the research and development departments than on the board of directors.

A further related distinction is also important—that between administrative and professional authority. The authority of the official is based upon his position in the bureaucratic hierarchy.

[1] V. L. Allen, *Power in Trade Unions* (1954).   [2] Ibid.
[3] B. C. Roberts, *Trade Union Government and Administration in Great Britain* (1956).

The authority of the professional, however, is based on knowledge.[1] His actions are based on his professional judgement and he alone, or in consultation with his professional colleagues (peers), is in a position to decide. The professor of physics, not the college administrator, decides what to teach. The surgeon, not the hospital administrator, decides whether to operate. In the sphere of professional conduct, therefore, the professional expects and demands freedom to exercise his own judgement: he expects professional autonomy.

Organizations have adopted a variety of solutions to the resulting problem. One method is to attach experts in an advisory capacity to the organization. They may have little or no executive authority. This is the solution frequently adopted by industry which distinguishes between *staff* (advisory) functions and *line* (executive) functions. But the difficulty is that the staff section may find itself out on a limb, isolated and playing little part in the life of the organization. The research and development department, for example, may frequently find itself in such a position. Or it may find that its primary function of development is being hindered by constant requests from production for 'trouble-shooting' help or product testing. In such circumstances, a struggle for power may develop in which research and development departments seek to dominate production. Another possible solution to such conflicts is that suggested by Burns and Stalker,[2] which has been mentioned earlier; the adoption of an *organic* as distinct from a *mechanistic* structure of control. They argue that instead of the hierarchical model in which communication and authority flow vertically, mainly from top to bottom, there should be a much more complex network of communication, horizontally as well as vertically.

One result of the growing insights which were inspired by the human relations approach was an increasing emphasis on machinery to improve communications between management and men in industry. To this end, works councils and works committees have been set up by many firms, while an elaborate consultative machinery was insisted upon in the nationalized industries. But there has been some ambiguity in the aims of such efforts. The dominant aim has been to reduce misunderstandings and conflicts between management and men, to put the workers in the picture and to ensure that they have a fuller appreciation of the goals of the firm. Some, however, have gone further and sought to increase the participation of workers in the decision-making process.

[1] A. W. Gouldner, 'Organizational Analysis', in Merton, Broom and Cottrell, op. cit.
[2] T. Burns and G. Stalker, op. cit.

Such efforts have come up against difficulties. We have seen in the previous chapter that workers experience varying degrees of alienation resulting from their roles in the socio-technical system of production. Consequently, many workers are simply calculatively and not normatively involved. Put another way, they are not work-centred. It is not surprising, therefore, to find that efforts to increase worker-participation have often met with apathy rather than hostility. There is little support for attending meetings during, or still less, after hours. This explanation is confirmed by the findings of an inquiry by Banks[1] that participation increases with the level of skill of the worker.

Communication and decision-making control variables are closely related. Decisions are based on information received from parts of the system and control is exercised by communications originating from decision-making centres.[2] The study of cybernetics has had considerable influence on this aspect of organization theory. Cybernetics is mainly concerned with problems of automation, and with devising feed-back and control mechanisms in engineering which function to maintain the system in equilibrium (homeostasis). Such notions of automatic and self-regulating control mechanisms are clearly attractive to administrators. The development of accounting and electronic data processing, for example, means that many decisions which were once taken on the basis of individual judgement, now emerge as the result of impersonal electronic data processing. Costing, quality control and critical path analysis are all ways in which rational decision and control mechanisms have been built into the organization.[3]

Closely related to this is the impact of technological innovations on management. A study of 100 firms in South-East Essex[4] showed considerable differences in their organization which were related to differences in techniques of production. Unit (batch) production firms were characterized by the centralization of authority, while delegation of authority was more general in mass production firms. In the process industry, there was a higher degree of specialization of functions such as production and marketing, combined with co-operative decision-making within each func-

[1] J. A. Banks, *Industrial Participation* (1963). See also W. H. Scott, *Industrial Leadership and Joint Consultation* (1952). For a development of methods of increasing participation, see Wilfred Brown, *Explorations in Management* (1960).
[2] K. W. Deutsch, 'On Communication Models in the Social Sciences', *Public Opinion Quarterly*, Vol. 16, 1952.
[3] S. Beer, *Cybernetics and Management* (1959); M. Rose, *Computers, Managers, and Society* (1971).
[4] Joan Woodward, *Management and Technology* (1958); *Industrial Organization: Behaviour and Control* (1970).

tion. Moreover, the most successful firms approximated to the medians of the group, indicating that each had devised a pattern of organization appropriate to its particular technology.[1]

INDIVIDUALS AND ORGANIZATIONS

In the last analysis, it is individuals who carry out the tasks in organizations. And as we have seen in Chapter 4, there may well be a lack of congruence between the characteristics which an individual brings with him to the performance of organizational roles and the characteristics which the role requires. Moreover, as we go down the organizational hierarchy, there is a decline in autonomy and skill. Tasks become increasingly fragmented and control over performance declines. We have seen that workers adopt a variety of responses, both individual (strategies of independence) and collective (occupational strategies including informal organization and trade union activities). And although socialization and selection function to minimize the discontinuities between the needs of individuals and organizations, there remains a gap between needs and satisfactions.[2]

Now the relevance of such data to organizational analysis is obvious. Division of labour, fragmentation of skills, subordination and lack of autonomy, all result from the fact that production (and teaching and research) is carried out by large-scale organizations. And the adaptive responses of individuals (absenteeism, restrictive practices, trade union demarcations, withdrawal from work and alienation) are unintended consequences of organization. In this section we are concerned with the organizational response to such problems.

Argyris argues that typical organizational responses exacerbate the problem.[3] At all levels, the consequence of the lack of congruence between the needs of individuals and organizations are dysfunctional for the achievement of organizational goals. Efforts to introduce a measure of control over the pace of work become

[1] See also F. J. Jasinski, 'Adapting Organization to New Technology', in J. A. Litterer, op. cit. See also W. H. Scott, op. cit.; F. C. Mann and L. R. Hoffman, *Automation and the Worker* (1960); A. Tourraine *et al.*, *Workers' Attitudes to Technical Change* (1965).

[2] C. Argyris quotes evidence to show that such needs as the opportunity for interesting work, to make decisions, exercise responsibility and make the most of capacities are not simply middle-class values. Moreover, the increased satisfactions resulting from job enlargement are evidence of the frustrations experienced by manual workers. Op. cit., pp. 82–6.

[3] See also A. Gouldner's discussion of punishment-centred bureaucracies. Op. cit. (1955).

institutionalized as informal group norms. Such institutionalization distorts the flow of communication by inhibiting information about the true state of affairs. Management reacts to apathy and restriction by stronger leadership, tighter controls and stiffer penalties. Even 'human relations' programmes may be perceived as attempts at manipulation. Such actions stimulate even stronger defensive reactions. 'This forms a closed loop of activity which is repetitive and compulsive; rather than solving the underlying causes, it actually helps to deepen them.'[1]

The solution suggested by Argyris to the problem of integrating the individual and the organization is to modify the organization in ways which release psychological energy for productive effort by devising conditions which make it possible for individuals to experience 'self-actualization', that is 'psychological success and opportunities for self-responsibility'. This will include work which uses the skills and abilities of the individual and is intrinsically satisfying. Above all, this involves a modification of the pyramidal structure of command which centralizes control at the top. Ways must be found to extend and increase autonomy and control down through the organization. This does not mean going to the other extreme and abolishing a hierarchical command structure entirely. Nor will the exact position be the same for all organizations, or for the different situations within the same organization. The degree of 'mix' is largely a matter to be determined by further empirical research.

As Argyris recognizes, his solution is similar to those suggested by Shepard, Burns and Stalker, and by Likert. He is proposing something very similar to Burns and Stalker's 'organic' type and to Likert's 'participative group'. The main difference claimed by Argyris is that his model, unlike the others, is derived from theoretical propositions about the characteristics of organizations. Moreover, Argyris suggests a continuum between two polar 'ideal types', the precise 'mix' differing according to circumstances.

Argyris recognizes that such modifications in organizations demand corresponding modifications in individuals. Working-class culture has institutionalized values and perspectives such as apathy, indifference and fatalism. The perpetuation of such values may be one mode of adjustment to the frustrations of work. To encourage the development of self-actualization without providing the opportunities would be damaging and dangerous. But the evidence suggests that the potential is there and that workers in fact respond to opportunities for increased skill and control.[2]

[1] C. Argyris, op. cit., pp. 110–12.
[2] S. Cotgrove, J. Dunham and C. Vamplew, *The Nylon Spinners* (1971).

The 'action perspective'

The work of Argyris is one example of a growing dissatisfaction with the approach of both the structural-functionalists and the more recent systems approach to the study of organizations, with their emphasis on consensus and order. Organizational psychology as exemplified by the work of Argyris draws attention to the fact that there is no necessary congruence between the goals of organizations and the needs of individuals. Indeed, to state the issue in this way is to draw attention to the fundamental weakness in an approach which assumes that organizations have goals 'out there'. Only individuals have purposes and goals. As we saw in the first section, interaction is a process which involves, among other things, perceiving the nature of the situation and discovering the perceptions of others. In other words, much of what organization theory takes for granted, is in fact problematic. We cannot assume that the goals of the 'organization' are perceived in the same way, or acceptable to all its members. In short, we come full circle, and are now in a position to relate what was said earlier on the interaction process to studies of organizations which have so far focused primarily on methods of achieving goals and maintaining order without paying much attention to the actors. The recent emergence of studies which explore this *action frame of reference* is an attempt to resolve this problem.[1]

The studies of the affluent workers discussed in Chapter 4 are a good example of this approach. Relations within the plant, it is argued, can only be understood in terms of the instrumental orientation to work which the workers bring with them from outside the factory gates. It is the meaning which work has for them which explains their satisfaction with their jobs and the relatively conflict-free industrial relations. The workers had taken the jobs for the money, and were satisfied with the effort-bargain. This does not imply a stable consensus, but rather a negotiated order. If the workers change their definition of the situation, and no longer consider the bargain fair, then conflict (not necessarily disruptive) will result. Indeed, the relative stability at the time of the study is perfectly consistent with recognizing the underlying conflict of interest between management and men. The problem becomes, how can both management and men achieve their somewhat different objectives through a process of bargaining? The emphasis shifts from a preoccupation with taking decisions and exercising control, to achieving compliance within a negotiated order. And since the involvement of the workers is (in Etzioni's

[1] For a critique of the structuralist–functionalist and systems approach and for an account of the action approach, see D. Silverman, *The Theory of Organizations* (1970), Chapters 6 and 7.

272

terms) calculative, then the wage-effort bargain is bound to be at the core of the interaction process. Of course, for those for whom work has a different (perhaps expressive) meaning, the negotiated order would have a different character.

The great value of this perspective is that it brings together the study of organizations and occupations. The structuralist and systems perspectives have tended to neglect the systematic study of the characteristics of those who occupy various roles in an organization. And to understand such characteristics, we need to take account of the processes of socialization and selection which lead individuals to become assembly-line operatives or scientists as well as the meanings and rewards which they seek and the strategies and negotiations which they adopt in their pursuit.

DISCUSSION

The image of *homo sociologicus* as a prisoner or puppet is no longer convincing. When we begin to look at interaction as a process, we become increasingly aware of the voluntaristic elements in society. Though it remains true that society makes man, there is also a sense in which man makes society. Reality is socially constructed: individual actors perceive situations, evolve meanings— and even a sense of personal identity—through interaction with others. Negotiation, bargaining and exchange are all indices of flexibility. Indeed, the analogy shifts from that of puppets acting parts to one of managing the presentation of self through the elaborate games which people play. But unlike cricket, the players may try to change the rules as they go along.

The study of interaction in more structured situations has similarly evolved, so that a point has now been reached where there is the possibility of substantial convergence between the various perspectives. Here again the emphasis has shifted. The structural-functionalist approach and the systems approach have tended to focus primarily on the strategies whereby organizations could allocate tasks and exercise control over their members in the pursuit of organizational goals. Managerial sociology, in particular, has been largely prescriptive, seeking to discover recipes for the effective control of organizational behaviour. Organizational psychology and the interactionist perspective have resulted in a more flexible approach which sees conflicts of interest not as aberrations but as part of the stuff of social interaction. From this perspective, order, norms, goals, are the outcome of interaction and negotiation, and there is no necessary consensus between the interests of actors. Of course, there are organizations, such as prisons, in which the possibility of such negotiation is limited, and order is largely imposed by coercive means. But even here, there is a substantial element of negotiation. In short, organization must be seen as a process and not as a rigid structure.

READING

C. Argyris, *Integrating the Individual and the Organization* (Wiley, 1964).

B. J. Biddle and E. J. Thomas (eds), *Role Theory: Concepts and Research* (Wiley, 1966).

P. M. Blau and W. R. Scott, *Formal Organizations* (Routledge, 1963).

F. G. Castles, D. J. Murray and D. C. Potter, *Decisions, Organizations and Society* (Penguin, 1971).

A. Etzioni, *Modern Organizations* (Prentice-Hall, 1964).

—— *A Sociological Reader in Complex Organizations* (Holt, Rinehart, 1969).

E. Goffman, *Asylums* (Anchor Books, 1961).

—— *The Presentation of Self in Everyday Life* (Allen Lane, 1969).

—— *Where the Action Is* (Allen Lane, 1969).

G. Hutton, *Thinking About Organization* (Bath University Press, 1970).

J. A. Litterer, *Organizations: Structure and Behaviour* (Wiley, 1964).

G. J. McCall and J. L. Simmons, *Identities and Interactions* (Free Press, 1966).

A. M. Rose (ed.), *Human Behaviour and Social Processes: An Interactionist Approach* (Houghton Mifflin, 1962).

D. Silverman, *The Theory of Organizations* (Heinemann, 1970).

K. Thompson and J. Tunstall, *Sociological Perspectives* (Penguin, 1971), Part 2.

J. Woodward, *Management and Technology* (HMSO, 1958).

—— *Industrial Organization: Theory and Practice* (Oxford University Press, 1965).

Chapter 9

ORDER AND CHANGE

The 'problem' of disorder is one which recurs at all levels of society—families break up, a classroom is disrupted, a workshop goes on strike; there is civil disorder within a community and war between nations. Not surprisingly, theories abound as to causes and remedies. On the one hand, there are those theories which emphasize the essentially selfish and aggressive nature of man and the need for constraint and regulation if conflict and disruption are to be contained. According to this view, it is difficult to see how society could have ever emerged. Indeed, the philosopher Hobbes argued that it was because life 'in a state of nature' was a war of each against all, that men were prepared to sacrifice some of their individuality, and contract to form a civil society which would control their disruptive tendencies.[1] For the sociologist Durkheim, hope lay in the building of consensus on norms and values; the achievement of a moral community.

The optimistic view of human nature, exemplified by the philosopher Rousseau and the writings of the young Marx, sees the 'noble savage' as potentially good. The problem is rather to build a society which permits the full development of human potential in harmonious relations with others. If the sources of exploitation and conflict are removed, then a spontaneous and harmonious community will evolve in which the coercive instruments of the state will wither away. On the one hand, then, society is held together and freedom is achieved either through regulation and order, or through the humanizing of man's animal nature by socialization; on the other hand, it is argued, the removal of obstructions to the full growth and expression of human potential will lead to a co-operative and united community.

Such grand theories are too general to be capable of rigorous testing. Indeed, for many, they are part of a personal philosophy of life, an ideology, which it would be uncomfortable to have challenged. Moreover, the polarity is overdrawn. Many would occupy an intermediate position, veering to one extreme or the

---

[1] See Talcott Parsons, 'Hobbes and the Problem of Order', and 'The Non-Contractual Elements in Contract', in Peter Worsley (ed.), *Modern Sociology: Introductory Readings* (1971), pp. 407–14.

other on specific issues. But as we have seen, the consensus versus conflict controversy underlies much recent sociological debate.[1] It is possible to test the usefulness of these perspectives for an understanding of a number of more manageable substantive issues central to the problem of order.[2] We will focus first on the relations between the individual and society, and at the ways in which the problems of individuals may threaten the social order or stimulate change. We will then shift the focus of attention to the level of systems analysis as a way of exploring some of the broader theories of change.

INDIVIDUALS AND SOCIETY

The question 'why do individuals conform?' has already been explored at a number of points, especially in the last chapter. Conformity to the norms of monogamy, to the rules of a school, to the requirements of a job—all raise essentially the same issue. We now switch the focus of attention to look specifically at those who do not conform.

Conformity and deviance

One of the most influential approaches to this problem stems from the functionalist perspective of R. K. Merton. He starts from a distinction between means and ends, and identifies four types of non-conformity derived from the differential acceptance of means and ends. In industrial societies such as America and Britain, great emphasis is placed on the achievement of success judged in terms of wealth and status. Such cultural emphasis on success goals plays an important part in encouraging the high levels of motivation which industrial societies require. But it also presents problems for those who are handicapped in the race for success, especially ethnic minorities and the children of manual workers. There is a variety of responses to such stress situations. *Innovation* involves the search for new means in addition to those already recognized and prescribed by the culture. Some such means may be condemned by society, such as fraud and robbery, while others are simply viewed unfavourably, such as institutionalized gambling.

[1] For a clear and simple exposition of these two positions in relation to the problem of order, see P. Worsley (ed.), *Introducing Sociology* (1970), Chapter 8. For a more extensive theoretical analysis, see P. S. Cohen, *Modern Social Theory* (1968), Chapter 2.
[2] These perspectives have also been explored, of course, in the chapters on politics and stratification.

Ritualism involves giving up the pursuit of ends and the search for security in a ritualistic involvement in means. By an undue emphasis on rules, the timid bureaucrat may allay the anxieties which the exercise of discretion might generate. The *retreatist* abandons both the goals and the sanctioned patterns of behaviour. He retreats from involvement in life to drink, drug addiction or simply melancholic withdrawal to the role of a fatalistic and passive onlooker. *Rebellion* is the total rejection of both culturally approved ends and means. It may take a political form which involves a rejection of the dominant values of society (for example, the rejection of the aristocracy in the French Revolution) together with an attempt to change the social structure. Or it may take the form of a social movement. Hippies, for example, reject the traditional values of society, such as material gain and success, and adopt socially disapproved means (drug-taking, deviant styles of dress) to achieve valued ends such as 'creative experiences'.

FIGURE 9.1

TYPES OF NON-CONFORMITY*

	Values (Ends)	Norms (Approved means)
1. Conformity	+	+
2. Innovation	+	−
3. Ritualism	−	+
4. Retreatism	−	−
5. Rebellion	±	±

* R. K. Merton, op. cit.

But Merton's paradigm is not a theory which accounts for conformity or deviance. It simply provides us with a list of the possible forms of nonconformity. We may take the analysis further by examining both the motivation to nonconformity and the constraints on nonconformity. In some cases, the constraints which ensure our conformity are external—legal sanctions with the threat of coercion and punishment, or incentives, such as production bonuses or chances of promotion, or fear of ridicule which leads us to comply with conventions. In others, the constraints are internal. The child learns through the socialization process that stealing and lying are wrong and accepts these as moral imperatives. The scientist values knowledge and feels impelled to publish his findings without distortion.

The relative importance of internal and external constraints will vary both between individuals and in different circumstances. In our work, for example, we may be calculatively involved, we may refrain from exceeding the speed limit simply because we fear a conviction, while we remain faithful to our wife because we think it is right to do so. Riesman[1] has suggested that there are three modes of conformity and that their relative importance varies in different periods. *Inner-directed* persons, for example, are dominated by conscience and inner drives. They have an internal gyroscope which keeps them on a fixed course. This type was dominant in nineteenth-century America. It corresponds to the rugged individualism of the protestant ethic and the entrepreneur. *Other-directed* persons have a radar-like sensitivity to others, particularly to the *significant others* whose opinions they value. They are sensitive to their expectations and adjust readily to social demands. The *other-directed* type is dominant in the modern era in which the emphasis is on consumption and performance in bureaucratic organizations. Conformity has become more important than self-assertion for getting on, and parents and schools have come to emphasize such values and to encourage their development in children. The third, *tradition-directed* type, is dominant only in relatively static societies.

In short, the functionalist approach argues that people break laws either because they are strongly motivated to perform particular acts, or because they have been inadequately socialized into the prevailing consensus. Now one difficulty with this approach is that it assumes cultural consensus. It defines deviancy as 'behaviour which violates institutionalized expectations, that is, expectations which are shared and recognized as legitimate within a social system.'[2] That is to say, such theories 'have given to society a moral consensus and normative integration that it so clearly lacks'.[3] But this does not mean that there is no crime or deviancy. 'Deviant behaviour is nothing less or more than it has always been: rule-breaking. It is behaviour which is proscribed by those who have the institutionalized power, and occasionally the consensual authority, to create rules; it is behaviour which places its perpetrator at risk of being punished . . .'[4] From this perspective, then, it is not surprising that attempts to discover the characteristics of deviants have been so unsuccessful. Despite great ingenuity, it has proved extremely difficult to discover any common features of deviants which could explain their behaviour. The reason being, claims Becker, because 'deviance is not a quality of the act the person commits, but rather a consequence of the application by others of rules and sanctions to an "offender". The deviant is one to whom the label has successfully been applied;

---

[1] D. Riesman, *The Lonely Crowd* (1950). Riesman's views have been criticized on theoretical and empirical grounds, but they are valuable for the insights they provide.

[2] A. K. Cohen, *Deviance and Control* (1966), p. 1.

[3] S. Box, *Deviance, Liability and Society* (1971), p. 8.   [4] Ibid., p. 9.

deviant behaviour is behaviour that people so label.'[1] It is important to be clear just what the 'labellists' are saying. Those 'labelled' deviant constitute only a proportion of those who commit similar acts. Official statistics refer only to crimes known to the police and to those convicted. To search for defining characteristics among those who are caught from a much larger group who are assumed to be conformist is not a very useful way of testing hypotheses about law-violating behaviour.[2]

But the labellists are doing more than draw attention to the doubtful validity of official statistics and the lack of cultural consensus. They also apply the insights of interactionist theory to argue that there is a further sense in which society makes 'deviants'. Labelling involves 'status degradation' and 'the mortification of self'. That is to say, conviction is the first step in the *career* of a criminal, which may lead him eventually to accept the *identity* of a criminal and engage in *secondary deviancy*. Social control may in this way result in the very behaviour it seeks to prevent.

It is now difficult to accept the functionalist view that deviance is the violation of expectations which are shared and recognized as legitimate. It has been argued that there are distinct subcultures, or perhaps 'contra-cultures', into which individuals are socialized. As we have seen in Chapter 8, an important element in the socialization process is the influence of others on our self-images. We are particularly influenced by *significant others*, those whose opinions we value and whom we accept as reference groups. Cohen and Short[3] distinguish between *normative reference groups* by which we measure the rightness of our behaviour. Such groups may provide justification for ambiguous actions, such as industrial stealing which is sanctioned by the norms of the work group. *Status reference groups* function in a similar way to confer acceptance and respect, in return for conformity to their standards. Committing an offence and being on probation, for example, have been observed as achieving status and respect in some delinquent groups. Such theories stress the fact that criminal roles are learnt by the same mechanisms as non-criminal roles. A well-known version of this view is Sutherland's theory of 'differential association' which argues that persons become criminals because they have frequent contacts with criminal behaviour patterns and because of isolation from anti-criminal patterns.[4] It is the ratio of

[1] Howard Becker, *Outsiders* (1963), pp. 8–9.

[2] For a more extended discussion of this issue, see S. Box, op. cit., Chapter 1.

[3] A. K. Cohen and J. F. Short, 'Juvenile Delinquency', in R. K. Merton and R. A. Nisbet, *Contemporary Social Problems* (1965).

[4] E. H. Sutherland and D. R. Cressey, *Principles of Criminology* (1955). For a summary and critique of Sutherland's theory, see R. K. Merton, L. Broom and L. S. Cottrell, *Sociology Today* (1965), pp. 520–13.

associations with definitions of situations favourable to law violation which is the significant variable.

A somewhat similar theory has been put forward by Taft[1] to explain the high crime rates of some nations such as America. He stresses the existence of 'criminogenic' influences in American culture, including its emphasis on material success, the destruction of primary group controls, rapid social change generating confusing definitions of morality, and a gulf between precept and practice which permits large-scale 'social swindles' to go unpunished. Such a culture will generate criminality, though its impact will vary between different segments of society and account for their specific form of criminal response. This explains the excess of male crime, since females are relatively protected from the stress of competition. Moreover, families which give security and affection provide more protection for their members from the criminogenic culture.

Now the weakness in these approaches is that only a minority of those exposed to deviant cultures become deviant. It is unlikely, therefore, that any single factor can account for deviant behaviour. One study attempts to combine the more traditional theories which stress special motivation with the delinquent sub-culture approach. A study of criminal areas in Croydon (Surrey) established that a hard core of 'psychiatric delinquency' is 'related to serious emotional disturbance in the family or mental ill health'.[2] About one-quarter of all the cases in each class are associated with such factors as parental dis-harmony, rejection, or separation, and inconsistent, severe, or lax discipline. But the residue is attributed to the cultural milieu and regarded as 'social delinquency'. Morris argues that the sub-culture of those 'at the bottom of the pile' is essentially criminal. Children exposed to a culture in which 'knocking-off' is a legitimate activity learn to comply with such normative expectations.[3] Moreover, housing policy and economic factors which combine to segregate 'unsatisfactory' tenants into homogeneous enclaves virtually ensures the perpetuation of the delinquent sub-culture. A child reared in these enclaves 'grows up in an atmosphere in which restraint is often conspicuous by its absence. . . . Punishment and indulgence follow in swift succession . . . play will be largely in the street in which he will form an autonomous social group with boys of his own age. . . . Whereas the

[1] D. R. Taft, *Criminology* (1956). For a summary, see D. R. Cressey, 'Crime', in R. K. Merton and R. A. Nisbet, op. cit., Chapter 1, pp. 61–3.
[2] T. Morris, *The Criminal Area* (1957), Chapters 10 and 11.
[3] See also J. B. Mays, *Growing Up in the City* (1954). Such areas are not 'disorganized' in the sense that they lack normative integration. On the contrary, there may be a high degree of consensus.

middle-class way of life tends to inhibit spontaneity, working-class culture tends to encourage it. In particular, aggression is seldom the subject of social disapproval'.[1] Furthermore, the working-class child is more likely to encounter the stressful situations with which he is ill-equipped to cope. Tensions and disagreements over money and sex occur publicly in the overcrowded conditions of sub-standard housing, while the single family living-room is a further source of discord and conflict. It is such factors it is argued, which account for the higher incidence of crime among lower working-class families, who are also to be found concentrated in delinquent enclaves in towns and cities.

Downes[2] similarly finds that the norms, values and beliefs of delinquents in East London do not differ markedly from those of the adult lower working class, though their emphasis on leisure justifies reference to the existence of sub-cultural variations. But he also identifies specific motivations to delinquent behaviour. Failure at school and at work for the lower working-class boy leads to the displacement of his search for achievement to non-work areas. The working-class 'corner boy' depends on leisure as a source of satisfying exploits. In other words, dissociation is the working-class male adolescent's normative response to semi- and unskilled work. It is to leisure that he turns for achievement. He starts out in a delinquency-prone situation. And the cultural values of the lower working-class areas help to shape the search for meaningful leisure.

The case against the functionalist approach and its various developments and modifications is, then, that it assumes a cultural consensus which does not exist, and accepts a legalistic definition of deviant behaviour. Even if we argue that not all delinquency is norm infraction, since we may exemplify behaviour in conformity with a delinquent culture, we are still faced with the problem that delinquent behaviour is episodic and confined to a minority. In short, the search for reasons why some are motivated to delinquent acts, but not others, has not so far been conspicuously successful.

It is this difficulty that the conflict theorists claim to be able to resolve. Daringly, it is argued, *all* are motivated to behave in ways labelled delinquent. The question is not, 'why do some break the law' but 'why don't we all break the law?' Instead of the pessimistic view that man is born wicked and needs to be controlled, it is society and its mechanisms of control that are the root of the matter: '. . . man is perceived as being morally neutral. He is born capable of engaging in an extremely wide diversity of acts. Thus,

[1] Ibid., pp. 171–3.
[2] D. M. Downes, *The Delinquent Solution* (1966).

281

in moral innocence, his passions could lead him to all manner of behavioural experimentation. . . . Unfortunately, society . . . cannot tolerate such diversity, for it is incompatible with orderly and predictable patterns of social interaction. Consequently, attempts are made to persuade youths and newcomers that they should restrict their potentially infinite activities to a comparatively small bundle . . .'[1]

Instead of looking for delinquent motivations, therefore, the conflict theorists explore the factors which influence the willingness of individuals to surrender their freedom to engage in diverse behaviour. Firstly, the *attachments* people form will influence the extent to which individuals are sensitive to what other people think. So, for example, Lemert found that among those who commit the characteristically middle-class crime of cheque forgery there is an unusually high rate of divorce and family alienation.[2] Lack of attachment may also account for the high rate of delinquency among those in the lower streams in the last year of school. *Commitment* refers to the extent of the individual's investment in any particular role or activity. Thus the married man with a good job has a lot to lose and would only risk what he has if the calculated rewards of deviancy were high. Finally, *beliefs* bring us back to the interactionist emphasis on the individual meanings and definitions of social reality. Individuals vary in the extent to which they believe they should obey the rules of society. Moreover, they exercise great ingenuity in neutralizing the moral bond of the law:[3] 'but no one really makes a completely honest tax return'; 'cannabis is no more harmful than alcohol'.[4]

The conflict approach certainly has considerable explaining power. But if the proponents of original sin have overstated their case, it could equally be argued that the labellists and conflict theorists seem to be brushing 'sin' under the carpet. Few commit murder, or rob with violence, but the optimistic view of human nature looks a little pale in the light of some of the more nasty kinds of brutality, beastliness, genocide and war-crimes. The present state of knowledge would not seem to justify a total rejection of the search for special motives for special crimes. And there may be more than a grain of truth in the Hobbesian approach that societies legislate against some kinds of behaviour precisely because they are generally accepted to be so unpleasant.

In the last analysis, the success of any theory is judged by its

[1] S. Box, op. cit., p. 140.   [2] Quoted in ibid., p. 142.
[3] For a persuasive statement of the conflict approach, see ibid., especially Chapter 5.
[4] There is, in fact, recent evidence of serious and irreversible brain damage from the use of cannabis.

ability to account for the known facts.[1] The labellists, for example, can give a plausible explanation of the observed association between crime and poverty and the differential class distribution of crime by questioning the validity of criminal statistics. Self-report studies which show that a very high proportion of the middle class admit to actions which would on conviction lead to imprisonment, have lent further weight to their argument. But it is more difficult to account for the fact that crime is outstandingly a male characteristic. The rate for men in all societies is very much higher than that for women. In some societies, such as Algeria and Ceylon, the ratio is several thousands to one, but in societies in which there is substantial equality and freedom for women, the ratio is nearer ten to one.[2] To explain this, the special motivation approach has some attraction. It has already been argued that all individuals face the problem of achieving a satisfactory self-concept, and social roles which enable them to achieve some sort of congruence between identity and role. Many aspects of male delinquency can be explained in these terms. Being tough, adventurous, daring—are all consistent with the way in which modern industrial societies define masculinity. Hence the boy who steals for 'kicks' (and much delinquency falls into this pattern) is seeking to express and establish his masculinity. Girls, by contrast, steal in a more rational way—typically clothing, cosmetics, jewellery. Such behaviour is *role-supportive* rather than *role-expressive*.[3] This theory may go some way to account for the peak years for delinquency in Britain occurring during the final year of compulsory education.[4] As Carter has shown, these are years of boredom for many, and delinquency may, under some circumstances, provide the compensatory kicks, and act as an expression of masculinity for those who resent the authority relations and subordination of many schools.[5]

Crime is seen as particularly threatening to the social order. But other forms of nonconformity such as drunkenness and drug addiction are also, to a lesser degree, disruptive and subject to attempts at social control. The most extreme form of opting out from society is suicide. Again, most societies seek to control such be-

[1] We must, of course, remember that theories also lead to the search for facts by focusing attention on their probable relevance.

[2] R. K. Merton and R. A. Nisbet, op. cit., pp. 33–5.

[3] For a more detailed account of this and related researches, see A. K. Cohen and J. F. Short, 'Juvenile Delinquency', in R. K. Merton and R. A. Nisbet, op. cit., Chapter 2.

[4] In the age group 14–17, 1,548 per 100,000 were found guilty of indictable offences, compared with 975 and 250 for the groups 17–21 and over 30. *Criminal Statistics for 1954.*

[5] M. Carter, *Home, School and Work*, pp. 101–3.

haviour since it is seen as a particular threat to the normative order. A brief analysis of these topics will provide further opportunities for exploring the various perspectives on the problem of order.

Suicide, drug addiction, alcoholism

Suicide constitutes a major form of death, accounting for about one per cent of all deaths in the United Kingdom. Over 5,000 suicides in England and Wales in 1959 far exceeds the 320 deaths by homicide and war.[1] The trends in most countries over the last fifty years have been fairly stable, but there have been more marked fluctuations in recent years.[2]

One of the pioneer works in scientific sociology, Durkheim's *Le Suicide*, challenged the view that the explanation of suicide was to be found simply in the psychology of the individual.[3] Durkheim adopted the epidemiological approach to the study of suicide and sought to establish the reasons for varying suicide rates. In a detailed statistical study, he claimed to demonstrate that suicide rates were a function of the integration of the individual in social groups. This, he argues, explains why the single, widowed or divorced are more prone to suicide than the married. Furthermore, Durkheim maintained, the inverse relation between religious subscription and suicide cannot be explained by the normative condemnation of suicide by religion. Such reasoning cannot explain the high incidence of suicide among Protestants and the lower incidence among Catholics and Jews, since all religions proscribe suicide.[4] The explanation, argues Durkheim, is again to be found in the fact that both Catholics and Jews form more close-knit communities, and it is this integration of the individual in a religious community which preserves him from suicide. This view has received some recent support from a study of suicide which showed a positive correlation between the number of single-member households and the suicide rate of London boroughs.[5]

Suicide which results from the lack of integration between the

---

[1] United Nations, *Demographic Yearbook* (1961). England and Wales has a lower rate than some other European countries (10·8 per 100,000 population compared with Austria 22·8, Sweden 17·8, France 15·9), but a higher rate than Norway 7·4 and Italy 6·1.

[2] United Nations, *Epidemiological and Vital Statistics Report*, Vol. 9, 1956, No. 4.

[3] The female rate for mental illness, for example, is higher than the male, yet more males commit suicide.

[4] It is, of course, possible to argue that the consequences of suicide for the Catholic deriving from the doctrine of mortal sin without repentance leads to attempts to avoid accepting deaths in the Catholic community as suicide, if it can be avoided, and hence to unreliable statistics. In fact, the uncertain reliability of statistics is a major weakness hindering adequate analysis.

[5] P. Sainsbury, *Suicide in London* (1955).

individual and the group, Durkheim called *egoistic* suicide. He distinguished this from *altruistic* suicide which results from actual group pressure to commit suicide under some circumstances, such as ritual suicide in Japan. A third type he identified as *anomic* suicide. This occurs when some social crisis, such as economic disaster, challenges the established norms and values which regulate society and restrain the actions of the individual. There is a collapse of what he calls the *collective conscience*, and the individual finds himself in a normless vacuum.

Such a disturbance of the norms and values of society, Durkheim maintains, may occur not only during periods of economic depression, but also during times of growing prosperity. This, he argues, may explain the higher incidence of suicide among the upper income groups, and the evidence which Durkheim claimed showed an increase near the peak of the economic cycle as well as the trough. This aspect of Durkheim's theory has, however, been challenged by more recent researches which find suicide to be associated with periods of business contraction.

An alternative explanation argues that both suicide and homicide are aggressive responses to frustration.[1] But whereas suicide increases with depression, homicide increases with prosperity among negroes, and decreases for whites. Moreover, suicide is concentrated in the high status categories, while homicide characterizes low status categories. A tentative explanation is that suicide and homicide are both responses to 'extreme frustration arising from loss of position in the status hierarchy relative to the status position of others in the same status reference group'.[2] It is further argued that relative status deprivation is highest among high status categories during business depression, since they have much to lose, hence the increase in suicide; while frustration is lowest among lower-class negroes during business contraction, hence the decrease in their homicide rate.

The argument is too complex and the data too scanty for a full treatment here, but enough has been said to outline the possibility of alternative hypotheses which remain basically sociological, since they identify the *aetiology* of suicide in the individual's role in the social system.

More recent studies have shown that other aspects of Durkheim's theory are challenged by more complete statistics.[3]

[1] A. F. Henry and J. F. Short, Jr, *Suicide and Homicide*, 1954.
[2] Ibid.
[3] There are also a number of methodological objections. For example, Durkheim's judgement of social integration is purely impressionistic, and he does not provide a definition of integration.

There are many cases, for example, in which Jews have higher rates than Protestants (Netherlands), or Catholics higher rates than Protestants (Toronto).[1] Moreover, although women generally have lower rates than men, the ratio varies extremely widely. But the search for alternative theories has so far failed to yield a satisfactory explanation of the variations between societies and statuses. The attempt to relate suicide to social disorganization, for example, is often essentially tautological since both are conceptualized as lack of conformity to social norms.[2] Nor does secularization account for high rates, since some highly secularized societies, such as the United States, Australia and England, have only moderate rates. All that we can say with any confidence is that psychological explanations which attribute suicide to some form of mental disorder fail to account for the frequent wide difference between the sexes, religions, occupations, and societies.

Drug addiction is a form of deviant behaviour which also appears to be primarily an escape from the strains of living. In America, it is particularly prevalent among negroes and adolescents, and is heavily concentrated in communities characterized by low socio-economic status, low proportions living in family groups, and high rates of a variety of social problems including crime and delinquency.[3] Within these areas, drug addiction is highest 'where income and education were at their lowest and where there was the greatest breakdown of normal family living arrangements'.[4] But this is not the only factor. Such facts do not by themselves explain why individuals turn to this particular form of retreatism. An additional consideration appears to be the sub-cultural stress on the search for 'kicks', together with support for behaviour which is contrary to the prevailing norms. The use of narcotics, together with criminality and violence in various forms, are sub-culturally approved means of enjoying the sub-culturally prescribed goal of excitement, which appeals to those who find difficulty in enjoying the more approved forms of satisfaction, or who experience the insecurity, sexual disturbance, and other behavioural disorders associated with a disturbed background.[5]

Drug addiction is not such a serious problem in England as in

[1] J. P. Gibbs, 'Suicide', in R. K. Merton and R. A. Nisbet, *Contemporary Social Problems* (1965), Chapter 5.

[2] Ibid., p. 252.

[3] J. A. Clausen, 'Drug Addiction', in R. K. Merton and R. A. Nisbet, op. cit., Chapter 4.

[4] Ibid., p. 192–3.

[5] See B. M. Spinley, *The Deprived and the Privileged: Personality Development in English Society* (1953).

the USA.[1] This may be due in part to the stronger cultural prohibitions in England. A contributory factor may be the much smaller size of an ethnic minority frustrated in their attempts to achieve socially approved success goals and seeking retreat into fantasy as a tension-management mechanism. The British system of drug control which permits the limited prescription of a maintenance dose on medical grounds has also helped to minimize the growth of an illicit traffic by drug-pushers and the associated criminality.

The control of drug addiction presents particular difficulties which reflect its aetiology in the social role of the addict. Synthetic drugs have been developed which minimize the abstinence syndrome (acute physical and psychological distress) which otherwise locks the sufferer in a vicious circle of addiction. But such treatment alone does nothing to alleviate the pressures to retreatism, and the return to a dependence on the in-group for support is almost inevitable, since addiction generally leads to alienation from the conventional culture. Consequently, recidivism is high.

Closely related to narcotic addiction is alcoholism, which presents similar problems of a withdrawal syndrome. Again, widespread group differences in its incidence indicate the existence of social factors. It is predominantly a male phenomenon, and strongly associated with ethnic groups in the USA, where the Irish and Scandinavians have high rates, and Southern Italians and Jews low rates. Synder[2] has suggested three main factors which may account for such differences. Firstly, there are *dynamic factors*, which refer to the level of acute psychic tensions within the group.[3] Secondly, there are *normative orientations*, including the norms, ideas and sentiments related to drinking in different groups. Thirdly, there are *alternative factors*; those culturally patterned behaviours which may act as functional alternatives. These factors together constitute the 'pressure' towards alcoholism. There are, for example, marked differences between Americans, Irish and Jews in the normative orientations toward drinking. Among Jews, 'cultural tradition locates the act of drinking squarely in the network of sacred ideas, sentiments, and activities'.[4] Drinking is primarily expressive and religiously symbolic. Socialization to this pattern begins early in life, and the orthodox Jew 'learns how to drink in a highly controlled, ritualized manner'.[5]

By contrast, in Irish culture drinking is not associated with a net-

[1] 350 compared with about 50,000 addicts: R. K. Merton and R. A. Nisbet, op. cit., p. 218.

[2] 'A Sociological View of the Aetiology of Alcoholism', in S. N. Eisenstadt, pp. 16–19.

[3] Cross cultural studies provide tentative support for this view. See D. Horton, 'The Functions of Alcohol in Primitive Societies', in ibid., pp. 20–5.

[4] Ibid., p. 17.   [5] Ibid., p. 18.

work of religious ideas and sentiments. Moreover, cultural traditions define the meaning of drinking so that the individual is likely to drink in situations of stress, simply to meet his needs to adjust as an individual.

This is a very tentative and hypothetical approach, but it does suggest that the current tendency to treat alcoholism simply as a disease resulting from chemical changes due to excessive drinking is likely to have only partial success. However, the attempts to establish support for alcoholics by the formation of 'alcoholics anonymous' groups may go some way to provide functional alternatives.

Private troubles and public issues[1]

Delinquency, drug addiction, divorce, suicide—these are all in a sense social *problems*. Unhappy marriages, by contrast, are not in general defined as social problems and therefore matters for legislation. On some issues, such as unwanted pregnancies, some groups have tried to get what has been considered a private misfortune defined as a public issue on which social action might be taken.

It is obvious that what constitutes a problem is itself problematic. We can adopt a 'labellist' perspective and say that a social problem is anything so defined by society. And we immediately face the same difficulty that we found in defining delinquency—that there is a lack of consensus on what constitutes a problem. Thus there are those who argue that drug taking is a problem only because society makes it one. If drug taking was not defined as immoral, there would be no problem. In short, every social problem consists of an objective condition and a subjective evaluation. Moreover, the fact that a condition is defined as a social problem by those who experience it does not ensure that other sections of society will share their definition. Poverty in the United States, for example, was for long defined as a private misfortune or, at best, an inevitable concomitant of an efficient economic system. In the latter part of the 1960s, vigorous attempts were made to politicize the issue as one for public action, and in this way to achieve a re-definition of poverty as a public issue.[2]

This approach also points to a possible trap for the unwary sociologist. Simply to accept a society's definition of a 'problem' would be to adopt a value position. This is not quite the same thing, of course, as talking about a *sociological* problem, for example a problem of theory or explanation which faces the sociologist. Even here, judgement, and in this sense *subjectivity*, is involved, but this is hardly a moral issue. For the sociologist, what is prob-

---

[1] On this distinction, see C. Wright Mills, *White Collar* (1951).
[2] R. E. Will and H. G. Vatter, *Poverty in Affluence* (1970), Part 7.

lematic is why society defines an issue as a problem, and the process by which an issue becomes a problem. Of course, sociologists can also contribute to the moral debate, both as citizens and as experts. Moral judgements rest on facts—about the consequences of a particular course of action. The objective inquiries of the sociologist can in this way contribute to a more informed judgement.[1]

If behaviour which is defined as a problem is that which deviates from some social norm, then this also raises issues of social control. Indeed, the policy adopted about an issue depends largely on the position adopted on the continuum from seeing it as a private misery to be alleviated, to its definition as a public issue to be controlled. If prostitution is seen mainly as a threat to the normative order and the values of society, then one way to deal with it is to get prostitutes off the streets by legislation controlling soliciting. Indeed, some have argued that most social work can be seen in this way: in many of its features, the social control function is dominant and the therapeutic function secondary. From this perspective, social work has emerged to cope with the problems of rapid social change resulting from industrialization. Thus, it is argued, social control is dominant not only in the treatment of criminals, but also in hospitals for the mentally ill, and in the agencies dealing with family breakdown. The social worker is armed with considerable coercive powers, including the withholding of benefits. Even the strategies of non-directive counselling, it is claimed, fail to avoid the authoritarian elements in the casework situation. A middle position is taken by those who argue that social work agencies can act as honest brokers, mediating in the conflict between interests in society. Thus, social work 'faces both ways' in its advocacy of therapy or individual measures to ameliorate social problems and reform, or structural changes which seek to eradicate these problems at their source.[2]

Innovation, achievement motivation and social change
Merton's paradigm locates delinquent acts in the category of those who strive for legitimate ends but by innovative means. Not all such 'deviant' acts will be condemned by society as morally culpable. Inventors and reformers are also examples of nonconformists, and, indeed, the line between reform and moral acceptability is often very hazy. In considering inventors and innovators, we are beginning to probe the boundary between

[1] On the definition of problems, see H. S. Becker, *Social Problems: A Modern Approach* (1966), Introduction, pp. 1–28.
[2] B. J. Heraud, *Sociology and Social Work: Problems and Perspectives* (1970), Chapter 8.

order and change. Indeed, as Durkheim has stressed, although a society which enforced rigid conformity would eliminate criminal behaviour, it would also be so rigid that change was impossible. In this sense, crime is a normal feature of all societies.

Although Merton's paradigm does not explain innovation and nonconformity, it contains the germ of an explanatory theory.[1] A number of writers have suggested that the source of innovation is to be found in socially structured strains experienced by the individual. Individuals experience needs which are not adequately satisfied by existing arrangements. For example, Hagen[2] argues that the innovators in a number of societies were individuals who experienced threats of status deprivation. They were the sons of fathers whose position in society was being undermined and who could not therefore provide their sons with an adequate role model.

Somewhat similar studies by McClelland, and Rosen and D'Andrade[3] have sought to explore the sources of high levels of achievement motivation and their connection with economic growth. McClelland considers that the entrepreneurs discussed by Weber were probably characterized by the need for high levels of achievement and were examples of a more general phenomenon in which levels of achievement motivation are correlated with economic growth. For historical periods, the existence of a high level achievement motivation was measured by the content analysis of imaginative literary documents or folk tales, and found to correlate strongly with economic growth and the existence of entrepreneurs. Comparable studies of contemporary nations confirmed this association between achievement motivation and economic growth. McClelland also demonstrates that those with high scores on achievement motivation, in fact possess the characteristics of entrepreneurs—willingness to innovate and to take risks. Fluctuations in achievement motivation scores are too rapid to be attributed to heredity. McClelland considers that the sources of high motivation must be attributed to parental influences.[4] A study by Inkeles of Russian emigrants also found that parents responded to extreme social changes resulting from the revolution by a marked decline in emphasis on traditional values in the

[1] A. K. Cohen, 'The Study of Social Disorganization and Deviant Behaviour', in R. K. Merton, L. Broom and L. S. Cottrell, op. cit.

[2] E. Hagen, *On the Theory of Social Change* (1964).

[3] David C. McClelland, 'The Achievement Motive in Economic Growth', in B. F. Hoselitz and W. E. Moore, *Industrialization and Society* (1963), Chapter 4, and D. McClelland, *The Achieving Society* (1961).

[4] See Chapter 7 for a discussion of the literature. See also D. F. Swift, 'Social Class and Achievement Motivation', *Educational Research*, February 1966.

upbringing of their children.[1] Moreover, he found that in the area of occupational choice, there was a marked decline in the importance attached to family traditions and an increased emphasis on self-expression and free choice.[2] His study, however, failed to find evidence of increased emphasis on achievement, but this he attributes to the possible greater importance attached to political considerations by his sample of refugees. The study does, however, serve to demonstrate the way in which parents respond to changing circumstances by mediating the values appropriate to the new situation which their children will face, rather than those to which they were themselves exposed during childhood.

Self and society

It has been argued that it is possible to escape from the determinist view of the relation between man and society and to discover voluntaristic possibilities through the interactionist perspective. However powerfully society moulds man, man may negotiate and bargain in both structured and unstructured situations. And in distinguishing between the 'I' and the 'me', we are also looking for ways in which man may play a bigger part in deciding 'who' he is.[3] It is a matter of temperament perhaps, certainly at this stage of knowledge, whether one emphasizes the pitiably small room for manoeuvre, or grasps the hope of increasing freedom through a greater realization of the sources of constraint. It is to this theme of man's search for an acceptable identity and its relation to the problems of order and change that we now turn.

The emphasis in Chapter 8 on the crucial role of social interaction in the formation of a self concept raises the possibility that the mechanisms may break down so that man can no longer find a satisfactory answer to the question 'who am I?' There is growing evidence to suggest that the formation of a satisfactory identity may become increasingly problematic in advanced industrial societies. The theme of alienation has claimed that industrialization prevents man from expressing his nature—that in his social life, man becomes separated from his self. Man is no longer able to realize his self through spontaneous and creative productive activity. 'Through the production of objects, an individual reproduces himself . . . actively and in a real sense, and sees his own reflection in a world which he has constructed.'[4] The

[1] A. Inkeles, 'Social Change and Social Character: The Role of Parental Mediation', A. and E. Etzioni, *Social Change: Sources, Patterns and Consequences* (1964), Chapter 37.

[2] Ibid., p. 350.

[3] See T. Parsons, 'The Position of Identity in the General Theory of Action', in C. Gordon and K. J. Gergen (eds), *The Self in Social Interaction* (1968), pp. 11–23.

[4] Quoted in R. Schacht, *Alienation* (1971), p. 76.

theme of the crisis of identity takes a slightly different form and argues that man is increasingly unable to evolve an identity.

Klapp defines identity as 'all things a person may legitimately say about himself—his status, his name, his personality, his past life.' The clue to the problem is to be found in the structural changes in society: '. . . if his social context is unreliable, it follows that he cannot say anything legitimately and reliably about himself. His statements of identity have no more reliability than a currency which depends upon the willingness of people to recognize and accept it.' An identity problem then is 'almost always associated with unsatisfactory "feed-back" from others.'[1]

A major source of this unsatisfactory feed-back is the plurality of roles which characterizes society with a high degree of division of labour. The fact that we have a number of role options available, plus the fact that status is achieved rather than ascribed, makes the task of discovering the self through role performance and interaction increasingly difficult. The choice between 'being' a doctor, solicitor, accountant, teacher, assembly-line operative or craftsman, has implications for the self. By contrast, in non-industrial societies where status is ascribed, the blacksmith's son knows that he will *be* a blacksmith: the process of identification is greatly simplified.

One way in which modern societies are particularly defective is in the loss of ritual and symbolism in conveying meaning. The meaning of a marriage, for example, and its emotional impact are conveyed in part by the rituals and ceremonies—the presence of others, music and exchanging of rings. The decline in ritual accompanying *rites de passage* is part of the symbolic poverty of modern societies.

The search for solutions takes many forms, both individual and collective. Some retreat into introspection, including artistic expression and the search for mystical experience as a source of meaning outside the self. Others seek affirmation of the self through encounters with others. Shopping around a variety of cults, religious and secular, is one way of searching for or confirming identity, 'through tests, ordeals, membership tokens, brotherhood rituals, badges and insignia'.[2] The pursuit of fashion and taking identity 'vacations'[3] are less extreme forms, while the alienated[4] totally reject the square world.

[1] O. Klapp, *Collective Search for Identity* (1969). See also M. Stein, A. J. Vidich and D. M. White, *Identity and Anxiety* (1960), Part 2.

[2] Ibid., p. 45.

[3] Presenting a different 'self' at weekends, at parties, or while on holiday, or even having a private ranch and being a cowboy at weekends.

[4] See K. Keniston, 'The Psychology of Alienated Students', in C. Gordon and K. J. Gergen (eds), op. cit., Chapter 41.

How far the crisis of identity is a threat to the social order and a source of new radical movements is a matter of current debate. Turner argues that a new sense of injustice is emerging, based not on anger about inequality or un-freedom, but 'for the first time in history, it is common to see violent indignation expressed over the fact that people lack a sense of personal worth—they lack an inner peace of mind which comes from a sense of personal dignity or a clear sense of identity.'[1] But how far this is likely to generate effective collective action is problematic. The Civil Rights movement in America, and the new radicalism of the CND and its successors in Britain have been largely moral protest movements.[2] In this sense, the lack of a sense of personal worth has come to be defined (certainly by youth) not as a private misfortune but as a public injustice. In some of its aspects, too, the Black Power movement is 'the demand for an identity which can give the ordinary individual dignity and self-respect.'[3]

It could, however, be argued that the responses to the identity problem have largely taken forms which do not constitute a radical revolutionary threat. Style rebellion in the form of flamboyant dress, loud and strident music, symbolizes a rejection of adult values. In its more extreme forms, it is a claim to personal anarchy. The drop-out movement, an even more total rejection of the values of adult society in the search for a new personal meaning, has even less political significance. But it could be argued that such protests may contribute to cultural transformations which could have more long-term effects on social action.

Collective action and social movements
The fact that individuals experience misfortunes and dissatisfactions does not imply that these will threaten the social order or generate pressures for change. The steps by which private misfortunes may become transformed into public issues have been spelt out by Zollschan. A discrepancy between what is desired or expected and an actual situation he defines as an *exigency*. 'To eventuate in social system changes . . . such exigencies must trigger a series of phase processes, namely, articulation—action—institutionalization'.[4] The discrepancies may be *cognitive* (between what is expected to happen and what happens), *evaluative* (between a legitimate arrangement and an actual situation), or *affective* (between what it desired and what it achieved). *Articula-*

[1] R. Turner, 'Contemporary Social Movements', *B.J.S.*, December 1969, p. 395.
[2] See Chapter 6.   [3] R. Turner, op. cit. (1969), p. 402.
[4] G. K. Zollschan and W. Hirsch, *Explorations in Social Change* (1964), p. 89.

tion involves the expression of what would otherwise remain as a free-floating discomfort. Articulation depends on the measure of discomfort generated by the exigency (saliency), and the extent to which the sources of discomfort can be identified and specified (*specification*). Moreover, there must be some measure of normative support for the articulation of a need (*justification*). Somewhat similar conditions are necessary before articulated needs evoke actions (valence, application, legitimation).

Collective action results when an action involves one or more others. Institutionalization is likely to occur when others bring to the situation similar needs and where the resulting interaction is mutually satisfying. A second variety of collective action occurs when the goal requires more than one person and where cooperation aids individuals in the achievement of similar or congruent goals. The collective activity which results does not necessarily achieve a state of equilibrium. There may be, for example, unintended (latent) consequences and, in this way, the creation of fresh exigencies. The existence of a stable state is, in fact, a special case since actions will create new exigencies. The theory does not, therefore, posit any fixed categories of needs.[1] Moreover, it takes account of the fact that exigencies emerge within the framework of established social systems with existing institutionalized patterns. The socialization process will have ensured that such institutionalized 'definitions of situations' and normative expectations are 'built in' to the personalities of members of society, and will function to determine the kind of responses adopted to an exigency.[2] The emergence of collective action does not necessarily lead to social change. Much will depend, as we have seen, on the societal response to such action. A full discussion of this requires us to move from an emphasis on the personality sub-system to the structural level of analysis.[3]

[1] Cf. Parsons's notion of functional imperatives. The author argues that 'social systems continue to satisfy functional requirements only as long as potential failures to meet them become exigencies. . . . States of equilibrium are special cases of dynamics . . .' (p. 122).

[2] 'It is in the socialization process that horizons of expectations and horizons of justification are formed in individuals. We are . . . suggesting that there exists a feedback process in which institutionalization leads to socialization of persons. . . . The horizons of expectations and horizons of justifications of socialized individuals thereupon enter into the determination of new articulations of exigencies and new patterns of institutionalization.' Ibid., p. 114.

[3] Much will depend, too, on the kind of control which a society exercises over innovations. For a discussion of this, see A. Boskoff, 'Functional Analysis as a Source of a Theoretical Repertory and Research Tasks in the Study of Social Change', in G. K. Zollschan and W. Hirsch, op. cit., pp. 231–4.

A linking concept which helps to bridge the transition to the collective level of analysis is the notion of *social movements*—largely neglected by sociologists until recently.[1] These may be thought of as a ground-swell of opinion and belief which brings together in loose and somewhat unstructured association those who share a like conviction. The CND, 'Women's Lib' and youth movements discussed in Chapter 6 are examples of social movements. Historically, we can identify the feminist movement[2] and co-operative movement in the nineteenth century and more recently the conservationist movement and the movement for social responsibility in science.[3] Social movements are examples of a lack of cultural consensus and constitute a challenge to some aspect of the dominant values or beliefs of society, seeking to raise the level of consciousness of a section of society (changing the definition of the situation) as a first step in the mobilization of action.

The essential feature of a social movement is then a powerful unifying idea; though this may lack clarity, and usually falls short of a systematically articulated ideology. Indeed, any attempt at more structured organized action brings to the surface the latent differences and antagonisms within the membership.

PERSPECTIVES ON CHANGE

The study of social change is by far the most complex of any topic in sociology. More than any other, it is necessary to go beyond description to explanation, and to attempt to arrive at generalizations. It is in this field that the claim of sociology to be a science is frequently challenged. The object of science, it is argued, is to be able to predict. And it is the inability of sociology to predict which indicates its immaturity. Such charges can be countered by distinguishing between prediction and prophecy.[4] The sociologist does not claim to be able to foretell the future. Prediction involves being able to say what is likely to happen to other variables in a system when one changes. Nevertheless, the difficulties of dealing with social change underline the undeveloped state of theory and the paucity of theory-oriented research.

[1] For an analysis of the concept, see J. A. Banks, *The Sociology of Social Movements* (1972).
[2] J. A. and D. Banks, 'Feminism and Social Change: A Case Study of a Social Movement', in G. K. Zollschan and W. Hirsch, op. cit.
[3] For a classification of types of social movement, see Paul Wilkinson, *Social Movement* (1971).
[4] K. Popper, *The Poverty of Historicism* (1957).

Meaning of change

One major difficulty presents itself at the outset. What precisely do we mean by social change? There is considerable conceptual confusion here, in which a wide variety of terms has been used to refer to various aspects of change, including evolution, development, adaptation, and social process. We must identify both the units for analysis, and the kind of changes which we wish to define as social change. We might, for example, look at the changes in the recruitment of the British Cabinet. But this may not involve changes in the structure of the Cabinet or its functions, and may not, therefore, be considered a significant social change. Again, we may demonstrate the emergence of more equalitarian relations within the family, or the institutionalization of industrial conflict through the establishment of arbitration machinery. These are changes *within* sub-systems and do not constitute major change *of* systems. An example of the latter would be the change from a feudal to a capitalist society. But here again, there are major problems of conceptualization. There is controversy, for example, as to whether the distinguishing features of feudalism are to be found in its economic system or its political system, or whether it is a configuration of economic and political variables. We are faced, that is to say, with the problem of devising a classification of types of society.

An alternative approach which avoids such taxonomic problems is to conceive of social change as a process of structural differentiation. This is the approach adopted by functionalists such as Parsons.[1] Smelser's[2] study of the industrial revolution, for example, shows how the decline of the domestic economy involved the structural differentiation of the family and the economic system, and their functional specialization.

It may also be useful to differentiate between social change and cultural change, and the interrelations between them. In fact, a major controversy in sociology has revolved around such a distinction. Marx, for example, argued that the ideological superstructure of society was built upon the material basis of society, and reflected the techniques of production and the mode of production to which these techniques gave rise. Ideology could only hasten or retard the process of change but could not in the long run stand against it. Weber, on the other hand, maintained that ideological changes were a necessary pre-condition for the evolution of capitalism, and attributed the emergence of the 'spirit of

---

[1] See T. Parsons, 'A Functional Theory of Change', in A. and E. Etzioni, op. cit.

[2] N. J. Smelser, *Social Change and the Industrial Revolution* (1959).

capitalism' to the influence of protestant sects. Ogburn[1] formulated a theory of 'cultural lag' in which he argued that there was a tendency for the 'non-material' culture to lag behind the 'material' culture.

Social conflict, disorganization and change

It is clearly difficult to account for change using a model of society which is preoccupied with demonstrating the integrative functions of norms. Hence writers, such as Rex and Dahrendorf, 'assert that social change is a result of the shifting balance of power between conflict groups'.[2] But as Lockwood has pointed tou, however much importance we attach to the role of conflict and coercion we still cannot ignore the importance of value systems and ideologies which play a key role in structuring the individual's definition of the situation and hence his response to it.

It is not, of course, being argued that strains and conflicts necessarily lead to social change. Only some of the possible range of societal responses will have this result. We are simply identifying a possible source of change in the strains and conflicts within sub-systems or between structural elements in the social system. Moreover, structural strains are not the same as individual strains. Dissatisfaction with low wages, for example, does not necessarily lead to trade unions and organized industrial conflict.

The maintenance of social integration depends not only on the existence and extent of conflict, but also on the effectiveness of the mechanisms which exist for its management. Conflicts occur between the structural elements in society. Those occupying dominant roles in one segment of the social system may seek to dominate other segments. The military elite, for example, may attempt to capture the political machinery, or the church may seek to dominate the state. This is a struggle between rival elites for dominance over other elites. A second type of conflict occurs within a sub-system of the social structure. There may be conflict for dominance between rival religious groupings, or contending political parties, or between workers and owners in the economic system over the distribution of incomes.

One of the most important factors influencing the intensity of conflict is the existence and perception of objective differences in the distribution of power, income, property, status. But equally important is the meaning attached to such differences. If, for

[1] W. F. Ogburn, *Social Change* (1922).
[2] D. Lockwood, 'Social Integration and System Integration', in P. Worsley (ed.), *Readings* (1970), Chapter 66. See also R. Dahrendorf, 'Towards a Theory of Social Conflict', in A. and E. Etzioni, op. cit., Chapter 13.

example, the contrast between 'The rich man in his castle, The poor man at his gate' is perceived, it is less likely to become a basis for social conflict if the distinction is judged to be legitimate, as the next two lines of the hymn suggest: 'God made them high or lowly, And order'd their estate.' Thus, as we saw in Chapter 7, the legitimation of inequality through the status system has contained and minimized class conflict in industrial societies. In short, a misfortune must be defined as an injustice. Hence the efforts of social movements such as 'Women's Lib' to change perceptions and legitimations through consciousness-raising strategies.

Two further conditions are necessary for the emergence of conflict; firstly, the perception of common interests by those who feel they have grounds for grievance, and secondly an awareness of the possibility of common action. A conflict may remain latent until the situation is defined as favourable for overt action. The severity of overt conflict will depend on the existence of societal machinery for channelling, accommodating and managing conflict—what Dahrendorf[1] calls the institutionalization of conflict. The development of arbitration machinery and industrial law, for example, has channelled and controlled industrial conflict.

Finally, a most important factor influencing the strength of conflict and the possibility of accommodation is the extent to which there is a super-imposition of differences so that they become cumulative and lead to unbridgeable dichotomies. If workers, for example, are members of the same religious groups, then religious similarities will reinforce economic interests and intensify the conflict with opposing groups. Hence, the particularly intransigent nature of racial conflict where economic, social, and even political discrimination is focused on ethnic minority groups.

In order to examine the implications of conflict for social disorganization, it is necessary to establish first the criteria for determining its existence. The simplest approach is to start from the notion of organization and consider what we mean by a breakdown of organization. It was shown in Chapter 8 that the essence of organization is the allocation of tasks and their co-ordination for the pursuit of goals in accordance with a set of constituted roles. Disorganization may occur therefore (a) when individuals are not adequately motivated to act out roles, (b) when there is no system of rules which adequately defines the behaviour of actors in the system (anomie). Such breakdowns of organization can, of course, occur in any of the sub-systems of society. But it is when such a breakdown threatens the stability of the total social system that we are faced with the possibility of a major social disorganization.

[1] R. Dahrendorf, *Class and Class Conflict in an Industrial Society* (1959).

298

Thus, as we have seen, conflict does not necessarily threaten disorganization. Much will depend on the responses of the system and the means it adopts to accommodate conflicts of interests. Those social systems which have elaborate mechanisms for the articulation and aggregation of interests are less likely to be threatened by a breakdown of organization, and are more likely to have achieved a consensus on ends and means. Conflict may stimulate the development of machinery for its resolution.[1] Arbitration is a means whereby a compromise is reached which is accepted as legitimate by both sides. By such means, conflict may be 'institutionalized', that is to say, regulated by an agreed set of rules. Once the parties act outside the rules, there is a degree of disorganization. Legislation on race relations, for example, is an attempt not only to devise a set of rules but also to influence the 'social definition' of the situation—to define racial discrimination as norm infraction.

Apart from attempts to modify rules or devise fresh rules to contain actions within an organized framework, efforts may be made to increase the motivations of the individual to abide by the rules. Appeals to higher obligations, efforts to increase the perceived legitimacy of the rules, or the threat of sanctions and coercion, may all contain actions within the framework of rules, while in no way lessening the basic dissatisfactions or conflicts of interest. Adaptations of the social system in these ways may be sufficiently basic to constitute a change within the system. The emergence of machinery for the handling of industrial disputes constitutes a change within the economic system, but not social change in the sense of change in the structure of the social system.[2]

The relation between order and change is therefore problematic. Social problems such as poverty do not necessarily become politicized. Inequality does not necessarily generate class conflict. Industrial or race conflict may be managed and contained in such ways that it does not result in social change, except in the limited sense of small changes within systems.

ALTERNATIVE FUTURES

Looking back on the early sixties, the mood among both social scientists and the general public was one of cautious optimism in the future. Science and technology it was widely believed would enable man to conquer nature and usher in an era of peace and plenty. Even the major Marxist critique of society with its predic-

[1] L. Coser, *The Functions of Social Conflict* (1956). See also the discussion of 'cleavage' in Chapter 5.
[2] See R. Dahrendorf, op. cit. (1959), for an elaboration of this distinction.

tions of the increasing impoverishment of the proletariat seemed less relevant in the face of growing affluence, declining support for radical politics, predictions of embourgeoisement and the end of ideology. By the end of the sixties, the mood had changed. Campus and racial riots, the rediscovery of poverty, an emerging radical attack on the threats to human freedom inherent in the technological society, the abuses of science and technology in the Vietnam war were associated with a growing disenchantment certainly among many of the better educated middle-class young, and the search for alternative life-styles, the rejection of science and rationality, and the growth of millenarianism. And to his has been added a growing awareness of the impact of industrialization on the environment, the rapid exhaustion of many metals and fossil fuels, and rising levels of pollution which have led some to predict that unless world population and economic growth can be controlled and stabilized, society as we know it faces catastrophe from pollution, famine or economic collapse by the year 2,000.

In general, apart from campus riots, such issues have received little attention from sociologists. The explosive interest in deviancy in the last decade has attracted many of the abler younger sociologists. Others of the new generation joined the crusade for ethnomethodology and became preoccupied 'with applying great ingenuity and sophistication to the personally sometimes problematic but societally insignificant difficulties of managing the first five seconds of conversations . . . or exchanging 'Good Mornings' in a world agonized by infinitely greater social problems to which, however, comparable inputs of sociological theoretical effort have not been applied'.[1]

It is such larger macro-issues about the future of human society that have been central to the work of the major founders of our subject—Weber, Durkheim, Marx—and with which we conclude this introduction to sociology.

The technological imperative
In any attempt to discover the dynamic forces underlying social change, the major candidate is undoubtedly technology. So for example, Clark Kerr (*et al.*) argues that the logic of industrialization is driving all advanced industrial societies towards a basic similarity—pluralistic industrialism. And underlying this thrust is technology. Although pluralistic industrialism may take several forms, 'the iron hand of technology tends to create relative uniformity in job structure, compensation differentials and technical

[1] Peter Worsley, 'The State of Theory and the Status of Theory', *Sociology* Vol. 8, No. 1 (Jan. 1974), p. 15.

training'.[1] Moreover, technology is everywhere much the same. 'There is one best technology; this affects economic relations and economic relations affect political realities . . .'.[2]

As in many theories of technological determinism, technology is conceived as a reified force, external to the intentions, interests and interactions of man in society. Kerr *et al.*, mistakenly attribute such a view to Marx. Yet Marx clearly distinguished between the *forces* of production (which included technological equipment and organized labour) and the *relations* of production (the legal and political framework within which the forces of production operate). It is the combination of these two elements as the *mode* of production which for Marx characterized the major forms of society. In short, for Kerr *et al.*[3] technology operates in a de-politicized world.

This approach is strongly criticized by those who challenge the notion that science and technology are autonomous, impersonal and 'neutral' forces. So, for example, Dickson marshals evidence to show that the new technologies of the industrial revolution were deliberately contrived to increase control over labour and the market. 'The factory was a managerial rather than a technical necessity.'[4]

Technology, growth and values
The point becomes clearer if we look at some of the proposals for 'alternative' technologies. These are rooted in what is basically a challenge to the *master value* of industrial society, the pursuit of economic growth. Current criticisms of society emphasize quality of life rather than quantity of output, such as protection of the environment from pollution and exploitation. Hence the search for alternative low-energy technologies which have minimal environmental impact. Even more radical proposals have challenged the notion of economic growth itself, arguing that the costs of growth in the form of urban sprawl, environmental degradation and other 'disutilities' have reached the point that they outweigh the advantages, and that society should now face up to the need for a stable state and zero-growth.[5] In short, such arguments not

[1] Clark Kerr, *et al.*, *Industrialism and Industrial Man* (1973), p. 292.
[2] Ibid., p. 298.
[3] For a critique of Kerr *et al.*, see Foreword to the 1973 edition by Roy Haddon.
[4] David Dickson, *Alternative Technology and the Politics of Technical Change* (1974), pp. 73–4.
[5] E. J. Mishan, *The Costs of Economic Growth* (1969). For a critique of the limits to growth debate, see H. S. D. Cole (ed.), *et al.*, *Thinking About the Future* (1974).

301

only challenge prevailing values, but bring out the intimate inter-relation between technology and values,[1] underlining the fact that technology is not an impersonal force, but the product of deliber-ate human intentions and is harnessed to serve consciously chosen human ends.

The politics of post-industrial society

The more advanced the technology, and the more capital-intensive the production process, the longer is the time-scale between the inception of, say, a new car model and its launching to a mass market, the more important it is to minimize uncertainty through central planning. It is such imperatives of technology, argues Galbraith,[2] which drive all modern industrial societies to similar organizational and political solutions—an increasingly close association between governments and producers, governments and trade unions, and governments and universities. All are brought into an organic relationship and all are harnessed to the over-riding objective of economic growth. This is what some see as the emergence of the *corporate state* in which the competing interest groups of pluralist democracies have been incorporated into a powerful centralized state-planning machine with the development of what Galbraith[3] calls *technostructures*. In such a knowledge-based society, politics is increasingly concerned with technical problems, which by their nature cannot be the subject of public discussion. A new class of technocrats rises to positions of power and influence. The political process becomes depoliticized[4]—a matter for experts. The values and goals of such a society are no longer open to challenge; the technocrats and the corporations share an implicit consensus on the political and economic objec-tives of society.

The issues raised are of great complexity, and have generated substantial controversy. Some would challenge the view that the technocrats can ever constitute a class and seize the apparatus of the state, though there would be little dissent from the view that experts are likely to become increasingly influential.[5] But more fundamental is the argument that it is not technology which is the force shaping the post-industrial society, but rather its overriding preoccupation with economic growth and defence. It is this which

---

[1] I. Taviss, *Our Tool-Making Society* (1972), especially pp. 47–58.

[2] J. K. Galbraith, *The New Industrial State* (1967).

[3] Ibid.

[4] J. Habermas, *Towards a Rational Society* (1971).

[5] On this debate, see J. Meynaud, *Technocracy* (1968), Chapter 3. For an optimistic view, see D. Bell, *The Coming of Post-Industrial Society* (1974), Chapter 6.

harnesses science and technology to industrial and military objectives, and subordinates social and political life to technological imperatives.[1]

Rationality, freedom and domination

Some of the most powerful critiques of the future facing industrial society have focused on its threats to human freedom. The technological society, it is argued, is one in which all aspects of social life are rationalized in the pursuit of economic goals. It is, Ellul asserts, a society dominated by technique, by the search for the one most rational, most efficient, best way.[2] Such rationalization, routinization and formalization of action results in the domination of the individual by technique, whether it be the assembly line or the operation of bureaucratic structures. Moreover, the ends of action are taken as given—it is a society preoccupied with what Weber called *instrumentally rational* action to the neglect of ends or *value-rational* action.[3] Judgements of value are seen not merely as non-scientific but as unscientific: they cannot be proved by experimental data ... 'technology cannot put up with intuitions and literature, it must don mathematical vestments. Everything in human life which does not lend itself to mathematical treatment must be excluded'.[4] And in this process, it is argued, science plays a key role as *the* contemporary ideology, legitimizing and justifying the actions of experts.

There is nothing new of course about such fears of the growth of impersonal, rational, bureaucratic efficiency. The contrast between *community*, characterized by affective, personal, face-to-face interaction, and the impersonal rule-governed formal relationships of *association* is familiar to students of sociology through the work of Tönnies and Weber. In Weber's writings on charismatic leaders, for example, 'one may readily discern the heritage of liberalism that has always confronted similar dichotomies: mass *versus* personality, the "routine" *versus* the "creative" entrepreneur, the conventions of ordinary people *versus* the inner freedom of the pioneering and exceptional man, institutional rules *versus* the spontaneous individual, the drudgery and boredom of everyday existence *versus* the imaginative flight of the genius'.[5]

[1] For an extended discussion, see S. Cotgrove, 'Technology, Rationality and Domination', *Science Studies*, 5 (Jan. 1975), and 'The Technological Society', *Technology and Society* (April 1974).

[2] J. Ellul, *The Technological Society* (1965).

[3] M. Weber, *Economy and Society* (1968), pp. 24–6.

[4] Ellul, op. cit., p. 43.

[5] H. H. Gerth and C. Wright Mills, *From Max Weber: Essays in Sociology* (1970), p. 53.

Value-dilemmas

In short, we are faced here with both empirical and value questions. Whether the inexorable march of technique and rationality is as inescapable as some would argue, is an empirical question. Whether spontaneity and unstructured situations are preferable to structured and rule-governed situations is a question of value. There are certainly signs of a growing challenge to routinization,[1] including attempts to break away from rigid stylized techniques in the arts, in music, painting and sculpture, and a move towards more flexible participative styles in administration and management.

What, then, can be challenged is the theory of change which sees technology as an autonomous mechanism, and man's future determined by forces over which he has no control. Technology operates within a social and political context, which includes values and preferred goals. It is these above all which shaped the objectives to which science and technology are harnessed. If technology opens up new options, it also points up moral dilemmas. To the extent to which man is free to choose the values by which he wishes to be guided, he has a stake in shaping his future. And the value dilemmas facing man today include the perennial questions of freedom and equality, sharpened up by the options which technology offers—economic growth with its possible threats to the quality of life; and efficiency at the possible cost of human values. Alternative futures involve both alternative values, and the development of appropriate technologies.

[1] For an analysis of the social structures which lead to spontaneity or formality and ritual, see Mary Douglas, *Natural Symbols* (1973).

J. A. Banks, *The Sociology of Social Movements* (Macmillan, 1972).

Howard S. Becker, *Social Problems* (Wiley, 1967).

D. Bell, *The Coming of Post-Industrial Society* (Heinemann, 1974).

Steven Box, *Deviance, Reality and Society* (Holt, Rinehart, 1971).

E. Butterworth and D. Weir, *Social Problems of Modern Britain* (Fontana, 1972).

N. Cross, D. Elliot, R. Roy, *Man-Made Futures* (Hutchinson, 1974).

R. Dahrendorf, *Class and Class Conflict in an Industrial Society* (Routledge, 1959).

D. Dickson, *Alternative Technology* (Fontana, 1974).

D. M. Downes, *The Delinquent Solution* (Routledge, 1966).

S. N. Eisenstadt, *Comparative Social Problems* (Collier-Macmillan, 1964).

J. Ellul, *The Technological Society* (Knopf, 1967).

A. and E. Etzioni (eds), *Social Change: Sources, Patterns and Consequences* (Basic Books, 1964).

J. Galbraith, *The New Industrial State* (Houghton-Mifflin, 1967).

J. Habermas, *Toward a Rational Society* (Heinemann, 1971).

Clark Kerr, *et all.*, *Industrialism and Industrial Man* (Penguin, 1973)

O. Klapp, *The Collective Search for Identity* (Holt, Rinehart, 1969).

R. K. Merton, L. Broom and L. S. Cottrell, *Sociology Today: Problems and Prospects* (Harper and Row, 1965).

R. K. Merton and R. A. Nisbet, *Contemporary Social Problems* (Hart-Davis, 1965).

Irene Taviss, *Our Tool-Making Society* (Prentice-Hall, 1972).

R. Williams, *Politics and Technology* (Macmillan, 1971).

INDEX: AUTHOR

306

309

310

INDEX: SUBJECT